ATLAS OF MICHIGAN

ATLAS OF MICHIGAN

Edited by

LAWRENCE M. SOMMERS

Professor and Chairman
Department of Geography
Michigan State University

Michigan State University Press

Distributed by Wm. B. Eerdmans Publishing Co.

LIBRARY OF CONGRESS CATALOG CARD NUMBER: 77-74637
ISBN NO. 0-87013-205-9
COPYRIGHT © 1977 BY MICHIGAN STATE UNIVERSITY PRESS
PRINTED IN THE UNITED STATES OF AMERICA

Typesetting by Central Trade Plant, Grand Rapids, Michigan
Lithography by KalaCraft, Inc., Kalamazoo, Michigan
Printed by The Printers, Inc., Grand Rapids, Michigan

MICHIGAN ATLAS STAFF

Cartographic Director
ROBERT W. McKAY
Department of Geography, MSU

Assistant Editor
STANLEY D. BRUNN
Professor
Department of Geography, MSU

Manuscript Editor
KATHLEEN M. SCHOONMAKER
Associate Editor
University Publications, MSU

Assistant to the
Cartographic Director
CHRISTINE FORCE
Department of Geography, MSU

Design
and Illustration
ROBERT BRENT

ATLAS STEERING COMMITTEE, MSU DEPARTMENT OF GEOGRAPHY

LAWRENCE M. SOMMERS, *Professor and Chairman*

STANLEY D. BRUNN, *Professor*

PHILIP KELLEY, *Assistant Professor*

JACK F. WILLIAMS, *Assistant Professor*

ROBERT I. WITTICK, *Associate Professor*

AUTHORS AND OTHER CONTRIBUTORS

ROLLIN H. BAKER, *Director*
Museum, MSU

RALEIGH BARLOWE, *Professor*
Department of Resource Development, MSU

J. ALLAN BEEGLE, *Professor*
Department of Sociology, MSU

ROBERT P. BOGER, *Director*
Institute for Family and Child Study, MSU

STANLEY D. BRUNN, *Professor*
Department of Geography, MSU

DIETER H. BRUNNSCHWEILER, *Professor*
Department of Geography, MSU

F. WILLIAM CAMBRAY, *Professor and Chairman*
Department of Geology, MSU

MICHAEL CHUBB, *Associate Professor*
Department of Geography, MSU

CHARLES CLELAND, *Professor*
Departments of Anthropology and
Racial and Ethnic Studies, MSU

WILLIAM COLBURN
Retired
Department of Natural Resources
State of Michigan

JOSEPH T. DARDEN, *Associate Professor*
Departments of Geography and
Racial and Ethnic Studies, MSU

CHARLES R. DOWNS, *Editor*
Environmental Quality
Department of Information Services, MSU

JAMES H. FISHER, *Professor*
Department of Geology, MSU

CARL GOLDSCHMIDT, *Professor and Director*
Department of Urban Planning and
Landscape Architecture, MSU

JAY R. HARMAN, *Associate Professor*
Department of Geography, MSU

JOHN L. HAZARD, *Professor*
Department of Marketing and
Transportation Administration, MSU

MADISON KUHN, *Professor*
Department of History, MSU

DELBERT L. MOKMA, *Assistant Professor*
Department of Crop and Soil Science, MSU

ROBERT C. MUTH, *Assistant to the Dean*
for Special Programs
College of Education, MSU

SADAYOSHI OMOTO, *Professor*
Department of Art, MSU

LAWRENCE SARBAUGH, *Assistant Dean*
and Associate Professor
College of Communication Arts, MSU

RICHARD M. SMITH, *Assistant Professor*
Department of Geography, MSU

LAWRENCE M. SOMMERS, *Professor and Chairman*
Department of Geography, MSU

WILLIAM C. TAYLOR, *Professor and Chairman*
Department of Civil and Sanitary Engineering, MSU

DAVID I. VERWAY, *Associate Professor*
Bureau of Business and Economic Research, MSU

JACK F. WILLIAMS, *Assistant Professor*
Department of Geography, MSU

HAROLD A. WINTERS, *Professor*
Department of Geography, MSU

STUDENT CONTRIBUTORS

DANIEL A. DUEWEKE
Research, layout, scribing, production,
specification, verification, corrections

GARY K. ALDEN
Research, photo-mechanics, film processing

CHRISTOPHER J. CIALEK
Layout, scribing, production

DAVID L. EDWARDS
Research, layout, scribing, production

PATRICIA A. ELLIS
Production, specification, verification

J. MICHAEL LIPSEY
Research, layout, graph design, scribing

DAVID P. LUSCH
Research, special projects, layout, production

WILLIAM M. MAYNARD
Research, layout, production, verification

L. PAUL SCHAFER
Layout, scribing, production, verification

CHARLENE E. WHITNEY
Design, layout, production, special art

DONALD BATKINS
Photographic acquisitions

WILLIAM GRIBB
Special problems

JOHN HARRINGTON
Climatological research

MARK NEITHERCUT
Computer graphics

RICHARD RIECK
Geomorphological research

THOMAS ROSS
Lithographic preparation

THEODORE ALTER
Research, natural environment

RICHARD SAMBROOK
Research, history

WILLIAM TILLINGHAST
Research, communication

MARY WOELFEL
Research, sociology

MARTIN BICK □ THOMAS DOSLAK □ SONJA ELINCHEV □ MICHAEL GRAFF
NANCY GRASSMICK □ VALERIE HEISLER □ DAVID HOWES □ THOMAS KRABACHER
CELESTE KREUZER □ GARY LaMUNION □ CHERYL LEIK □ SHERRI MEYER
SIDNEY MOOK □ JOHN NYE

ACKNOWLEDGMENTS

The production of the *Atlas of Michigan* was possible only through the generous contributions of numerous individuals at Michigan State University as well as throughout the state. The initial idea and outline were developed by the Department of Geography faculty. The atlas was endorsed by a university ad hoc land-use committee, and the early stages were strongly encouraged and supported financially by Dr. John Nellor, then acting director of the Center for Environmental Quality. The publication was intended to begin to satisfy the data base needs in the land-use area. The atlas was also approved as an official bicentennial project of the university.

The university-wide nature of this effort is indicated by the participation of faculty, graduate students, undergraduate students, and staff from 12 different colleges in the planning, research, cartographic, writing, and production phases. The scope of this involvement is indicated on the preceding pages. My deepest appreciation goes to all these individuals for their essential and valuable contributions.

Special recognition needs to be given to a number of individuals. Dr. Stanley D. Brunn has served as a valued adviser and contributor throughout the project. Robert W. McKay provided cartographic innovation and supervision that makes this volume distinct among state atlases. Kathleen M. Schoonmaker provided expertise much beyond copy editing; the flow of the writing and the organizational accuracy of the volume are largely due to her dedicated ability. The design and color selection contributions and graphic illustrations of Robert Brent add considerably to the eye appeal which the volume possesses. Sheila Hoeve, executive secretary in the Department of Geography, provided accurate manuscript typing and was responsible for many essential record keeping details on student personnel and budget. The steering committee provided the daily and periodic advice and monitoring of the atlas that were so necessary to its completion. William Colburn, recently retired from the Michigan Department of Natural Resources, made helpful suggestions throughout, particularly in the recreation section.

I am deeply indebted to the faculty authors of the section introductions and of the text portions on the map pages. The many student cartographers, researchers, and compilers have provided vital talent; part of their reward must be in the form of the valuable experience they have gained, which I hope will help them throughout their careers.

The project would not have been possible without the generous financial support from Michigan State University. I am also pleased to acknowledge gratefully the sizeable grant from the Michigan State University Foundation.

A number of administrators provided essential support: Dr. Herman King took over university administrative responsibility for the project in midstream; George Kooistra provided publication management expertise and other contributions; Gwen Andrew gave much support as dean of the College of Social Science; and Lyle Blair contributed as director of the MSU Press. I would also like to acknowledge the contributions of Leslie W. Scott, Vice President for University Development, and Leo G. Erickson, Professor of Marketing and Transportation.

Finally, I wish to thank the many individuals, librarians, and agencies that supplied data, maps, photographs, and ideas which were essential to the completion of the atlas. It is impossible to list here all those who have contributed to this project, but their efforts are much appreciated and many are identified in the preceding lists.

LAWRENCE M. SOMMERS

PHOTOGRAPHIC CREDITS

By G. A. Amman, DNR (Ret.)
Woodcock, p. 192

By "Atlas of Michigan" Project
All photos, pp. 118-19
All photos, p. 125
Photo #3, p. 127
All photos, p. 132
All photos except #8, p. 133
Beef cattle, p. 148
All photos except hogs and poultry, p. 149
Cattle, p. 150
American Center, p. 162
Ford Motor Company, p. 163
All photos, p. 200
Ore ship, p. 213
All photos, p. 215

By A. J. Burgess, U.S.G.S.
Relief of Isle Royale, p. 58

Courtesy of Burton Historical Collections
William Hull, p. 126

Courtesy of Chicago Historical Society
Lewis Cass, p. 126

Courtesy of Chrysler Corporation
Chrysler headquarters (upper left corner), p. 162

By Michael Chubb, MSU
Canoeing, p. 195

Courtesy of Clements Library, Ann Arbor, Mi.
Both map photos, p. 107
Michigan, 1841, p. 117

Courtesy of Detroit Ethnic Festival Program
Photo #12, p. 202

Courtesy of Detroit Parks and Recreation Department
Checkers championship, p. 199

Courtesy of Detroit Public Information Office
Swimmobile, p. 199

Courtesy of Ford Motor Company
Three photos of assembly lines, pp. 162-63

By H. D. Foth, MSU
Brookston profile, p. 37

Courtesy of General Motors Corporation
General Motors headquarters, p. 163

Courtesy of Henry Ford Museum and Greenfield Village
Photo #3, p. 201

By Robert W. McKay, MSU
Photo #9, p. 202

Courtesy of Michigan Department of Commerce,
Michigan Tourist Council
Lake of the Clouds, Sleeping Bear Dunes, and Tip
of the Thumb, pp. 22-23
Fort Mackinac, p. 112
Photo #8, p. 133
General farm scene, p. 148
Fruit trees and wheat harvest, p. 150
Dunes and lake, p. 184
All photos except #2, p. 186
All photos, p. 187
Canada goose, p. 192
Both photos, p. 194
Top photo and second from bottom photo, p. 195
Bottom photo, p. 196
Photos #1 and #18, p. 201
Photos #10 and #13, p. 202

Courtesy of Michigan Department of Natural Resources,
Fisheries Division
All photos, pp. 188-89

Courtesy of Michigan Department of Natural Resources,
Information and Education Division
Rabbit, p. 191

Courtesy of Michigan Department of Natural Resources,
Parks Division
Pictured Rocks, p. 22
Photo #2, p. 186
Yankee Springs (top), p. 196
Photo #22, p. 201

Courtesy of Michigan Department of Natural Resources,
Waterways Division
Marina (second from top), p. 195

Courtesy of Michigan Department of Natural Resources,
Wildlife Division
Both photos, p. 190
Four bottom photos, p. 192
White-tailed buck, p. 193

From the collections of Michigan Secretary of State,
Michigan History Division
Poster photo, p. 120
All photos, pp. 123-24
All photos except Hull, Cass, and Milliken, pp. 126-27
All black and white photos, pp. 162-63

By Delbert Mokma, MSU
Morley, Oakville, and Kalkaska profiles, p. 37

Courtesy of National Aeronautics and Space Administration
Skylab photo, p. 73

Courtesy of National Cherry Festival, Inc.
Photo #17, p. 202

Courtesy of National Red Cherry Institute
Fruits, p. 148

By Bob Newman, MSU
Hogs and poultry, p. 149
Milking parlor, p. 150

Courtesy of Office of the Governor
Milliken, p. 126

Courtesy of Oldsmobile Public Relations
Assembly line (bottom), p. 163

Courtesy of U.S. Army Corps of Engineers
Soo Locks, p. 213

Courtesy of U.S. Department of Interior,
Pictured Rocks National Lakeshore
Miner's Castle, p. 184

PREFACE

This full color *Atlas of Michigan* portrays the major characteristics of the state's natural, man-made, and human resources, largely in graphic form. A combination of maps, graphs, photographs, text, and sketches reveals the complexity of this Great Lakes state. Introductory text to each of eight sections provides the reader with an overview, while the text blocks on the map pages explain in detail the patterns and distributions delineated by the maps and graphs. Major emphasis, however, is on maps. They portray significant aspects of Michigan's economy, history, culture, social structure, and natural environment.

The atlas is intended as a basic reference volume on Michigan for the general reader, as well as for students, teachers, and specialists. Although it contains much complex information, every attempt has been made to clarify terminology and geographic concepts for the nonspecialist reader. In most instances the graphic material is self-explanatory.

The ideas and data for this atlas came from a variety of sources. Existing maps and statistics were used wherever possible, but for some of the subjects exhaustive research was necessary and some pages are completely new contributions to published geographic material on Michigan. References for the sources of maps and diagrams are found in the bibliography, which itself is a useful list of sources for material on the state of Michigan and a guide to the many offices in the state where valuable information can be obtained. The appendix also contains selected statistical data for counties. Metric equivalents are used in the text throughout the volume.

Among the unique features of this atlas is a new map projection that gives the reader a perspective of the state as seen from an orbiting satellite. Also, a computer was used to draw some of the maps and to determine class intervals for data on many of them. Each of the eight sections of the atlas has a different background color, and each map page carries a key word or phrase to indicate the subject matter covered.

As a basic reference volume, the *Atlas of Michigan* should serve a wide variety of users. Our major objective was to present the nature of Michigan in a way that would foster better understanding of this important Great Lakes state as it exists in the 1970s.

CONTENTS

INTRODUCTION

Michigan's varied physical and cultural characteristics make it unique among the 50 states of the United States. This uniqueness is first obvious from the state's shape and location. The two peninsulas, surrounded by four of the five Great Lakes, give the state vital land and water resources. Michigan leads the nation with 3,100 miles (4,960 kilometers) of freshwater shoreline, and it has 38,575 square miles (100,295 square kilometers) of the Great Lakes within its political boundaries. Thus the state is central in any Great Lakes' development. Bridges span the waterways at Mackinac Straits and to Canada at Sault Sainte Marie, Port Huron, and Detroit. The Windsor Tunnel under the Detroit River is another important connection to Canada. Michigan's long common international boundary with Canada and its strategic position near Ontario, one of the best-developed provinces of Canada, are also significant aspects of its location.

Michigan's 58,216 square miles (151,362 square kilometers) of land area place it twenty-third among the 50 states. The straight-line distance from the northwest to the southeast corner of the state is 456 miles (734 kilometers)—about 640 miles (1,030 kilometers) by highway. This same mileage would reach from Detroit to Columbus, Georgia.

The land area of the state has an interesting and diverse natural landscape that is largely the work of the Great Ice Age. Glacial ridges such as moraines, eskers, and kames alternate with till plains and lake bottoms to give Michigan a variety of topography. Much of the state was and still is poorly drained, and thus it has thousands of lakes and large acreages of swampy land. Rocks outcropping in the western Upper Peninsula are some of the oldest in the world, consisting of hard, crystalline, igneous formations that contain copper and iron ore. The eastern part of the Upper and all of the Lower Peninsula are underlain by sedimentary rocks containing deposits of petroleum, natural gas, poor-quality coal, lime, salt, and gypsum.

Soils also differ greatly throughout the state because of the varying nature of the glacial deposits, bedrock source material, natural vegetation, and climatic conditions. The soils of the southern third of the Lower Peninsula are generally more fertile and thus more productive agriculturally, but this is in part due to the longer growing season and larger amounts of level land. The climate of the southern Lower Peninsula is moderate, with higher summer temperatures, less severe winter temperatures, and smaller amounts of winter snowfall than the Upper Peninsula. The sur-

1

2

rounding Great Lakes, particularly Lake Michigan to the west, help moderate cold temperatures. The Upper Peninsula is characterized by a humid, continental-type climate with long, severe winters and short, mild summers.

Originally the entire state was covered by native coniferous and deciduous forests. The coniferous pine trees in the north were cut to provide lumber and other forest products. The broad-leaf forests in the south were removed to make way for agriculture. Second-growth forests are now prospering in both peninsulas, but they probably will never equal the original trees in size and quality.

It is against this varied natural background that man has developed the present economic, political, and social character of Michigan. The state has played a key role in the evolution of the western Great Lakes area of North America. The Indians first saw its value as a rich hunting, fishing, trapping, and farming area and contested with the white man for its control in the 1700s and early 1800s. Michigan was an important battleground in the French and Indian War as well as in the War of 1812. The Michigan Territory became a state in 1837. In the nineteenth and early twentieth centuries, many immigrants from Europe settled in Michigan. Recent ethnic additions have been the large number of blacks in Detroit and urban southern Michigan and the Spanish-speaking migrants who came largely as itinerant laborers for the fruit and vegetable specialty areas of the state.

During the present century Michigan has become one of the principal manufacturing states in the United States. Manufacturing, an important recreation industry, and varied agriculture are the three major bases of the state's economic development. Beginning with the sawmills of the lumbering heyday in the late 1800s, manufacturing became the dominant source of employment in Michigan. However, the full force of the Industrial Revolution was not felt in Michigan until the arrival of the automobile. Currently about 31 percent of the automobiles assembled in the United States are produced in Michigan.

Michigan is a highly urbanized and industrial state. A large proportion of its more than 9 million people live south of a line from Muskegon to Bay City. Within southern Michigan, the Detroit metropolitan area dominates the state's manufacturing and retail and wholesale trade. The automotive industry is dominant here, but the region produces many other products as well, such as machinery and metals, chemicals, food products, and glass. The other large cities of southern Michigan, such as Grand Rapids, Flint, Lansing, Kalamazoo, Battle Creek, and the Midland—Bay City—Saginaw area, have extensive industry. In fact, about 73 percent of Michigan's people live in cities of more than 2,500 people, and the main base of their livelihood is industry.

Even though the south and southeast dominate the state economically, politically, and socially, the various regions of Michigan complement each other. This is demonstrated by the fact that the second most important industry in the state is recreation. Michigan's many water areas, both those inland and the Great Lakes, provide summer recreation opportunities. Its winter climate provides rather reliable snow conditions for skating, snowmobiling, and ice fishing, and many glacial hills provide much winter skiing. Thus there is a balance between winter and summer recreation as well as between city and rural or wilderness activities.

The third major industry, agriculture, is also quite varied. Dairying and mixed farming are common, but highly specialized production also exists, such as the growing of fruits and vegetables in western Michigan and navy beans in the Saginaw Bay lowlands. Michigan leads the nation in the production of tart cherries, dry edible beans, and cucumbers for processing.

Organization of the Atlas

The *Atlas of Michigan* presents the major characteristics of the state. The initial pages provide basic reference maps to orient the reader to Michigan. The natural environment section establishes the landforms, climate, soils, flora, fauna, minerals, and water resources that are available to the people of the state. This is followed by a portrayal of the characteristics of the state's population and society; the distribution and density of the population and demographic as well as social variables are covered. The next section on Michigan's history and culture surveys major historical and political events, from the Indian period to the present. Then the significant economic features of Michigan are presented, with emphasis upon manufacturing and agriculture, to show the many ways that the people of Michigan make their living. Recreation and tourism are treated in a separate section because of their exceptional importance and variety in Michigan. Likewise, transportation and communication are examined independently to depict how goods, people, and ideas move within the state. Finally, there is a section not commonly found in most atlases, a look at what Michigan might be like in the future.

Special Features of the Atlas

Some features of this atlas need explanation so that the reader can better enjoy and benefit from its use.

Data for the atlas came from a wide variety of sources, many of them already published, such as statistical data books, state and national government publications, monographs, scholarly studies of various kinds, and published maps. This vast amount of information was transformed into maps, graphs, and charts using special methods and techniques. Much of the raw data was first coded for computer analysis and the initial plotting of maps. Fortunately, a variety of maps on Michigan topics already existed and could be incorporated directly into the atlas with only minor changes and redrafting. The major portion of the atlas, however, required production of original maps.

This atlas relies primarily upon two basic types of maps—the *isoline map* and the *choropleth map*. An isoline is a line connecting points of equal value. Hence an isoline map shows spatial distributions by lines connecting "control points," or points for which values are known. In some cases these values, as rainfall or temperature, are actually measured at those specific points. In other cases, however, the data are collected on the basis of areal units, such as counties, and the value for that unit is assigned an artificial control point in the the center of the unit. These values are most commonly shown in derived form, such as ratios, means, or percentages. Isolines are always located by interpolation, or estimation, on the basis of the locations and values of the control points. The accuracy and detail of an isoline map depend on the number of control points and the quality of the data. Since field work to collect original raw data was not possible, efforts were made to obtain the most recent, detailed, and reliable published data. Data for the early 1970s were used in most instances, but for some topics statistics for the late 1960s were the latest available. In some cases three-year averages were used in order to give a more accurate indication of trends.

The number of control points for counties is obviously limited to the 83 counties in Michigan. Even for other data the number of measuring stations in the state generally is not large. For example, there are only about 90 stations in Michigan collecting weather and climate data. Once the isolines are drawn, the data are ranked from highest to lowest and divided into several categories or "classes," normally five or six. Colors are assigned to each class to give the perception of relative increasing density from lowest to highest class. Thus, the isoline map should not be interpreted as an exact depiction of reality. Rather it is intended to show broad spatial patterns of selected phenomena across the state.

The choropleth map is also based on data aggregated on an areal basis—in the case of this atlas, on the county level. It differs, however, from the isoline map in that the boundaries of the counties, rather than isolines, delimit the classes of data. In using and interpreting the choropleth map, it is important to realize that the mean value for each county or statistical unit is shown. Hence,

Macatawa	mack a TAW wa
Mackinac Island	MACK in awe island
Mackinaw City	MACK in awe city
Marengo	mer ENG go
Manistique	man iss TEEK
Manitoulin	man i TOOL in
Marenisco	mare n ESS koe
Marlette	mar LET
Marquette	mar KET
Mecosta	ma COST a
Medora	ma DOOR a
Menominee	men AH ma knee
Mesick	ME sick
Michigamme	mich i GAHM me
Milakokia	mill a COKE a
Milan	MILE un
Millecoquins	mill a COKE in
Missaukee	mi SAW ki
Montague	MONT a gew
Munising	MEW ni sing
Munuscong	mun US kong
Muskalonge	MUSK a lunge
Muskegon	muss KEY gun
Nahma	NAY ma
Naomikong Pt.	nay AHM i kong point
Naubinway	NAW bin way
Neebish	KNEE beesh
Negaunee	na GONE ee
Nisula	NISS oo la
Nunica	NOON ick a
Ocqueoc	AH key ock
Ogemaw	OH ga maw
Okemos	OAK em us
Onekama	oh NECK a ma
Onondaga	on an DAY ga
Ontonagon	on ton AH gun
Osceola	ah see OH la
Oscoda	ahs CODE a
Ossineke	AH sin eek
Owosso	oh WAH so
Pequaming	pe KWAHM ing
Petoskey	pe TAH ski
Pinconning	pin CON ning
Pinnebog	PIN a bog
Pte. Aux Pins	point oh pan
Pte. Mouillee	point moo YEA
Pt. Aux Barques	point oh barks
Pt. Aux Chenes	point oh shane
Pokagon	poh KAY gun
Pontiac	PON tee ack
Pori	POUR eye
Potaganissing	pot a GAN iss sing
Presque Isle	presk eel
Quanicassee	kwahn icka SEE
Quinnesec	KWIN ness sec
Sagola	sa GO la
St. Jacques	saint jocks
Sanilac	SAN ill lack
Saugatuck	SAW ga tuck
Sault Ste. Marie	sue saint ma ree
Sebewaing	SEE ba wing
Seney	SEE knee
Seul Choix Pt.	SISH wah point
Shiawassee	shy a WAH see
Skandia	SKAN dee a
Stambaugh	STAM baw
Tahquamenon	ta KWAH men un
Tapiola	tappy OH la
Tawas	TAH wahss
Tecumseh	te COME SUH
Tekonsha	te KON sha
Tittabawassee	tit a ba WAH see
Toivola	TIE voh la
Topinabee	TOP in a bee
Traunik	TRAW nik
Trenary	tren AIRY
Wacousta	wa KOOSE ta
Wahjamega	wah ja ME ga
Watervliet	water v'LEET
Waugoshance	wah go SHAUNTS
Ypsilanti	ip sill ANT ee

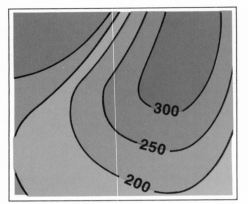
Isoline technique

Choropleth technique

the choropleth map is used only to show general impressions of relative distributions and not the exact values for specific places.

The degree of detail and accuracy of the maps in the atlas is also directly influenced by the projections and scales used. The traditional vertical map is a *polyconic projection,* a widely used compromise projection well suited to Michigan's shape and latitude, which provides minimal distortion in all directions and maintains relatively true areas, shapes, and distances. One innovation in this atlas, however, is an oblique view of the state as it would look when observed at an angle from space. This *isometric projection* was derived by computer and selected because it saved page space and added variety to the graphics. Because there is greater distortion of areas, shapes, and distances on such a projection, it was generally used for data that did not require the higher degree of exactness of the polyconic projection.

Both projections have been used in a wide range of scales. Map scale refers to the ratio of distance between two known points on the map and the same two points on the earth's surface. Most maps in the atlas are at very small scales, meaning that Michigan is shown on a map covering a small area on the page. The nature of most topics covered makes measurement with a scale unnecessary because the information being shown is highly generalized, regardless of whether it is portrayed by isolines, choropleths, or some other technique. Finally, some of the displays show time series or chronological sequences. For these, maps of the same scale have been used throughout each series in order to avoid implying greater relative importance of any given time period.

Another feature of this atlas is the complete bibliography of all data sources used in the production of the graphics, which will help the reader assess the reliability of a map or graph and provide sources for further information. Numbers at the end of each bibliographic entry indicate the pages for which the reference was used as a source.

Using the Atlas

The atlas comprises eight sections that logically present major themes. Each begins with an introductory essay, which is followed by a series of map pages showing the different topics making up the section's theme. Each series of map pages has a specific background color to facilitate immediate identification of a major section or theme. At the top of each map page is a key word or phrase indicating the topic on that page. Topics may also be located by using the table of contents or the comprehensive index at the back of the volume. The index is not intended to be a complete gazeteer, however.

The atlas may also be used for comparative analysis. For example, by comparing various climatic maps, such as precipitation, temperature, and length of growing season with the maps of soils and agricultural activities, a better understanding of the reasons for the location and nature of agriculture in the state should be possible. Strong correlations will also be noted between the successful agricultural areas and the population distribution maps. The most important value of comparative analysis, however, is the awareness that the human or cultural landscape is closely related to the physical or natural landscape, and that everything in the state is the result of many interacting factors. Comprehension of these basic relationships is the key to understanding the state of Michigan.

Lawrence M. Sommers
Jack F. Williams

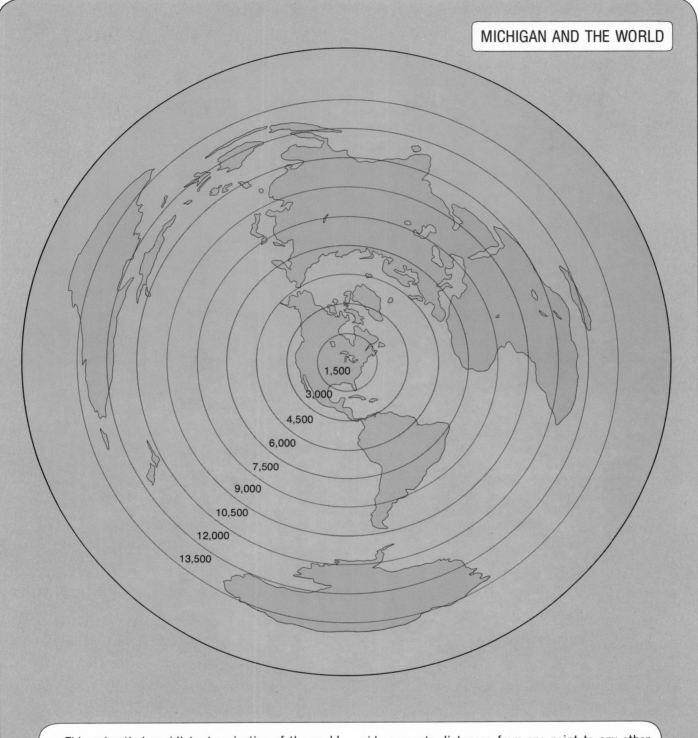

MICHIGAN AND THE WORLD

1,500
3,000
4,500
6,000
7,500
9,000
10,500
12,000
13,500

This azimuthal equidistant projection of the world is centered on Lansing, Michigan. Such a map projection shows true distances in all directions from the central point. Every point on the map is a true direction (azimuth) from the center point or Lansing. The concentric circles represent distances in increments of 1,500 miles (2,415 km) from Lansing to other parts of the world. The major advantage of this map is to pro-vide accurate distances from one point to any other given point. The projection does, however, result in great distortion of area and shape as one moves out-ward from the center. Distortion is especially severe in the outermost rings. An equidistant azimuthal projection is the only kind that can show the entire world; other azimuthals cover only one hemisphere.

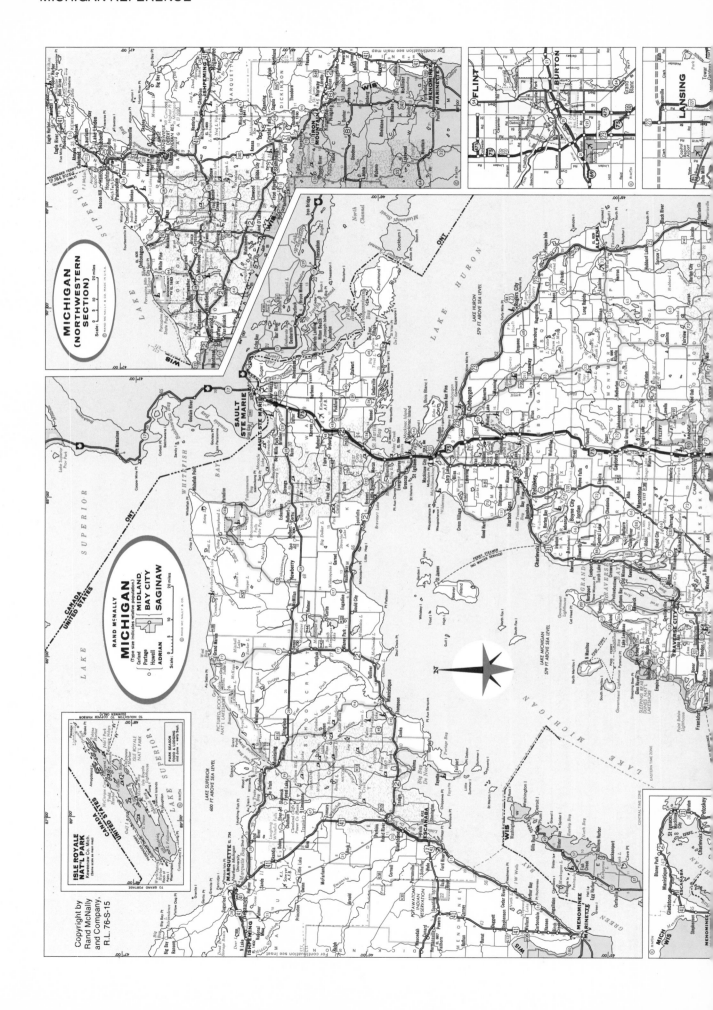

MICHIGAN (NORTHWESTERN SECTION)

Scale: 0 5 10 15 20 miles

RAND McNALLY
MICHIGAN
(Type size indicates relative population)

MIDLAND
BAY CITY
SAGINAW
Portage
Cleland
Howell
Adrian

Scale: 0 10 20 30 miles

ISLE ROYALE NAT'L PARK
Keweenaw Co. Mich.
(Same scale as main map)

FLINT

BURTON

LANSING

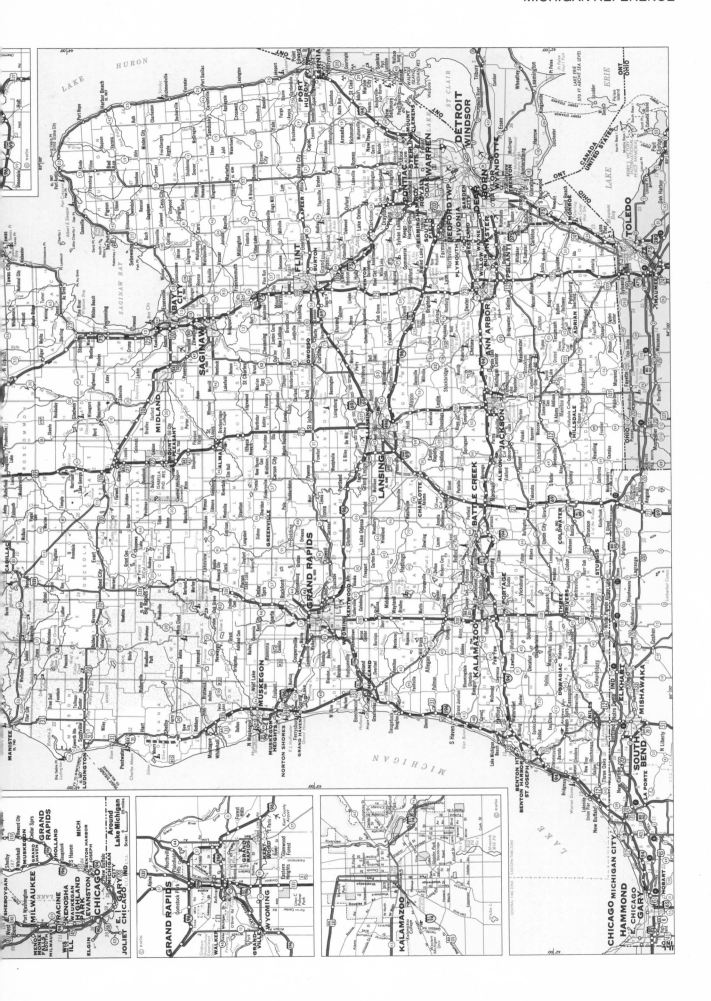

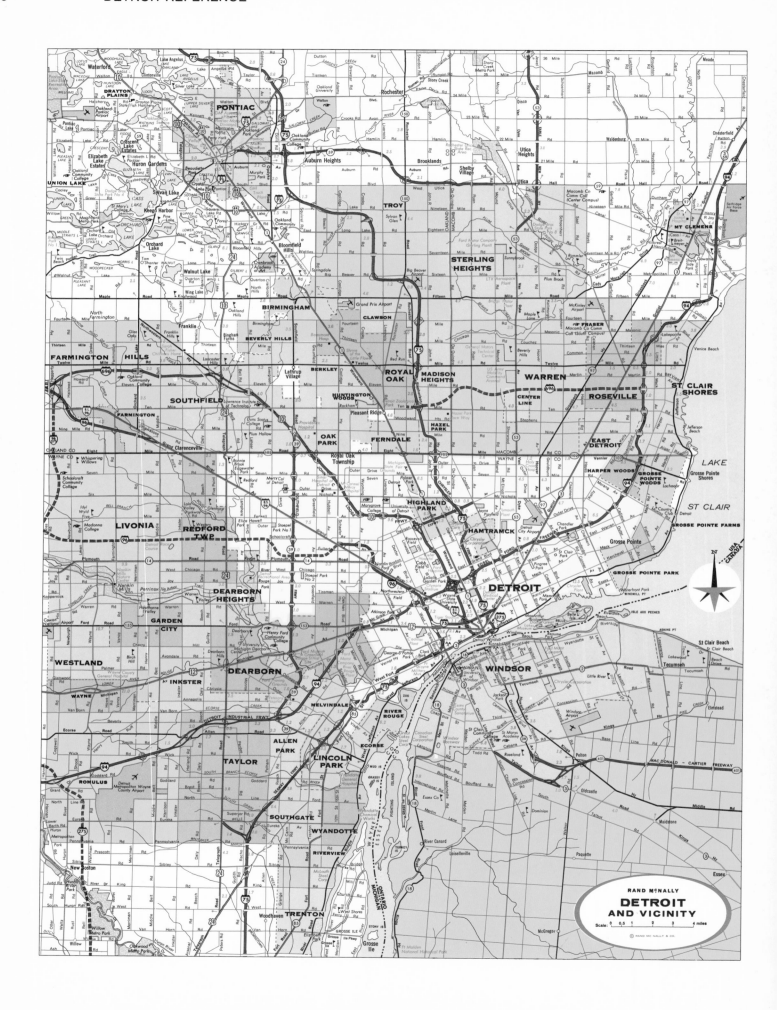

RAND McNALLY

DETROIT
AND VICINITY

Scale: 0 .5 1 2 3 4 miles

© RAND McNALLY & CO.

Distances between Selected Michigan Communities

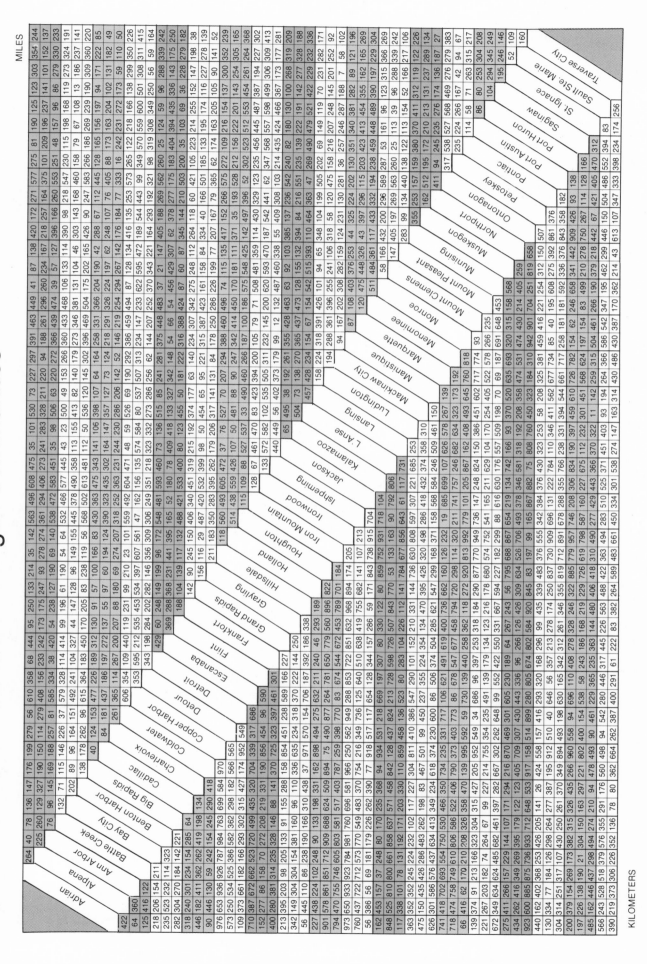

MILES

KILOMETERS

Source: Adapted from Michigan. Department of State Highways and Transportation. State Highway Commission. "Official Michigan Highway Map." Lansing, 1976.

MAJOR INHABITED ISLANDS

Inhabited islands of Michigan are found predominantly in the northern parts of both Lakes Michigan and Huron. The major exceptions are Isle Royale in Lake Superior (discussed on p. 58) and Belle Isle in the Detroit River in Detroit.

Mackinac Island, the best known of the northern islands shown on these two pages, is located less than four miles (6.4 km) east of St. Ignace. Its year-round population of 583 is increased considerably during the summer by tourists and people owning summer homes. Mackinac Island contains a state park, a museum emphasizing the history of the area, the famous Grand Hotel, and a number of interesting landforms and rock formations. No motor vehicles are allowed on the island. Ferry service is available from both St. Ignace and Mackinaw City.

Drummond Island, reached by ferry from De Tour, is a favorite place for hunting, fishing, and camping.

Beaver Island, the largest island in Lake Michigan, lies 30 miles (48.3km) off the shore of Emmet County. Ferry connections are available from Charlevoix during the tourist season. The island is most famous for the Mormon settlement established in 1847 and led by a tyrannical politician named James Jesse Strang. This colony was eliminated by force in 1856. Some Irish and a few Indians live on Beaver Island today, and many sportsmen come for fishing and hunting.

North and South Manitou Islands, reached during the summer by ferry from Leland, are largely wilderness areas that are now part of the Sleeping Bear Dunes National Lakeshore.

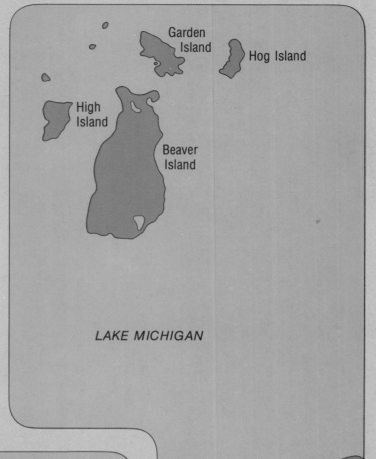

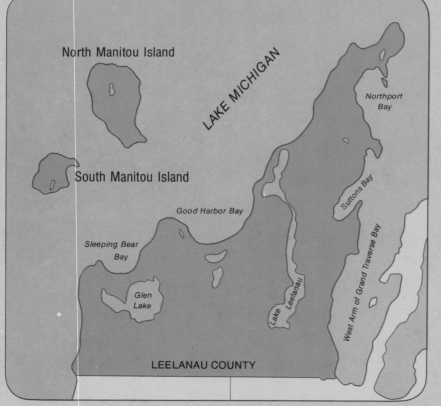

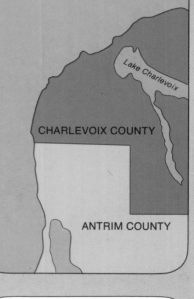

MILES

0   5   10

Scale For All Maps

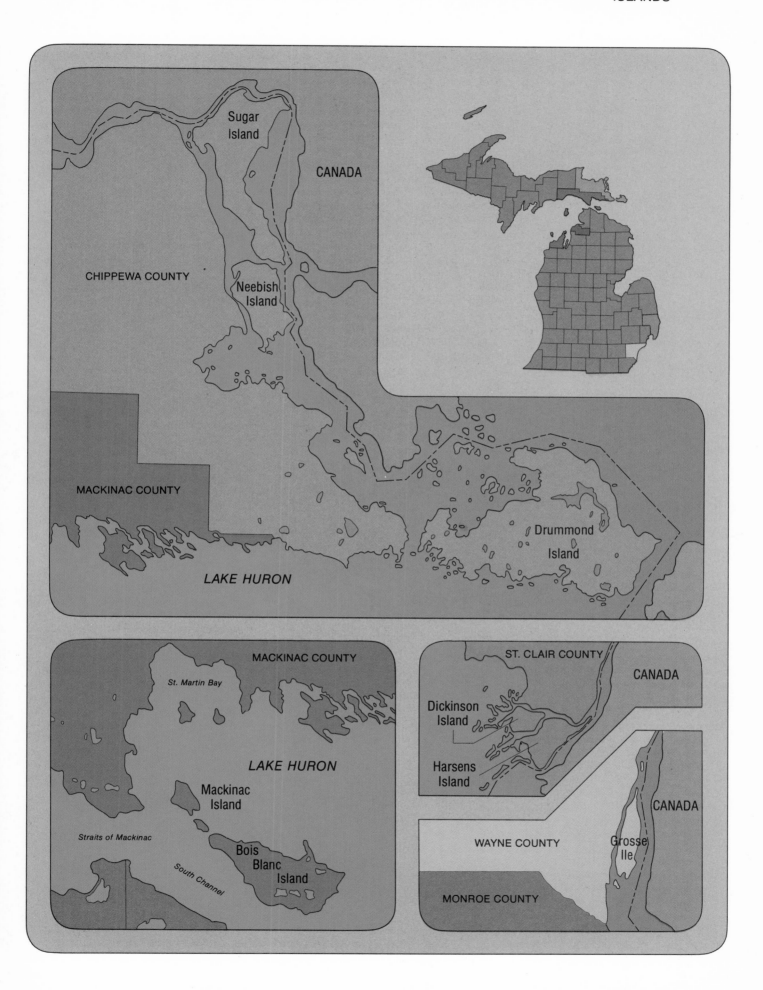

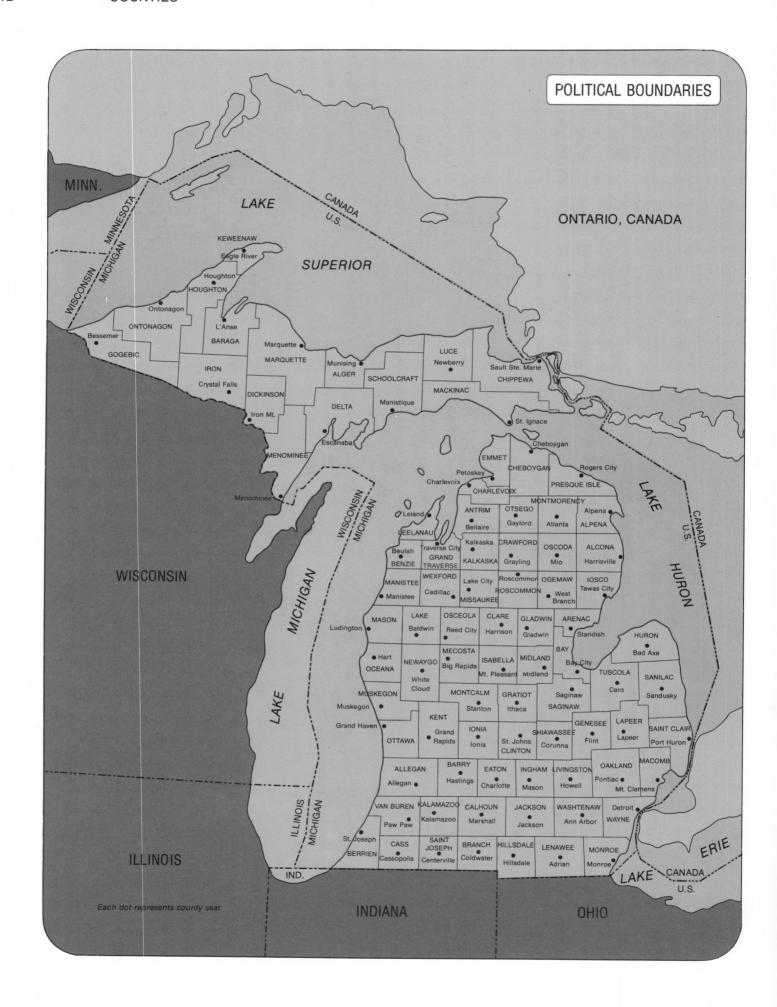

POLITICAL BOUNDARIES

MINN.

MINNESOTA

WISCONSIN

MICHIGAN

LAKE SUPERIOR

CANADA
U.S.

ONTARIO, CANADA

KEWEENAW
Eagle River

Houghton
HOUGHTON

Ontonagon

ONTONAGON

L'Anse
BARAGA

Bessemer

GOGEBIC

IRON
Crystal Falls

DICKINSON
Iron Mt.

Marquette
MARQUETTE

Munising
ALGER

DELTA
Manistique

SCHOOLCRAFT

LUCE
Newberry

MACKINAC

Sault Ste. Marie
CHIPPEWA

LAKE HURON

CANADA
U.S.

Escanaba

MENOMINEE

Menominee

WISCONSIN

WISCONSIN
MICHIGAN

LAKE MICHIGAN

St. Ignace

Cheboygan

EMMET
Petoskey

Charlevoix
CHARLEVOIX

Leland

LEELANAU

Beulah
BENZIE

MANISTEE
Manistee

CHEBOYGAN

MONTMORENCY

ANTRIM
Bellaire

OTSEGO
Gaylord

Atlanta

Rogers City
PRESQUE ISLE

Alpena
ALPENA

WISCONSIN

Traverse City
GRAND
TRAVERSE

Kalkaska
KALKASKA

CRAWFORD
Grayling

OSCODA
Mio

ALCONA
Harrisville

WEXFORD
Cadillac

Lake City
MISSAUKEE

Roscommon
ROSCOMMON

OGEMAW
West
Branch

IOSCO
Tawas City

MASON
Ludington

LAKE
Baldwin

OSCEOLA
Reed City

CLARE
Harrison

GLADWIN
Gladwin

ARENAC
Standish

HURON
Bad Axe

Hart
OCEANA

NEWAYGO
White
Cloud

MECOSTA
Big Rapids

ISABELLA
Mt. Pleasant

MIDLAND
Midland

BAY
Bay City

TUSCOLA
Caro

SANILAC
Sandusky

MUSKEGON
Muskegon

Grand Haven

OTTAWA

MONTCALM
Stanton

KENT
Grand
Rapids

GRATIOT
Ithaca

SAGINAW
Saginaw

IONIA
Ionia

St. Johns
CLINTON

SHIAWASSEE
Corunna

GENESEE
Flint

LAPEER
Lapeer

SAINT CLAIR
Port Huron

ALLEGAN
Allegan

BARRY
Hastings

EATON
Charlotte

INGHAM
Mason

LIVINGSTON
Howell

OAKLAND
Pontiac

MACOMB
Mt. Clemens

WISCONSIN

LAKE MICHIGAN

ILLINOIS
MICHIGAN

VAN BUREN
Paw Paw

KALAMAZOO
Kalamazoo

CALHOUN
Marshall

JACKSON
Jackson

WASHTENAW
Ann Arbor

Detroit
WAYNE

ILLINOIS

St. Joseph
BERRIEN

CASS
Cassopolis

SAINT
JOSEPH
Centreville

BRANCH
Coldwater

HILLSDALE
Hillsdale

LENAWEE
Adrian

MONROE
Monroe

ERIE

LAKE
CANADA
U.S.

Each dot represents county seat

INDIANA

IND.

OHIO

Since the late 1800s the U.S. Geological Survey has compiled topographic maps of much of the United States. The unit of survey is a quadrangle bounded by parallels of latitude and meridians of longitude. The most detailed maps, published at the scale of 1:24,000 (1 inch = 2,000 feet), cover 7½ minutes of latitude and longitude. Maps covering 15 minutes of latitude and longitude are printed at the scale of 1:62,500 (1 inch = approximately 1 mile).

Eventually, all of the country including the state of Michigan will be mapped, or remapped, with metric measures. Two map series are planned: a 1:25,000 (7½ minutes) series to replace the 1:24,000 maps, and 1:100,000 (1° x 30') quadrangles to supplant the 15 minute, 1:62,500 sheets. Completion of the 1:24,000 series mapping probably will be accomplished before the metric scale maps are begun.

A little less than half of Michigan's surface has been mapped in 7½ minute quadrangles. Michigan ranks fortieth among the states in percentage of topographic map coverage. Most of the land surface yet to be covered by this scale of mapping is in the western halves of both the Lower and Upper Peninsulas. Topographic maps provide useful information for fishermen, hunters, hikers, other recreationists, builders, and various private and public agencies.

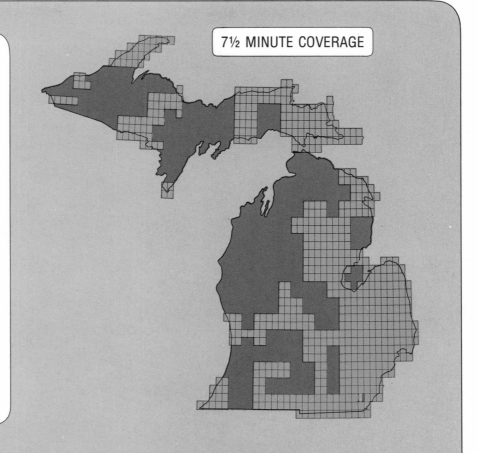

7½ MINUTE COVERAGE

15 MINUTE COVERAGE

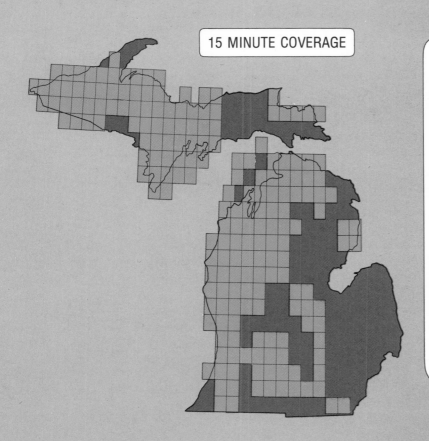

Each topographic map is designated by the name of a city, town, or prominent natural feature within its boundaries. The indexes to topographic maps of Michigan shown on this page list each quadrangle by name and date of publication. The quadrangles are available from the Michigan Geological Survey Office, Department of Natural Resources, Lansing, Michigan.

The older 15 minute quadrangles cover most of the Upper Peninsula and the western two-thirds of the Lower Peninsula. The newer 7½ minute maps were begun in the areas not yet covered by the 15 minute quadrangles. No new mapping at the 1:62,500 scale is being done. Maps of practically all of the state are currently available in one or the other of these two series.

Topographic maps are generally printed in four colors. Cultural features, such as roads, are shown in red. Black is used for other man-made objects including railroads and buildings, and all lettering is in this color. Blue is used to depict water features. Most quadrangles are available with a green overprint delimiting woodlots. Elevations of the land above sea level are indicated by brown contour lines. Although the contour interval is dependent on the map scale and terrain ruggedness, 10 and 20 foot intervals are common on Michigan quadrangles.

NATURAL ENVIRONMENT

Si quaeris peninsulam amoenam, circumspice—if you seek a beautiful peninsula, look about you. This legend on the great seal of the state of Michigan is evidence of the feeling Michigan's early leaders had for their natural environment. The rich and varied resources that Michigan still offers its residents are the subjects of this section.

Geology

Geologic formations in Michigan span a vast period of time. The period called Precambrian — that is, before 570 million years ago — covers 87 percent of geologic time. On the basis of isotope dating the U.S. Geological Survey has broadly divided this vast period into the classifications shown in the margin on the next page. Using this classification we can outline the history of Michigan's Precambrian.

Michigan's oldest rocks belong to the Precambrian W period and consist of gneisses, some of which are probably older than 3.5 billion years, and greenstones. The extrusion of the greenstones, which are probably volcanic in origin and bear some similarities to the basalts found on modern ocean floors, was followed by a period of granite intrusion.

The state's next oldest rocks, Precambrian X, are metamorphosed sediments that were deposited unconformably about 2 billion years ago on the deformed Precambrian W rocks and subsequently deformed and metamorphosed themselves. They consist of quartzites, carbonates, slates, and volcanics. Among the more spectacular deposits are the Kona dolomite, which contains well-preserved algal structures, and the famous banded iron formations, which are the source of Michigan's iron ore.

In the Precambrian Y period a basin developed into which the Keweenawan rocks were deposited. The formations consist of sandstones, conglomerates, and shales together with more than 12,000 feet (3,600 meters) of mafic volcanics. These rocks are best known for the native copper deposits that have been mined since the 1840s. Pure copper occurs in the spaces left by gas bubbles in the lavas, in fractures, and between pebbles within the conglomerates. It also occurs as a sulphide in the Nonsuch shale, from which it is extracted at White Pine. These rocks are separated from the rest of the Precambrian rocks by the Keweenaw fault. All these rocks were deformed into large synclines of which the Keweenaw Peninsula is one limb and Isle Royale the other.

Underlying the Cambrian sandstones to the west is perhaps Michigan's only representative of the Precambrian Z period, the Jacobsville sandstone. It is not deformed, except where it approaches the Keweenaw fault, and it lacks fossils. Estimates of its age vary from Keweenawan to Cambrian.

During most of the Cambrian period Michigan was exposed to erosion. Seas encroached late in the period and deposited a thick layer of sand that was indurated to stone over the entire state. Portions of this sandstone are exposed in the famous Pictured Rocks along the Lake Superior shoreline in the Upper Peninsula. The seas became widespread over much of North America during Ordovician time, and a warm, mild climate developed that produced extensive layers of carbonate rocks. During the deposition of these rocks the Michigan basin, a broad saucer-shaped depression, first developed. Later fracturing of these Ordovician carbonates along a fault led to the formation of the giant Albion-Scipio oil field in south central Michigan, which will eventually produce more than 100 million barrels of oil.

The warm, mild climate continued, and middle Silurian time saw the development of a massive barrier reef, 600 feet (180 meters) thick, made up of corals and algae, that completely encircled the Lower Peninsula. Along the basinward side of this feature small finger-like reefs called pinnacles grew in great numbers. After burial they acted as traps for oil and gas migrating outward from the deeper basin. These Silurian pinnacle reefs have provided the impetus for extensive petroleum exploration, first in Saint Clair County (1957), then in Grand Traverse and Kalkaska counties (1969), and later in Ingham County (1970).

By late Silurian time the climate had become arid and vast thicknesses of salt were precipitated in a rapidly subsiding Michigan basin. The greatest thickness of salt, some 1,600 feet (480 meters), exists in the subsurface near the southwest end of Saginaw Bay and is partly responsible for the extensive chemical industry there.

During the onset of the Devonian period, which was marked by crustal instability, periods of marine deposition resulting principally in sandstones and limestones were interrupted by frequent uplifts and erosion. By middle Devonian time the basin had stabilized and was covered by a warm, shallow sea. At times the climate became arid and salt deposits formed, mostly in the northern half of what is now the Lower Peninsula. As the arid climate abated, normal salinity was restored in the extensive shallow seas covering Michigan, and widespread deposits of limestone were laid down. These limestones form the basis of the quarrying industry at Rogers City, one of the largest limestone quarries in the world, and also yield the famous Petoskey stones — wave-polished fragments of colonial corals that grew in the Devonian seas. The early development of the oil industry in Michigan was based on petroleum traps in anticlines in which Devonian carbonates serve as the reservoir rock. Extensive oil pools were developed in the central part of the state. Toward the end of Devonian time the seas became stagnant and limestone deposition gave way to black muds that eventually formed a thick black shale over much of the Lower Peninsula.

Shale deposition continued during the Mississippian period, but conditions on the sea floor were normal and the shales are typically gray to greenish-gray in color. As the period progressed there were intervals when the seas became extremely shallow, producing blanket sandstones and some evaporites, notably gypsum. The gypsum is close enough to the surface at Grand Rapids to be mined commercially. At the end of the Mississippian time uplift and erosion were predominant in the United States, and the Michigan area was subjected to a mild episode of folding. By Pennsylvanian time, uplift was occurring in the Appalachian region, and vast quantities of sediment were carried into Michigan by westward-flowing streams. Swampy deltaic and coastal environments alternated with shallow marine conditions as the sea fluctuated in and out of the area. The swampy terrain eventually led to the formation of thin

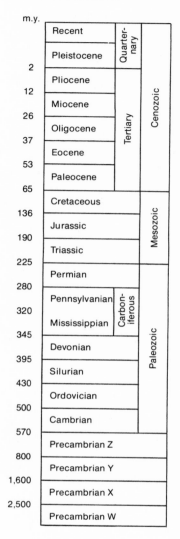

GEOLOGIC TIME SCALE

m.y.			
Recent	Quarternary		Cenozoic
Pleistocene			
2			
Pliocene	Tertiary		
12			
Miocene			
26			
Oligocene			
37			
Eocene			
53			
Paleocene			
65			
Cretaceous		Mesozoic	
136			
Jurassic			
190			
Triassic			
225			
Permian		Paleozoic	
280			
Pennsylvanian	Carboniferous		
320			
Mississippian			
345			
Devonian			
395			
Silurian			
430			
Ordovician			
500			
Cambrian			
570			
Precambrian Z			
800			
Precambrian Y			
1,600			
Precambrian X			
2,500			
Precambrian W			

m.y. = million years before present

coal beds, primarily in east central Michigan, that were mined periodically from 1860 to the 1970s.

Michigan underwent a very long period of erosion of more than 100 million years following the Pennsylvanian period. The Michigan basin had essentially stabilized by the end of Mississippian time, sinking only slightly during the Pennsylvanian. A brief incursion of the sea in late Jurassic time left a few thin red beds that filled in low spots in the terrain. The total Paleozoic sedimentary accumulation at the thickest point in the Michigan basin is about 15,000 feet (4,500 meters) in Arenac County, immediately north of Saginaw Bay.

The next recorded geologic event in the state was the advent of glaciers during parts of the Pleistocene epoch. Evidence of the last three of the four major glacial advances during this ice age can be seen in Michigan. Glaciers scoured the surface, moved millions of tons of surface burden to new locations further south, and left glacial ridges such as moraines, till, kames, eskers, and other deposits as they receded. During the warmer weather that occurred between the ice ages of this period new plants and animals moved north, and mammoths, mastodons, giant beavers, musk-oxen, and other vertebrates were known to have lived in Michigan.

Glaciers from the last ice age retreated from Michigan approximately 15,000 to 9,500 years ago, leaving behind the Great Lakes. These waters drained first to the south, later to the east across Ontario to the Saint Lawrence River, and still later via Lake Saint Clair, the Detroit River, and Lake Erie as they do now.

Landforms

The past geologic events, especially glaciation, have provided Michigan with a variety of landforms: highlands, hilly uplands, hill-lands, upland plains, rolling plains, plains, and lake-border plains. The levelness and low-lying nature of the lake-border plains attest to their relatively recent inundation. Scattered moraines, till plains, and connecting patterns of outwash plains characterize much of the rest of the state.

Michigan's old mountain remnants and hill-lands with the highest altitudes are found in the western Upper Peninsula. Brockway Mountain in Keweenaw County, the Huron Mountains in northern Marquette County, and the Porcupine Mountains in Ontonagon County are familiar examples of these highland areas. The highest sites in the state, with elevations of about 1,800 feet (531 meters), are found in the hilly uplands south of the more familiar mountains of the Upper Peninsula. Other highlands are found in the north central part of the Lower Peninsula and in Hillsdale and Lapeer counties in Lower Michigan. These lands range from 1,000 to 1,600 feet (295 to 472 meters) in elevation. The steep slopes of the highlands in the northern half of the Lower Peninsula make them logical sites for winter skiing and associated recreational uses.

Most of the remaining surface land of Michigan lies between 600 and 1,000 feet (177 and 295 meters) above sea level. Considerable expanses of relatively level lands that were once submerged by glacial lakes are found in the Saginaw Valley and along Lake Saint Clair, the Detroit River, and Lake Erie.

Topographic variations do not stop at the edges of the Great Lakes. Lake Superior, with its average water level of about 600 feet (177 meters) above sea level, is both the largest and deepest of the Great Lakes, at one point dropping to a maximum depth of 1,333 feet (393 meters). Lakes Michigan and Huron, with an average water level of 579 feet (171 meters), are somewhat shallower, Lake Michigan having a maximum depth of about 925 feet (273 meters) and Lake Huron about 725 feet (214 meters). Lake Erie, in turn, is relatively shallow. Its average surface level is 570 feet (168 meters) above sea level, and only a small area in the eastern part of the lake reaches depths of 200 feet (59 meters).

Soils

As indicated, most of Michigan's bedrock is buried under layers of glacial deposits. These parent rocks provided the primary materials from which the soils were formed, aided by such factors as topography, climate, types of vegetative cover, and time.

Wisconsin calcareous glacial drift is the parent material for most of the soils in the Lower Peninsula and in the south central portion of the Upper Peninsula. Sandy glacial drift is the parent material for soils in the eastern part of the Upper Peninsula and also in the northwestern and west central parts of the Lower Peninsula. Most of the soils in the western Upper Peninsula were formed from slightly calcareous or noncalcareous Wisconsin drift, whereas the soils in a few areas such as the northwestern and eastern Upper Peninsula and along the Detroit River and Lake Erie were formed from lacustrine and till deposits.

Michigan soils, because of the state's moderately rolling topography, ordinarily retain adequate moisture to enjoy optimum aeration and oxidation and to facilitate desirable biological activity and chemical alterations. Soils on flat areas, however, often have a zone of saturation near the surface that restricts aeration and oxidation and leads to gleying (development of gray colors). In general, Michigan soils receive considerable precipitation and are affected by the state's lower summer and winter temperatures, shorter periods of frost-free weather, and greater depths of frost penetration. Freezing and thawing can facilitate the breaking down of parent rock materials, but shorter periods of warm weather are a deterrent to needed biological action.

Vegetation has also affected Michigan's soil types. Except for a few small prairies in southwest Michigan where the soils were conditioned by the annual growth and decay of tall prairie grasses, all of Michigan's upland soils were formed under forest cover. Southern Michigan was covered with a well-developed deciduous forest in which oak and hickory trees prevailed on the better-drained lands, and beech, elm, maple, and basswood predominated on the less well-drained lands. The northern Lower Peninsula and the Upper Peninsula, in turn, were covered with a forest of conifers and mixed hardwoods.

On the basis of their composition, characteristics, water holding capacities, and infiltration rates, Michigan's soils have been classified by series and associations within the six orders shown in the margin. A significant portion of the southern counties is covered with Hapludalfs (well-drained Alfisols) that developed in a humid, temperate climate under deciduous forest cover. They are moderately productive and are responsive to good agricultural management. Ochraqualfs (somewhat poorly drained Alfisols) and Haplaquepts (poorly drained Inceptisols) predominate in the Thumb area, the Saginaw Valley, and in various other parts of southern Michigan. These soils, which were formed from level or nearly level lacustrine or till deposits, usually have a high potential for agricultural use but suffer from poor natural drainage. Southern Michigan also has areas with mixtures of Hapludalfs, Ochraqualfs, and Haplaquolls (poorly drained Mollisols). Tracts of organic soils, Histosols, developed from partially decomposed woody and herbaceous plant materials, also occur at many sites in old glacial lake beds and in bottomland areas.

Most of northern Michigan is covered with Haplorthods (well-drained Spodosols). These soils were formed under coniferous and mixed hardwood cover. Some of the finer textured soils have a good potential for agricultural use. The more shallow and sandy soils are best used for forest culture. Tracts of Eutroboralfs (well-drained Alfisols), which were formed from more calcareous and finer textured materials, also are found in the eastern Upper Peninsula and in the northern part of the Lower Peninsula.

Although Michigan's soils are not the most productive in the nation, the state has considerable area that boasts soil and climatic characteristics appropriate for specialized uses and high yields. Areas near Lake Michigan capitalize on climatic advantages for fruit production. Many other sites, such as some of Michigan's muck land farms, have good soils for vegetables and other specialty crops. Other lands are best suited at the present time for forestry and recreation.

SOIL HORIZONS

A Horizon

The surface layer and normally the highest in organic matter

B Horizon

The middle layer where minerals accumulate

C Horizon

The bottom layer consisting of relatively unaltered parent material

SIX SOIL ORDERS
IN MICHIGAN

Alfisols

Soils with accumulations of clay in the B horizon

Spodosols

Soils with accumulations of iron, aluminum, and humus or partially decayed organic material in the B horizon

Mollisols

Soils with dark, thick A horizons

Entisols

Soils with little or no evidence of B horizon development

Inceptisols

Soils with weakly developed B horizons

Histosols

Soils such as mucks and peats developed from organic materials

Water

Michigan prides itself as being the nation's "Water Wonderland," an image well deserved. Of the state's official gross water and land area of 61,946,160 acres (25,088,194 hectares), some 40 percent or 24,688,000 acres (9,998,640 hectares) is covered by the Great Lakes, and another 841,000 acres (340,605 hectares) are covered with inland lakes and ponds. The state lies within the drainage basin of the Great Lakes. It has 3,251 miles (5,202 kilometers) of shoreline on the Great Lakes and 36,350 miles (58,160 kilometers) of inland streams. About 35,000 mapped lakes and ponds each cover areas of more than a tenth of an acre (.04 of an hectare.) Including the 20 large inland lakes, Michigan has about 6,500 lakes that each cover ten acres (four hectares) or more and about 15,800 that cover two acres (.8 hectares) or more.

Early explorers found much of the Michigan area swampy or poorly drained. Surface and tile drains have been extensively used, and practically all of the land area of southern Michigan is included in drainage districts. An estimated 50,000 individual drainage projects of varying size are now in operation throughout the state.

Groundwater is readily available from bedrock or from glacial deposits at most sites in the state, although there are places in the western Upper Peninsula and in southern Michigan where well yields are low. There are also areas in the state where underlying salt deposits make the supplies of groundwater unfit for normal household use.

The Great Lakes are one of the largest freshwater sources in the world. Many coastal settlements and several inland communities depend on the Great Lakes for their water supply. Water supply problems in the state are complicated by the uneven distribution of population. Most of the domestic and industrial need for water is concentrated in the southern third of the state. The Detroit area experiences both the greatest pressure upon surface and groundwater supplies and the greatest threat of pollution of existing sources.

Flora

More than half of Michigan's surface area is now covered with trees. The predominant species are maple, birch, hemlock, aspen, spruce, and fir in the Upper Peninsula and maple, beech, birch, aspen, and pine in southern Michigan. Most of the elms of Michigan's presettlement forest have disappeared and many of the earlier pine stands of northern Michigan have been replaced with aspen and birch.

Michigan is a broad transition zone between the broadleaf deciduous forests of the eastern United States and the needleleaf evergreen forests of Canada. Its flora thus consists of species common to both regions, and plants occupy physical sites similar to those characteristic of their original centers of distribution. For example, species common to the Canadian boreal forest are found principally on acid, infertile soils of bogs or sandy uplands. In constrast, the deciduous or broadleaved species widespread in the eastern United States, such as beech, sugar maple, and red oak, prefer the more fertile clay or loam upland soils. The alternation of forest communities is largely due to the sorting of plants in relation to local soil properties and terrain characteristics.

Patterns of both the original and present forest reflect gradients of climate and soil texture. South of a transition zone extending from near Muskegon to Saginaw Bay the presettlement forest consisted of deciduous trees on all but the wettest, most acid sites. Black oak, white oak, red maple, and shagbark hickory were found on dry, well-drained uplands, but sugar maple, beech, basswood, and red oak were prevalent on more moist, somewhat finer (but still upland) soils. In the counties near Lake Michigan, beech and maple were more widespread than elsewhere, possibly because of the drought-reducing effect of the lake. On low muck, alluvial, or lake plain soils, as in the Saginaw Bay lowland, forests of ash, American elm, silver and red maples, and swamp white oak were common.

North of this transition zone where northern species were more prevalent, coarse, sandy soils are more widespread, the climate is cooler, and the growing season is shorter. Lower temperatures in summer reduce the rate at which moisture is depleted from the soil, and coarse textures result in more acid upland soils. These conditions permitted boreal plants to occupy a greater variety of northern sites in Michigan. As a result, beech and sugar maple were mixed with white pine, hemlock, and yellow birch on all but the most well-drained uplands, particularly in northwestern Lower Michigan where precipitation is greater. In drier northeastern and north central Lower Michigan, these species were confined to the finer, moister upland soils; elsewhere, dry-site oaks or pines were common. The great Michigan white and red pine stands, of which Hartwick Pines State Park is a small uncut remnant, were spread over the lower sandy soils in a wide swath from Montmorency and Alpena counties to Oceana and Newaygo counties.

In the presettlement landscape of the Upper Peninsula similar forest patterns had developed, with pines generally on sandy, acid soils. However, cooler summer weather there led to a higher percentage of northern drought-sensitive species in the upland forests, and thus hemlock, yellow birch, balsam fir, and white spruce were more common than in northern Lower Michigan, particularly in the Keweenaw Peninsula. A greater number of the poorly drained sites were sufficiently cold and acid that bog communities of black spruce and larch were a conspicuous part of the landscape.

Since settlement by white man nearly all of Michigan's forested landscape has been subjected to disturbances of various types. Change was most pronounced on the coarser soils of northern Michigan where white and red pine dominated. There, heavy logging and subsequent fires, ending by the 1930s, converted the forest to one of oaks, jack pine, and, on the slightly better soils, aspen and white birch. In contrast, logging on the best upland soils (where beech, yellow birch, sugar maple, and hemlock dominated) had much less effect on the composition of subsequent successional stands. It was generally assumed that the plow would continue to follow the axe, but much of the northern land proved unsuitable for farming, and a "cutover" land problem resulted. Most of the cutover lands have since reverted to forests and now support a growing tree cover that provides a valuable forestry and recreational resource. Because so much poorer, sandy soil was subjected to the logging and fire sequence, forest communities of oak, aspen, and white birch are among the most common in northern Lower Michigan today. Like the pines, they are intolerant of shade and, without disturbance again, will be succeeded by sugar or red maple over large areas. The habitat favorable for deer, which thrive on young aspen stands, and other species, such as Kirtland's Warbler which is specific to young jack pine stands, will slowly change.

Because of Michigan's wide array of habitats and its transitional position between the boreal and eastern forests of North America, many plants have very local distributions within the state. The dunes along portions of both Lakes Michigan and Superior have long captured the attention of botanists because of the unique habitats and tree and dune grass vegetation found there. In southwestern Lower Michigan, especially Saint Joseph, Cass, and Kalamazoo counties, patches of upland prairie interrupted the presettlement forest. Covered by grass species common to the prairies of Illinois and Iowa, they are thought to be remnants of more extensive prairies that developed several thousand years ago across southern Lower Michigan during a post-glacial dry period and persisted because of locally favorable soils. Blueberries also occur locally across much of the state. Requiring acid soils, they are found on both sandy pinelands and low, boggy sites in northern Michigan, but are more restricted to bogs in southern Lower Michigan. Thimbleberry, a northern raspberry, is so abundant in the Keweenaw Peninsula that it is used for making jam. In some bogs across the state wild cranberry is sufficiently plentiful to make collecting worthwhile. Mushrooms, especially morels, are common in the forests of the northwestern portion of the Lower Peninsula and are avidly sought in the spring in places such as Mesick.

Fauna

Humans have also disrupted Michigan's wildlife. Hunting and settlement have contributed to the disappearance of the initial populations of caribou, moose, elk, wild turkeys, and grayling. Although squirrel and deer have been greatly reduced, a population of 1 million deer still inhabits much of Michigan, especially the northern Lower Peninsula and the Upper Peninsula. The size of the herd is controlled by the amount of hunting that is allowed and the amount of winter feed. Of the deer population, 300,000 are found in the Upper Peninsula and 700,000 in the Lower Peninsula.

Michigan possesses a wide assortment of birds, fish, and wild animals. Elk and wild turkeys have been reintroduced into the state. New species such as pheasants, rainbow and brown trout, and coho, king, and Atlantic salmon have been brought in, and unwanted species such as sea lamprey and alewives have entered the Great Lakes via the Saint Lawrence Seaway. Opossums have come to the state without human encouragement. The inland lakes and rivers are inhabited by perch, bass, pike, crappie, and trout. Whitefish, lake trout, perch, and smelt are native to the Great Lakes. The many birds that pass through the state on spring and fall migrations augment the great variety of native birds. Ducks, geese, quail, and pheasant are much sought by hunters during open seasons. Fur-bearing animals are common; trade in furs was important in the state's early history. Major species include bear, mink, rabbit, fox, muskrat, otter, and racoon. Although Michigan is called the "Wolverine State," that animal no longer exists in the state.

Climate

One of the most important factors determining Michigan's climate is the state's position within the westerly wind belt. Circling the earth north of about 30 degrees latitude, the westerlies influence the climate of most of North America. They are characterized by a procession of centers of high and low atmospheric pressure during much of the year and ensure the day-to-day changeability so typical of Michigan weather. Because of the eastward movement of air in the westerlies, most weather changes within the state occur first in the western counties. Surface winds are much affected by the high and low pressure systems moving across the state and may be from any direction at a given time, even though the systems themselves move generally eastward.

During winter the westerlies envelop much of North America, including Michigan, and weather changes are often as frequent and abrupt in the southern Lower Peninsula as in the Upper Peninsula. In July and August, however, the main belt of eastward-moving weather disturbances often shifts northward, carrying the zone of greatest weather changeability with it. As a result prolonged spells of hot, humid, and often rainless weather may occur in southern Lower Michigan but are less likely elsewhere in the state and are rare in the Upper Peninsula. For the same reason, brief summer showers are somewhat more frequent in the northern parts of the state, whereas no rain may fall for prolonged intervals in the south.

Another factor contributing to the climate of Michigan is its location in the eastern two-thirds of North America, a large zone in which the lack of major mountain barriers allows air masses of contrasting properties—moist tropical air from the South, mild but dry air from the West, and bitter cold air from the Arctic—to converge, assuring the potential for extreme weather changes. Passing storms do, however, provide beneficial rain or snowfall. Most of the precipitation falling in Michigan (except to the lee of the Great Lakes) originates as moisture in northward-moving air masses from the Gulf of Mexico that interact with cold or dry air masses of northern origin.

At times the pattern of weather movement within the westerlies is not exactly west to east; it may, for example, possess a northerly component so that weather disturbances originating in Canada are steered southeastward over Michigan. Such a pattern may produce very cold weather that can last for weeks, particularly in winter. At other times, the movement of weather may have a southerly component, and a series of storms from the southern Great Plains may pass northeastward over Michigan.

The Great Lakes also affect the climate of Michigan. During the winter they are usually warmer than the air passing over them; thus, the heat they add to the overlying atmosphere results in moderated temperatures in leeshore areas, particularly on exceptionally cold nights. In addition, moisture acquired by the cold air as it passes over the warmer lake water usually results in cloudiness that moves eastward with the airflow and covers these leeshore areas sometimes 20 miles (32 kilometers) or more inland. Acting like a blanket, this cloud cover moderates nighttime minimum temperatures and often keeps leeshore stations up to 20 degrees Fahrenheit (9.0 degrees Centigrade) warmer than stations in the interior. As a result of these influences, average January temperatures generally are less cold in leeshore areas. Even during the first frosty days of autumn the lakes retain some summer warmth and may prevent early freezes and so extend the growing season of adjacent downwind areas and peninsulas until well after it has ended in the interior.

A further influence of the Great Lakes on the climate of downwind areas is the generation of so-called "lake-effect" snow. This snowfall occurs if the moisture acquired by cold air passing over the unfrozen waters of the lakes promotes the development of clouds sufficiently thick to yield precipitation. Normally, if a substantial difference between the temperature of the lake and the air prevails, many inches of snow may fall, and the associated cloudiness may cover much of the state. Commonly, only areas within about 20 miles (32 kilometers) of the lakeshore receive measurable snow. Some northern Michigan areas along Lakes Superior and Michigan receive snowfall almost daily during the winter months. About half of this snowfall comes from passing storms and the rest from cold-air-generated lake-effect clouds.

The Great Lakes also modify the climate of leeshore areas during the warm season. Because they are cooler than the surrounding land areas in summer, they chill the adjacent shore areas, sometimes for several miles inland. Extreme maximum temperatures are lower, therefore, on east shore and peninsular sites than in the interior.

Michigan's climate also is affected by elevation and topography. The areas of greatest local relief in northern Lower Michigan and in the Keweenaw Peninsula, Huron Mountains, and Porcupine Mountains of the Upper Peninsula are regions of heavy average annual snowfall. Hilly topography also favors the development of frost and low temperature pockets under calm nighttime conditions. The unusually low minimum temperatures associated with these pockets are not necessarily representative of regional conditions.

Raleigh Barlowe
F. William Cambray
James H. Fisher
Jay R. Harman
Delbert L. Mokma

Pictured Rocks

Lake of the Clouds

Sleeping Bear Dunes

Tip of the Thumb

PERSPECTIVE PHYSIOGRAPHIC DIAGRAM

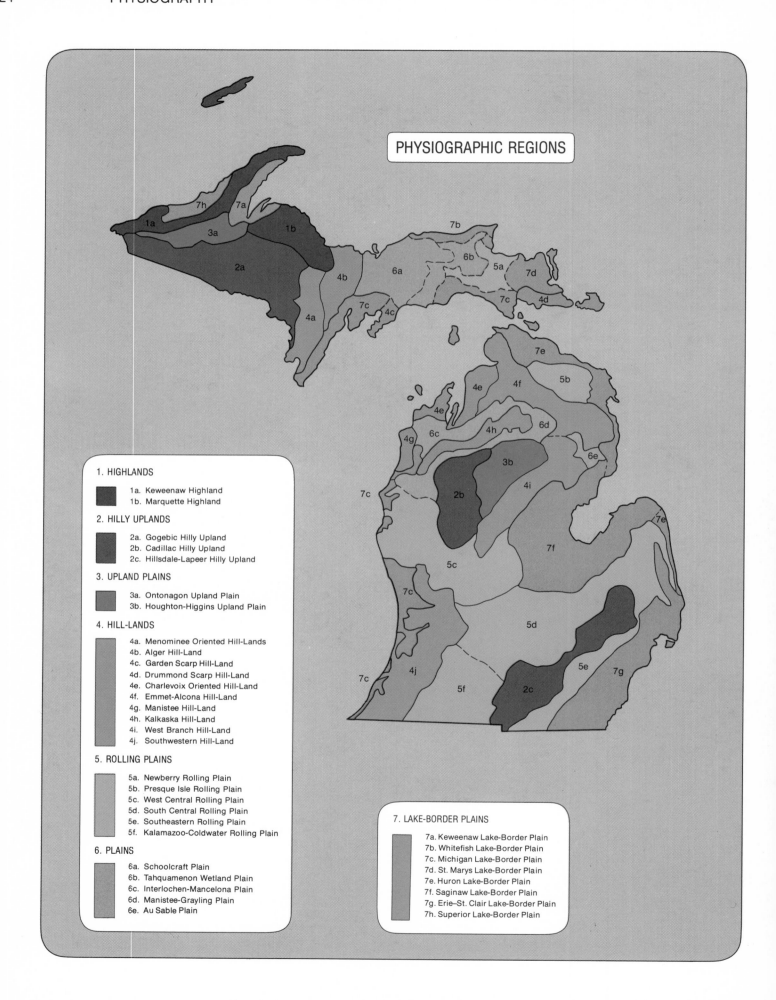

PHYSIOGRAPHIC REGIONS

1. HIGHLANDS

1a. Keweenaw Highland
1b. Marquette Highland

2. HILLY UPLANDS

2a. Gogebic Hilly Upland
2b. Cadillac Hilly Upland
2c. Hillsdale-Lapeer Hilly Upland

3. UPLAND PLAINS

3a. Ontonagon Upland Plain
3b. Houghton-Higgins Upland Plain

4. HILL-LANDS

4a. Menominee Oriented Hill-Lands
4b. Alger Hill-Land
4c. Garden Scarp Hill-Land
4d. Drummond Scarp Hill-Land
4e. Charlevoix Oriented Hill-Land
4f. Emmet-Alcona Hill-Land
4g. Manistee Hill-Land
4h. Kalkaska Hill-Land
4i. West Branch Hill-Land
4j. Southwestern Hill-Land

5. ROLLING PLAINS

5a. Newberry Rolling Plain
5b. Presque Isle Rolling Plain
5c. West Central Rolling Plain
5d. South Central Rolling Plain
5e. Southeastern Rolling Plain
5f. Kalamazoo-Coldwater Rolling Plain

6. PLAINS

6a. Schoolcraft Plain
6b. Tahquamenon Wetland Plain
6c. Interlochen-Mancelona Plain
6d. Manistee-Grayling Plain
6e. Au Sable Plain

7. LAKE-BORDER PLAINS

7a. Keweenaw Lake-Border Plain
7b. Whitefish Lake-Border Plain
7c. Michigan Lake-Border Plain
7d. St. Marys Lake-Border Plain
7e. Huron Lake-Border Plain
7f. Saginaw Lake-Border Plain
7g. Erie–St. Clair Lake-Border Plain
7h. Superior Lake-Border Plain

With elevation above sea level and local relief serving as the two major distinguishing criteria, the Michigan landscape can be divided into seven first-order topographic types, illustrated below. Further subdivision into physiographic regions, shown on the map to the left, is possible on the basis of surface materials, drainage, microrelief, and other selected landform characteristics. The boundaries of these regions may be distinct, such as the inner margin of the lake-border plains or the Keweenaw highland (la), or they may be transitional (indicated by dashed lines), such as those between the Schoolcraft and Tahquamenon wetland plains (6a and 6b). A comparison of the map to the left with the maps showing the geologic age of bedrock (p. 30) and surface formations (p. 32) reveals some distinct correspondence: the trends of the Precambrian bedrock formations underlie the more rugged terrain of the western half of the Upper Peninsula, whereas the recessional moraines, outwash plains, interlobate complexes, and lacustrine plains of Pleistocene age stand out in the Lower Peninsula. Most of these physiographic regions can also be recognized in the preceding physiographic diagram of Michigan's landscape.

The only portions of the state that may be called mountainous are located near the western half of the Lake Superior shore (la). Here the igneous and metamorphic formations of the Keweenaw Peninsula, the Porcupine and Huron mountains, and also Isle Royale support large tracts of considerable local relief. The topographic diversity of this part of the state results largely from differences in the geologic age and resistance to weathering and erosion of the bedrock units, as well as from variations in the thickness of glacial drift.

The hilliest portions of the Lower Peninsula are found in the interlobate moraine tracts (see surface formations, p. 32). These hill-and-lake areas form the axis of the Thumb (called Hillsdale–Lapeer hilly upland, 2c) and the rather massive hills of the Cadillac area (2b). They easily stand out as some of the most markedly rolling terrain in Michigan. The hill-lands reach somewhat lower elevations, but still exhibit a pronounced relief and contain some of the locally most distinctive landforms in the state. To this category belong the striking drumlin concentrations (see selected landforms, p. 33) in the west central part of the Upper Peninsula (4a) and the Traverse Bay vicinity (4e), and the well-defined recessional moraines, which impose a linear grain to the landscape of the northern interior (4f to 4i) and extreme southwest (4j) of the Lower Peninsula.

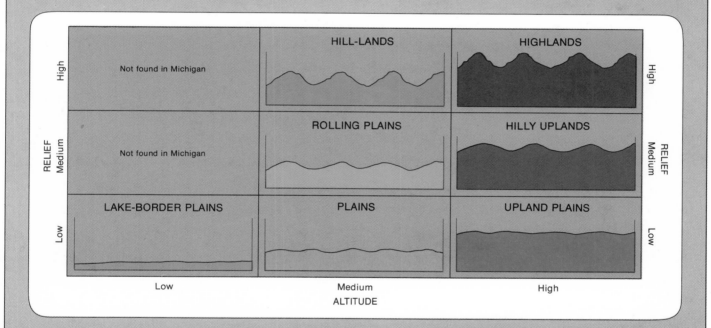

Physiographic regions of distinct character are more difficult to define in the low-relief categories. Boundaries between them may follow drainage divides, delimit isolated flatlands large enough to be shown on small-scale maps, or set off the relatively large areas of poorly or somewhat poorly drained lake-border plains. In the case of the rolling plains of southern lower Michigan (5c to 5f), the boundaries between the suggested subdivisions are based more on location than on distinct topographic differences: till plains and low-relief recessional moraines alternating with outwash plains give this large portion of the state a rather homogeneous physiographic character. The south central rolling plain is notable, however, for the large number of eskers (see selected landforms, p. 33). The extensive complexes of outwash and deltaic deposits in the eastern portion of the Upper Peninsula (6a and 6b), in the northern Lower Peninsula (6c and 6d), and in the lower Au Sable valley (6e) are grouped together in a physiographic category. Similar in origin and appearance, but at higher elevations are the Ontonagon and Houghton-Higgins upland plains (3a and 3b).

Minimal elevational differences characterize vast stretches of land in Michigan bordering the Great Lakes, but these lake-border plains (identified as lacustrine plains on the surface formations map, p. 32) are not entirely featureless. Beach ridges, indicative of former higher lake levels, and inland dune fields are noteworthy, especially in the Saginaw and Erie–St. Clair sectors (7f and 7g), as are the numerous sharply defined valleys cut into some of these lake-border plains, particularly the Superior region (7h) and the southern part of the Huron lake-border plain (7e). Distinctive and sometimes massive dunes are characteristic of much of the Lake Michigan border as well as the Grand Marais area along the southern shore of Lake Superior.

These lakeshore dunes are one of the most unique landforms in Michigan. They are largely a result of the combined action of waves and the prevailing westerly winds piling up sands along the eastern and southern shores of Lakes Michigan and Superior. In some cases the dunes are built upon glacial moraine deposits.

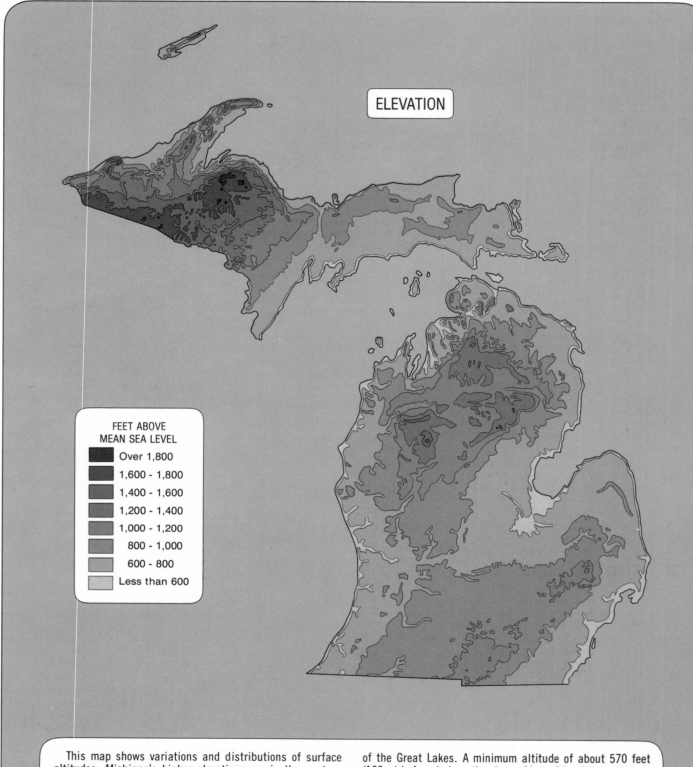

ELEVATION

FEET ABOVE
MEAN SEA LEVEL

Over 1,800
1,600 - 1,800
1,400 - 1,600
1,200 - 1,400
1,000 - 1,200
800 - 1,000
600 - 800
Less than 600

This map shows variations and distributions of surface altitudes. Michigan's higher elevations are in the western Upper Peninsula, the highest hilltop, Mount Curwood in north central Baraga County, being 1,980 feet (594 m). Much of the western Upper Peninsula is underlain by old resistant bedrock that has a thin cover of glacial drift in places. The lowest areas in the state are along the shorelines of the Great Lakes. A minimum altitude of about 570 feet (169 m) is found along the shore of Lake Erie. Although maximum variation in altitude within the state is about 1,400 feet (413 m), most of the Lower Peninsula and the eastern half of the Upper Peninsula have elevations that vary from 600 to 1,000 feet (177 m to 295 m). Extreme variations in altitude are uncommon.

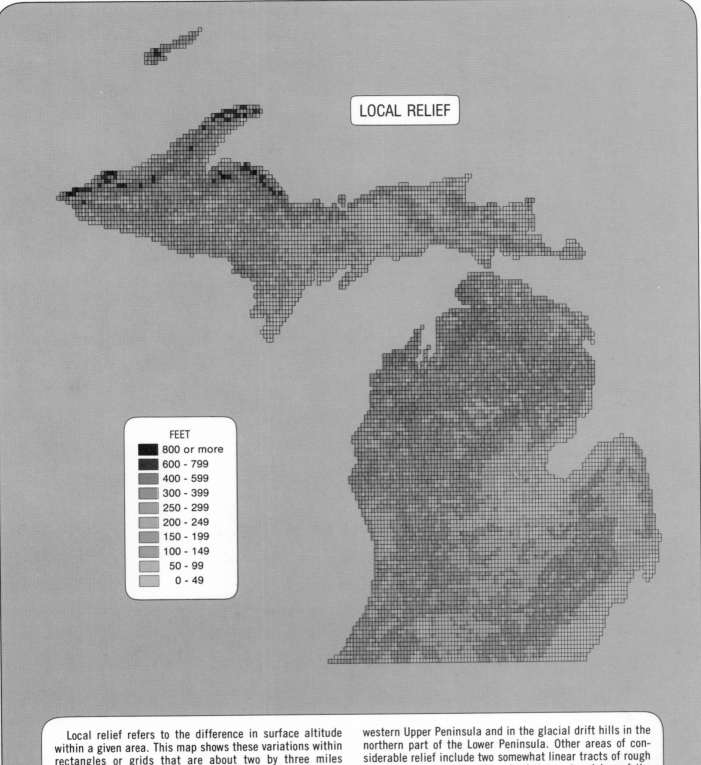

LOCAL RELIEF

FEET

- 800 or more
- 600 - 799
- 400 - 599
- 300 - 399
- 250 - 299
- 200 - 249
- 150 - 199
- 100 - 149
- 50 - 99
- 0 - 49

Local relief refers to the difference in surface altitude within a given area. This map shows these variations within rectangles or grids that are about two by three miles (3.2 by 4.8 km) in size. The areas with lowest relief are located along the Lake Erie–Lake St. Clair shoreline, within the Saginaw lowland, and in the eastern portion of the Upper Peninsula. Many of these low-relief tracts, especially in the Lower Peninsula, are due to former glacial lakes. The greatest amount of local relief exists in the bedrock highlands in the western Upper Peninsula and in the glacial drift hills in the northern part of the Lower Peninsula. Other areas of considerable relief include two somewhat linear tracts of rough interlobate topography (deposits between two lobes of the glacier) in the southern part of the Lower Peninsula as well as certain coastal areas of the Great Lakes where both erosion and glacial deposits have produced rugged topography, such as the dunes along Lakes Michigan and Superior.

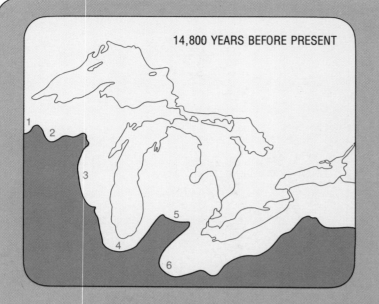

14,800 YEARS BEFORE PRESENT

It is generally accepted that the Great Lakes did not exist in preglacial times but are the cumulative result of several phases of glaciation that took place during the Pleistocene. It is also believed that some sort of system of large lakes existed in conjunction with the earlier glacial and interglacial episodes, but the character and configuration of the present Great Lakes are the products of the final deglaciation of their drainage basin that began around 14,800 radio-carbon years before the present (14,800 B.P.). At that time several major lobes characterized the margin of the continental glacier within the Great Lakes area. These included, from west to east, the Superior (1), Chippewa (2), Green Bay (3), Michigan (4), Saginaw (5), and Huron-Erie (6) lobes. As the margins of these lobes retreated, melt-water and precipitation drained southward to the Gulf of Mexico because higher land or glacial ice blocked flow in other directions.

By 14,000 B.P. a considerable area of the Lower Peninsula was deglaciated, and the three lobes affecting the area were more clearly separate. Drainage continued southward to the Gulf of Mexico, but further retreat of the margins of the Michigan and Huron-Erie lobes resulted in the impoundment of water between the ice margin and moraines formed previously by the glaciers. This is the first phase of the complex development of the present Great Lakes, which are the result of such factors as erosion and deposition by the glaciers, blockage of drainage by glacial ice, subsidence of the land beneath the glacier's immense weight followed by rebounding of land during and after glaciation, and postglacial lowering of lake outlets by erosion. The following stages summarize some important aspects of the further development of the lakes.

14,000 YEARS BEFORE PRESENT

? = Position questionable

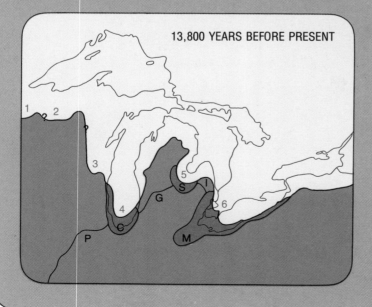

13,800 YEARS BEFORE PRESENT

The first glacial lakes to form were Maumee (M) and Chicago (C), associated with the Huron-Erie and Michigan lobes, respectively. Initially excess water from Glacial Lake Maumee flowed southwest to the Wabash River, and Glacial Lake Chicago drained west and south by way of the Illinois River (P). Further retreat of the ice margin resulted in the formation of Glacial Lake Saginaw (S) by about 13,800 B.P. This lake drained westward through the Maple River–Grand River (G) lowland to Glacial Lake Chicago. The recession of the ice margin in southeast Michigan also uncovered lower north-flowing outlets for Glacial Lake Maumee. One of these, referred to as the Imlay Outlet (I) after the city of the same name, permitted water to drain from Lake Maumee into Lake Saginaw. At this time, about one-half of the Lower Peninsula was deglaciated, but ice still covered all of the Upper Peninsula.

About 12,500 B.P. another lower drainage way referred to as the Ubly outlet (U) was uncovered in southeast Michigan by the retreating ice margin, and it carried water northward from the Erie basin. The result was Glacial Lake Whittlesey (W), which had a lower level than its predecessor, Maumee. Ubly outlet drained into Glacial Lake Saginaw, which had increased in size because of marginal retreat by the Saginaw lobe. Excess waters of the glacial lake continued to drain westward to Glacial Lake Chicago by way of the Maple River–Grand River lowland. Glacial Lake Chicago continued to drain southward, but its level and that of Lake Saginaw were somewhat lower because of downcutting and erosion by their outlet streams.

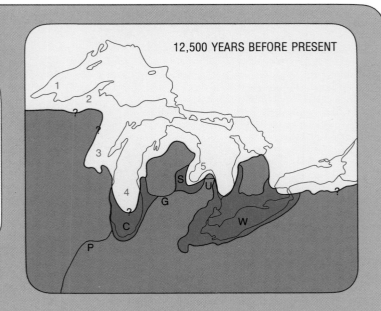

By 11,000 B.P. most, if not all, of the basins of Lakes Michigan and Huron were deglaciated, and one large body of water, Lake Algonquin (A), resulted from the coalescence of Glacial Lakes Saginaw and Chicago. This lake was more extensive than the present Lakes Michigan and Huron (582 ft or 175 m above sea level) because its altitude was more than 20 feet higher (605 ft or 182 m). Drainage of Lake Algonquin changed with time from the previously established Glacial Lake Chicago outlet (P) to the Lake Erie Basin by way of the St. Clair–Detroit River (SD), and eventually by even lower outlets across what is now Ontario. Water in the Erie basin (E) drained eastward over an ancestral Niagara Falls into Glacial Lake Iroquois (I), which discharged into the Hudson River of New York by way of the Rome outlet (R). The predecessor to Lake Superior, Glacial Lake Duluth (D), formed at this time and drained southward by way of the St. Croix River (SC).

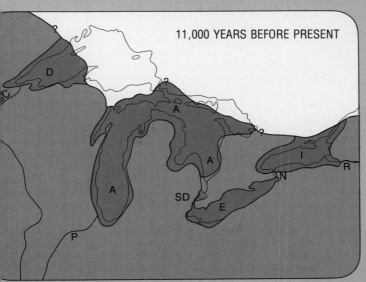

Final deglaciation of the state took place about 9,500 B.P. and permitted Glacial Lake Duluth to grow in area and at the same time drain by lower outlets, first southward across the central Upper Peninsula and later eastward by way of the St. Marys River. The marginal retreat of the ice from land depressed by the former weight of the glacier permitted unusual low-water lake levels in both the Michigan (Glacial Lake Chippewa—CP) and Huron (Glacial Lake Stanley—ST) basins. This was accomplished by the presence of such low-level drainage ways across Ontario as the Ottawa River (O), which drained into the Champlain Sea (CS), an estuary of the Atlantic Ocean. Lake Erie continued to drain eastward via Niagara Falls (N), which were slowly retreating because of erosion. The present-day Great Lakes formed as the earth's crust, depressed from the weight of the ice sheets, rebounded with deglaciation. This raised the level of the Ottawa River outlet, drained the Champlain Sea, formed the St. Lawrence River, and eventually reestablished the St. Clair–Detroit River outlet for Lake Huron.

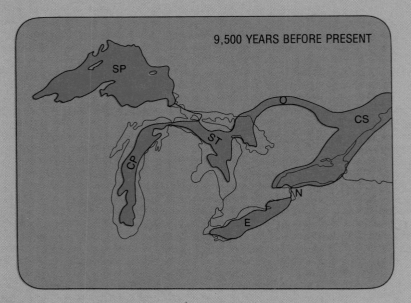

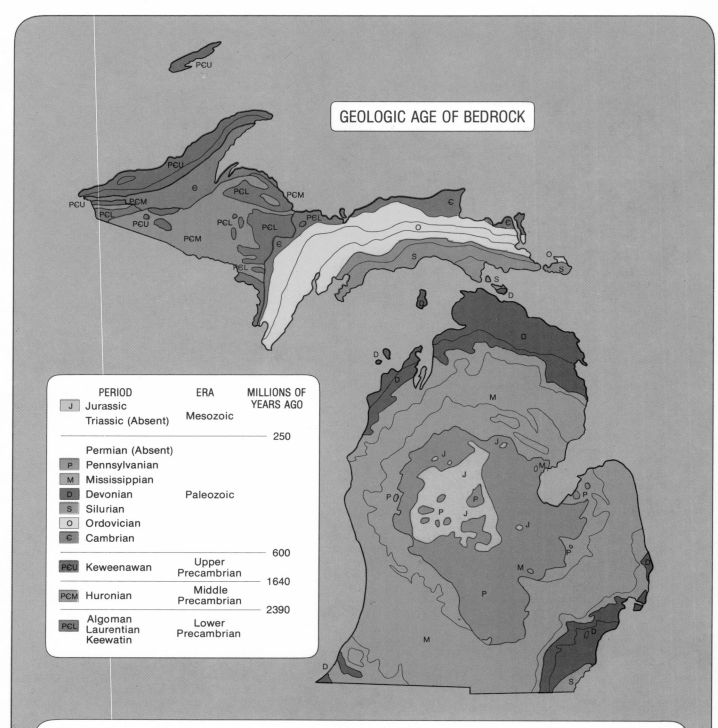

GEOLOGIC AGE OF BEDROCK

PERIOD		ERA	MILLIONS OF YEARS AGO
J	Jurassic	Mesozoic	
	Triassic (Absent)		
			250
	Permian (Absent)		
P	Pennsylvanian		
M	Mississippian		
D	Devonian	Paleozoic	
S	Silurian		
O	Ordovician		
Є	Cambrian		
			600
PЄU	Keweenawan	Upper Precambrian	
			1640
PЄM	Huronian	Middle Precambrian	
			2390
PЄL	Algoman Laurentian Keewatin	Lower Precambrian	

The consolidated rock formations of Michigan, referred to as bedrock, range from about 150 million to more than 3 billion years in age. The oldest, known as the Precambrian, are exposed at the surface at many places in the western part of the Upper Peninsula and most are either igneous or metamorphic. The most important metallic mineral resources of the state, iron and copper, are associated with some of these formations. Collectively they form the basement rocks of the state. On this map the Jacobsville sandstone has been included in the Cambrian series.

During Paleozoic time, from 600 million to 250 million years ago, the surface of these rocks tended to subside to form a basin structure centered at about the mid point of the Lower Peninsula. As subsidence took place sediments accumulated in this basin to form the rocks that range from the older and outermost Cambrian through the younger and inner Pennsylvanian and post-Paleozoic Jurassic formations. The succession of deposition in the basin and subsequent erosion resulted in the concentric pattern of saucer-like layers on the map. Lakes Michigan and Huron occupy basins eroded into weaker rock units and conform to the concentric pattern. Important nonmetallic resources including petroleum, natural gas, limestone, gypsum, and brines are associated with some of the Paleozoic sedimentary formations.

Mineral-collecting areas are predominant in the Upper Peninsula in the complex igneous rocks of the Canadian Shield. The fossil-collecting sites are located where sedimentary rocks are close to the surface and rock quarries are generally found. There are no fossil locations in that portion of the Lower Peninsula where the glacial drift is deep. The two lower maps indicate that Pleistocene-age vertebrates predominated in the southern half of the Lower Peninsula where climate, food, and habitat were favorable. Both plains and Arctic species of vertebrates have been found in Michigan.

FOSSIL- AND MINERAL-COLLECTING LOCALITIES

I Fossil Location
• Mineral Location

RECORDED DISCOVERY SITES OF PLEISTOCENE-AGE MAMMOTHS AND MASTODONS

DISCOVERY SITES OF OTHER PLEISTOCENE-AGE VERTEBRATES

INCLUDES GIANT BEAVER, PECCARY, BISON, MOOSE, CARIBOU, AND MUSK-OX

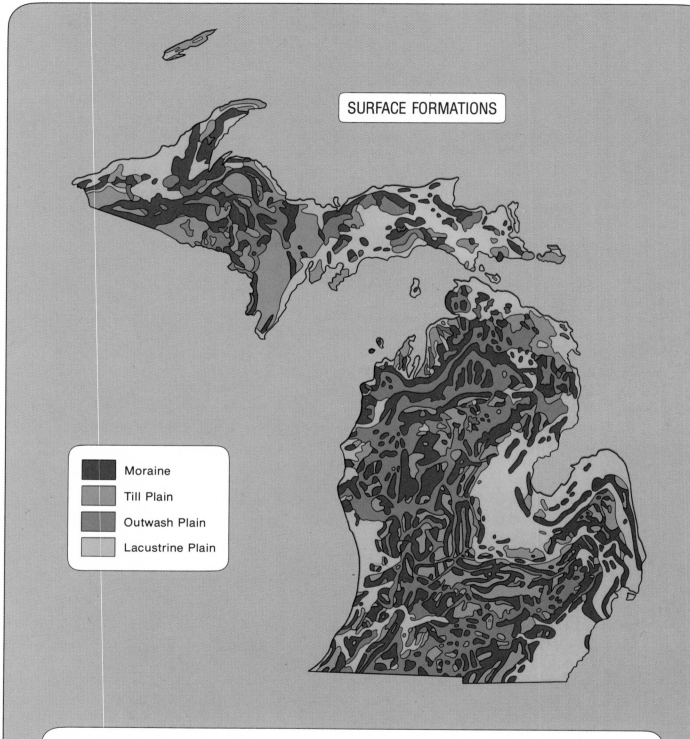

SURFACE FORMATIONS

Moraine

Till Plain

Outwash Plain

Lacustrine Plain

The surface formations of Michigan are largely late-glacial and postglacial in age. **Moraines,** linear hilly belts, were formed by the deposition of debris (sand, gravel, rocks, clay, and so forth) at the margins of the glacier when the rate of ice advance equaled the amount of melting at the periphery. In today's landscape, a moraine represents the former position of an ice border or margin. Numerous linear and curved moraines exist because the margins of several glacial lobes held a number of positions during deglaciation. **Till plains,** gently rolling topography that also resulted from deposition by ice, may have formed as an ice margin retreated from one position to another. **Outwash plains,** stratified deposits of clay, silt, sand, and gravel, were formed by the numerous melt-water streams that carried sediments away from the glacier. **Water-deposited plains** resulted from clays, silt, and other finer sediments in glacial and postglacial lakes that have since been drained.

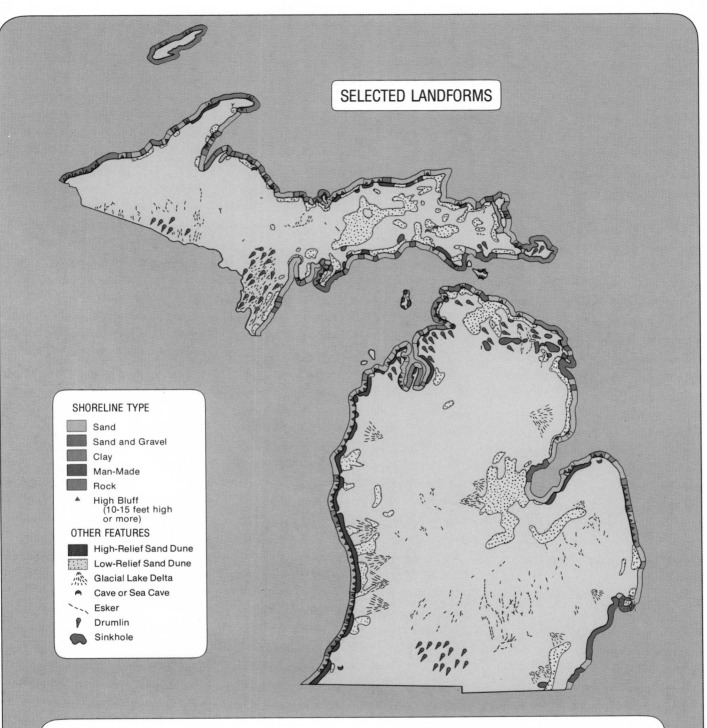

SELECTED LANDFORMS

SHORELINE TYPE

Sand

Sand and Gravel

Clay

Man-Made

Rock

▲ High Bluff
   (10-15 feet high
   or more)

OTHER FEATURES

High-Relief Sand Dune

Low-Relief Sand Dune

Glacial Lake Delta

Cave or Sea Cave

Esker

Drumlin

Sinkhole

With the limited relief of Michigan's land surface, great contrasts in landforms are not to be expected, but there are distinctions nevertheless. The high bluffs that cut into the moraines and the active dunes of the Lake Michigan shore of the Lower Peninsula contrast with the lacustrine flats—former lake floors—along the eastern coast. The rocky stretches of the igneous, northwestern Upper Peninsula give way to predominantly sandy and gravelly shores in its eastern, sedimentary portion. The rocky coasts near Big Bay De Noc and around Drummond Island reflect the presence of the resistant Niagara dolomite that rims this part of the Michigan basin. The bedrock outcrops at Rogers City, Petoskey, and Grindstone City form the most extensive rocky shores of the Lower Peninsula. Another distinctive feature of Michigan's coastline are the sand dunes along various portions of the Great Lakes.

Of the many landforms produced by glacial action in Michigan, the drumlins (tear-drop shaped hills) and eskers (sinuous ridges of sand and gravel) are particularly noteworthy. Large expanses of flat lacustrine (glacial-lake deposited) plains with low beach ridges are found in several places in Michigan, and fossil sand dunes are located in the Saginaw Bay lowland.

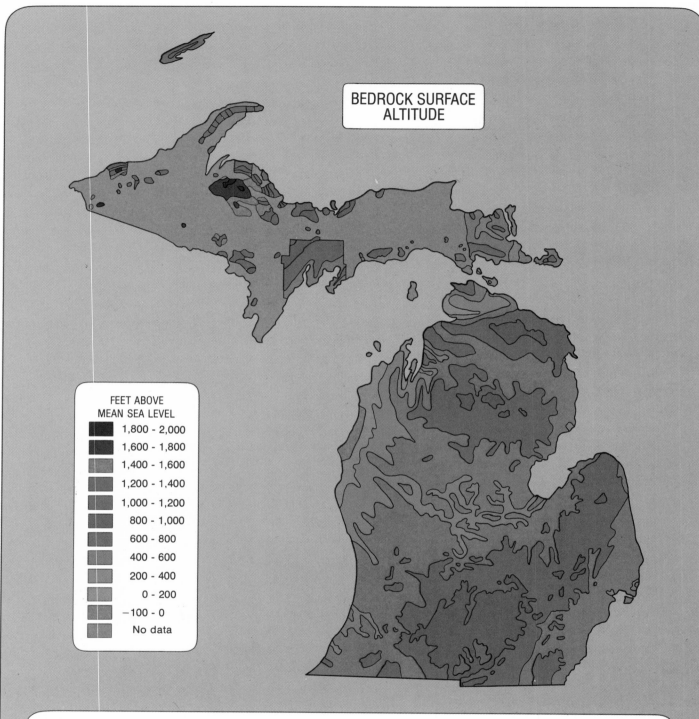

BEDROCK SURFACE
ALTITUDE

FEET ABOVE
MEAN SEA LEVEL

1,800 - 2,000
1,600 - 1,800
1,400 - 1,600
1,200 - 1,400
1,000 - 1,200
800 - 1,000
600 - 800
400 - 600
200 - 400
0 - 200
−100 - 0
No data

   This map shows the approximate altitude of the bedrock surface that is buried beneath unconsolidated Pleistocene or younger deposits in much of the state. The map is compiled largely from water- and petroleum-well data, which are much more abundant for the Lower Peninsula. The surface is the result of differential weathering and erosion of the bedrock in preglacial times and the gradational effects of glaciation. Higher altitudes are usually associated with more resistant bedrock and lower surfaces with weaker formations. The highest bedrock elevations are within the area of resistant Precambrian rocks in the western part of the Upper Peninsula, but toward the east, where weaker Paleozoic rocks exist, the altitude is considerably lower. The bedrock surface of the Lower Peninsula is in the form of two plateaus surrounded by lower surfaces. These plateaus, one in the northern part and the other in the Thumb, are supported by more resistant Paleozoic rocks. Adjacent areas underlain by weaker rocks formed during the same era were eroded to lower levels before and during glaciation to form, at least in part, the lowlands now occupied by the Great Lakes. In some places, most notably beneath Lakes Superior and Michigan, the bedrock surface is lower than the present sea level. Thus there are more than 2,000 feet (600 m) between the highest and lowest point on the bedrock surface within the state.

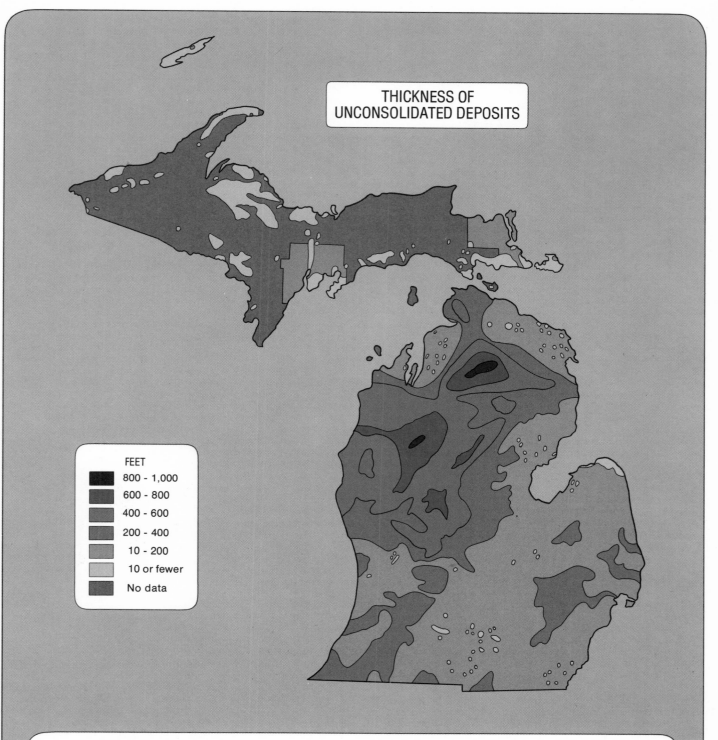

THICKNESS OF
UNCONSOLIDATED DEPOSITS

FEET
800 - 1,000
600 - 800
400 - 600
200 - 400
10 - 200
10 or fewer
No data

Across much of Michigan unconsolidated sediments, largely deposited by glaciation and often referred to as "drift," overlay bedrock, but their thickness varies from 0 to more than 600 feet (180 m). In the western part of the Upper Peninsula, where resistant Precambrian rocks exist, these deposits may average less than 10 feet (3 m) in thickness and are absent over considerable areas. Deposits are also shallow or absent across much of the Keweenaw Peninsula, Isle Royale, and the area overlaying a Silurian formation (Niagaran dolomite) extending from the Garden Peninsula to Drummond Island. Elsewhere in the Upper Peninsula these deposits tend to be thicker than 50 feet (15 m).

The average thickness of drift and related unconsolidated deposits is greater in the Lower Peninsula but varies considerably. These sediments tend to be thickest where the bedrock surface is lowest and in glacial interlobate areas and thinnest where the bedrock surface is highest. Thus it is evident that the uneven deposition of these glacial sediments upon the irregular bedrock surface made the topography of the state less rugged.

SOIL ASSOCIATIONS

PREDOMINANTLY ALFISOLS

A. Ochraqualfs and Argiaquolls
 1. Pewamo, Corunna, Selfridge
 2. Blount, Pewamo, Metamora
 3. Hoytville, Nappanee, Pewamo
B. Ochraqualfs and Haplaquepts
 1. Wisner, Essexville, marsh
 2. Parkhill, Capac, Sims, Kawkawlin
C. Hapludalfs, Ochraqualfs and Argiaquolls
 1. Miami, Conover, Brookston
 2. Morley, Blount, Pewamo
D. Hapludalfs
 1. Fox, Oshtemo
 2. Hillsdale, Spinks, Boyer
 3. Boyer, Oshtemo
E. Eutroboralfs and Haplaquepts
 1. Nester, Kawkawlin, Sims
 2. Watton, Ontonagon, Pickford
 3. Ontonagon, Pickford, Rudyard

PREDOMINANTLY SPODOSOLS

F. Haplorthods and Eutroboralfs
 1. Longrie, Detour, Johnswood
 2. Emmet, Leelanau, Onaway
 3. Marlette, Guelph, McBride
G. Haplorthods and Udipsamments
 1. Rubicon, Kalkaska, Grayling
H. Haplorthods and Fragiorthods
 1. Vilas, Gogebic, rockland
 2. Keweenaw, Kalkaska, Gogebic
 3. Emmet, Trenary, Leelanau
 4. Gogebic, Iron River, rockland
 5. Gogebic, Trenary, Kalkaska
 6. Munising, Skanee, Keweenaw
 7. Gogebic, Tula, Wakefield
 8. Iron River
 9. Munising, Allouez, rockland
I. Haplorthods and Haplaquods
 1. Au Gres, Rubicon, Iosco
J. Haplorthods
 1. Onota, Waiska
 2. Leelanau, Emmet, Kalkaska
 3. Montcalm, McBride, Rubicon
K. Haplorthods and rockland
 1. Baraga, Champion, rockland

PREDOMINANTLY ENTISOLS

L. Udipsamments and Haplaquolls
 1. Oakville, Tedrow, Granby

PREDOMINANTLY INCEPTISOLS

M. Haplaquepts and Haplaquods
 1. Brevort, Iosco, Parkhill
 2. Angelica, Brimley, organic soils

PREDOMINANTLY HISTOSOLS

N. Histosols, Psammaquents and Haplaquods
 1. Roscommon, Au Gres, organic soils
 2. Organic soils

Morley Profile

Oakville Profile

Soil is the collection of natural bodies in the earth's crust that supports living plants. They differ because of (1) parent material, (2) topography and natural drainage, (3) natural vegetation, (4) climate, and (5) length of weathering. Because soils are products of these factors, they will be similar wherever these conditions are the same.

Soil series are groups of soil bodies that have similar physical, chemical, and biological properties. Each series is named for a town or other geographical feature near the place where the soil series was first recognized.

Michigan's soils vary widely in thickness, color, texture (particle size), chemical and mineralogical composition, biological characteristics, and productivity. In Michigan more than 350 soil series have been mapped by soil scientists. On the map to the left, soils are grouped into general **associations** of usually two or more soil series that occur together. An association is named after the dominant soils in the area but contains many minor soils also.

Soils are classified according to their properties in a system adopted for use in the United States in 1965. Six of the ten Orders of soils are found in Michigan:

Alfisols, with accumulations of clay in the B horizon

Entisols, with little or no evidence of development in the B horizon

Histosols, developed from organic materials

Inceptisols, with weakly developed B horizons

Mollisols, with dark, thick A horizons

Spodosols, with accumulations of iron, aluminum, and humus in the B horizon

Lower soil categories are the Suborder, Great Group, Subgroup, Family, and Soil Series. The Great Group level of the system is used to classify soil series and associations on the map to the left. Four soils representative of Michigan are classified as follows: the Morley series (C2) is in the Alfisol Order and the Hapludalfs Great Group; the Oakville series (L1) in the Entisol Order and the Udipsamments Great Group; the Kalkaska series (H2) in the Spodosol Order and the Haplorthods Great Group; and the Brookston series (C1) in the Mollisol Order and the Argiaquolls Great Group.

A **soil profile** is a vertical section through all the horizons or layers of a soil. The profiles of the Morley, Oakville, Kalkaska, and Brookston soils shown on this page are representative of the soils found in Michigan. Horizons are labeled with capital letters in the alphabetical order in which they occur beneath the soil surface. Each of these major horizons may be subdivided into layers or subhorizons with different properties.

The A horizon includes the surface soil layers to which partially decayed organic matter or humus has been added by growing plants and from which the finer mineral particles and soluble materials have been leached or removed by moving water. The B horizon or subsoil includes the layers in which some of the fine particles and some of the less easily dissolved or leached materials have been deposited by the percolating water. The C horizon is the parent material, which is relatively unaltered by leaching or by the action of plant roots. In Michigan these horizons were formed by (1) accumulation of organic matter, (2) leaching of carbonates (lime) and other minerals, (3) reduction and transfer of iron, (4) formation and translocation of silicate clay minerals.

In the Morley soil, organic matter has accumulated in the surface horizon, carbonates and other bases have been leached, and clay minerals have been transferred from the A horizon and accumulated in the B horizon. In the Oakville soil, organic matter has accumulated in the A horizon and carbonates and other minerals have been leached from the profile. The accumulation of organic matter, leaching of carbonates and other minerals, and the translocation of iron, aluminum, and humus from the A to the B horizon has occurred in the Kalkaska soil. In the Brookston soil, organic matter has accumulated in the A horizon, carbonates and other bases have been leached from the profile, iron has been reduced and transferred, and clay minerals have translocated from the A horizon and accumulated in the B horizon. The grayish color of the subsoil horizons indicates the reduction and loss of iron, or gleying.

The Morley, Oakville, and Kalkaska soils developed in well-drained conditions with water tables or zones of saturation below 40 inches (102 cm). Because of good aeration and oxidation their subsoils are uniformly bright in color. Brookston soils developed in poorly drained areas where the zone of saturation was near the surface of the soil for several months of the year. Because of poor aeration and reducing conditions, the subsoil is gray.

Kalkaska Profile

Brookston Profile

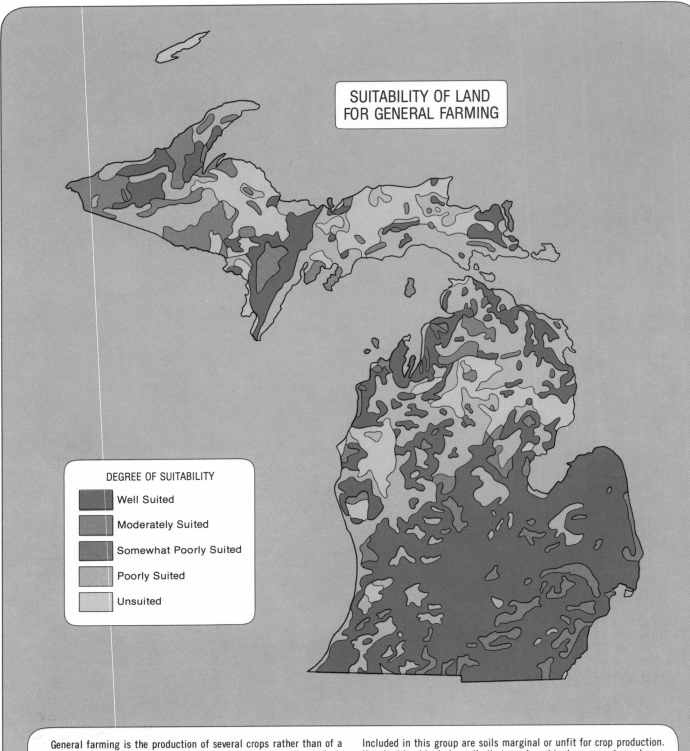

SUITABILITY OF LAND
FOR GENERAL FARMING

DEGREE OF SUITABILITY

Well Suited

Moderately Suited

Somewhat Poorly Suited

Poorly Suited

Unsuited

General farming is the production of several crops rather than of a single crop. Land well suited to general farming has soils with relatively high natural fertility, good tilth (easy to cultivate), level or gently undulating topography, and good capacity to hold available water. Such soils are capable of producing high yields. Land moderately suited has lower natural fertility, poorer tilth, or steeper slopes; it includes some soils that are marginal for crop production. Land somewhat poorly suited has a large proportion of soils that are not well suited for crop production, including some that are not usable for general farming. Land poorly suited has soils with low natural fertility, poor tilth, or steep slopes.

Included in this group are soils marginal or unfit for crop production. Unsuited land includes soils that are droughty, have very steep slopes, have very low fertility, or are very wet.

Because of the agricultural origin of many cities, the major urban areas of the state are located on soils that are well suited to general farming. Urban growth thus means further loss of good agricultural land. In the northern part of the state there are many thousands of acres of soils that are also well suited to general farming, but because the growing season of these areas is less than the optimum of 140 days, some crops cannot be grown or have low yields.

Soil properties affect many processes that occur in the soil. The infiltration rate, or the rate at which water enters the soil, is determined by the properties of the upper layers of the soil. The minimum infiltration rates were based on measurements made on surface layers of soils that had been in sod for more than two years. Soils used for crop production, especially those subject to crusting, might have lower infiltration rates than those shown.

The infiltration rate affects the amount of soil that will be removed by water erosion. Sandy soils have a rapid infiltration rate: most rainfall enters the soil, only a small amount runs off, and little soil is removed by water erosion. Clayey soils have slow infiltration rates: much water runs off and significant amounts of soil are removed by water erosion. Other types of soils have infiltration rates between the extremes of sand and clay.

The water holding capacity of soil is a measure of the amount of water held by the soil in a field situation. The water holding capacity of the upper three feet (88 cm) of soil reflects the amount of water available for plants. Sandy soils have a low water holding capacity and thus tend to be droughty in the summer. Medium-textured soils have a high water holding capacity and can normally hold enough water for plants to grow through the dry summer months. Clayey soils also hold large amounts of water, but much of it is held so tightly by the soil particles that plants cannot use it.

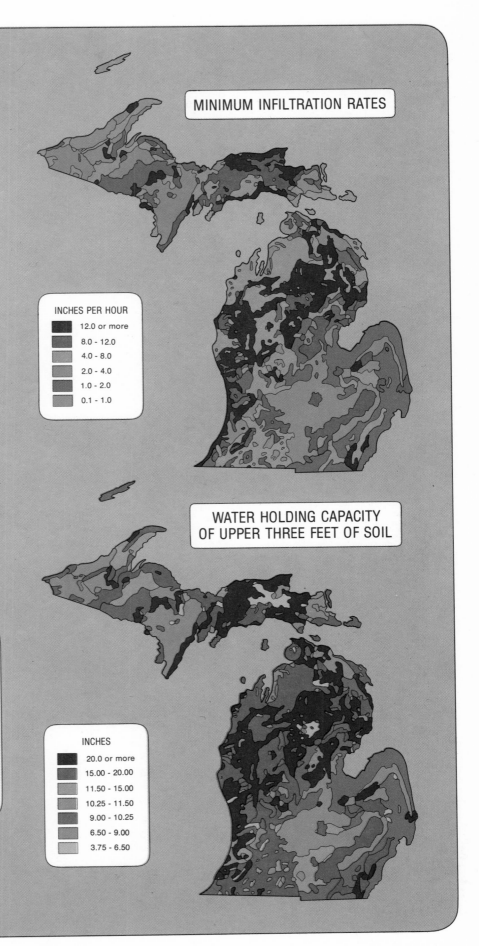

MINIMUM INFILTRATION RATES

INCHES PER HOUR

- 12.0 or more
- 8.0 - 12.0
- 4.0 - 8.0
- 2.0 - 4.0
- 1.0 - 2.0
- 0.1 - 1.0

WATER HOLDING CAPACITY OF UPPER THREE FEET OF SOIL

INCHES

- 20.0 or more
- 15.00 - 20.00
- 11.50 - 15.00
- 10.25 - 11.50
- 9.00 - 10.25
- 6.50 - 9.00
- 3.75 - 6.50

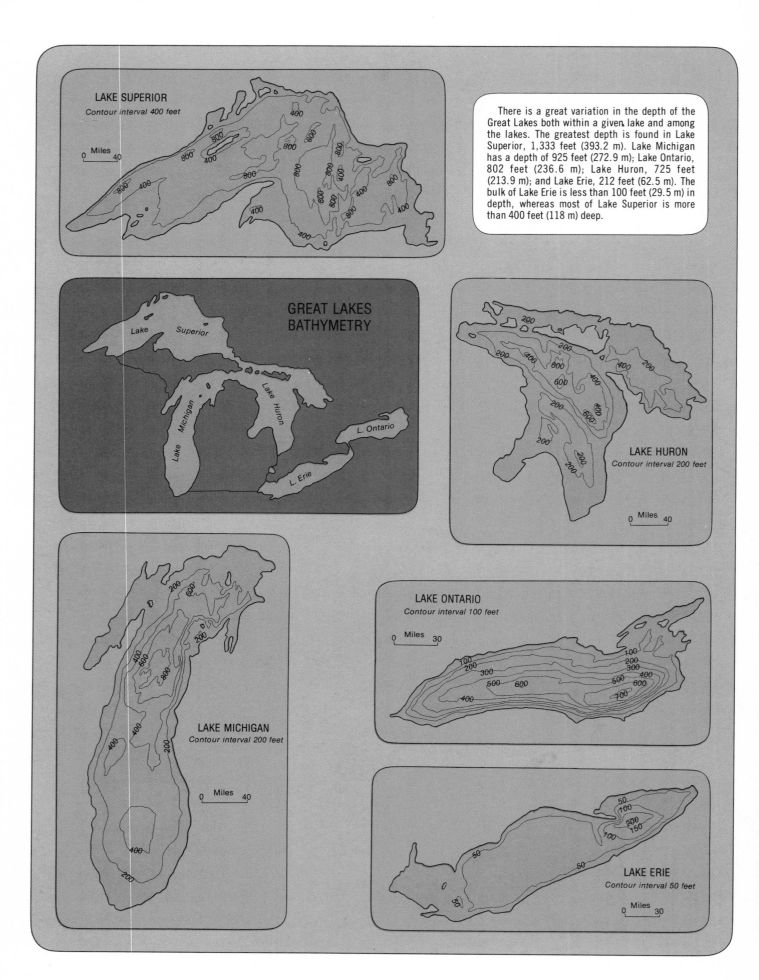

LAKE SUPERIOR
Contour interval 400 feet

Miles
0   40

There is a great variation in the depth of the Great Lakes both within a given lake and among the lakes. The greatest depth is found in Lake Superior, 1,333 feet (393.2 m). Lake Michigan has a depth of 925 feet (272.9 m); Lake Ontario, 802 feet (236.6 m); Lake Huron, 725 feet (213.9 m); and Lake Erie, 212 feet (62.5 m). The bulk of Lake Erie is less than 100 feet (29.5 m) in depth, whereas most of Lake Superior is more than 400 feet (118 m) deep.

GREAT LAKES BATHYMETRY

Lake Superior
Lake Michigan
Lake Huron
L. Ontario
L. Erie

LAKE HURON
Contour interval 200 feet

Miles
0   40

LAKE MICHIGAN
Contour interval 200 feet

Miles
0   40

LAKE ONTARIO
Contour interval 100 feet

Miles
0   30

LAKE ERIE
Contour interval 50 feet

Miles
0   30

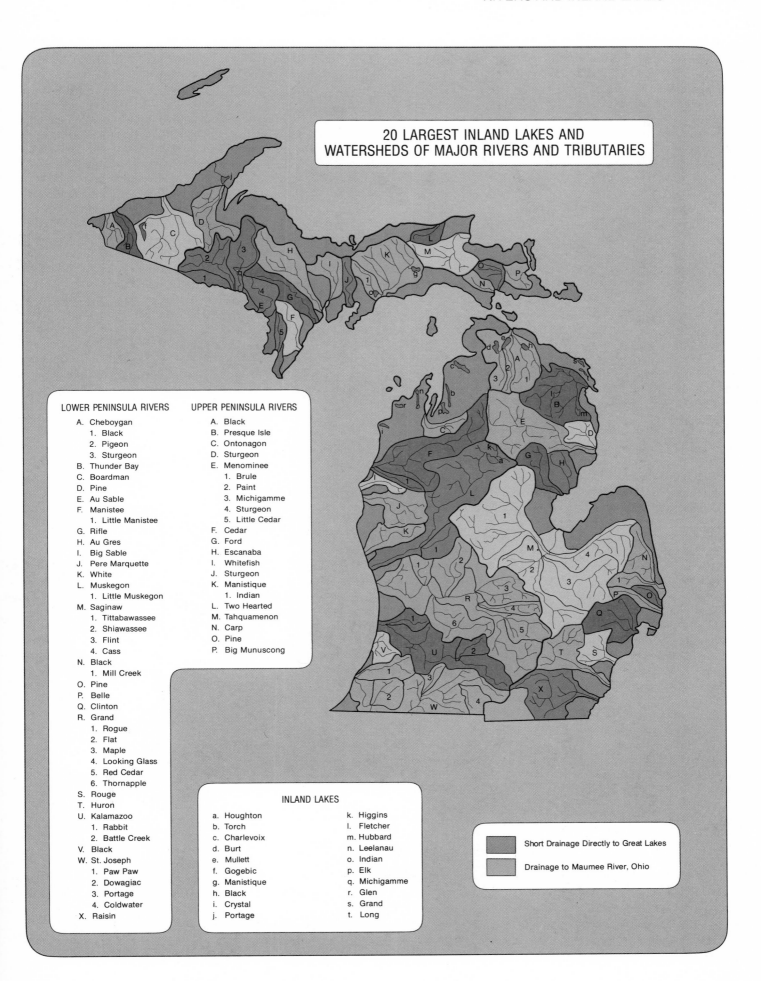

20 LARGEST INLAND LAKES AND WATERSHEDS OF MAJOR RIVERS AND TRIBUTARIES

LOWER PENINSULA RIVERS

A. Cheboygan
   1. Black
   2. Pigeon
   3. Sturgeon
B. Thunder Bay
C. Boardman
D. Pine
E. Au Sable
F. Manistee
   1. Little Manistee
G. Rifle
H. Au Gres
I. Big Sable
J. Pere Marquette
K. White
L. Muskegon
   1. Little Muskegon
M. Saginaw
   1. Tittabawassee
   2. Shiawassee
   3. Flint
   4. Cass
N. Black
   1. Mill Creek
O. Pine
P. Belle
Q. Clinton
R. Grand
   1. Rogue
   2. Flat
   3. Maple
   4. Looking Glass
   5. Red Cedar
   6. Thornapple
S. Rouge
T. Huron
U. Kalamazoo
   1. Rabbit
   2. Battle Creek
V. Black
W. St. Joseph
   1. Paw Paw
   2. Dowagiac
   3. Portage
   4. Coldwater
X. Raisin

UPPER PENINSULA RIVERS

A. Black
B. Presque Isle
C. Ontonagon
D. Sturgeon
E. Menominee
   1. Brule
   2. Paint
   3. Michigamme
   4. Sturgeon
   5. Little Cedar
F. Cedar
G. Ford
H. Escanaba
I. Whitefish
J. Sturgeon
K. Manistique
   1. Indian
L. Two Hearted
M. Tahquamenon
N. Carp
O. Pine
P. Big Munuscong

INLAND LAKES

a. Houghton
b. Torch
c. Charlevoix
d. Burt
e. Mullett
f. Gogebic
g. Manistique
h. Black
i. Crystal
j. Portage
k. Higgins
l. Fletcher
m. Hubbard
n. Leelanau
o. Indian
p. Elk
q. Michigamme
r. Glen
s. Grand
t. Long

Short Drainage Directly to Great Lakes

Drainage to Maumee River, Ohio

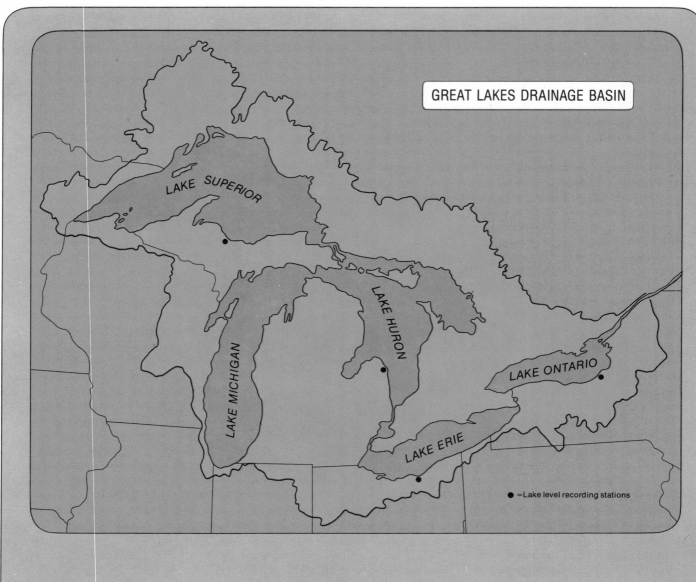

GREAT LAKES DRAINAGE BASIN

LAKE SUPERIOR

LAKE HURON

LAKE MICHIGAN

LAKE ONTARIO

LAKE ERIE

● =Lake level recording stations

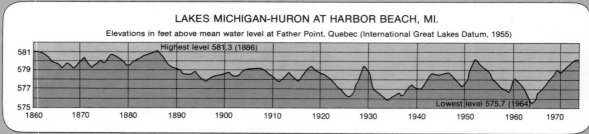

LAKES MICHIGAN-HURON AT HARBOR BEACH, MI.

Elevations in feet above mean water level at Father Point, Quebec (International Great Lakes Datum, 1955)

Highest level 581.3 (1886)

Lowest level 575.7 (1964)

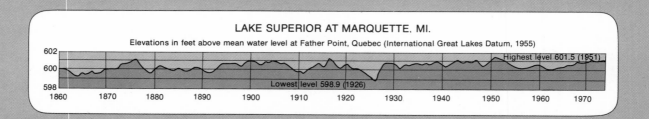

LAKE SUPERIOR AT MARQUETTE, MI.

Elevations in feet above mean water level at Father Point, Quebec (International Great Lakes Datum, 1955)

Highest level 601.5 (1951)

Lowest level 598.9 (1926)

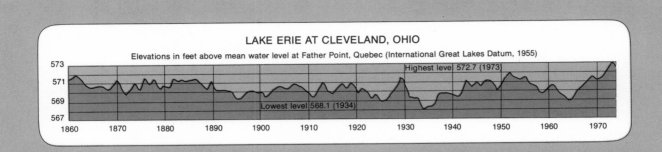

LAKE ERIE AT CLEVELAND, OHIO

Elevations in feet above mean water level at Father Point, Quebec (International Great Lakes Datum, 1955)

Highest level 572.7 (1973)

Lowest level 568.1 (1934)

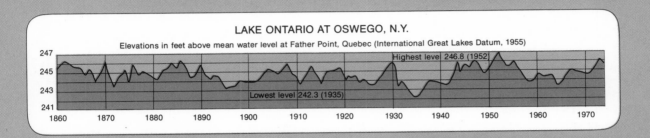

LAKE ONTARIO AT OSWEGO, N.Y.

Elevations in feet above mean water level at Father Point, Quebec (International Great Lakes Datum, 1955)

Highest level 246.8 (1952)

Lowest level 242.3 (1935)

About 40,000 square miles (103,600 sq km) of the Great Lakes, the largest system of connected freshwater lakes in the world, are within the boundaries of Michigan. Lake Superior's surface altitude averages about 600 feet (177 m) above sea level and is drained by the St. Marys River. The surface of Lakes Huron and Michigan, which are connected by the Straits of Mackinac, averages about 580 feet (171 m) in altitude. These lakes are drained by way of the St. Clair River, Lake St. Clair, and the Detroit River to the smaller Lake Erie, which has a surface altitude of 570 feet (168 m). Drainage continues by way of Lake Ontario and the St. Lawrence River to the Atlantic Ocean. During the last century the maximum variation for the level of Lake Superior has been only 2.6 feet (.77 m), whereas the surface of Lakes Huron and Michigan has fluctuated 5.6 feet (1.65 m). During the same period, Lakes Erie and Ontario have changed a maximum of 4.6 (1.36 m) and 4.5 feet (1.33 m), respectively.

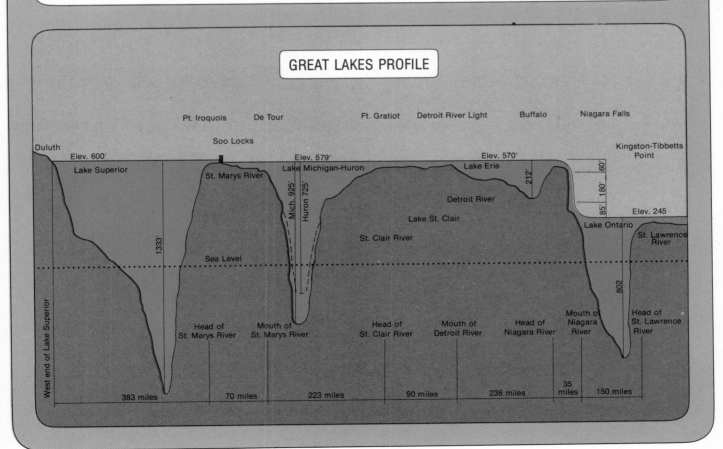

GREAT LAKES PROFILE

The availability of groundwater is generally related to the porosity and permeability of the bedrock and unconsolidated materials in any given area. Michigan is fortunate in that it has both bedrock and unconsolidated glacial deposits that are relatively reliable sources of groundwater. The sedimentary rocks of the Michigan Basin contain sandstones and porous limestones, which are excellent storage beds for groundwater. These sedimentary rocks dip toward the center of the basin, and in some cases artesian wells are found which result from the water pressure in the sedimentary rock beds. The Saginaw sandstone formation, which can be easily reached by drilling in central Michigan, is an excellent water-bearing rock.

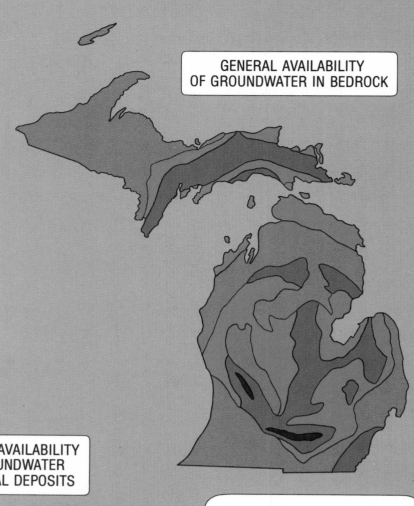

GENERAL AVAILABILITY OF GROUNDWATER IN BEDROCK

GENERAL AVAILABILITY OF GROUNDWATER IN GLACIAL DEPOSITS

The availability of groundwater in glacial deposits depends on the thickness and character of unconsolidated sediments. The best groundwater resources are found in the glaciofluvial (water-laid) deposits of the central and northern Lower Peninsula.

WELL YIELDS

- More than 500 gallons per minute from wells 10" or more in diameter
- 100 to 500 gallons per minute from wells 10" or more in diameter
- 10 to 100 gallons per minute
- less than 10 gallons per minute

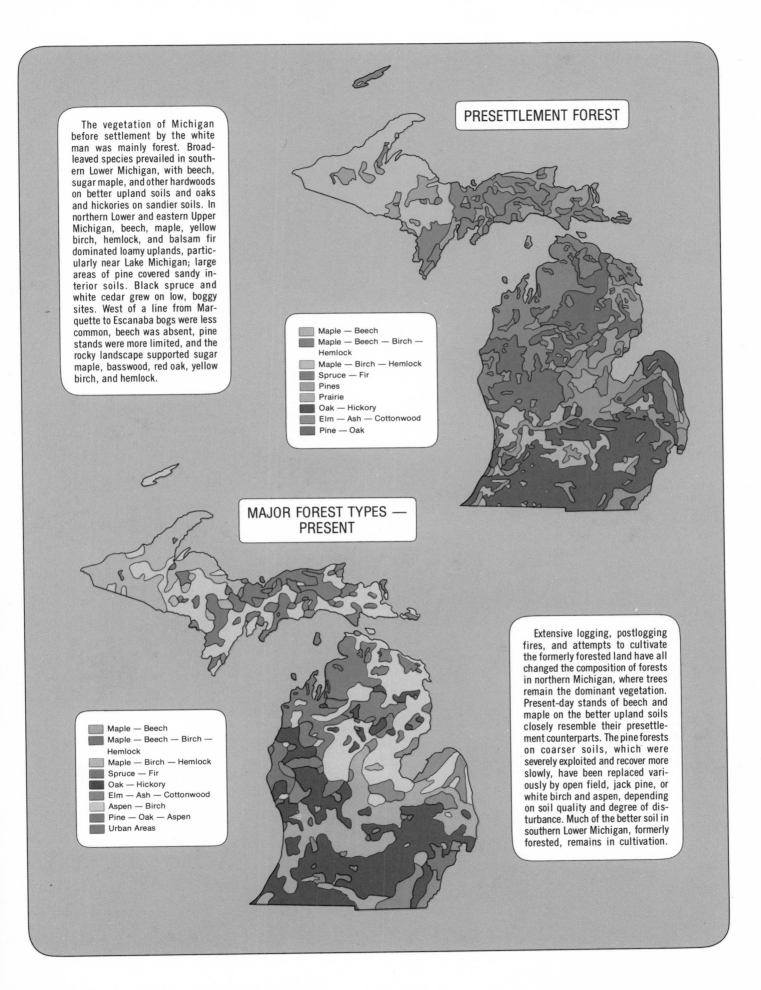

The vegetation of Michigan before settlement by the white man was mainly forest. Broad-leaved species prevailed in southern Lower Michigan, with beech, sugar maple, and other hardwoods on better upland soils and oaks and hickories on sandier soils. In northern Lower and eastern Upper Michigan, beech, maple, yellow birch, hemlock, and balsam fir dominated loamy uplands, particularly near Lake Michigan; large areas of pine covered sandy interior soils. Black spruce and white cedar grew on low, boggy sites. West of a line from Marquette to Escanaba bogs were less common, beech was absent, pine stands were more limited, and the rocky landscape supported sugar maple, basswood, red oak, yellow birch, and hemlock.

PRESETTLEMENT FOREST

- Maple — Beech
- Maple — Beech — Birch — Hemlock
- Maple — Birch — Hemlock
- Spruce — Fir
- Pines
- Prairie
- Oak — Hickory
- Elm — Ash — Cottonwood
- Pine — Oak

MAJOR FOREST TYPES — PRESENT

- Maple — Beech
- Maple — Beech — Birch — Hemlock
- Maple — Birch — Hemlock
- Spruce — Fir
- Oak — Hickory
- Elm — Ash — Cottonwood
- Aspen — Birch
- Pine — Oak — Aspen
- Urban Areas

Extensive logging, postlogging fires, and attempts to cultivate the formerly forested land have all changed the composition of forests in northern Michigan, where trees remain the dominant vegetation. Present-day stands of beech and maple on the better upland soils closely resemble their presettlement counterparts. The pine forests on coarser soils, which were severely exploited and recover more slowly, have been replaced variously by open field, jack pine, or white birch and aspen, depending on soil quality and degree of disturbance. Much of the better soil in southern Lower Michigan, formerly forested, remains in cultivation.

Geographic patterns in mean annual precipitation arise from differences in either atmospheric moisture or the number of passing disturbances (fronts and storms). Greatest average precipitation falls in southwestern Lower Michigan and over the higher terrain in western Upper Michigan. Southwestern Lower Michigan is nearest the Gulf of Mexico, the source of moist air for much of the state's rain and snow, and the average atmospheric moisture is higher there than in northern areas of the state. In western Upper Michigan snowfall created by cold air crossing the relatively warmer surface of Lake Superior contributes greatly to that area's total precipitation. Lower average annual precipitation in northeastern Lower Michigan than in the northwest results from less lake-effect snowfall and from limited summertime atmospheric moisture. The contrast in precipitation between northwestern and northeastern Lower Michigan is caused by the uplands in Kalkaska and Otsego counties which locally augment lake-effect snowfall.

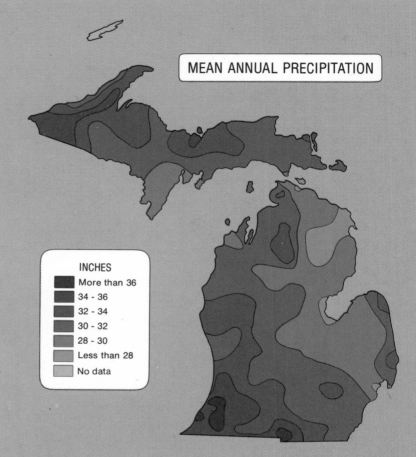

MEAN ANNUAL PRECIPITATION

INCHES
- More than 36
- 34 - 36
- 32 - 34
- 30 - 32
- 28 - 30
- Less than 28
- No data

MEAN ANNUAL TEMPERATURE

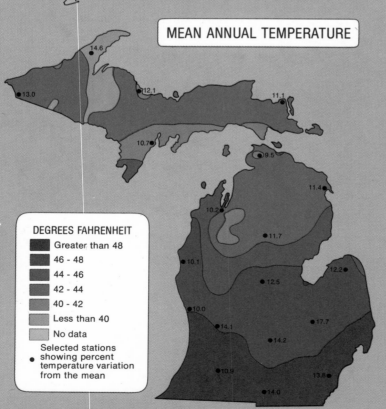

DEGREES FAHRENHEIT
- Greater than 48
- 46 - 48
- 44 - 46
- 42 - 44
- 40 - 42
- Less than 40
- No data
- ● Selected stations showing percent temperature variation from the mean

Differences in mean annual temperature across Michigan result from variations in the relative importance of air masses crossing the state as well as from the moderating influence of the Great Lakes. In any season warm intervals in Michigan are produced by an influx of air from the southern United States or Great Plains, whereas cold periods are the result of the invasion of air from Canada or the Arctic. Lying nearest these northern sources, the Upper Peninsula is often affected by cool air masses, whereas warm southerly air masses are more frequent in southern Lower Michigan. Thus average temperatures are lower in northern Michigan during all seasons, even in summer when it experiences longer days than any other part of the state. Snow cover, persistent in northern Michigan during winter, promotes nighttime cooling and also lowers mean temperatures. The Great Lakes, which retain heat, modify the climate of near-shore areas by cooling extremely hot summer days. They also moderate the bitter cold of winter by directly releasing heat and generating local cloudiness.

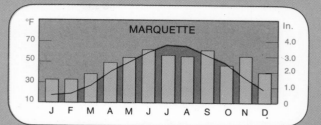

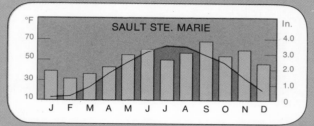

This series of climagraphs illustrates the major precipitation and temperature differences from north to south and west to east in Michigan. This kind of graph has long been the traditional method of indicating the annual precipitation and temperature variations for a given weather station, and it allows comparison between stations. The period of record is from 1940 to 1974.

The range in temperature is roughly similar at the six stations but, as expected, winter and summer averages are lower in the north. The higher winter precipitation at both Sault Ste. Marie and Muskegon is the result of greater lake-effect snowfall. The average annual snowfall is more than 100 inches (254 cm) at Sault Ste. Marie, compared to 93 (236 cm) at Muskegon, 86 (218 cm) at Alpena, and 50 (127 cm) at Lansing. Detroit and Lansing show a greater concentration of precipitation in the warm season; they receive little lake-effect snowfall in winter and higher summertime humidity favors more thunderstorms.

The following table of daily maximum and minimum temperature averages indicates differences from north to south and variations between coastal and inland locations. Note that although Muskegon and Lansing are at approximately the same latitude, Muskegon has a higher minimum temperature in January and Lansing has a higher maximum in July. Lake Michigan lessens extremes of temperature at coastal locations, resulting in a greater range between winter and summer temperatures at inland stations.

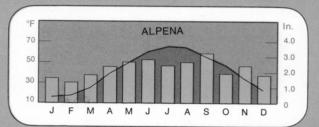

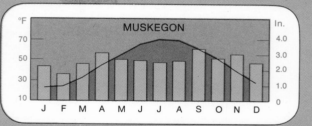

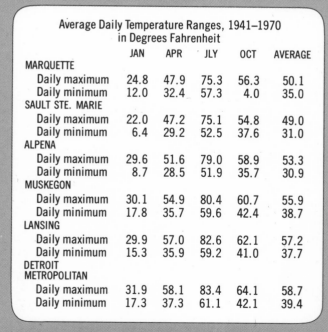

Average Daily Temperature Ranges, 1941–1970 in Degrees Fahrenheit					
	JAN	APR	JLY	OCT	AVERAGE
MARQUETTE					
Daily maximum	24.8	47.9	75.3	56.3	50.1
Daily minimum	12.0	32.4	57.3	4.0	35.0
SAULT STE. MARIE					
Daily maximum	22.0	47.2	75.1	54.8	49.0
Daily minimum	6.4	29.2	52.5	37.6	31.0
ALPENA					
Daily maximum	29.6	51.6	79.0	58.9	53.3
Daily minimum	8.7	28.5	51.9	35.7	30.9
MUSKEGON					
Daily maximum	30.1	54.9	80.4	60.7	55.9
Daily minimum	17.8	35.7	59.6	42.4	38.7
LANSING					
Daily maximum	29.9	57.0	82.6	62.1	57.2
Daily minimum	15.3	35.9	59.2	41.0	37.7
DETROIT METROPOLITAN					
Daily maximum	31.9	58.1	83.4	64.1	58.7
Daily minimum	17.3	37.3	61.1	42.1	39.4

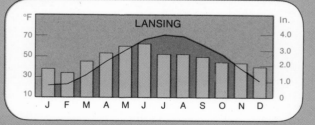

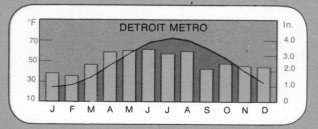

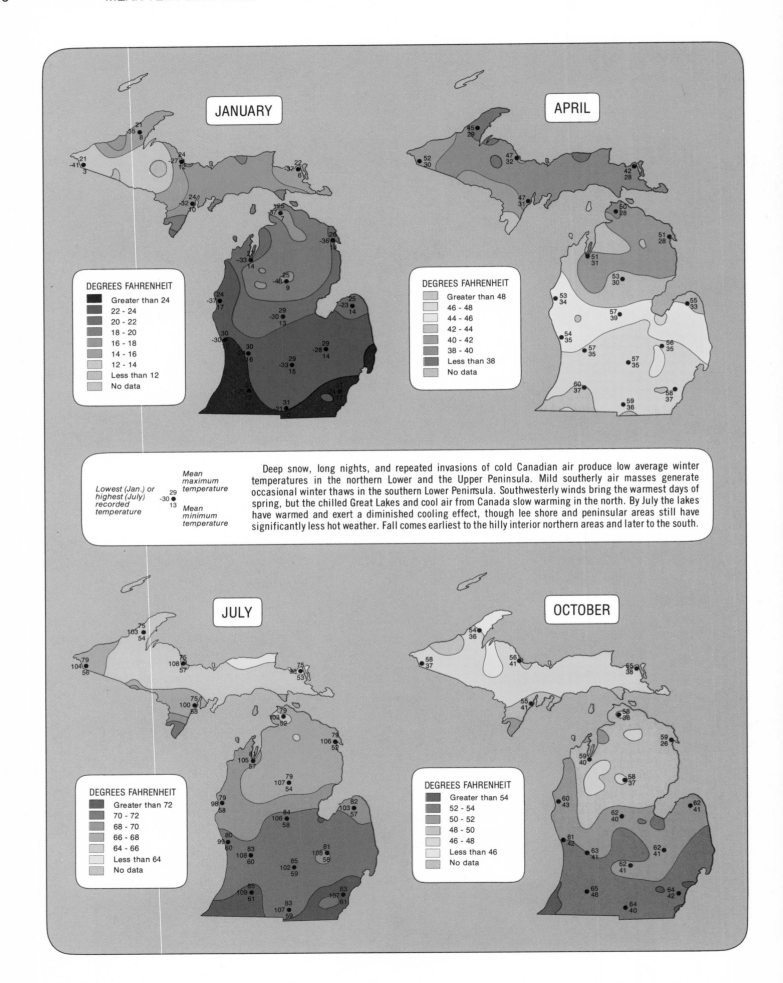

JANUARY

APRIL

DEGREES FAHRENHEIT

| Greater than 24 |
| 22 - 24 |
| 20 - 22 |
| 18 - 20 |
| 16 - 18 |
| 14 - 16 |
| 12 - 14 |
| Less than 12 |
| No data |

DEGREES FAHRENHEIT

| Greater than 48 |
| 46 - 48 |
| 44 - 46 |
| 42 - 44 |
| 40 - 42 |
| 38 - 40 |
| Less than 38 |
| No data |

Lowest (Jan.) or highest (July) recorded temperature — Mean maximum temperature / Mean minimum temperature

Deep snow, long nights, and repeated invasions of cold Canadian air produce low average winter temperatures in the northern Lower and the Upper Peninsula. Mild southerly air masses generate occasional winter thaws in the southern Lower Peninsula. Southwesterly winds bring the warmest days of spring, but the chilled Great Lakes and cool air from Canada slow warming in the north. By July the lakes have warmed and exert a diminished cooling effect, though lee shore and peninsular areas still have significantly less hot weather. Fall comes earliest to the hilly interior northern areas and later to the south.

JULY

OCTOBER

DEGREES FAHRENHEIT

| Greater than 72 |
| 70 - 72 |
| 68 - 70 |
| 66 - 68 |
| 64 - 66 |
| Less than 64 |
| No data |

DEGREES FAHRENHEIT

| Greater than 54 |
| 52 - 54 |
| 50 - 52 |
| 48 - 50 |
| 46 - 48 |
| Less than 46 |
| No data |

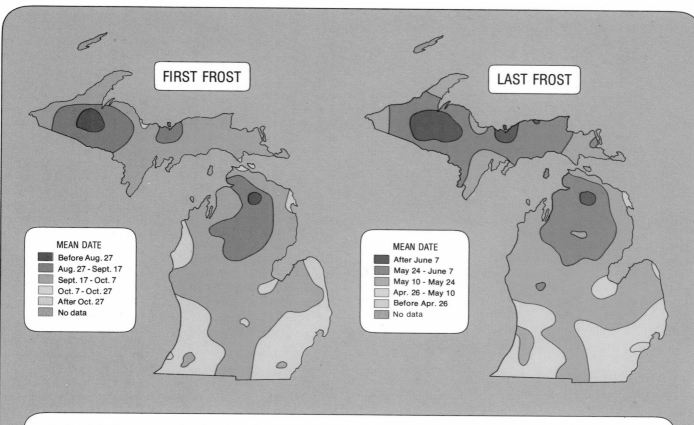

FIRST FROST

MEAN DATE
- Before Aug. 27
- Aug. 27 - Sept. 17
- Sept. 17 - Oct. 7
- Oct. 7 - Oct. 27
- After Oct. 27
- No data

LAST FROST

MEAN DATE
- After June 7
- May 24 - June 7
- May 10 - May 24
- Apr. 26 - May 10
- Before Apr. 26
- No data

The latest frosts in spring and earliest frosts in autumn generally occur in northern areas away from the influence of the Great Lakes. Lee shore locations benefit from the warm lake waters that moderate cold winds, delay the frost, and lengthen the growing season. Thus, for example, cold-sensitive crops such as fruit can be cultivated near the lee of Lake Michigan. The number of growing degree days, a measure of the average annual accumulation of daily mean temperatures above 42° F (5.6° C), is greatest generally in the southern half of the Lower Peninsula, to the lee of Lake Michigan in the northern Lower Peninsula, and in the Keweenaw region of the Upper Peninsula.

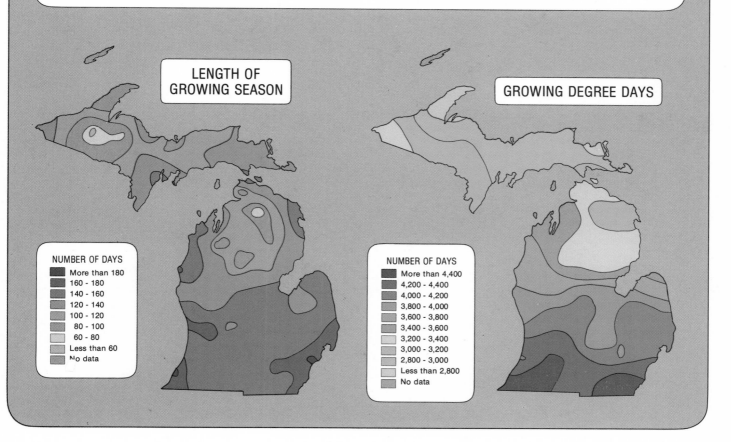

LENGTH OF GROWING SEASON

NUMBER OF DAYS
- More than 180
- 160 - 180
- 140 - 160
- 120 - 140
- 100 - 120
- 80 - 100
- 60 - 80
- Less than 60
- No data

GROWING DEGREE DAYS

NUMBER OF DAYS
- More than 4,400
- 4,200 - 4,400
- 4,000 - 4,200
- 3,800 - 4,000
- 3,600 - 3,800
- 3,400 - 3,600
- 3,200 - 3,400
- 3,000 - 3,200
- 2,800 - 3,000
- Less than 2,800
- No data

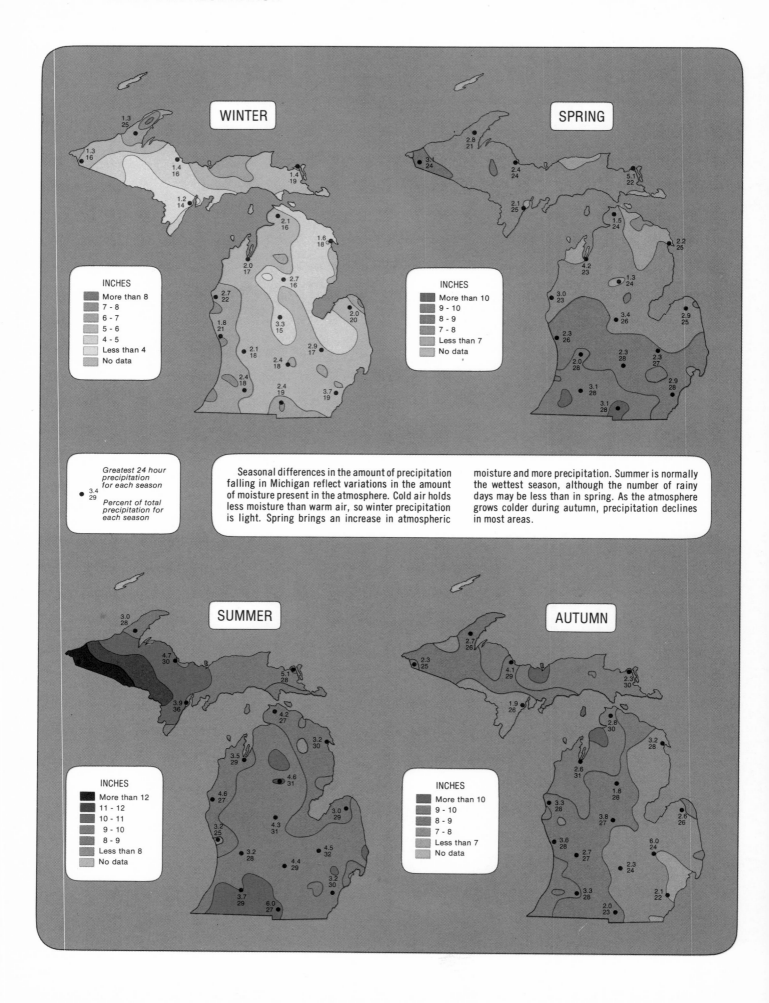

WINTER

1.3
25

1.3
16

1.4
16

1.4
19

1.2
14

2.1
16

1.6
18

2.0
17

2.7
16

INCHES
More than 8
7 - 8
6 - 7
5 - 6
4 - 5
Less than 4
No data

2.7
22

1.8
21

3.3
15

2.0
20

2.1
18

2.4
18

2.9
17

2.4
18

2.4
19

3.7
19

SPRING

2.8
21

3.1
24

2.4
24

5.1
22

2.1
25

1.5
24

2.2
25

4.2
23

1.3
24

INCHES
More than 10
9 - 10
8 - 9
7 - 8
Less than 7
No data

3.0
23

3.4
26

2.9
25

2.3
26

2.0
28

2.3
28

2.3
27

3.1
28

2.9
28

3.1
28

Greatest 24 hour
precipitation
for each season

• 3.4
29

Percent of total
precipitation for
each season

Seasonal differences in the amount of precipitation falling in Michigan reflect variations in the amount of moisture present in the atmosphere. Cold air holds less moisture than warm air, so winter precipitation is light. Spring brings an increase in atmospheric moisture and more precipitation. Summer is normally the wettest season, although the number of rainy days may be less than in spring. As the atmosphere grows colder during autumn, precipitation declines in most areas.

SUMMER

3.0
28

4.7
30

5.1
28

3.9
36

4.2
27

3.2
30

3.5
29

4.6
31

4.6
27

3.0
29

3.2
25

4.3
31

INCHES
More than 12
11 - 12
10 - 11
9 - 10
8 - 9
Less than 8
No data

3.2
28

4.5
32

4.4
29

3.2
30

3.7
29

6.0
27

AUTUMN

2.7
26

2.3
25

4.1
29

2.3
30

1.9
26

2.8
30

3.2
28

2.6
31

1.8
28

3.3
28

INCHES
More than 10
9 - 10
8 - 9
7 - 8
Less than 7
No data

3.8
27

2.6
26

3.6
28

6.0
24

2.7
27

2.3
24

3.3
28

2.1
22

2.0
23

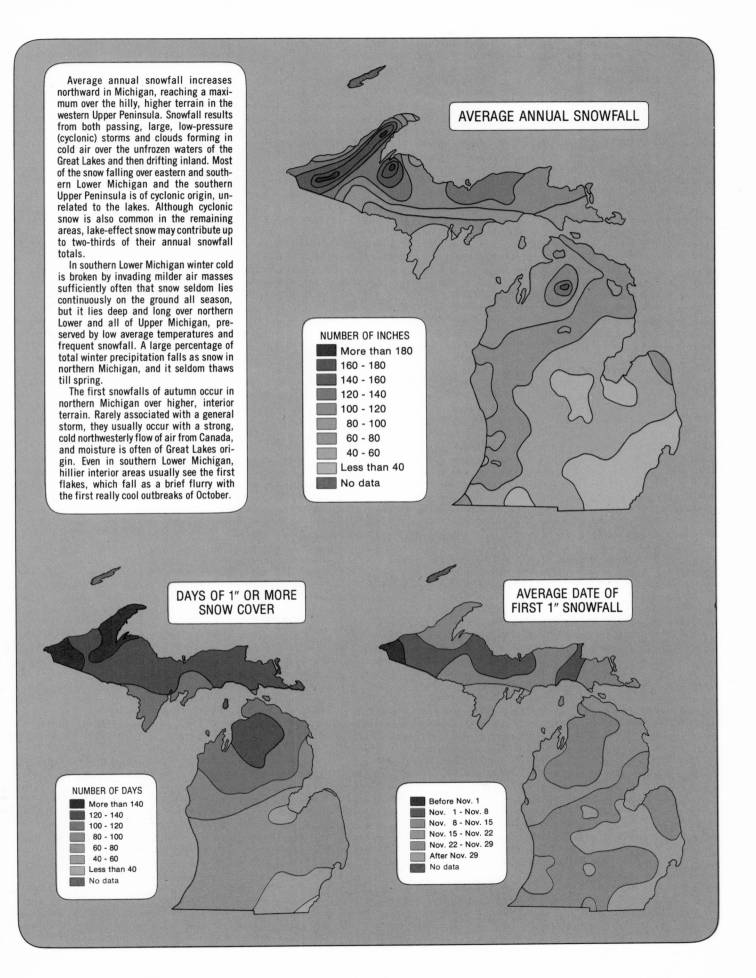

Average annual snowfall increases northward in Michigan, reaching a maximum over the hilly, higher terrain in the western Upper Peninsula. Snowfall results from both passing, large, low-pressure (cyclonic) storms and clouds forming in cold air over the unfrozen waters of the Great Lakes and then drifting inland. Most of the snow falling over eastern and southern Lower Michigan and the southern Upper Peninsula is of cyclonic origin, unrelated to the lakes. Although cyclonic snow is also common in the remaining areas, lake-effect snow may contribute up to two-thirds of their annual snowfall totals.

In southern Lower Michigan winter cold is broken by invading milder air masses sufficiently often that snow seldom lies continuously on the ground all season, but it lies deep and long over northern Lower and all of Upper Michigan, preserved by low average temperatures and frequent snowfall. A large percentage of total winter precipitation falls as snow in northern Michigan, and it seldom thaws till spring.

The first snowfalls of autumn occur in northern Michigan over higher, interior terrain. Rarely associated with a general storm, they usually occur with a strong, cold northwesterly flow of air from Canada, and moisture is often of Great Lakes origin. Even in southern Lower Michigan, hillier interior areas usually see the first flakes, which fall as a brief flurry with the first really cool outbreaks of October.

AVERAGE ANNUAL SNOWFALL

NUMBER OF INCHES
More than 180
160 - 180
140 - 160
120 - 140
100 - 120
80 - 100
60 - 80
40 - 60
Less than 40
No data

DAYS OF 1" OR MORE SNOW COVER

NUMBER OF DAYS
More than 140
120 - 140
100 - 120
80 - 100
60 - 80
40 - 60
Less than 40
No data

AVERAGE DATE OF FIRST 1" SNOWFALL

Before Nov. 1
Nov. 1 - Nov. 8
Nov. 8 - Nov. 15
Nov. 15 - Nov. 22
Nov. 22 - Nov. 29
After Nov. 29
No data

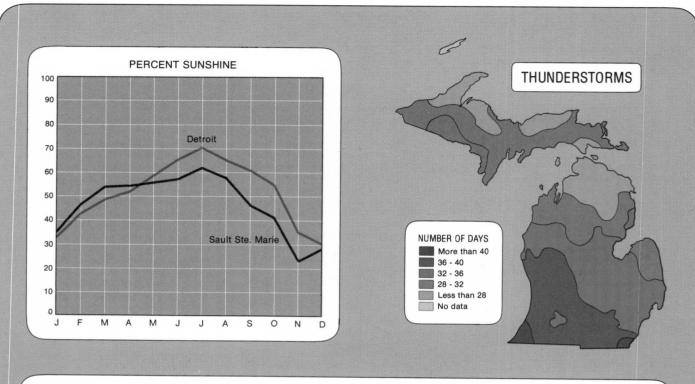

PERCENT SUNSHINE

Detroit

Sault Ste. Marie

THUNDERSTORMS

NUMBER OF DAYS
- More than 40
- 36 – 40
- 32 – 36
- 28 – 32
- Less than 28
- No data

Michigan residents see less of the sun than residents of most other states. Cloudiness is generated both by cyclonic storms, which are larger, stronger, and more frequent in winter, and by the condensation of water vapor released by the Great Lakes. During fall and winter the Great Lakes are warmer than the atmosphere and liberate enough moisture to increase the percentage of cloudiness. During summer, however, storminess declines, and the lakes are cooler than the atmosphere and therefore do not create additional cloud cover.

Tornadoes, and thunderstorms with which tornadoes are associated, require the presence of warm, moist air for formation. Only a few exceptional thunderstorms spawn tornadoes because an ideal and rare com-

bination of conditions is needed. Most Michigan thunderstorms are produced by the approach of an atmospheric disturbance such as a cold front when warm, moist air overlays part of the state. Storms and fronts cross Michigan at all seasons, but a warm, humid air mass is most likely to precede them during the summer. Humid air normally enters Michigan from the southwest, originating in the Gulf of Mexico, and spreads northward until a disturbance moving eastward across the state disperses it with cooler, drier air. Moisture-laden air infrequently has time to penetrate into northern Michigan before a new disturbance moves in, so the prime ingredient for thunderstorms and tornadoes is often absent there.

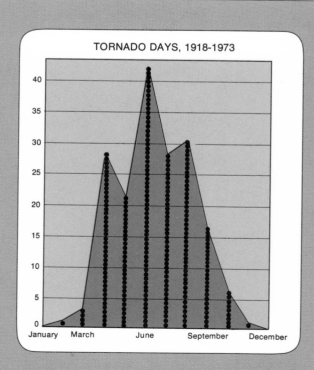

TORNADO DAYS, 1918-1973

January   March   June   September   December

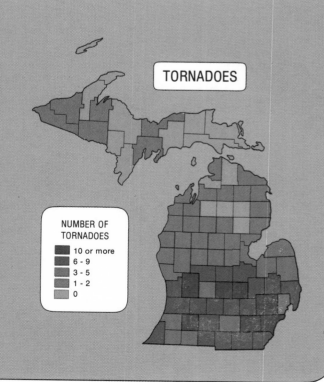

TORNADOES

NUMBER OF TORNADOES
- 10 or more
- 6 – 9
- 3 – 5
- 1 – 2
- 0

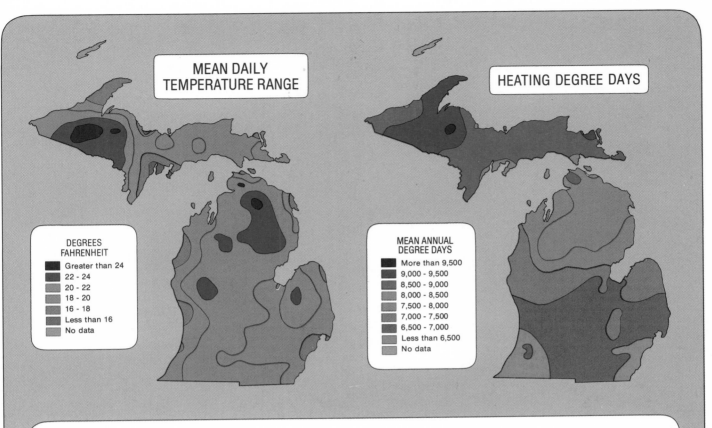

MEAN DAILY TEMPERATURE RANGE

DEGREES FAHRENHEIT
- Greater than 24
- 22 - 24
- 20 - 22
- 18 - 20
- 16 - 18
- Less than 16
- No data

HEATING DEGREE DAYS

MEAN ANNUAL DEGREE DAYS
- More than 9,500
- 9,000 - 9,500
- 8,500 - 9,000
- 8,000 - 8,500
- 7,500 - 8,000
- 7,000 - 7,500
- 6,500 - 7,000
- Less than 6,500
- No data

The average range of daily temperature is greatest in the interior of the northern Lower Peninsula and the central western portion of the Upper Peninsula and least near the shores of the Great Lakes because of the modifying effect of the water. Heating degree days, a measure of the average annual accumulation of daily mean temperatures below 60° F (15.6° C), follow a similar pattern. Daily winds can be from any direction but are predominantly westerly. Shoreline stations along the Great Lakes experience a high frequency of summer on-shore lake breezes. Evaporation rates are highest in the southern Lower Peninsula where summer temperature averages are the highest.

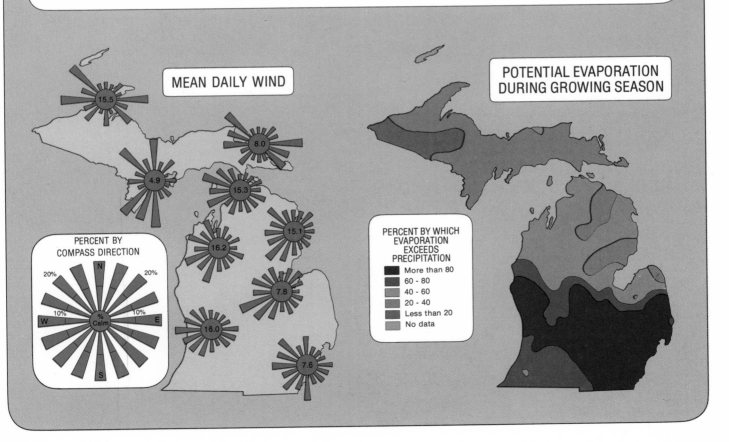

MEAN DAILY WIND

PERCENT BY COMPASS DIRECTION

N
20%   20%
10%   10%
W   E
% Calm
S

15.5
8.0
4.9
15.3
15.1
16.2
7.8
16.0
7.6

POTENTIAL EVAPORATION DURING GROWING SEASON

PERCENT BY WHICH EVAPORATION EXCEEDS PRECIPITATION
- More than 80
- 60 - 80
- 40 - 60
- 20 - 40
- Less than 20
- No data

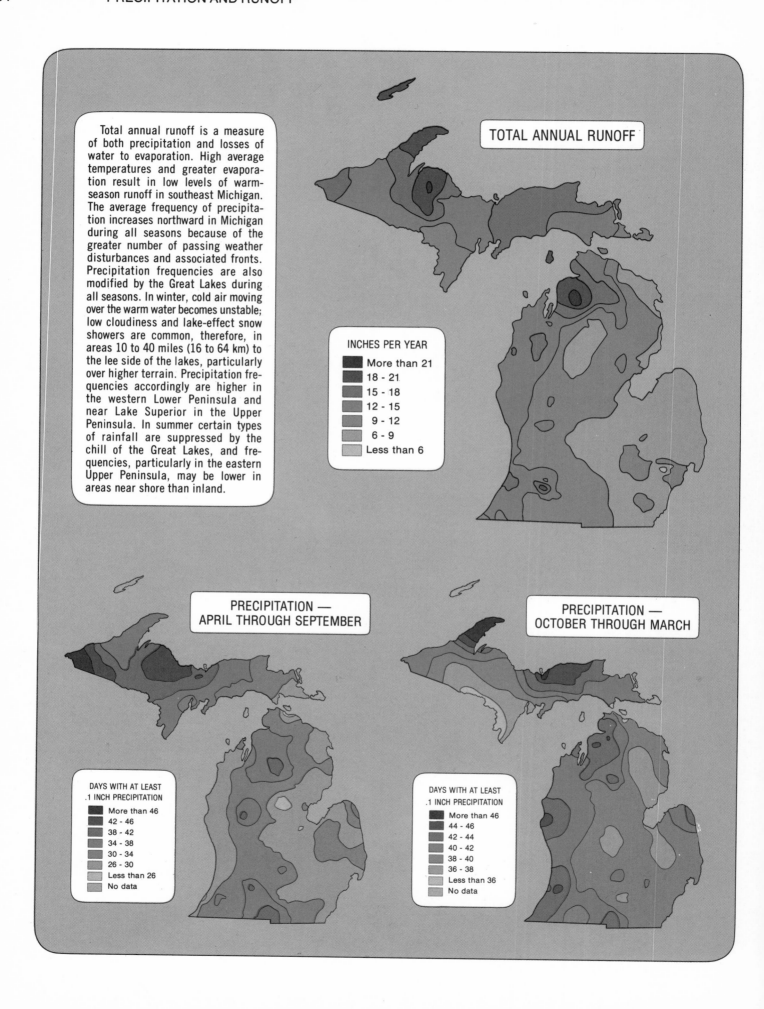

Total annual runoff is a measure of both precipitation and losses of water to evaporation. High average temperatures and greater evaporation result in low levels of warm-season runoff in southeast Michigan. The average frequency of precipitation increases northward in Michigan during all seasons because of the greater number of passing weather disturbances and associated fronts. Precipitation frequencies are also modified by the Great Lakes during all seasons. In winter, cold air moving over the warm water becomes unstable; low cloudiness and lake-effect snow showers are common, therefore, in areas 10 to 40 miles (16 to 64 km) to the lee side of the lakes, particularly over higher terrain. Precipitation frequencies accordingly are higher in the western Lower Peninsula and near Lake Superior in the Upper Peninsula. In summer certain types of rainfall are suppressed by the chill of the Great Lakes, and frequencies, particularly in the eastern Upper Peninsula, may be lower in areas near shore than inland.

TOTAL ANNUAL RUNOFF

INCHES PER YEAR
- More than 21
- 18 - 21
- 15 - 18
- 12 - 15
- 9 - 12
- 6 - 9
- Less than 6

**PRECIPITATION —
APRIL THROUGH SEPTEMBER**

DAYS WITH AT LEAST
.1 INCH PRECIPITATION
- More than 46
- 42 - 46
- 38 - 42
- 34 - 38
- 30 - 34
- 26 - 30
- Less than 26
- No data

**PRECIPITATION —
OCTOBER THROUGH MARCH**

DAYS WITH AT LEAST
.1 INCH PRECIPITATION
- More than 46
- 44 - 46
- 42 - 44
- 40 - 42
- 38 - 40
- 36 - 38
- Less than 36
- No data

A wide variety of weather affects Michigan throughout the year. Each episode of weather lasting only a day or two can be identified with a particular distribution of air masses and fronts over eastern North America. Although these weather conditions change continuously, many types repeat themselves over periods of time. The examples below and on the following pages represent a few of the more distinctive situations that might occur in any given year. On the surface maps, the lines bearing symbols represent fronts that separate different air masses; centers of high and low atmospheric pressure are indicated with letters; and unmarked curving lines (isobars) connect areas of equal pressure. Curved lines on the 500 millibar maps suggest air movement, prevalently from the west.

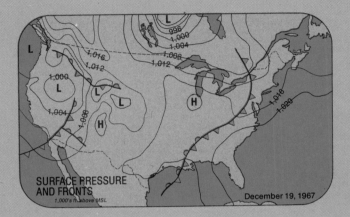
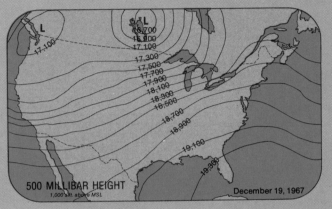

WINTER WARM SPELL

Warm periods during the winter are most often associated with the movement of mild Pacific air masses across the Great Plains into Michigan. The air, after crossing the Rocky Mountains, is dry but mild and may produce widespread thaws in the Great Lakes area. Such an air mass is shown on the surface map above (left) over Illinois, and another is following behind the front trailing across Nevada and Arizona. The movement of these mild air masses is promoted by the broad current of air from the southwest as indicated on the 500 millibar map above (right.)

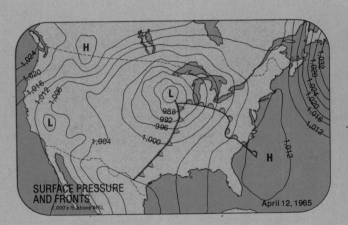
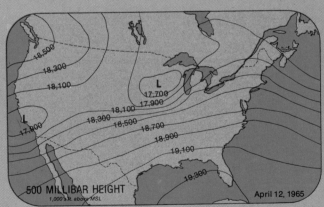

TORNADOES

Tornadoes are usually spawned by an advance of a strong cold front into a mass of warm, moist air from the Gulf of Mexico, the presence of dry air over the frontal zone at middle levels of the atmosphere, and high-speed winds aloft fostered by the jet stream. Such conditions, although they combine relatively infrequently in Michigan, have resulted in some devastating tornadoes in the state. During the weather situation shown on the maps above, numerous destructive tornadoes touched down in Michigan and nearby states. The storms formed near the cold front extending along the Mississippi River and within several hours had raced as far east as Ohio before they began to weaken, with average forward speeds as high as 60 miles (96 km) per hour. Winds spiraled around individual tornadoes at velocities estimated between 200 and 300 miles (320 and 480 km) per hour.

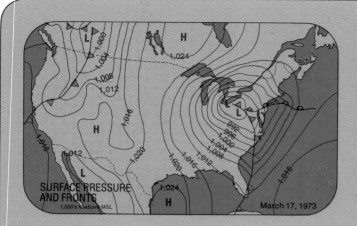

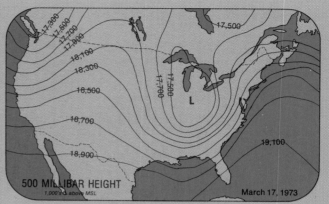

WINTER STORM

Storms originating from a number of different regions can produce adverse weather in Michigan. Some generate mainly high winds that usher a cold wave into the state, whereas others are associated with heavy falls of snow or rain. Generally those storms that develop in the southwestern United States and draw moist air northward into their circulation from the Gulf of Mexico produce the heaviest snowfall in Michigan as they move northeastward across Indiana and Ohio. Moisture from the Great Lakes contributes little to the snowfall from these general storms except in the immediate lee shore areas. Heaviest snow usually falls in a band 150 to 200 miles (240 to 320 km) wide just north of the storm path. Rain occurs south of the snow zone while north of the heavy

snow only light snow may fall or none at all. Between the areas of rain and heavy snow may be a zone of sleet and freezing rain; all precipitation north of the storm center's path is accompanied by surface winds from the northeast even though the storm itself approaches from the southwest in response to southwesterly flow aloft. Heavy cyclonic snow conditions such as those shown in the maps above are particularly common in March when the storm track across the United States is in a more southerly position. This storm left 12 to 14 inches (31 to 36 cm) of snow across parts of the southern Lower Peninsula, and strong northeasterly winds accompanying the snow produced road-blocking drifts.

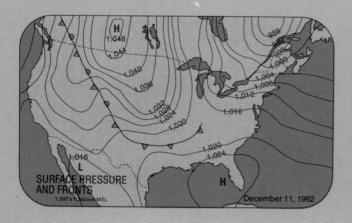

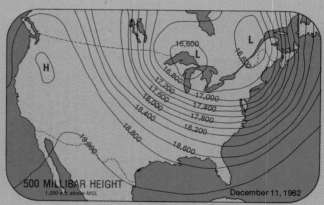

WINTER COLD OUTBREAK

The coldest weather in the Midwest during the winter months is associated with air masses that move from the Arctic, traveling southward through Canada east of the Rocky Mountains. Such a movement of surface weather is produced as the main current of winds in the middle atmosphere (the jet stream) swings far northward over the Pacific Ocean and then moves southward over central North America, as depicted by the lines on the 500 millibar chart above. The associated air mass, represented on the surface map by the center (H) of high atmospheric pressure over southern Canada, therefore would be dry and bitter cold with temperatures far below 0°F (−18°C) over much of Michigan. The dryness of the air mass is partly responsible for the absence of

snow that usually accompanies such Arctic outbreaks. On Great Lakes lee shore areas, however, the movement of very cold air, with much cold air present in the middle atmosphere as well, over the warm, usually unfrozen waters of the lakes leads to instability and the development of stratocumulus or heavy moisture-bearing clouds. Drifting eastward with the wind, these clouds may cause intense snowfall in near-shore areas while residents in eastern Michigan may be experiencing sunny, cold conditions. Arctic weather is not dominant in Michigan because the jet stream configuration needed to produce it occurs only a small percentage of the time during most winters.

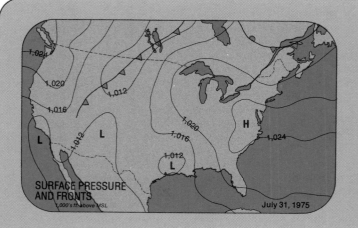

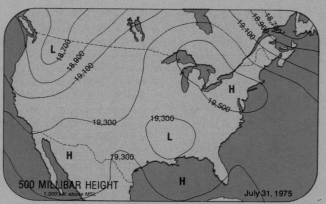

SUMMER HEAT WAVE

Periods of high summer temperatures and high relative humidity in Michigan are usually associated with an influx of air originating over the Gulf of Mexico. Although hot, humid air is found much of the summer over the southeastern United States, its movement into Michigan is favored by the presence of a slow-moving high-pressure center over the mid-Atlantic states and low pressure over the Great Plains as indicated on the above maps. Moving northward from the Gulf under these conditions, the moist, tropical air brings Michigan its most uncomfortable summertime weather. Establishment and persistence of this pattern are dependent upon the configuration of the circulation (the jet stream) in the middle atmosphere. During such periods the upper level air flow over the Plains is normally from the southwest, while over Michigan the air aloft is warm and the circulation weak, circumstances which often lead to high levels of atmospheric pollution in the southern larger industrialized urban areas of the state. In spite of the heat and humidity, general rainfall may not occur for days, because the air aloft is too warm and prevents convectional currents of sufficient strength to develop clouds of the depth necessary for rain.

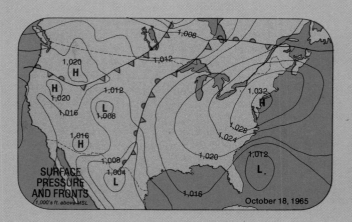

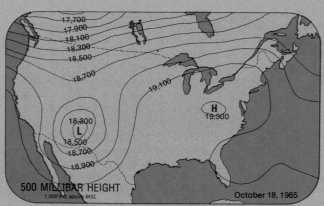

INDIAN SUMMER

Periods of dry, mild, and stagnant weather in October and November that are referred to as Indian summer are usually associated with a slow-moving weather pattern as indicated above. This type of weather often begins as a cool air mass of Pacific or polar origin that might even have brought widespread frosts or freezes to the Midwest. Moving southeastward over the eastern United States, the air mass warms slowly, and the return flow of mild dry westerly air ushers in possibly several days of stable, pleasant weather. Because the air mass is dry, clear skies are characteristic, and the days warm quickly, though the lengthening nights at this season coupled with the clear skies permit rapid nighttime cooling. Heavy dew and radiation fog that is due to the loss of heat in the lower layers of air are therefore typical of the early morning hours. Under such surface conditions, the principal circulation aloft is eastward over Canada, and a large ridge of warm air and weak winds sprawls over the southern Great Lakes region, favoring atmospheric stability and the buildup of pollutants in the lower layers that contribute to the haziness so typical of Indian summer.

Isle Royale is densely covered with northern mixed forest. Because summer heat is moderated by the surrounding cool waters of Lake Superior, boreal plants such as black and white spruce and balsam fir are common forest species, particularly along the low shorelines. The higher interior regions support predominantly deciduous forests of red and sugar maples, yellow birch, and northern red oak. The forest provides excellent cover for certain larger animals, including the only self-sustaining population of timber wolves in Michigan. Wolves apparently reached the island from Ontario on ice that formed during an exceptionally cold winter. The present population, averaging 20 or so animals, relies chiefly on the local moose population for food, primarily the sick or aged animals. Populations of both animals appear to be stable. The shy timber wolves are seldom seen by hikers but can be heard occasionally.

TIMBER WOLF

ISLE ROYALE

MOOSE

The topography of Isle Royale reflects the types and structures of the underlying bedrock. Layers of weak and strong rocks of Keweenawan age are inclined southeastward toward a structural trough located between the island and the Keweenaw Peninsula. As a result, rocks of the same age and characteristics, including the presence of native copper, exist at both places. Differential erosion on the edges of the inclined beds has resulted in ridges that run from northeast to southwest and that are associated with stronger rock formations and parallel lowlands where less resistant layers exist. A second smaller cross-cutting series of erosional lowlands is related to fracture patterns in the bedrock.

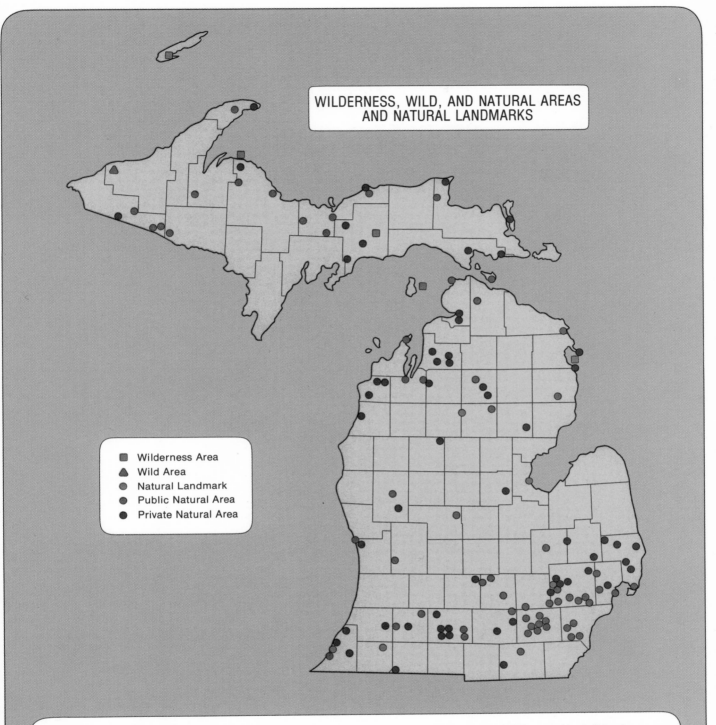

WILDERNESS, WILD, AND NATURAL AREAS
AND NATURAL LANDMARKS

■ Wilderness Area
▲ Wild Area
● Natural Landmark
● Public Natural Area
● Private Natural Area

Michigan enacted a Wilderness and Natural Areas Act in 1972 to protect small natural enclaves of wild areas in the urban, industrial, and agriculturally dominated southern third of the state and larger wilderness areas in the less populated northern two-thirds of the state. These areas are valuable, fragile natural sites where combinations of biological communities, geological bedrock, or complex glacial topography have resulted in features of particular scientific, educational, or scenic value. State designated wilderness areas are 3,000 or more acres (1,200 or more ha) of land, or an island of any size, that are primitive, offer outstanding opportunities for solitude or an unconfined type of recreation, and contain notable natural features with ecological, geological, scenic, or historical value. Wild areas are similar but are

smaller and comprise less than 3,000 acres of land. Natural areas are usually still smaller in size and generally confined to a single distinct land type or an unusual biotic, geologic, or scenic feature. Natural areas may be public or privately owned and frequently are located near schools and population centers. The bulk of natural areas are in southern Michigan, especially in the southeast near Detroit. Natural landmarks, administered by the National Park Service, are true and essentially unspoiled examples of nature. Five sites in Michigan have been registered: Warren Woods Natural Area in Berrien County, Tobico Marsh in Bay County, Highland Haven Hill Natural Area in Oakland County, Deadstream Swamp in Roscommon County, and Fred Russ Natural Area in Cass County.

SELECTED WILDLIFE

BLACK BEAR

OTTER

The wildlife species shown on these two pages have distinct patterns of distribution. All but the wild turkey are concentrated in the northern Lower and the Upper Peninsula, where extensive wilderness has facilitated their survival. The wild turkey has been reintroduced to Michigan in several areas, including Allegan County. In 1918 the elk (Wapiti) was reintroduced to the state in the Pigeon River Valley. By the early 1960s the original 7 animals had increased to a herd of 1,000 to 2,000, but by 1974 they reached a new low in number. Now the herd, estimated to number more than 200, is making a comeback, partly because elk are protected from poaching. They currently range over a 600-square-mile (1,560 sq km) area, and their protection is included in a state plan to protect wildlife. Oil drilling in the Pigeon River area, however, presents potential conflicts for game management.

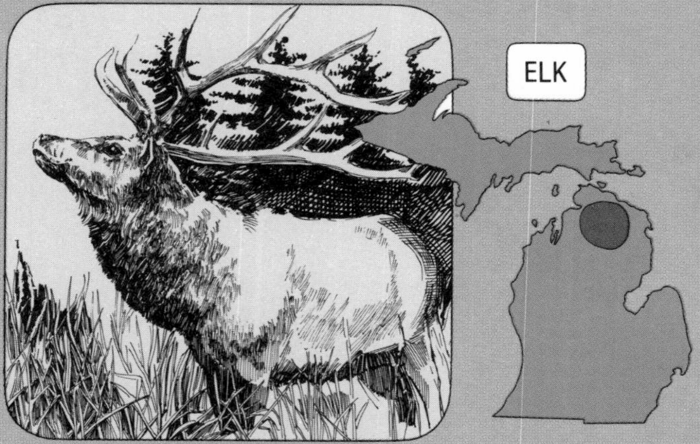

ELK

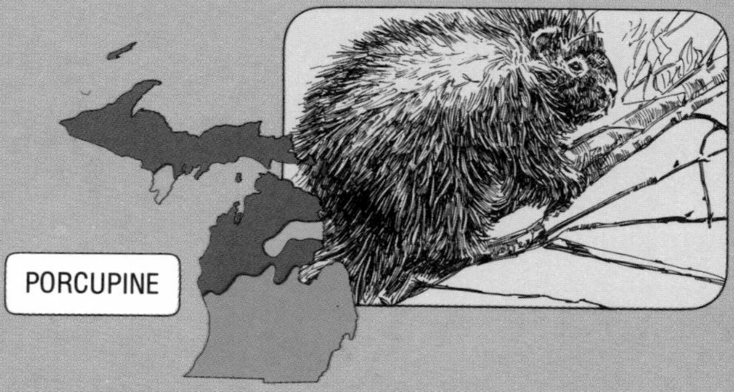

PORCUPINE

OSPREY

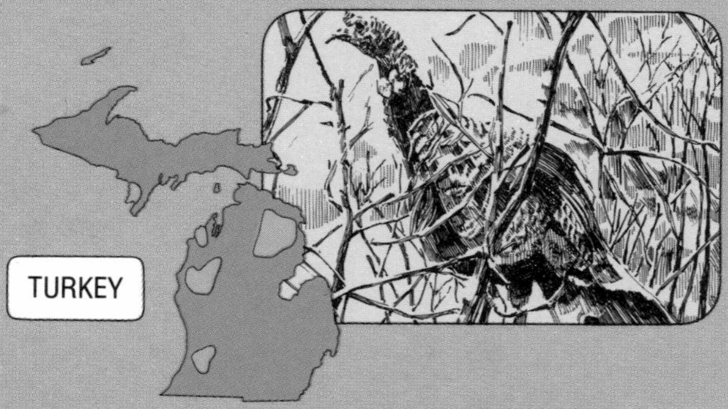

TURKEY

BALD EAGLE

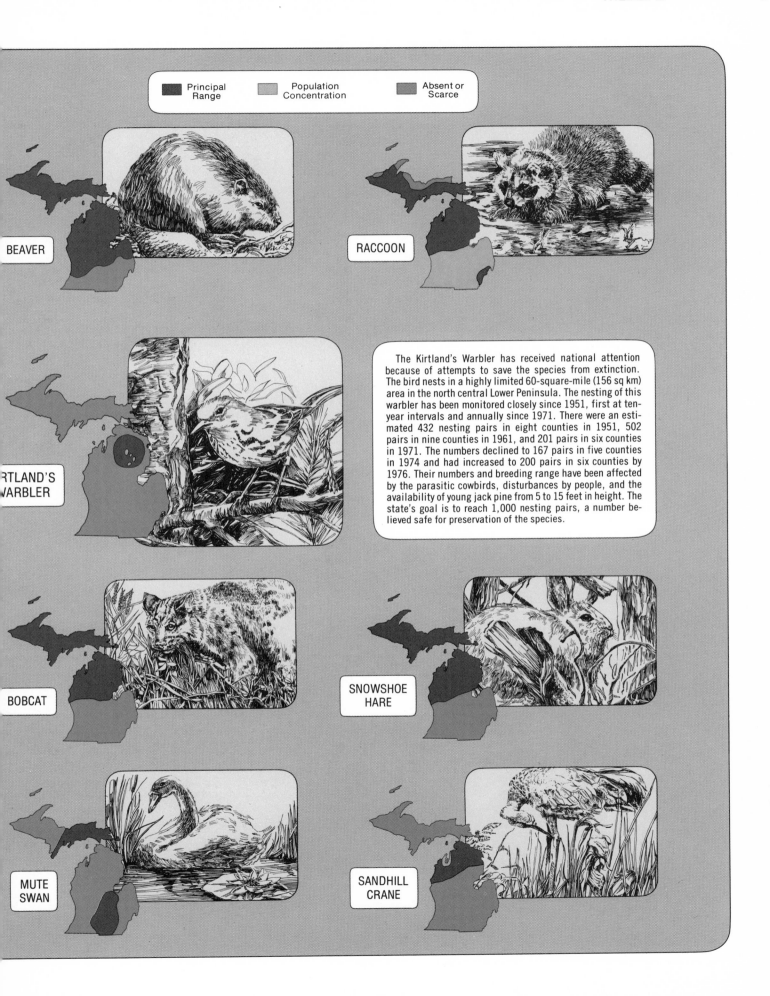

Principal Range   Population Concentration   Absent or Scarce

BEAVER

RACCOON

KIRTLAND'S WARBLER

The Kirtland's Warbler has received national attention because of attempts to save the species from extinction. The bird nests in a highly limited 60-square-mile (156 sq km) area in the north central Lower Peninsula. The nesting of this warbler has been monitored closely since 1951, first at ten-year intervals and annually since 1971. There were an estimated 432 nesting pairs in eight counties in 1951, 502 pairs in nine counties in 1961, and 201 pairs in six counties in 1971. The numbers declined to 167 pairs in five counties in 1974 and had increased to 200 pairs in six counties by 1976. Their numbers and breeding range have been affected by the parasitic cowbirds, disturbances by people, and the availability of young jack pine from 5 to 15 feet in height. The state's goal is to reach 1,000 nesting pairs, a number believed safe for preservation of the species.

BOBCAT

SNOWSHOE HARE

MUTE SWAN

SANDHILL CRANE

PEOPLE AND SOCIETY

Michigan, the seventh most populous of the United States, contains approximately nine million people, who account for 4.4 percent of the national population. In area, Michigan, with its two peninsulas, ranks twenty-third among the states, and has an average density of 156.2 persons per square mile (404.5 per square kilometer). Although the density of Michigan's population is more than two and a half times the national average, it would be even greater if the entire state were as densely populated as the southern third of the state. For example, no county in the Upper Peninsula has a density greater than 35.4 persons per square mile (91.7 per square kilometer), whereas three counties in southern Michigan have densities in excess of 1,000 persons per square mile (2,590 per square kilometer).

The Michigan territory, as defined in 1810, had a population of only 4,762. After a number of boundary changes, the population in 1840 in the area presently constituting this state numbered 212,267. In these pages we will look at the nature of Michigan's population, its growth, organization, and adaptation to the resources of its environment.

Changing Modes of Adaptation

It is useful to think of different styles of life as representing particular adaptations to an environment for the purpose of gaining a livelihood and of satisfying human needs. Populations create a social organization of a particular kind and use appropriate tools and skills to develop the resources of the environment. The essential components in the process of adaptation include population, organization, environment, and technology. Change in any one of these components brings about new forms of adaptation and, indeed, societal transformations.

At least three phases in the adaptation to the environment may be distinguished in Michigan. The first about which we know something is the hunting-fishing-gathering phase of tribes primarily belonging to the Algonquian linguistic group. The best known of these tribes occupying the Michigan territory were the Chippewa, Ottawa, Potawatomi, Miami, Menominee, and the Huron. The economy of these tribes was woodland hunting, deer being the chief food animal. The women cultivated plots of maize, squash, and beans. Tools were simple and made of stone, wood, bone, or shell. The Indians were skilled in the art of tanning deerskins and in spinning twine from the fibers of weeds and bark. They were a Stone Age people who knew nothing of iron and little about copper. They did make simple utilitarian pottery and textiles, but these skills were not highly developed or sophisticated. The

Algonquian Indians were religious people, whose beliefs and ceremonies displayed a great reverence and respect for nature. Tribal identification was strong. Members of the household had well-defined roles that were based upon age and sex. It is not known with any certainty how many Indians inhabited the Michigan territory. One estimate places the number at 15,000, with perhaps 3,000 inhabiting the Upper Peninsula. It is certain the number was never large and would represent only a small fraction of today's large urban-industrial population.

With the exploration of the Michigan territory by Étienne Brulé in the early 1600s and its subsequent settlement, the hunting-fishing-gathering phase was gradually displaced by an agricultural economy. This agricultural phase had its real beginning after 1800. It involved settlement, bringing the land under cultivation, and the organization of small, trade-centered communities. Early agricultural production was, to a large extent, self-sufficient. The farmer was a jack-of-all-trades who, with the help of his family, grew an assortment of crops and livestock. Only much later was farming to become more specialized and oriented to the marketplace. Soon the landscape became filled with small, more or less autonomous communities inhabited almost exclusively by farmers. At the center of these communities was a trade center that served the needs of the farmers. In 1840, 96 percent of the population of Michigan was rural, and it was not until 1920 that the urban population outnumbered the rural.

The agricultural mode of adaptation, however, eventually gave way to an urban-industrial mode. Technological changes in power sources, communication, and the organization of industrial production were among the innovations that increased the support for a growing population, made a large-scale organization possible, and rendered the previous agricultural mode of adaptation obsolete. Technological changes in the farm sector brought increased farm size, specialization, and increased production for the market. Farming as a way of life yielded to farming as a market-oriented business enterprise. The agricultural mode of adaptation became history, the self-contained communities of farmers disintegrated, and agriculture assumed the traits of the new urban-industrial method of adaptation. Surplus farm laborers, as well as established farmers who failed to adapt to the new conditions, became a part of the great rural-to-urban migration streams that only recently began to show signs of drying up. Today more than three-fourths of the state's people reside in metropolitan areas. Only a small fraction of those residing outside metropolitan areas are related to agriculture.

Is the urban-industrial phase here to stay or are we about to embark on a postindustrial phase? The emergence of a new phase seems to be suggested by the relative decline of employment in manufacturing and increase in governmental and service occupations, by the blighting and decline of the centers of our great cities, by residential suburbanization, and by the reduced migration from, and even growth in, some nonmetropolitan areas.

Each successive facet of adaptation has been characterized by changes in the size and composition of the population, by new and more elaborate technology, and by increasingly complex and interrelated social organization. Successive phases not only have brought new roles and new organizational forms, but also have superseded and replaced earlier forms of social organization.

Patterns of Growth, Fertility, Mortality, and Migration

Population growth (or decline) in Michigan, as in any population group, is a consequence of the rate at which infants are born, the rate at which people die, and the rate of in- and out-migration. Since Michigan became a state in 1837 (having the same boundaries as today), its population has grown at an extraordinarily rapid rate. This rapid growth has been a result of high rates of natural increase combined with high rates of migration into the state. Except during the two decades from 1890 to 1910, Michigan's population grew more rapidly than that of the nation as a whole; and except for the depression years,

1930 to 1940, when Michigan's population increased 8.5 percent (and the nation's 7.3 percent), its rate of growth during each decade has never fallen below 13.4 percent, the figure for 1960 to 1970. Before 1890 the growth rate during each decade was often greatly in excess of 25 percent. The rate of growth in Michigan, as well as in the United States, is now slowing. Between 1970 and 1974 Michigan's population was estimated to have increased by 223,000 persons, a percentage increase of only 2.5 percent. During the same period it is estimated that the state lost 102,000 persons through net out-migration.

In broad outline the pattern of Michigan's birthrate since the 1930s has had the same contours as that of the nation. Following low levels in the 1930s the birthrate rose during the mid-1940s into the 1950s, then fell rapidly (with one minor rise in 1970) through 1974. In 1957, the high point of Michigan's "baby boom," 208,488 infant births were registered; in 1974 the number of registered live births was only 137,414. Since 1950 the live birthrate in Michigan has been slightly above that for the United States. Marked changes affecting family formation and dissolution have been evident in recent years. The number of annual divorces in Michigan has risen sharply — from 17,479 in 1963 to 41,850 in 1974. Furthermore, increasing numbers of people are remaining single, and the average age at marriage is on the increase. All these trends tend to support a continuation of a low birthrate.

Although some variations in birthrates are found within Michigan's population, differences between groups tend to be small. Among the significant trends has been the disappearance of large fertility differences by social class, rural and urban residence, and race. Several comments about childbearing are worth noting. First, women are having children earlier in life and childbearing is confined to an increasingly brief time span. In 1973 in Michigan slightly more than 56 percent of all live births were to mothers age 24 or under. Second, higher order births (i.e., third, fourth, fifth, and above) are declining markedly. Fourth order and higher births accounted for approximately 34 percent of all births in Michigan in 1963, whereas these birth orders constituted only about 14 percent of all births in the state in 1973. Finally, births to unwed mothers in Michigan, as elsewhere in the nation, are increasing rapidly. The number of births to unwed mothers per 1,000 total live births in Michigan rose from 49 in 1963 to 143 in 1973, an increase of 193 percent.

Because of improved sanitation and medical technology, among other factors, mortality rates have declined and a newborn infant may expect to live longer than ever before. Death rates, however, do not adequately reflect these improvements because the average age of Michigan's population is rising. The peak death rate among Michigan residents in this century was 15.6 per 1,000 people, which occurred in 1918 during the flu epidemic; in 1974 the rate was 8.4 per 1,000. Death rates among Michigan counties vary widely, and are primarily due to the age structure of county populations. In 1974, for example, death rates of 15 or more per 1,000 people were recorded in Gogebic, Iron, Keewenaw, Lake, and Montmorency counties, all of which have large proportions of older people. In contrast, death rates of less than 7 per 1,000 were registered for the relatively young populations of Clinton, Eaton, Ingham, Isabella, Kalamazoo, Lapeer, Livingston, Macomb, Midland, Oakland, Ottawa, and Washtenaw counties.

Mortality rates in Michigan, as in the nation as a whole, are higher for males than females and for blacks than whites. The median age at death for Michigan males in 1973 was 67, and for Michigan females 74. Comparable median ages for all blacks and all whites in the state are 57 and 71 respectively.

Today the leading causes of death may be described as predominantly chronic, degenerative conditions. At the turn of the century the leading causes were predominantly infectious diseases. The ten leading causes of deaths for Michigan residents in 1973 were: (1) diseases of the heart, (2) malignant neoplasms, (3) cerebrovascular diseases, (4) accidents, (5) influenza and pneumonia, (6) diabetes mellitus, (7) cirrhosis of the liver, (8) homicide, (9) arteriosclerosis, and (10) suicide. These ten causes accounted for 84 percent of all deaths, heart diseases being the single largest cause of death in Michigan as well as in the United States. Diseases of the heart account for more deaths than the next four leading causes combined (cancer, stroke, accidents, and influenza).

Throughout much of Michigan's history, the high rates of net migration into the state greatly amplified natural increase to produce rapid growth. Immigrants from abroad, as well as migrants from the New England and Middle Atlantic states, poured into Michigan during the 1800s. With the state's growing industrial and manufacturing complex, migrants from other areas, particularly from the South, both blacks and whites, moved into Michigan. The flow of people into Michigan now appears to be diminishing and even reversing itself. Net migration into Michigan during the 1950–60 decade is estimated at approximately 156,000 people and during the 1960–70 decade at about 30,000. Between 1970 and 1974 the estimated net loss through migration was about 102,000 people. These losses occurred in the metropolitan areas of the state, whereas the nonmetropolitan areas experienced net gains. The retirement of older people to many of the nonmetropolitan counties in the northern Lower Peninsula has contributed to this pattern.

Urban-Rural and Age-Sex Composition

As suggested by our characterization of the urban-industrial economy, Michigan is among the highly urban states. Employment in nonagricultural occupations gives the state an even more markedly urban character than suggested by the 73.8 percent of the population classed as "urban" in the 1970 census. Many people classified among the 26.2 percent "rural" population reside in areas outside cities, but commute to work and form a part of the urban labor force. The extent of Michigan's urban nature is suggested by the fact that, in 1970, approximately 77 percent of the population resided in 11 Standard Metropolitan Statistical Areas (SMSAs). These areas, defined as an entire county or group of contiguous counties having at least one city of 50,000 people or more and constituting a socially and economically integrated unit, include: Ann Arbor (Washtenaw County), Bay City (Bay County), Detroit (Macomb, Oakland, and Wayne counties), Flint (Genesee and Lapeer counties), Grand Rapids (Kent and Ottawa counties), Jackson (Jackson County), Kalamazoo (Kalamazoo County), Lansing (Clinton, Eaton, and Ingham counties), Muskegon and Muskegon Heights (Muskegon County), Saginaw (Saginaw County), and Toledo, Ohio-Michigan (Monroe County).* More than three-fourths of Michigan's total population reside in 17 of the 83 counties.

The age-sex composition of Michigan's population in 1970 differed from that of the total U.S. population in relatively minor ways. Michigan's population was somewhat younger and had a higher sex ratio (number of males per 100 females) for both whites and nonwhites. Overall, dependency ratios (number of persons under 20 plus number of persons 65 and over, divided by the number of persons 20 to 64, multiplied by 100) were higher in Michigan than in the United States. The population pyramids for Michigan (as well as for the United States) reveal two major trends: the ongoing aging of the population and a reduced birthrate beginning during the 1960s. Between 1960 and 1970 the 75-year-old-and-over age group in Michigan increased by 41 percent. During the same period the age group under 5 years of age declined by about 18 percent. Michigan had about 165,000 fewer children under 5 years old in 1970 than in 1960. In addition to the growth of older age groups and the decline of the youngest age group, the population pyramids for Michigan show especially small cohorts between ages 30 to 34 and 35 to 39. People of these ages in 1970 were born in the decade of the 1930s, a period of especially

*Counties included in the SMSA delineation as of 1970. Additional counties were added to some of the state's SMSAs in 1974.

low birthrates. Changes in age structure have far-reaching economic and social consequences. For example, the age structure of a population affects the size of the work force, which in turn affects the incidence of savings, investment, retirement insurance, and annuity costs. There is a close relationship between age composition and the number of teachers, classrooms, and other educational facilities needed. A population's age composition also is related to family formation and the types of goods and social services required.

Marked differences in age-sex structure exist among the counties of Michigan. Such differences are largely due to varying patterns of in- and out-migration. In general, and until very recently, the direction of migration streams has been from the rural, nonmetropolitan counties to metropolitan or adjacent counties. Largely because of extensive out-migration and the consequent overall aged character of the residual county population, seven counties in Michigan are characterized by "natural decrease"—that is, deaths exceeded births in at least three of the five years between 1966 and 1970. Other differences in age structure among counties are due to the presence of institutions (such as colleges, universities, reformatories, and mental hospitals) and military installations. Furthermore, county variations may be due to large proportions of blacks, whose age structure is markedly younger than that of whites. In general, metropolitan areas contain larger proportions of economically productive people. The comparatively younger nonwhite population in both metropolitan and nonmetropolitan areas is a persistent difference. Sex ratios are usually higher in nonmetropolitan than in metropolitan areas. Sex ratios for blacks are often lower than for whites. Dependency ratios are higher among blacks than whites, but vary greatly for both groups in metropolitan and nonmetropolitan counties.

Racial and Cultural Composition

The population of Michigan today is a collage of diverse races and cultures. Immigrants from abroad played an important role in the early phase of agricultural development as well as in later periods of industrial expansion. The influx of foreign-born people was very large around the turn of the century before federal legislation established national origin quotas. Many ethnic groups played a role in the development and use of Michigan's resources: the Finns and Welsh were associated importantly with iron and copper mining; the Dutch and Germans with agriculture; and the Italians, Poles, and Hungarians with manufacturing. Each ethnic group in Michigan has its own unique history in terms of reasons for leaving the homeland, period of immigration, employment, and problems associated with adaptation to the new environment.

Racial composition, as identified by the U.S. Bureau of the Census, consists of whites, blacks (which refers to the census category "Negroes"), and other races (comprising Indians, Japanese, Chinese, Filipinos, and all others). In 1970 whites accounted for 88.3 percent of Michigan's inhabitants; blacks, 11.2 percent; and other races, 0.5 percent. The state's black population (991,066 in 1970) has grown exceptionally rapidly; there were only about 60,000 blacks in Michigan 50 years ago. The black population is largely confined to the state's metropolitan areas. Approximately one-third of the population of the central cities of the state's metropolitan areas is black. Other races in Michigan numbered only 50,543 in 1970. Indians, the largest single group, accounted for 16,854 and are more widely distributed than the Japanese, Chinese, and Filipinos, who are largely confined to the larger cities. In 1970 the Japanese, Chinese, and Filipinos numbered 5,221, 6,407, and 3,657 respectively.

The ethnic diversity of Michigan's population is also evident from data on nativity and parentage. In 1970 foreign-born residents of Michigan numbered 424,309, or 4.8 percent of the total population. The "foreign stock" (foreign-born plus native-born of foreign or mixed parentage), however, numbered 1,259,961 or 14.2 percent of the total population. Because of reduced immigration from abroad, the proportions of both foreign-born and foreign stock are declining. In 1900, for instance, more than 22 percent of Michigan's population was born abroad and slightly more than 61 percent was of foreign stock.

Data concerning the country of origin of foreign stock reveal that most countries of the world have sent immigrants to Michigan. In 1900 the five most numerous countries of origin, in order, were Germany, Canada, United Kingdom, Ireland, and Poland. These five countries of origin accounted for 46 percent of the total foreign stock in Michigan. Ranking just below the first five were people with origins in Scandinavia—the Swedes, Norwegians, and Danes. In 1970, by contrast, the leading countries of origin for Michigan were Canada, Poland, Germany, United Kingdom, and Italy, which together accounted for slightly more than 60 percent of all foreign stock. In addition to shifts in the ranking, Italy now appears among the first five, and Ireland has disappeared from the list. Such a ranking fails to call attention to many less numerous enclaves of ethnic groups in Michigan. Many of them, such as the Scandinavians and Dutch, came during earlier periods and are now largely counted as native-born. The once strong ethnic character of numerous rural areas of the state has become diluted through migration.

Special mention should be made of the Mexican-Americans in Michigan, many of whom initially came into the state as migrant farm laborers and later settled out from the migrant stream. Relatively few are counted as foreign stock, since many of them were born in Texas and other southwestern states and thus are native-born. In 1970 the census enumerated 31,579 people of Mexican foreign stock in Michigan. At the same time, people of "Spanish origin or descent" (including origins other than Mexico) numbered slightly more than 151,000.

Social Institutions and Services

Up to this point Michigan's human resources have been stressed as have the dynamics of population growth and of changes taking place in the state's population. Of equivalent significance, although less amenable to graphic representation, is the system of institutions and services created to meet human needs.

A major concern in all societies is health care, and in Michigan an elaborate system of hospitals, with medical and dental professionals, has been created as a response to this need. In addition to maps showing air quality, variations in the distribution of physicians, dentists, nurses, and hospital beds are depicted. A series of maps and charts are presented concerning housing, which relates to the quality of life and is a mirror of some aspects of life style and, of course, suggests variations in socioeconomic status. Among the problems faced in all states is law enforcement, which requires an organized effort to ensure compliance. Maps and charts are presented to show the incidence of various crimes and the location of police posts and personnel.

An increasingly elaborate system for the transmission of skills, norms, and values has been developed in Michigan. The growth of facilities for education at all levels, as well as the rising level of educational attainment of Michigan's population, is depicted in a series of maps and graphs. Social services form another organizational system developed to meet the needs of an increased population. Variation with respect to income and social service payments is presented. Variations between counties in the incidence of poverty and in the distribution of personal income of $15,000 or more are of special interest. In summary, the nature and diversity of the people and society in Michigan are presented in graphic form in the following pages.

J. Allan Beegle

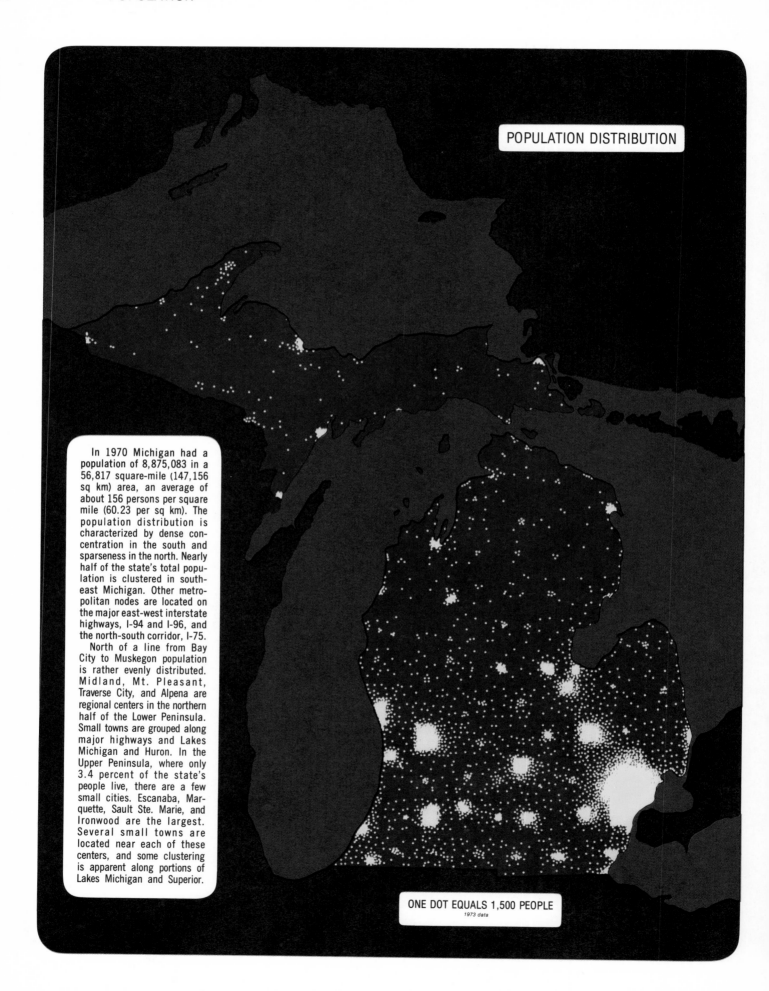

POPULATION DISTRIBUTION

In 1970 Michigan had a population of 8,875,083 in a 56,817 square-mile (147,156 sq km) area, an average of about 156 persons per square mile (60.23 per sq km). The population distribution is characterized by dense concentration in the south and sparseness in the north. Nearly half of the state's total population is clustered in southeast Michigan. Other metropolitan nodes are located on the major east-west interstate highways, I-94 and I-96, and the north-south corridor, I-75.

North of a line from Bay City to Muskegon population is rather evenly distributed. Midland, Mt. Pleasant, Traverse City, and Alpena are regional centers in the northern half of the Lower Peninsula. Small towns are grouped along major highways and Lakes Michigan and Huron. In the Upper Peninsula, where only 3.4 percent of the state's people live, there are a few small cities. Escanaba, Marquette, Sault Ste. Marie, and Ironwood are the largest. Several small towns are located near each of these centers, and some clustering is apparent along portions of Lakes Michigan and Superior.

ONE DOT EQUALS 1,500 PEOPLE
1973 data

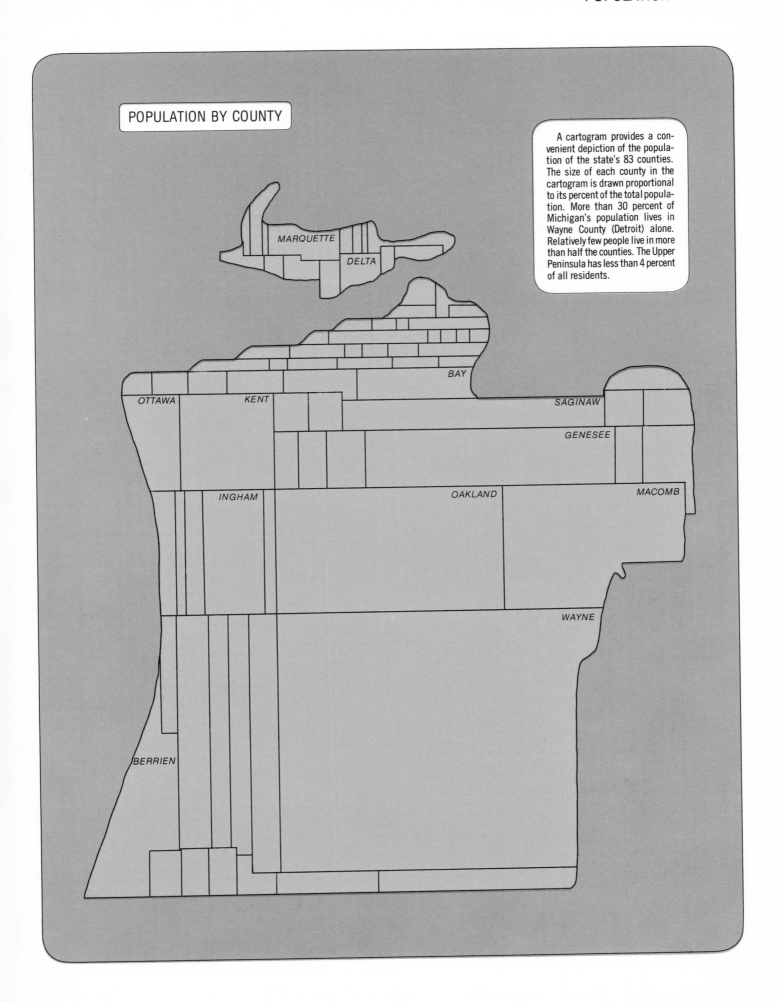

POPULATION BY COUNTY

A cartogram provides a convenient depiction of the population of the state's 83 counties. The size of each county in the cartogram is drawn proportional to its percent of the total population. More than 30 percent of Michigan's population lives in Wayne County (Detroit) alone. Relatively few people live in more than half the counties. The Upper Peninsula has less than 4 percent of all residents.

MARQUETTE

DELTA

BAY

OTTAWA

KENT

SAGINAW

GENESEE

INGHAM

OAKLAND

MACOMB

WAYNE

BERRIEN

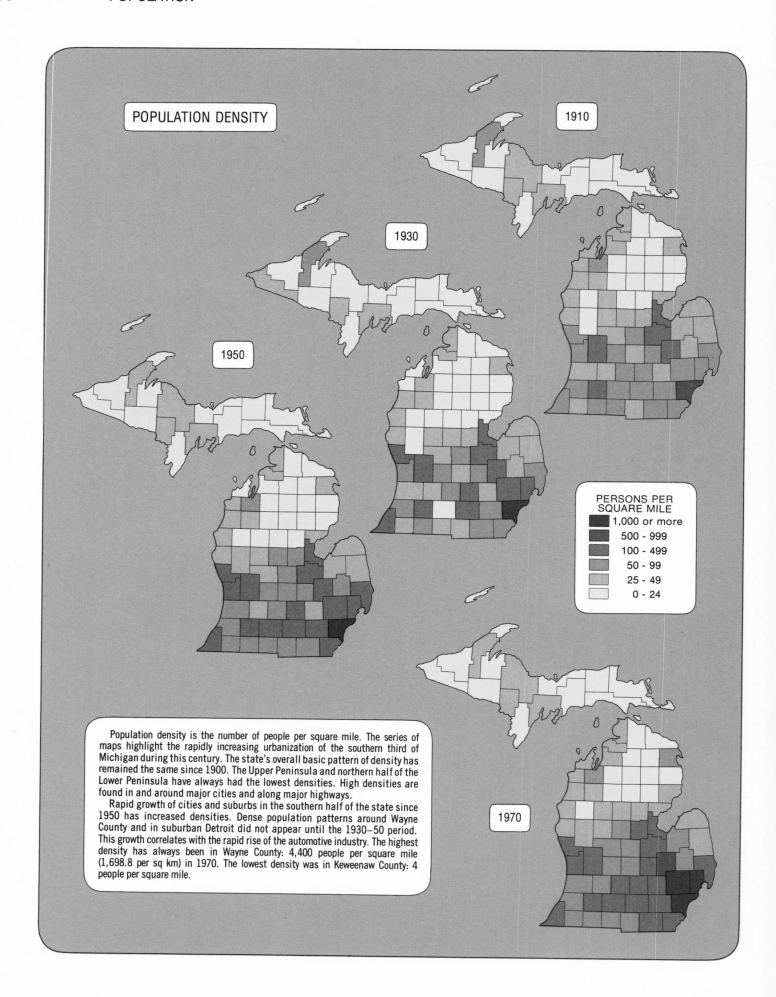

POPULATION DENSITY

1910

1930

1950

PERSONS PER
SQUARE MILE

1,000 or more
500 - 999
100 - 499
50 - 99
25 - 49
0 - 24

    Population density is the number of people per square mile. The series of
maps highlight the rapidly increasing urbanization of the southern third of
Michigan during this century. The state's overall basic pattern of density has
remained the same since 1900. The Upper Peninsula and northern half of the
Lower Peninsula have always had the lowest densities. High densities are
found in and around major cities and along major highways.
    Rapid growth of cities and suburbs in the southern half of the state since
1950 has increased densities. Dense population patterns around Wayne
County and in suburban Detroit did not appear until the 1930–50 period.
This growth correlates with the rapid rise of the automotive industry. The highest
density has always been in Wayne County: 4,400 people per square mile
(1,698.8 per sq km) in 1970. The lowest density was in Keweenaw County: 4
people per square mile.

1970

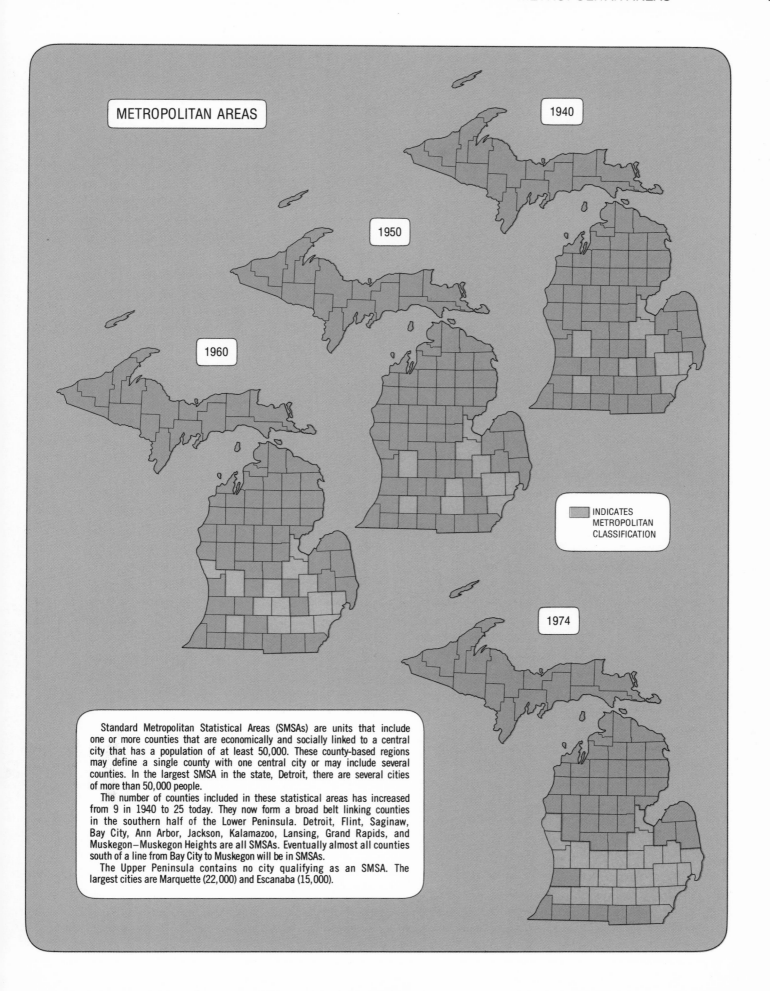

METROPOLITAN AREAS

1940

1950

1960

INDICATES
METROPOLITAN
CLASSIFICATION

1974

Standard Metropolitan Statistical Areas (SMSAs) are units that include one or more counties that are economically and socially linked to a central city that has a population of at least 50,000. These county-based regions may define a single county with one central city or may include several counties. In the largest SMSA in the state, Detroit, there are several cities of more than 50,000 people.

The number of counties included in these statistical areas has increased from 9 in 1940 to 25 today. They now form a broad belt linking counties in the southern half of the Lower Peninsula. Detroit, Flint, Saginaw, Bay City, Ann Arbor, Jackson, Kalamazoo, Lansing, Grand Rapids, and Muskegon—Muskegon Heights are all SMSAs. Eventually almost all counties south of a line from Bay City to Muskegon will be in SMSAs.

The Upper Peninsula contains no city qualifying as an SMSA. The largest cities are Marquette (22,000) and Escanaba (15,000).

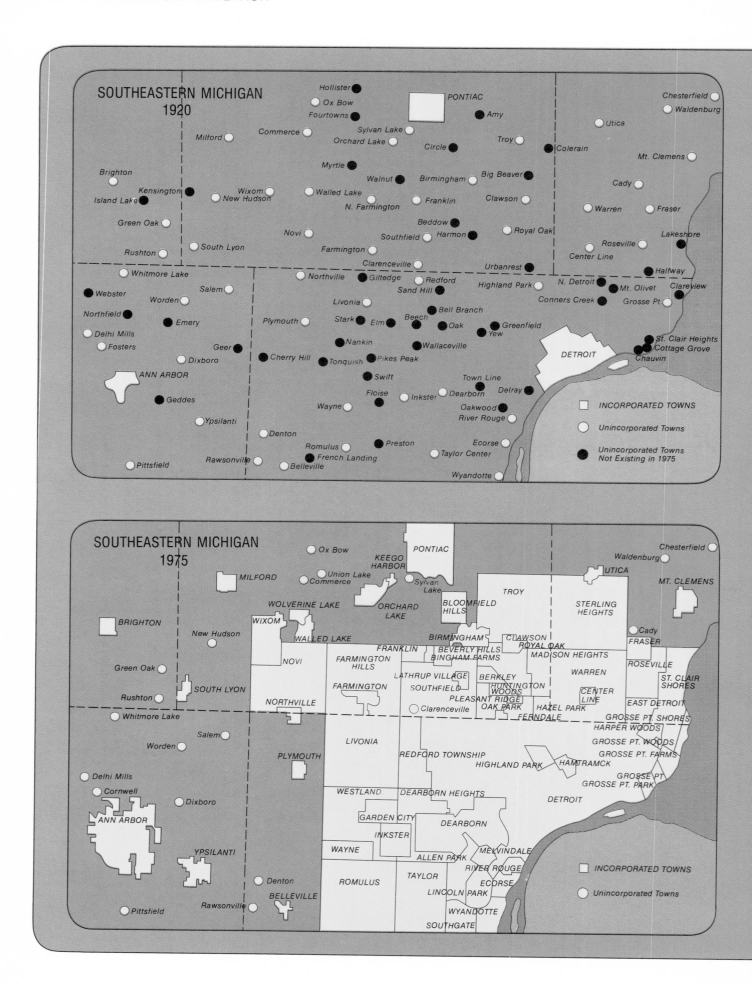

SOUTHEASTERN MICHIGAN 1920

Hollister
Ox Bow
Fourtowns
PONTIAC
Amy
Chesterfield
Waldenburg
Utica
Commerce
Sylvan Lake
Milford
Orchard Lake
Troy
Colerain
Mt. Clemens
Circle
Myrtle
Walnut
Birmingham
Big Beaver
Cady
Brighton
Kensington
Wixom
New Hudson
Walled Lake
Franklin
Clawson
Warren
Fraser
Island Lake
N. Farmington
Green Oak
Beddow
Royal Oak
Lakeshore
Novi
Southfield
Harmon
Roseville
Rushton
South Lyon
Farmington
Center Line
Whitmore Lake
Clarenceville
Urbanrest
Halfway
Northville
Giltedge
Redford
Highland Park
N. Detroit
Clareview
Webster
Salem
Sand Hill
Mt. Olivet
Worden
Livonia
Bell Branch
Conners Creek
Grosse Pt.
Northfield
Plymouth
Stark
Elm
Beech
Oak
Greenfield
Delhi Mills
Emery
Yew
St. Clair Heights
Fosters
Geer
Nankin
Wallaceville
Cottage Grove
Dixboro
Cherry Hill
Tonquish
Pikes Peak
Chauvin
ANN ARBOR
Swift
DETROIT
Geddes
Floise
Inkster
Dearborn
Town Line
Delray
Ypsilanti
Wayne
Oakwood
Denton
River Rouge
Romulus
Preston
Ecorse
Taylor Center
Pittsfield
Rawsonville
French Landing
Belleville
Wyandotte

INCORPORATED TOWNS
Unincorporated Towns
Unincorporated Towns Not Existing in 1975

SOUTHEASTERN MICHIGAN 1975

Ox Bow
PONTIAC
KEEGO HARBOR
Chesterfield
Waldenburg
UTICA
MILFORD
Union Lake
Commerce
Sylvan Lake
WOLVERINE LAKE
ORCHARD LAKE
TROY
MT. CLEMENS
BLOOMFIELD HILLS
STERLING HEIGHTS
BRIGHTON
New Hudson
WIXOM
WALLED LAKE
BIRMINGHAM
CLAWSON
ROYAL OAK
Cady
FRASER
Green Oak
NOVI
FRANKLIN
BEVERLY HILLS
BINGHAM FARMS
MADISON HEIGHTS
ROSEVILLE
FARMINGTON HILLS
LATHRUP VILLAGE
BERKLEY
WARREN
ST. CLAIR SHORES
Rushton
SOUTH LYON
FARMINGTON
SOUTHFIELD
HUNTINGTON WOODS
CENTER LINE
EAST DETROIT
NORTHVILLE
PLEASANT RIDGE
OAK PARK
HAZEL PARK
Whitmore Lake
Clarenceville
FERNDALE
GROSSE PT. SHORES
Salem
HARPER WOODS
Worden
LIVONIA
GROSSE PT. WOODS
GROSSE PT. FARMS
PLYMOUTH
REDFORD TOWNSHIP
HIGHLAND PARK
HAMTRAMCK
Delhi Mills
Dixboro
GROSSE PT
GROSSE PT. PARK
Cornwell
WESTLAND
DEARBORN HEIGHTS
DETROIT
ANN ARBOR
GARDEN CITY
YPSILANTI
INKSTER
DEARBORN
Denton
WAYNE
ALLEN PARK
MELVINDALE
Pittsfield
Rawsonville
BELLEVILLE
ROMULUS
TAYLOR
RIVER ROUGE
ECORSE
LINCOLN PARK
WYANDOTTE
SOUTHGATE

INCORPORATED TOWNS
Unincorporated Towns

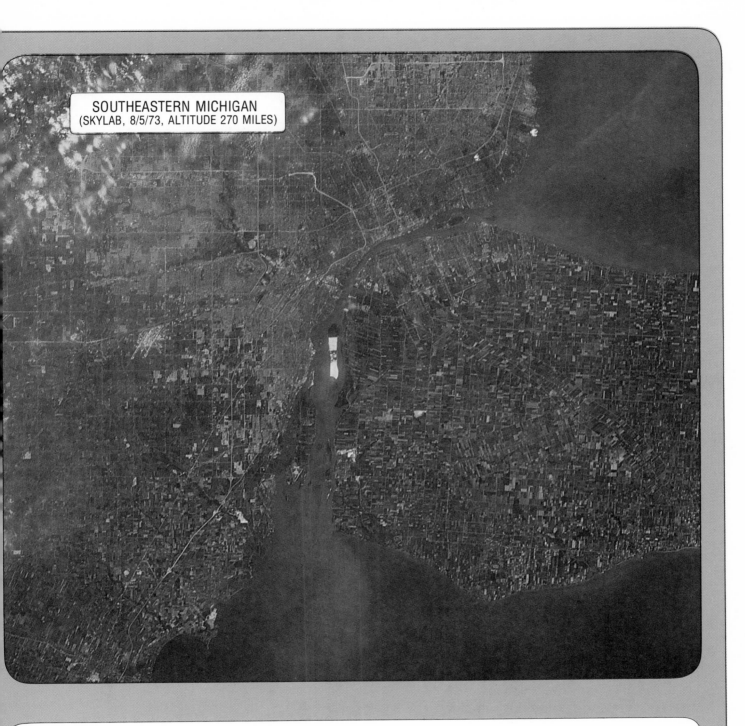

SOUTHEASTERN MICHIGAN
(SKYLAB, 8/5/73, ALTITUDE 270 MILES)

A satellite photograph taken from the Skylab III mission on August 5, 1973 reveals the Detroit area and beyond in a unique manner. Although partially obscured by cloud formations in the upper left corner, this perspective (north is at the top of the photograph) provides an opportunity to examine the striking physical and cultural characteristics of Michigan's largest metropolitan environment. Even from a height of 270 miles (435 km), certain general features may be recognized easily. The extent of urban sprawl, for example, is much more intense in Michigan than on the Canadian side of the Detroit River.

The large islands in the Detroit River, such as Grosse Isle, Belle Isle, and Fighting Island (indicated by white areas in the center of the photograph), are easily distinguished. In Lake Saint Clair (upper right) and Lake Erie (lower portion) light colored plumes of sediment denote agricultural runoff and industrial discharge. Shipping channels, always areas of sediment disruption, are seen as light linear forms above the plumes.

The Rouge, Huron, and Raisin rivers are evident by the conspicuous absence of urban development immediately adjacent to them. Close examination of the urban areas permits identification of major thoroughfares, expressways, and airports. The rectangular grid pattern in the countryside is highlighted by different crop types and field patterns. The peculiar long-lot land tenure systems developed during settlement by the French are visible in the field patterns on the Canadian side of the Detroit River near Fighting Island.

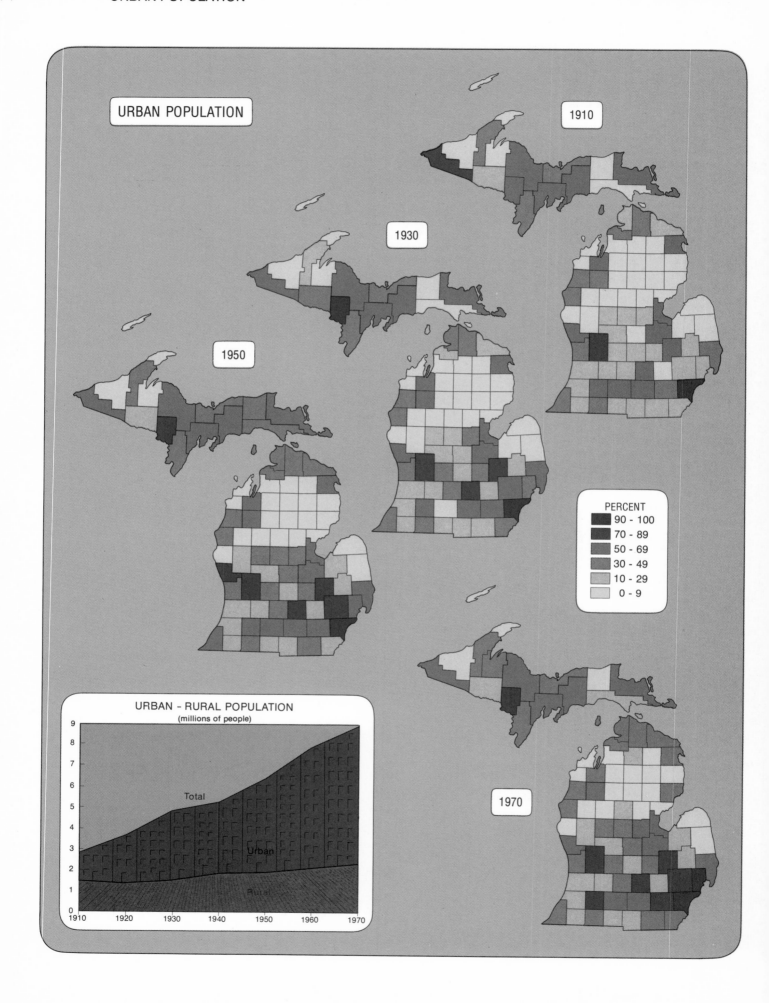

URBAN POPULATION

1910

1930

1950

PERCENT
90 - 100
70 - 89
50 - 69
30 - 49
10 - 29
0 - 9

URBAN - RURAL POPULATION
(millions of people)

Total

Urban

Rural

1910   1920   1930   1940   1950   1960   1970

1970

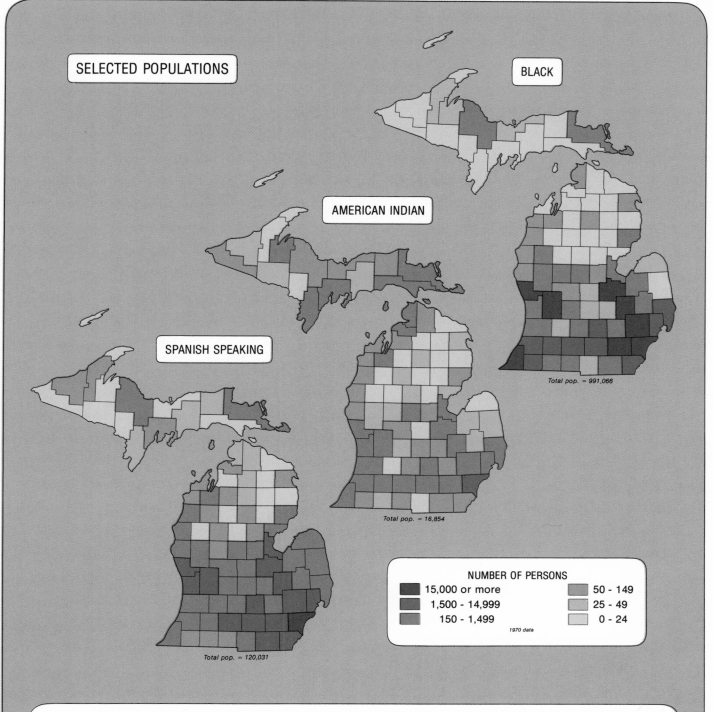

SELECTED POPULATIONS

BLACK

AMERICAN INDIAN

SPANISH SPEAKING

Total pop. = 991,066

Total pop. = 16,854

Total pop. = 120,031

NUMBER OF PERSONS

15,000 or more

1,500 - 14,999

150 - 1,499

50 - 149

25 - 49

0 - 24

1970 data

Blacks, Spanish-Americans, and native Indians are three major minority groups found in Michigan. According to the 1970 census, there are nearly one million blacks, about 120,000 Spanish-speaking residents, and nearly 17,000 native Indians.

The black population is concentrated in the Lower Peninsula, especially in the Detroit metropolitan area and in major urban centers having heavy industry. Wayne, Oakland, Macomb, Genesee, Kent, Berrien, Ingham, and Saginaw counties have the largest number of blacks. More than 720,000 live in Wayne County alone. There are few blacks in the northern half of the Lower Peninsula or in the Upper Peninsula.

The Spanish-speaking population primarily includes Mexican-Americans and Cuban-Americans. They live in both urban and rural regions, but are concentrated in southeast Michigan, especially in the Detroit metropolitan area. Smaller concentrations are found in Flint, Saginaw, and Bay City. The rural Spanish-speaking people live in the western half of the Lower Peninsula, where many originally came as seasonal employees in fruit and vegetable production.

Native Indians live primarily in the rural and sparsely populated counties and in Detroit (Wayne County). Some concentrations are also found in the western half of the Lower Peninsula and in the Upper Peninsula. It is noteworthy that the native Indian population is largely located in rural areas and small towns, where very few blacks and Spanish-speaking residents live.

FOREIGN STOCK

Throughout Michigan's past, but especially in the nineteenth century, people from a number of ethnic groups, primarily Europeans, have moved into the state. Some were attracted to rural areas for agriculture, mining, and lumbering. Others migrated to urban areas for industrial employment or to establish a business.

As these new immigrants came, whether in the 1800s or early in this century, they tended to be attracted to locations similar to their areas of origin and to settlements of those having a similar cultural background. First- and second-generation Michiganians, whether from central, southern, or northern Europe, were prone to retain the social and cultural patterns of their homeland. The net result of more than a century of settlement by various ethnic groups is a cultural mosaic, an important part of the state's heritage and tradition.

The 1970 census provides the composition of the state's population by country of birth. By far the largest number of immigrants came from Canada, which is not unexpected considering the proximity of our neighbor and its similar settlement histories. Most Canadians live in the cities and in the rural southeast parts of the state.

Other groups that immigrated to Michigan in large numbers came from Germany, Poland, Great Britain, and Italy. Germans and British are found throughout most of the state. Those of Polish and Italian extraction are most often found in the largest urban areas.

Other major European groups have also settled here in large numbers. The Upper Peninsula is populated by Finns, especially in the western mining regions, and by Norwegians and Swedes. Hungarians, Austrians, Czechs, Russians, French, and Irish are scattered throughout the state; many live side by side. The Dutch are concentrated around Grand Rapids and Holland. The relatively few Chinese, Cubans, and Japanese reside mainly in the large cities.

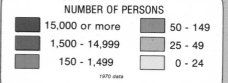

NUMBER OF PERSONS

15,000 or more	50 - 149
1,500 - 14,999	25 - 49
150 - 1,499	0 - 24

1970 data

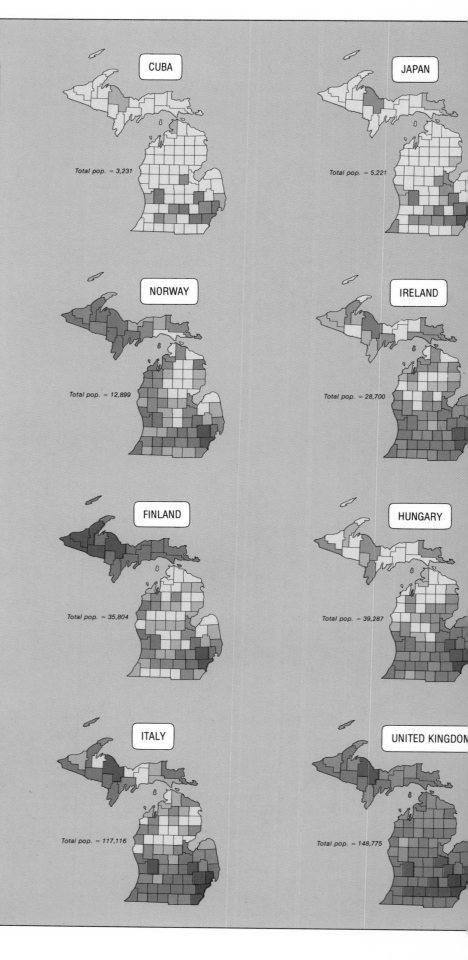

CUBA — Total pop. = 3,231

JAPAN — Total pop. = 5,221

NORWAY — Total pop. = 12,899

IRELAND — Total pop. = 28,700

FINLAND — Total pop. = 35,804

HUNGARY — Total pop. = 39,287

ITALY — Total pop. = 117,116

UNITED KINGDOM — Total pop. = 148,775

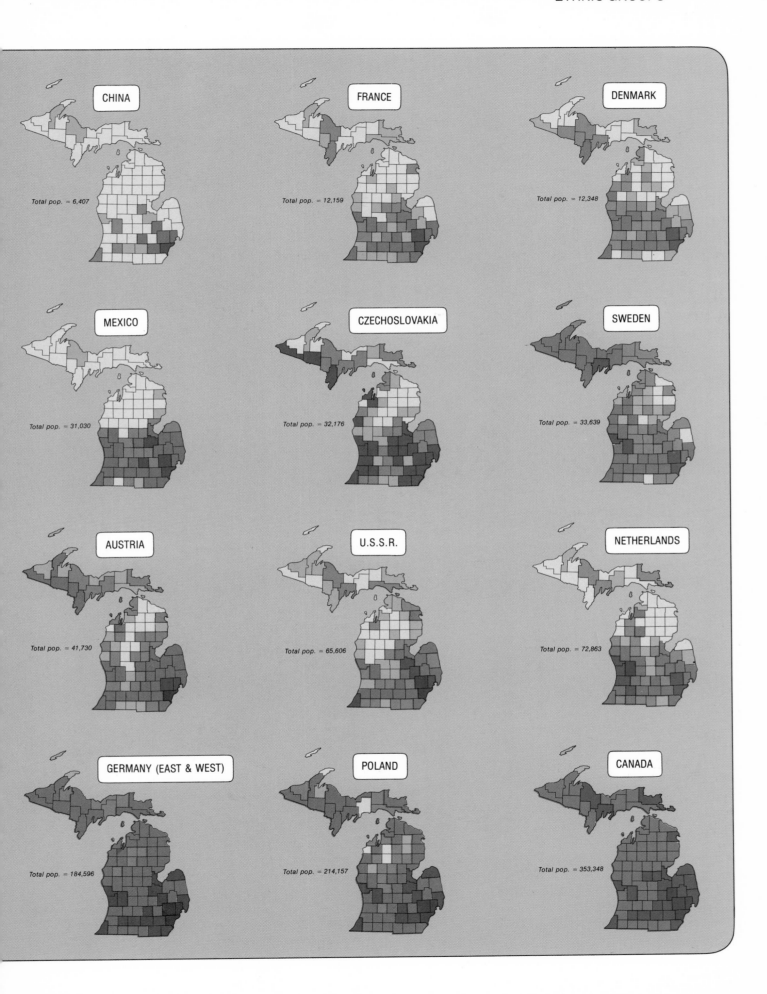

CHINA
Total pop. = 6,407

FRANCE
Total pop. = 12,159

DENMARK
Total pop. = 12,348

MEXICO
Total pop. = 31,030

CZECHOSLOVAKIA
Total pop. = 32,176

SWEDEN
Total pop. = 33,639

AUSTRIA
Total pop. = 41,730

U.S.S.R.
Total pop. = 65,606

NETHERLANDS
Total pop. = 72,863

GERMANY (EAST & WEST)
Total pop. = 184,596

POLAND
Total pop. = 214,157

CANADA
Total pop. = 353,348

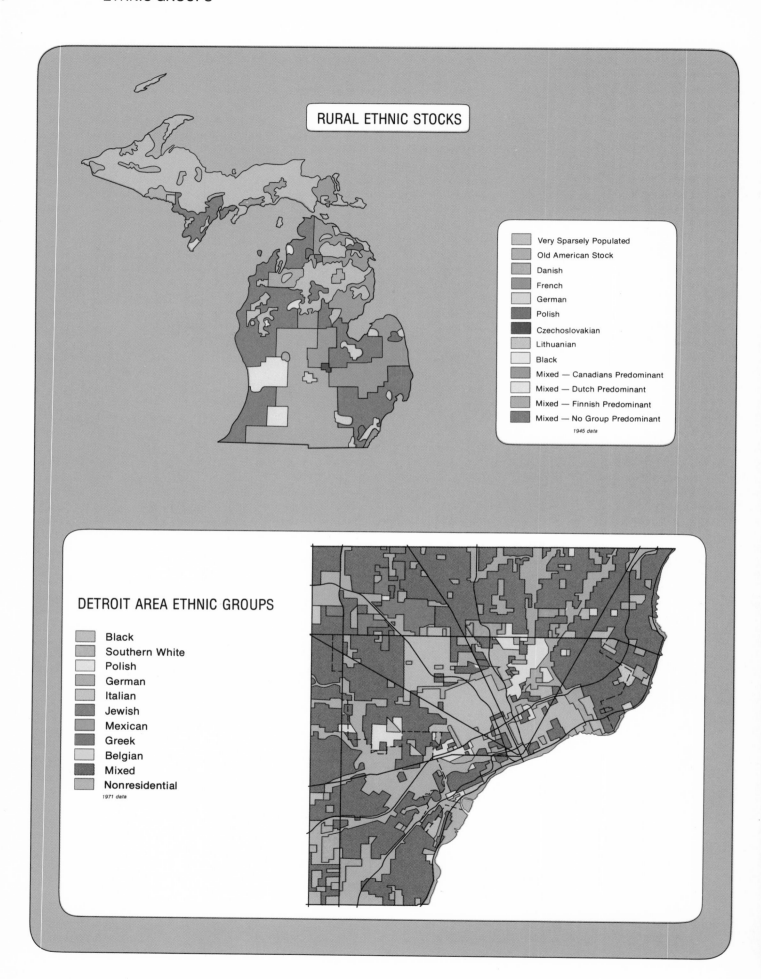

RURAL ETHNIC STOCKS

Very Sparsely Populated
Old American Stock
Danish
French
German
Polish
Czechoslovakian
Lithuanian
Black
Mixed — Canadians Predominant
Mixed — Dutch Predominant
Mixed — Finnish Predominant
Mixed — No Group Predominant

1945 data

DETROIT AREA ETHNIC GROUPS

Black
Southern White
Polish
German
Italian
Jewish
Mexican
Greek
Belgian
Mixed
Nonresidential

1971 data

Catholics, Jews, and numerous Protestant groups are found throughout Michigan. The largest group, Roman Catholics (more than 2.2 million in 1971), reside in largest numbers in the Detroit area and around Bay City and Saginaw. Concentrations also exist in the Upper Peninsula. Ethnic groups from Germany, Poland, Italy, Czechoslovakia, Hungary, and Ireland make up the bulk of the Catholics. More recently, Spanish-speaking groups have augmented the Catholic population, especially in Detroit and other large cities. In 29 counties more than half of the total religious population are Catholics, and in another 41 counties they constitute from 25 to 49 percent of all adherents.

Jewish congregations are found in the larger cities, particularly in the Detroit metropolitan area. The largest protestant denominations are Lutherans (510,000), Methodists (345,000), and Presbyterians (188,000). Methodists and Lutherans are found in largest relative numbers in the Upper Peninsula and in areas settled by Germans, Swedes, Danes, Norwegians, and Finns. The state's Dutch heritage is reflected in the Christian Reformed Church and the Reformed Church of America, both of which are strong around Holland and Grand Rapids (Kent County in particular). Mennonites are concentrated in Oscoda County and members of the United Church of Christ in Lake County.

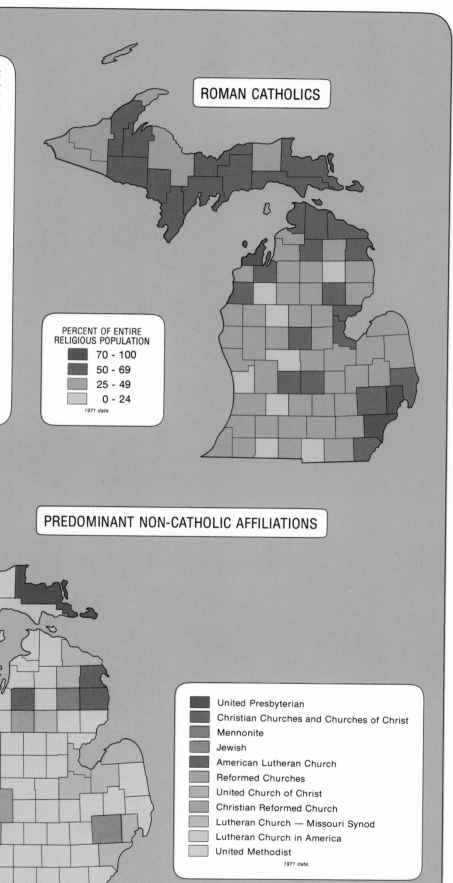

ROMAN CATHOLICS

PERCENT OF ENTIRE
RELIGIOUS POPULATION

70 - 100
50 - 69
25 - 49
0 - 24

1971 data

PREDOMINANT NON-CATHOLIC AFFILIATIONS

United Presbyterian
Christian Churches and Churches of Christ
Mennonite
Jewish
American Lutheran Church
Reformed Churches
United Church of Christ
Christian Reformed Church
Lutheran Church — Missouri Synod
Lutheran Church in America
United Methodist

1971 data

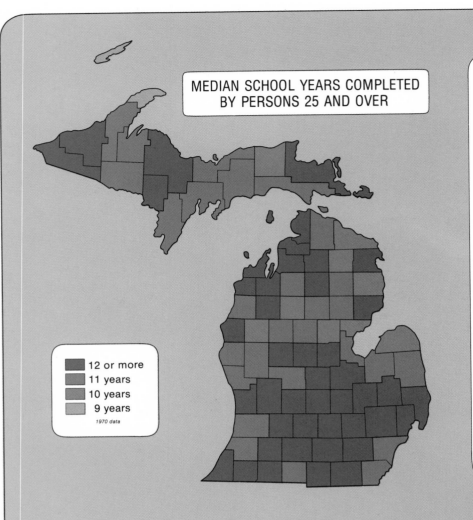

MEDIAN SCHOOL YEARS COMPLETED BY PERSONS 25 AND OVER

- 12 or more
- 11 years
- 10 years
- 9 years

1970 data

The median number of school years completed by Michigan residents 25 years old and over in 1970 was 12.1. (Median is that value under and over which half the distribution falls.) The highest medians are found in those counties with large numbers of college and university students and of professionals. The largest number of counties having median school years completed below the state average were rural and were in the northern parts of the state.

Washtenaw County (University of Michigan) had a median of 12.6 years, followed by Midland (Dow Chemical Company) with 12.5 years and Oakland (suburban Detroit) and Ingham (Michigan State University and the state capital) each with 12.4 years. The lowest median, 9.0, was in Keweenaw County.

Public school enrollments have increased gradually over time, in part as a result of the growing population. Since 1970, however, the declining birthrate has signaled lower enrollments in grade schools. On the other hand, the number of Michiganians with college training has risen rapidly.

The number of school districts has declined, especially since 1940. Migration from rural to urban areas has forced most one-room schools to consolidate with larger schools. There are many new schools in the state that attract students residing in several adjacent counties.

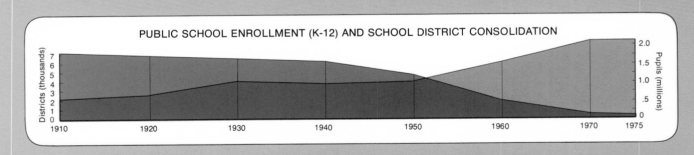

PUBLIC SCHOOL ENROLLMENT (K-12) AND SCHOOL DISTRICT CONSOLIDATION

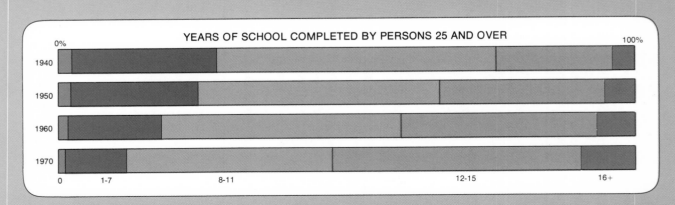

YEARS OF SCHOOL COMPLETED BY PERSONS 25 AND OVER

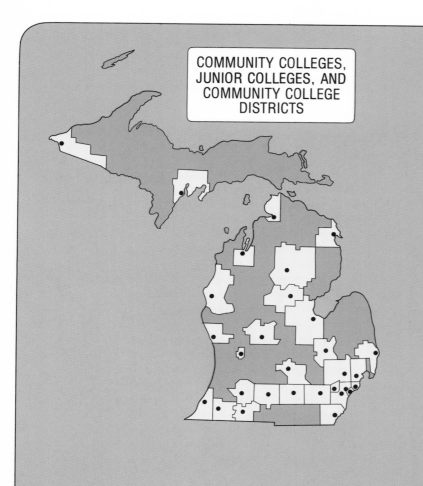

COMMUNITY COLLEGES, JUNIOR COLLEGES, AND COMMUNITY COLLEGE DISTRICTS

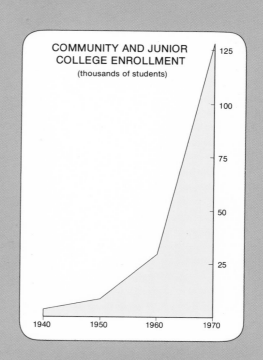

COMMUNITY AND JUNIOR COLLEGE ENROLLMENT

(thousands of students)

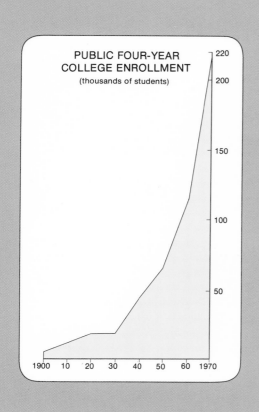

PUBLIC FOUR-YEAR COLLEGE ENROLLMENT

(thousands of students)

PUBLIC FOUR-YEAR COLLEGES AND UNIVERSITIES

1. Central Michigan U., Mt. Pleasant
2. Eastern Michigan U., Ypsilanti
3. Ferris State College, Big Rapids
4. Grand Valley State College, Allendale
5. Lake Superior State College, Sault Ste. Marie
6. Michigan State U., E. Lansing
7. Michigan Tech U., Houghton
8. Northern Michigan U., Marquette
9. Oakland U., Rochester
10. Saginaw Valley College, University Center
11. U. of Michigan, Ann Arbor
12. U. of Michigan, Dearborn
13. U. of Michigan, Flint
14. Wayne State U., Detroit
15. Western Michigan U., Kalamazoo

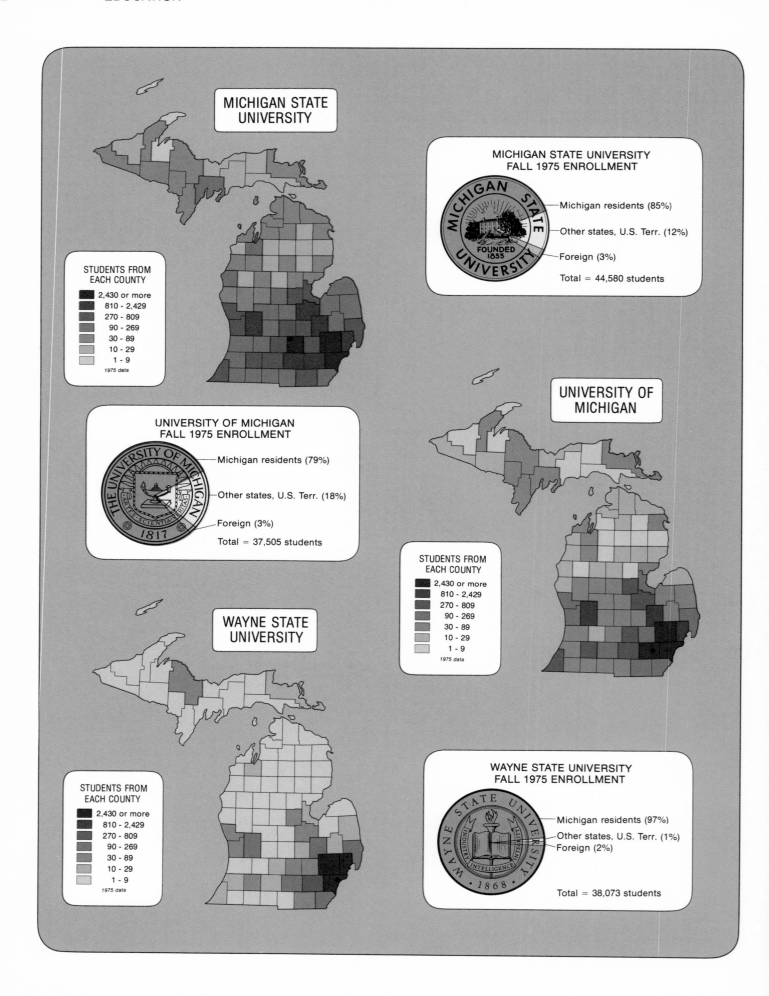

MICHIGAN STATE
UNIVERSITY

MICHIGAN STATE UNIVERSITY
FALL 1975 ENROLLMENT

—Michigan residents (85%)

—Other states, U.S. Terr. (12%)

—Foreign (3%)

Total = 44,580 students

STUDENTS FROM
EACH COUNTY

2,430 or more
810 - 2,429
270 - 809
90 - 269
30 - 89
10 - 29
1 - 9
1975 data

UNIVERSITY OF MICHIGAN
FALL 1975 ENROLLMENT

—Michigan residents (79%)

—Other states, U.S. Terr. (18%)

—Foreign (3%)

Total = 37,505 students

UNIVERSITY OF
MICHIGAN

STUDENTS FROM
EACH COUNTY

2,430 or more
810 - 2,429
270 - 809
90 - 269
30 - 89
10 - 29
1 - 9
1975 data

WAYNE STATE
UNIVERSITY

STUDENTS FROM
EACH COUNTY

2,430 or more
810 - 2,429
270 - 809
90 - 269
30 - 89
10 - 29
1 - 9
1975 data

WAYNE STATE UNIVERSITY
FALL 1975 ENROLLMENT

—Michigan residents (97%)

—Other states, U.S. Terr. (1%)
—Foreign (2%)

Total = 38,073 students

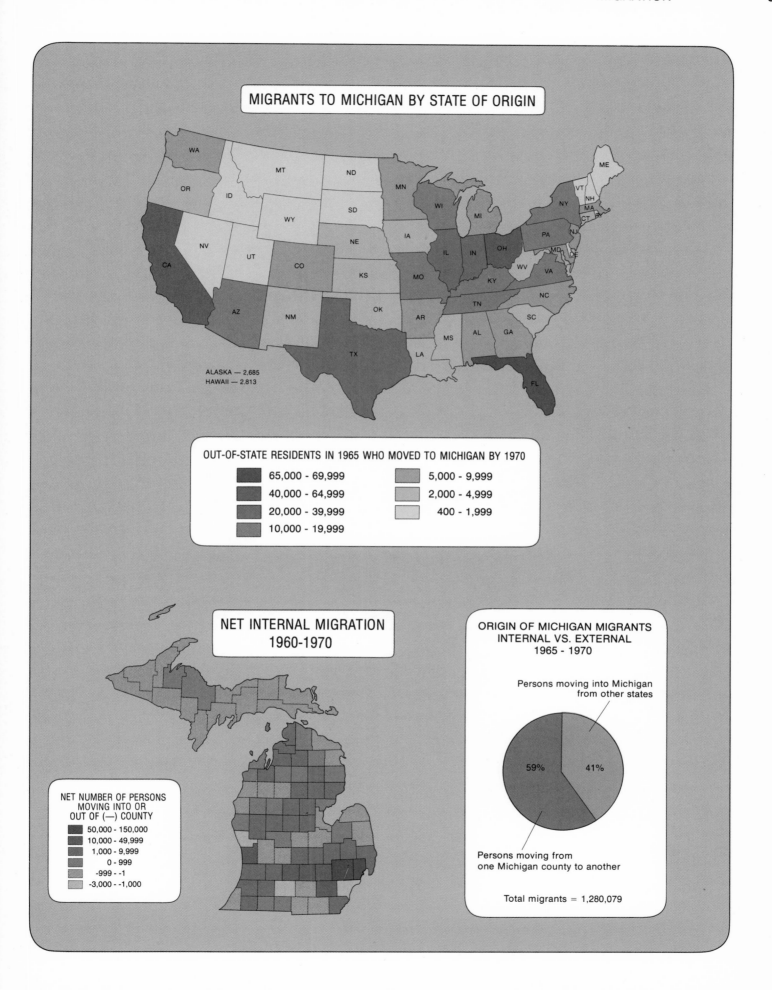

MIGRANTS TO MICHIGAN BY STATE OF ORIGIN

ALASKA — 2,685
HAWAII — 2,813

OUT-OF-STATE RESIDENTS IN 1965 WHO MOVED TO MICHIGAN BY 1970

- 65,000 - 69,999
- 40,000 - 64,999
- 20,000 - 39,999
- 10,000 - 19,999
- 5,000 - 9,999
- 2,000 - 4,999
- 400 - 1,999

NET INTERNAL MIGRATION
1960-1970

NET NUMBER OF PERSONS MOVING INTO OR OUT OF (—) COUNTY

- 50,000 - 150,000
- 10,000 - 49,999
- 1,000 - 9,999
- 0 - 999
- -999 - -1
- -3,000 - -1,000

ORIGIN OF MICHIGAN MIGRANTS INTERNAL VS. EXTERNAL
1965 - 1970

Persons moving into Michigan from other states

59%   41%

Persons moving from one Michigan county to another

Total migrants = 1,280,079

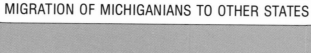

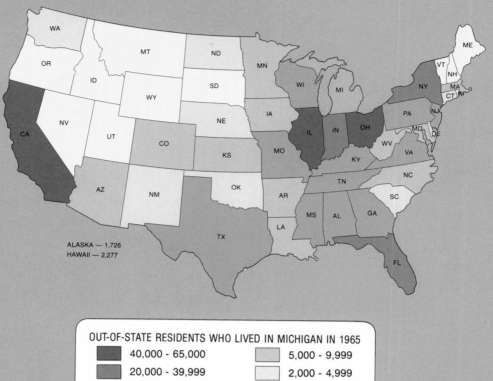

MIGRATION OF MICHIGANIANS TO OTHER STATES

OUT-OF-STATE RESIDENTS WHO LIVED IN MICHIGAN IN 1965

- 40,000 - 65,000
- 20,000 - 39,999
- 10,000 - 19,999
- 5,000 - 9,999
- 2,000 - 4,999
- 400 - 1,999

ALASKA — 1,726
HAWAII — 2,277

From 1965 to 1970 more than 490,000 Michiganians left the state for residence in a different state. The destinations for these young, middle-aged, and retired residents of Michigan had two distinct patterns: first to surrounding states in the Northeast and Middle West, and second to selected sun-belt states in the South and Southwest. Overall, the largest number moved to two states, Florida and California. The nearby states of Ohio, Illinois, and Indiana attracted the next largest numbers. Texas and Arizona attracted sizable numbers. Only a small number of people moved to the New England, South Atlantic, Great Plains, and Rocky Mountain states.

The statistics below indicate the leading states to which Michigan residents migrated and the leading states from which people moved to Michigan in the 1965–70 period. Inmigrants to Michigan exceeded outmigrants in the nearby states of Ohio, Illinois, and Indiana; the eastern states of New York, Pennsylvania, and New Jersey; and the southern states of Alabama, Mississippi, and Arkansas.

Destinations of Outmigrating Michigan Residents, 1965-70

Florida	65,642	Virginia	11,585
California	60,484	Missouri	10,246
Ohio	43,743	Georgia	9,417
Illinois	37,330	Colorado	9,131
Indiana	26,215	North Carolina	8,568
Texas	20,173	Minnesota	8,562
Wisconsin	18,066	New Jersey	8,290
New York	16,165	Washington	7,611
Arizona	14,353	Alabama	6,281
Kentucky	14,346	Arkansas	4,782
Pennsylvania	13,182	Mississippi	2,723
Tennessee	12,711		

Leading Sources of Inmigrants to Michigan, 1965-70

Ohio	58,350	Missouri	11,510
Illinois	50,381	Virginia	11,211
California	40,127	New Jersey	9,831
Indiana	36,433	Georgia	9,461
New York	23,761	Mississippi	9,157
Florida	18,880	Arkansas	8,070
Pennsylvania	18,036	Minnesota	7,922
Wisconsin	17,801	North Carolina	7,189
Texas	17,486	Colorado	5,713
Kentucky	16,004	Arizona	5,109
Tennessee	15,466	Washington	4,148
Alabama	15,439		

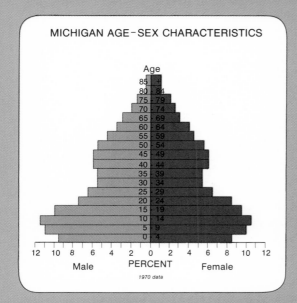

MICHIGAN AGE-SEX CHARACTERISTICS

Age

85 +
80 - 84
75 - 79
70 - 74
65 - 69
60 - 64
55 - 59
50 - 54
45 - 49
40 - 44
35 - 39
30 - 34
25 - 29
20 - 24
15 - 19
10 - 14
5 - 9
0 - 4

12 10 8 6 4 2 0 2 4 6 8 10 12

Male   PERCENT   Female

1970 data

The age and sex cohorts constituting a population can be graphically illustrated by what is referred to as a population pyramid. A true pyramid would have fewer individuals within each successive five-year age category. A population pyramid is also usually characterized by more males at the young ages and more females at the older ages. Michigan's population does not form a true pyramid, in part because of the recent decline in births that began in the 1960s.

In Michigan there are fewer children in the 0-to-4 and 5-to-9 cohorts than in the next older groups. A large proportion of the population, nearly 35 percent, is between 25 and 29 and 50 and 54, and there are slightly more females than males. Especially small are the 30-to-34 and 35-to-39 age groups. These people were born in the 1930s, when birthrates were low.

The median age for the state in 1970 was 26.3 years, which means that half of the residents were younger and half older than that age. An aging population is evident near the top of Michigan's pyramid. Almost 490,000 (5 percent) of the state's 8.8 million residents in 1970 were 70 years old and older. At this age, there is a much larger number of females than males.

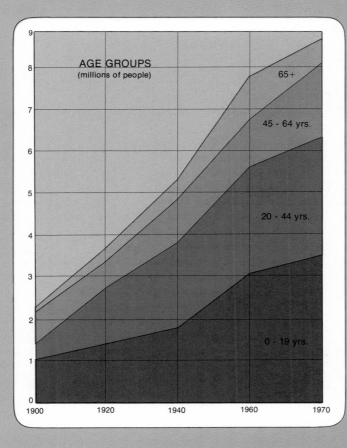

AGE GROUPS
(millions of people)

65+

45 - 64 yrs.

20 - 44 yrs.

0 - 19 yrs.

1900   1920   1940   1960   1970

Since 1900 some major changes in the numbers of Michiganians in specific age groups have occurred. At the turn of the century, the largest age cohort was comprised of those 19 years old and younger. Similarly, in 1970, almost 40 percent (3.5 million) of Michigan's population was under 21 years old, whereas 20-to-44-year-old people made up a much larger percentage of the population than they did in 1900—23 percent. Within recent years, the sharpest growth has been in the 40-to-64-year-old age group (26 percent) and in the group of those 65 years old and older (almost 9 percent).

In general, Michigan's population is characterized by more adults, both middle-aged and older, than children. These changes are accounted for by a declining birthrate and a longer life span for both males and females.

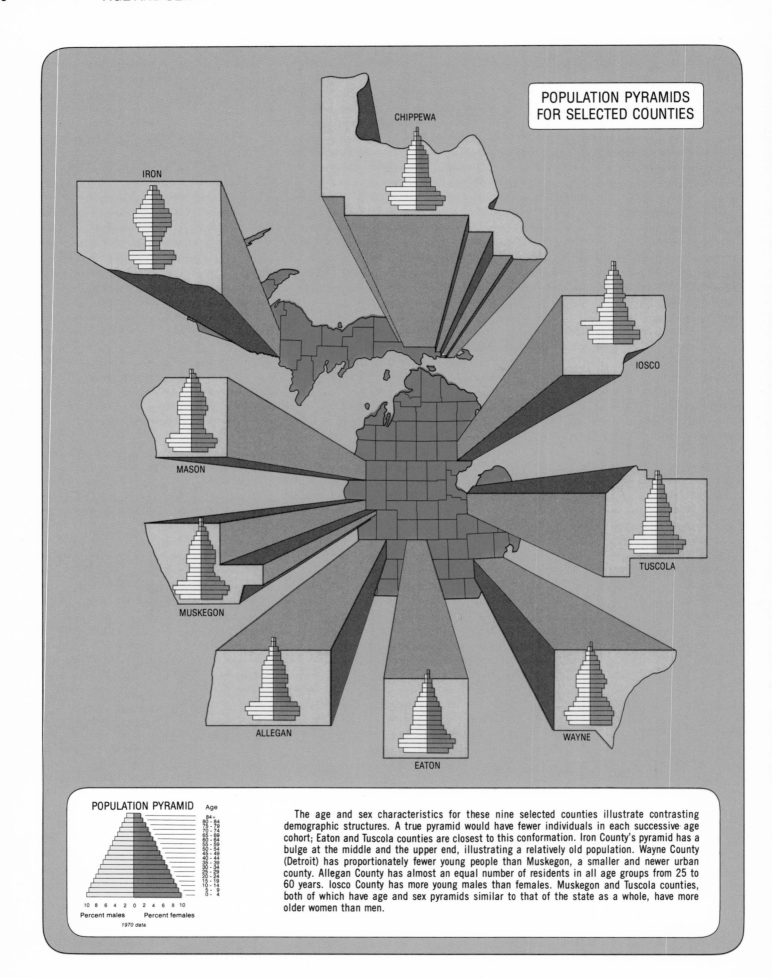

POPULATION PYRAMIDS
FOR SELECTED COUNTIES

CHIPPEWA

IRON

IOSCO

MASON

TUSCOLA

MUSKEGON

ALLEGAN

WAYNE

EATON

POPULATION PYRAMID

Age

84+
80 - 84
75 - 79
70 - 74
65 - 69
60 - 64
55 - 59
50 - 54
45 - 49
40 - 44
35 - 39
30 - 34
25 - 29
20 - 24
15 - 19
10 - 14
5 - 9
0 - 4

10 8 6 4 2 0 2 4 6 8 10

Percent males   Percent females

1970 data

The age and sex characteristics for these nine selected counties illustrate contrasting demographic structures. A true pyramid would have fewer individuals in each successive age cohort; Eaton and Tuscola counties are closest to this conformation. Iron County's pyramid has a bulge at the middle and the upper end, illustrating a relatively old population. Wayne County (Detroit) has proportionately fewer young people than Muskegon, a smaller and newer urban county. Allegan County has almost an equal number of residents in all age groups from 25 to 60 years. Iosco County has more young males than females. Muskegon and Tuscola counties, both of which have age and sex pyramids similar to that of the state as a whole, have more older women than men.

Median age is that value that divides the population in half, one half being younger and the remainder older than the median value. In 1970 the median age for the state was 26.3 years, which was slightly lower than that for the nation, 28.3 years. The median age for the state's urban areas, 26.4, was lower than that for the rural areas, 29.6.

Counties display marked differences in median age. The youngest or lowest median ages were in counties with colleges and universities — Isabella, 21.2 (Central Michigan University); Washtenaw, 23.5 (University of Michigan); Ingham, 24.1 (Michigan State University) — and in counties with rapidly growing suburbs — Mecosta (22.1), Ottawa (24.1), and Genesee (24.5). On the other hand, the highest median ages were found in rural counties and those losing population, especially in the northern Lower Peninsula. The median age values are more than 40 years in Iron and Roscommon counties, and more than 35 in seven others. A population of older and retired residents coupled with the outmigration of young people for several decades contributes to such high median ages.

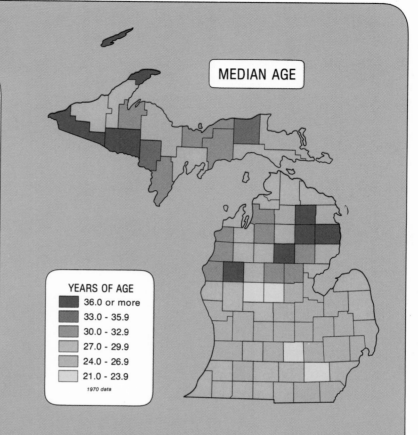

MEDIAN AGE

YEARS OF AGE

36.0 or more
33.0 - 35.9
30.0 - 32.9
27.0 - 29.9
24.0 - 26.9
21.0 - 23.9

1970 data

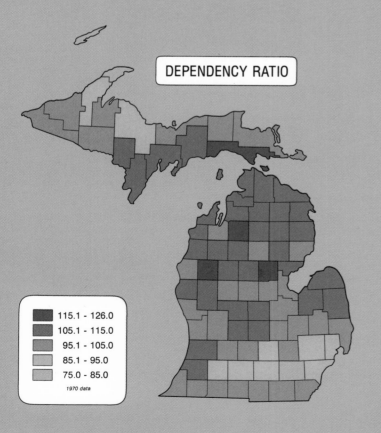

DEPENDENCY RATIO

115.1 - 126.0
105.1 - 115.0
95.1 - 105.0
85.1 - 95.0
75.0 - 85.0

1970 data

The dependency ratio is a rough measure of economic dependency in a total population. The ratio is based on the population under 20 years of age plus those 65 years and older (the dependents) divided by the population between 20 and 64 (the work force). The resulting value is multiplied by 100 to yield the dependency ratio. A ratio of more than 100 indicates that there are more dependent people (very young and very old) than those in the working ages (20 to 64). A ratio of less than 100 means that there are more people in the working ages than in the young and over-65 groups.

Of the 8.8 million people in the state in 1970, roughly 3.6 million were less than 20 years of age and 750,000 were 65 and over. The dependency ratio for the state was 95.4. Some metropolitan areas like Detroit and Lansing had ratios below the state average. Washtenaw County's ratio was the lowest at 78, followed by Ingham's 87 and Wayne's 90. However, not all large urban counties had low ratios. Upper Peninsula counties and those in the northern part of the Lower Peninsula had the highest ratios: Lake County's 125 was followed by Kalkaska's 116, Mackinac's 115, and Missaukee's 114. Interspersed with the counties that had high ratios were some with low values. Counties with a large percentage of people in the labor force and in the middle-age brackets tended to have the lowest dependency ratios. Those counties with large numbers of retired people had high ratios. Many of these same counties, being rural in character, have suffered population declines for several decades.

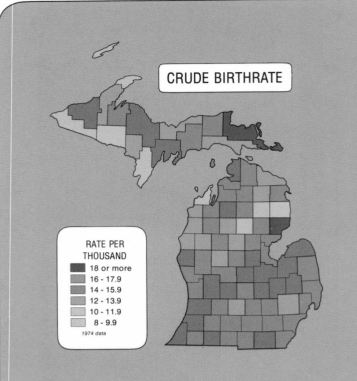

CRUDE BIRTHRATE

RATE PER THOUSAND

- 18 or more
- 16 - 17.9
- 14 - 15.9
- 12 - 13.9
- 10 - 11.9
- 8 - 9.9

1974 data

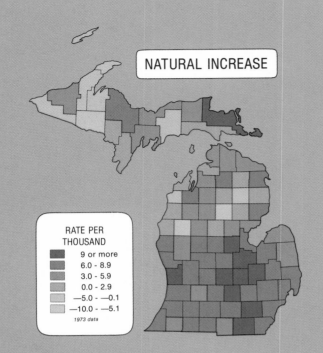

NATURAL INCREASE

RATE PER THOUSAND

- 9 or more
- 6.0 - 8.9
- 3.0 - 5.9
- 0.0 - 2.9
- −5.0 - −0.1
- −10.0 - −5.1

1973 data

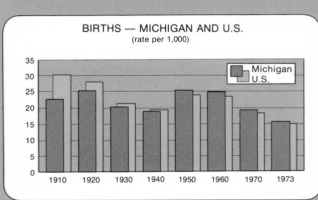

BIRTHS — MICHIGAN AND U.S.
(rate per 1,000)

Michigan / U.S.

1910 · 1920 · 1930 · 1940 · 1950 · 1960 · 1970 · 1973

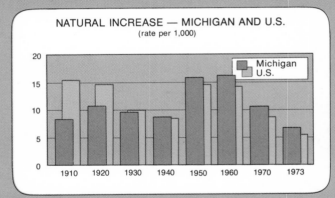

NATURAL INCREASE — MICHIGAN AND U.S.
(rate per 1,000)

Michigan / U.S.

1910 · 1920 · 1930 · 1940 · 1950 · 1960 · 1970 · 1973

The crude birthrate is defined as the number of births per 1,000 people by county of residence. The base population for this rate includes males and females as well as children and old people. The state average in 1974 was 15.1.

There was a marked variation in the birthrate within the state, ranging from a low of 8.9 in Iron County to a high of 19.7 in Chippewa County, both in the Upper Peninsula. It is difficult to provide regional interpretation of the county birthrates since high and low rates frequently do not show consistent patterns. Some of the more rural, sparsely populated, and economically poor counties in the northern sections of the state had high birthrates, yet others with these same characteristics had low rates. The Upper Peninsula, for instance, has counties with the lowest and highest birthrates.

Counties with large urban populations have rates approximating the state average: Wayne County (Detroit) has 15.2, Genesee County (Flint) 16.2, and Kent County (Grand Rapids) 16.1. Washtenaw County's (Ann Arbor) rate is below the state average at 14.6, which is in part explained by the large student body at the University of Michigan.

The crude birthrate minus the crude death rate yields the rate of natural increase. Migration is not considered in measuring natural increase. On the basis of 1973 data, ten counties in Michigan lost population in that they had more deaths than births. Most of these counties were in the Upper Peninsula in the more rural, economically depressed areas. Iron County had a 9 percent decline and Lake County nearly 7 percent.

The highest rates of increase were in suburban counties around large cities and in some small cities, where more births than deaths are expected. Washtenaw County increased by 9.8 percent, Genesee County by 9.7 percent, and Clinton County by 9.6 percent. The highest rate was in Chippewa County — 11.3 percent. Natural increases in the southern half of the Lower Peninsula were generally above the state average of 6.9 percent. Wayne County's 6.0 was much lower than that of surrounding suburban counties.

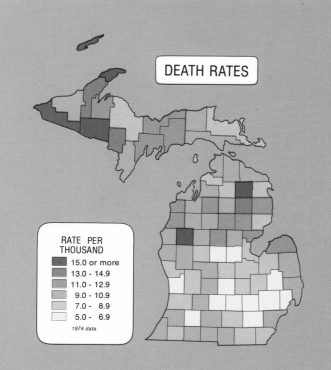

DEATH RATES

RATE PER
THOUSAND

■ 15.0 or more
■ 13.0 - 14.9
■ 11.0 - 12.9
■ 9.0 - 10.9
■ 7.0 - 8.9
□ 5.0 - 6.9

1974 data

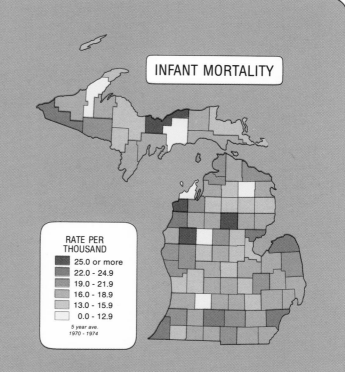

INFANT MORTALITY

RATE PER
THOUSAND

■ 25.0 or more
■ 22.0 - 24.9
■ 19.0 - 21.9
■ 16.0 - 18.9
■ 13.0 - 15.9
□ 0.0 - 12.9

5 year ave.
1970 - 1974

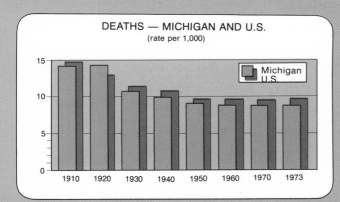

DEATHS — MICHIGAN AND U.S.
(rate per 1,000)

Michigan
U.S.

1910 1920 1930 1940 1950 1960 1970 1973

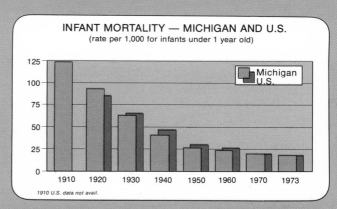

INFANT MORTALITY — MICHIGAN AND U.S.
(rate per 1,000 for infants under 1 year old)

Michigan
U.S.

1910 1920 1930 1940 1950 1960 1970 1973

1910 U.S. data not avail.

Death rate is defined as the number of deaths per 1,000 people. In 1974, 76,143 persons died in Michigan, an average death rate of 8.4. The rate varied from 5.5 in Washtenaw County to 15.9 in Keweenaw County. Overall the highest rates were in the rural, sparsely populated counties in the Upper Peninsula. Large numbers of elderly people have remained in these counties, while many younger and middle-age residents migrated to urban centers nearby. Very low and very high death rates are found side by side in the Upper Peninsula, illustrating the declining rural and growing urban populations. Iron, Gogebic, and Keweenaw counties had more than 15 deaths per 1,000 people compared to 8.1 per 1,000 in Marquette County.

The lowest death rates were in rapidly growing suburban counties in the Lower Peninsula. Suburban counties around Detroit and Grand Rapids as well as those containing Lansing and East Lansing, Kalamazoo, and Ann Arbor had large numbers of young families and students attending major universities. Both conditions lead to lower death rates. Washtenaw County's value was 5.5, Ingham's 6.0, Macomb's 6.1, and Oakland's 6.8. Wayne County had a rate of 9.8, slightly above the state average.

Because of improved health delivery systems and medical care, the death rate has generally declined since 1910. The state's average, which has been slightly below the national average for the past 50 years, has remained relatively constant since 1950.

Infant deaths still occur in spite of improved medical practices, sanitation, and nutrition. The infant and neonatal deaths per 1,000 live births for the state from 1970 to 1974 averaged 17.6. The highest rates were in Lake (35.8), Benzie (26.2), Roscommon (25.8), and Alger (25.4) counties. The lowest rates were in Osceola (11.3), Montmorency (11.7), Barry (12.0), and Houghton (12.0) counties.

The geographical pattern of infant deaths is complex and difficult to interpret. Counties without hospitals, such as Lake and Roscommon, and those where residents have lower income levels and must travel long distances to hospitals have some of the highest rates. Counties with high and low values exist side by side. The number of infant deaths dropped sharply from 1910 to 1940. Since 1950 there has been little change in the state figures, which approximate the national average.

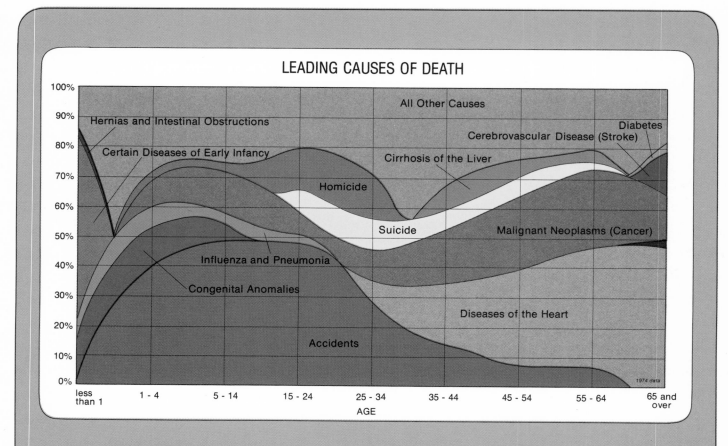

LEADING CAUSES OF DEATH

All Other Causes

Hernias and Intestinal Obstructions

Diabetes

Cerebrovascular Disease (Stroke)

Certain Diseases of Early Infancy

Cirrhosis of the Liver

Homicide

Suicide

Malignant Neoplasms (Cancer)

Influenza and Pneumonia

Congenital Anomalies

Diseases of the Heart

Accidents

1974 data

AGE: less than 1 · 1 - 4 · 5 - 14 · 15 - 24 · 25 - 34 · 35 - 44 · 45 - 54 · 55 - 64 · 65 and over

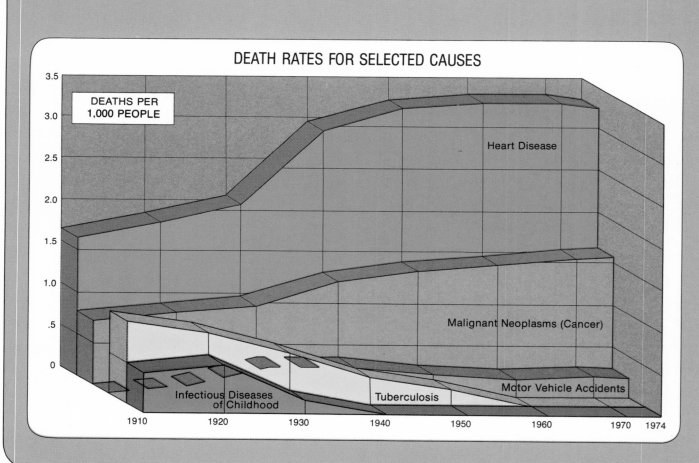

DEATH RATES FOR SELECTED CAUSES

DEATHS PER 1,000 PEOPLE

Heart Disease

Malignant Neoplasms (Cancer)

Infectious Diseases of Childhood

Tuberculosis

Motor Vehicle Accidents

1910 · 1920 · 1930 · 1940 · 1950 · 1960 · 1970 · 1974

SUSPENDED PARTICLES IN THE AIR

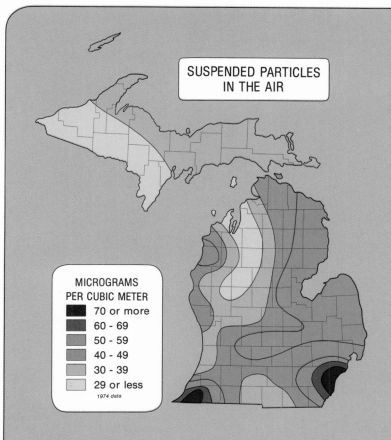

MICROGRAMS PER CUBIC METER

- 70 or more
- 60 - 69
- 50 - 59
- 40 - 49
- 30 - 39
- 29 or less

1974 data

The quality of the air can be measured by determining the amount of pollutants and suspended particulate matter per given volume of air. The degree of air contamination usually is related to the type and amount of industry, the population density, and the strength and shift in direction of prevailing winds.

There is considerable variation in the quality of air Michiganians breathe. The highest amounts of particulate matter and pollutants are in central Detroit and around Benton Harbor in southwest Michigan. Other industrial centers such as Lansing, Flint, and Saginaw have high levels of pollution. The cleanest air is found in the rural areas in the western half of the Upper Peninsula and in the west central Lower Peninsula. Except for those living in the southwest corner of the state, the population along Lake Michigan's shoreline breathes relatively clean air.

The air quality for the Detroit metropolitan area has sharply contrasting patterns. When using micrograms of suspended particulates per cubic meter, a measuring index developed by federal agencies to measure air pollution, the highest levels in 1974 were recorded in the industrial regions of southeast Michigan and in Detroit's inner city. The rest of Detroit had lower values or slightly cleaner air. Medium values included much of south central Wayne County and adjacent Macomb County. High-income areas of Oakland County had the cleanest air in the metropolitan region. The quality of air for these three counties is inversely related to the medium income levels and the value of owner-occupied homes. High concentrations of particulate matter occur in areas where the poor reside.

24-HOUR CONCENTRATIONS OF SUSPENDED PARTICULATES IN EXCESS OF FEDERAL STANDARDS — DETROIT AREA

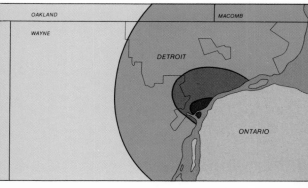

FEDERAL STANDARDS*

- Primary standard exceeded 5 times
- Primary standard exceeded 2 times
- Secondary standard exceeded 2 times

*(Not to be exceeded more than once per year)

Primary = 260 micrograms per cubic meter
Secondary = 150 micrograms per cubic meter

1974 data

AVERAGE OF SUSPENDED PARTICULATES IN THE AIR — DETROIT AREA

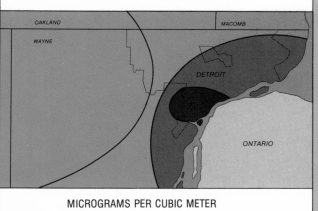

MICROGRAMS PER CUBIC METER

- 125 or more
- 75 - 124
- 60 - 74
- less than 60

Federal Standard: not more than 75 micrograms per cubic meter

1974 data

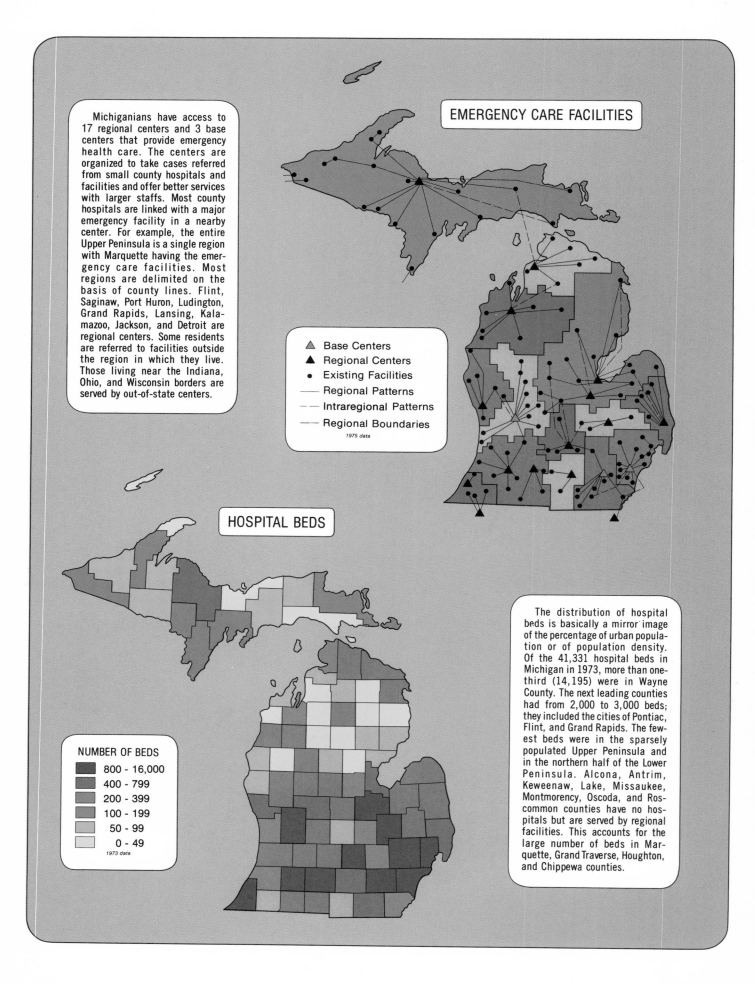

EMERGENCY CARE FACILITIES

Michiganians have access to 17 regional centers and 3 base centers that provide emergency health care. The centers are organized to take cases referred from small county hospitals and facilities and offer better services with larger staffs. Most county hospitals are linked with a major emergency facility in a nearby center. For example, the entire Upper Peninsula is a single region with Marquette having the emergency care facilities. Most regions are delimited on the basis of county lines. Flint, Saginaw, Port Huron, Ludington, Grand Rapids, Lansing, Kalamazoo, Jackson, and Detroit are regional centers. Some residents are referred to facilities outside the region in which they live. Those living near the Indiana, Ohio, and Wisconsin borders are served by out-of-state centers.

△ Base Centers
▲ Regional Centers
● Existing Facilities
— Regional Patterns
-- Intraregional Patterns
— Regional Boundaries
1975 data

HOSPITAL BEDS

NUMBER OF BEDS
800 - 16,000
400 - 799
200 - 399
100 - 199
50 - 99
0 - 49
1973 data

The distribution of hospital beds is basically a mirror image of the percentage of urban population or of population density. Of the 41,331 hospital beds in Michigan in 1973, more than one-third (14,195) were in Wayne County. The next leading counties had from 2,000 to 3,000 beds; they included the cities of Pontiac, Flint, and Grand Rapids. The fewest beds were in the sparsely populated Upper Peninsula and in the northern half of the Lower Peninsula. Alcona, Antrim, Keweenaw, Lake, Missaukee, Montmorency, Oscoda, and Roscommon counties have no hospitals but are served by regional facilities. This accounts for the large number of beds in Marquette, Grand Traverse, Houghton, and Chippewa counties.

In 1976 there were 11,649 doctors of medicine (M.D.s), 2,267 doctors of osteopathy (D.O.s), 4,851 dentists (D.D.S.s), 1,136 veterinarians (D.V.M.s), and 80,895 nurses (registered—R.N.s—and licensed practical—L.P.N.s) in Michigan. The actual number of health care specialists in the most populous counties of Michigan is shown in the table below.

Medical professionals are clustered mainly in urban areas; their numbers are roughly in proportion to population density. The largest numbers live in Wayne, Oakland, and Macomb counties (the Detroit metropolitan area). Within these three counties are roughly half of all the state's medical doctors and dentists, 60 percent of its osteopathic physicians, and 40 percent of its nurses. Fewer health providers are found in the Upper Peninsula: 250 medical doctors, 16 osteopathic physicians, 151 dentists, and 3,152 nurses.

The number of health care specialists in certain counties is also correlated with the location of long-established training schools. For example, Washtenaw County has a sizable number—1,216 medical doctors and 3,440 nurses—as a result of the medical schools and research facilities in the Ann Arbor area. Ingham County has a large number of veterinarians because of the College of Veterinary Medicine at Michigan State University.

Outside the Detroit area there are high ratios of medical personnel per 10,000 people in major urban counties such as Genesee (Flint), Kent (Grand Rapids), Kalamazoo (Kalamazoo), Ingham (Lansing and East Lansing), and Saginaw (Saginaw). The lowest ratios were found generally in counties with small and sparse populations and particularly those with large rural populations.

COUNTY	M.D.s	D.O.s	D.D.S.s	D.V.M.s	R.N.s & L.P.N.s
Genesee	456	155	188	47	4,487
Ingham	457	117	174	116	2,824
Jackson	133	21	69	19	1,289
Kalamazoo	377	13	128	44	2,379
Kent	640	93	274	46	4,773
Macomb	488	223	353	52	4,824
Muskegon	131	55	76	12	1,556
Oakland	2,110	506	784	159	8,921
Ottawa	102	14	70	18	1,678
Saginaw	252	57	110	29	2,103
Saint Clair	103	13	55	17	1,078
Washtenaw	1,216	21	308	40	3,440
Wayne	3,333	577	1,208	139	19,378
STATE TOTAL	11,649	2,267	4,851	1,136	80,895

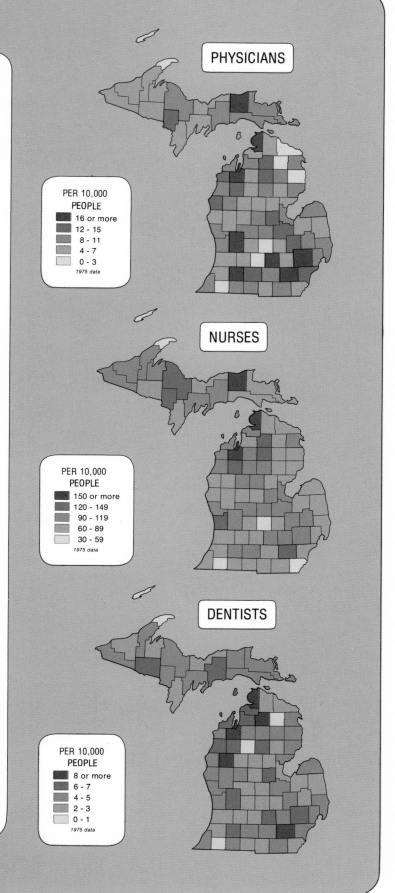

PHYSICIANS

PER 10,000 PEOPLE
16 or more
12 - 15
8 - 11
4 - 7
0 - 3
1975 data

NURSES

PER 10,000 PEOPLE
150 or more
120 - 149
90 - 119
60 - 89
30 - 59
1975 data

DENTISTS

PER 10,000 PEOPLE
8 or more
6 - 7
4 - 5
2 - 3
0 - 1
1975 data

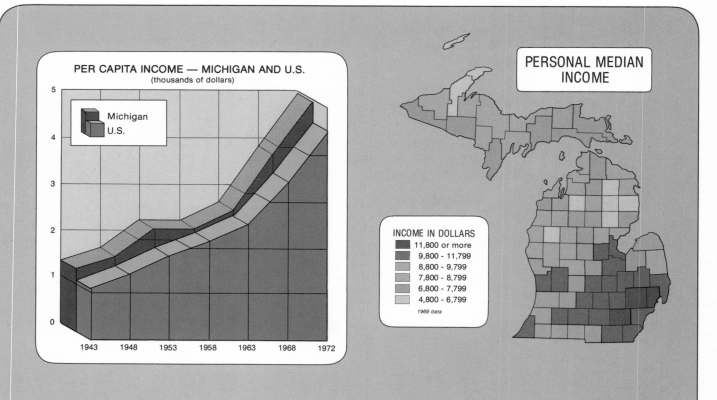

PER CAPITA INCOME — MICHIGAN AND U.S.
(thousands of dollars)

Michigan
U.S.

1943 1948 1953 1958 1963 1968 1972

PERSONAL MEDIAN INCOME

INCOME IN DOLLARS
- 11,800 or more
- 9,800 - 11,799
- 8,800 - 9,799
- 7,800 - 8,799
- 6,800 - 7,799
- 4,800 - 6,799

1969 data

The median family income for Michigan was $11,072 in 1969, $1,115 above the national average of $9,957. The highest incomes were in the suburban counties around Detroit—Oakland ($13,826), Macomb ($12,110), and Washtenaw ($12,294)—rather than in Wayne County ($11,351). A broad region of urban and suburban counties in the Lower Peninsula report the highest values.

The Upper Peninsula and northern half of the Lower Peninsula had family incomes below the state's median. Fifteen counties had medians below $7,500. Keweenaw ($4,809), Alcona ($5,842), and Montmorency ($5,851) counties report the lowest medians. The exodus from rural areas in these counties has left many retired people who depend on fixed social security incomes.

Among families that earn $15,000 or more there is a similar pattern. Suburban counties around Detroit are the wealthiest. Of families in Oakland County, 43 percent earned more than $15,000 in 1969. For Macomb and Washtenaw counties the percentages are 36 and 35, respectively. Relatively few families with such high income are located in the Upper Peninsula. According to the 1969 census, only 3 percent of the families in Keweenaw County earned $15,000 or more; in Gogebic and Iron counties, 5 and 6 percent. The state's per capita income over time has been slightly above the national average, a pattern not unexpected considering the state's wealth.

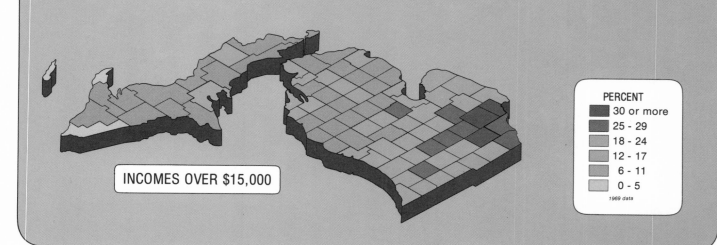

INCOMES OVER $15,000

PERCENT
- 30 or more
- 25 - 29
- 18 - 24
- 12 - 17
- 6 - 11
- 0 - 5

1969 data

According to the 1970 census, 7.3 percent of all families in the state had incomes below the poverty level. The incomes are calculated by weighing such factors as family size, sex of the family head, number of children under 18 years old, and whether the residence is farm or nonfarm. The percentage of families with poverty incomes ranged from lows of 3.6 and 3.8 in Macomb and Oakland counties, to 21.8 and 22.9 in Keweenaw and Lake counties. In most of the southern half of the Lower Peninsula less than 10 percent of all families live in poverty. On the other hand, more than 15 or 20 percent of the families in the rural and economically depressed counties of the Upper Peninsula and northern Lower Peninsula had poverty-level incomes. In a number of cases, counties with medium-size cities or larger suburban populations had fewer poverty families than the most populous counties. Wayne County's 8.1 percent was higher than its suburban counties. Lansing and East Lansing, Kalamazoo, Grand Rapids, and Bay City had lower values than surrounding counties with rural and small-town populations.

Social service payments include the absolute dollar amount each county was allocated during 1974 for a variety of programs: Old Age Assistance, Aid to the Blind, Aid to Disabled, and Aid to Dependent Children. The amount each county spent was directly proportional to its total population. Wayne County spent $279 million, nearly nine times more than Genesee County (Flint), which spent $33 million. Oakland, Kent, Saginaw, Ingham, and Macomb counties spent more than $15 million each. Fewer dollars were used by the smaller and poorer counties. In the Upper Peninsula, in particular, the dollar amounts were less than $500,000. Keweenaw County spent $95,000 for these social programs. The range for 13 other counties was from $100,000 to $500,000.

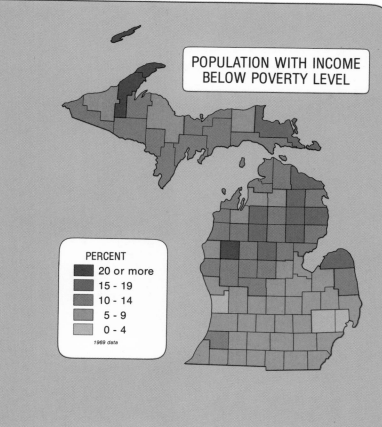

POPULATION WITH INCOME BELOW POVERTY LEVEL

PERCENT
20 or more
15 - 19
10 - 14
5 - 9
0 - 4

1969 data

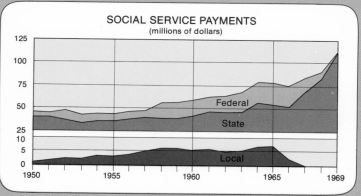

SOCIAL SERVICE PAYMENTS
(millions of dollars)

Federal

State

Local

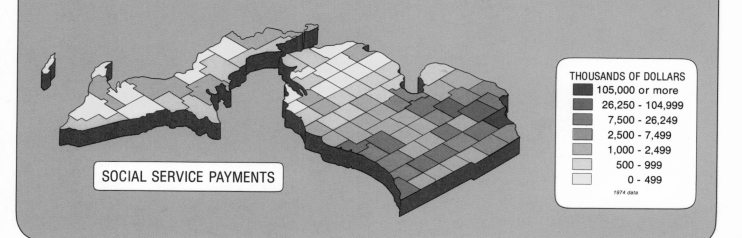

SOCIAL SERVICE PAYMENTS

THOUSANDS OF DOLLARS
105,000 or more
26,250 - 104,999
7,500 - 26,249
2,500 - 7,499
1,000 - 2,499
500 - 999
0 - 499

1974 data

OWNER-OCCUPIED HOUSING

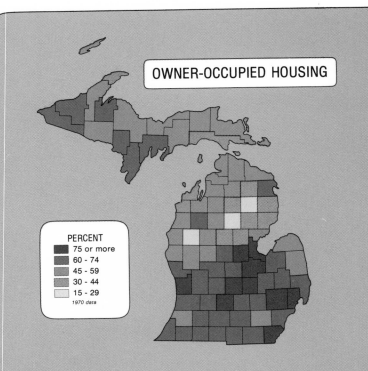

PERCENT
75 or more
60 - 74
45 - 59
30 - 44
15 - 29
1970 data

SINGLE-FAMILY UNITS — MICH. AND U.S.
(as a percentage of all housing)

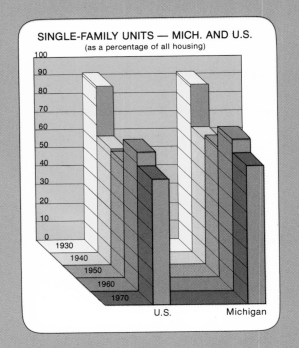

1930 1940 1950 1960 1970

U.S.   Michigan

A good indicator of housing quality is the median value of owner-occupied housing for a single family. According to the 1970 census the median value for Michigan was $17,590. The values vary from a low of $4,720 in Keweenaw County to $23,321 in Washtenaw County. Population growth and urbanity are related directly to the median housing values. In general, the highest values are in the suburban Detroit counties and those counties in which Lansing, Midland, Flint, Saginaw, and Grand Rapids are located. In addition to Washtenaw County, Oakland and Macomb counties had median values in excess of $22,000. Wayne County's value was $18,098, slightly above the state median. Counties in poor or marginal agricultural, forested, or mineral lands had values far below the state median.

Of nine counties with values less than $9,000, seven are in the Upper Peninsula.

Housing density measures the number of persons per housing unit, whether apartments, mobile homes, or single-family dwellings. In 1970 the state average was 3.3 persons per unit. The highest densities were in the suburban counties and the broad belt of urban counties in southern lower Michigan. Macomb County had the highest density, 3.6 persons per unit. Keweenaw and Roscommon counties had the fewest persons per unit, 2.7. Wayne County's value of 3.2 was slightly less than that of the surrounding suburban counties.

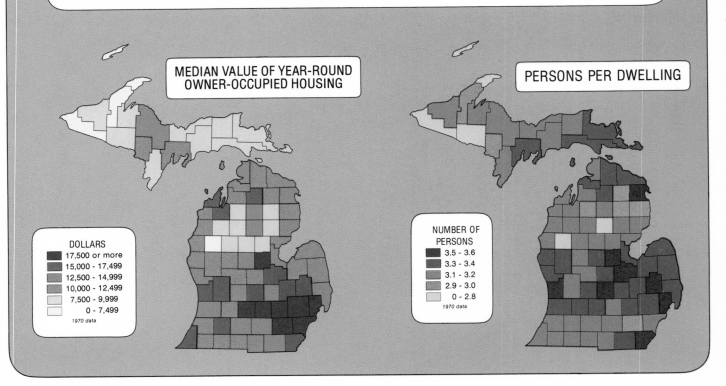

MEDIAN VALUE OF YEAR-ROUND OWNER-OCCUPIED HOUSING

DOLLARS
17,500 or more
15,000 - 17,499
12,500 - 14,999
10,000 - 12,499
7,500 - 9,999
0 - 7,499
1970 data

PERSONS PER DWELLING

NUMBER OF PERSONS
3.5 - 3.6
3.3 - 3.4
3.1 - 3.2
2.9 - 3.0
0 - 2.8
1970 data

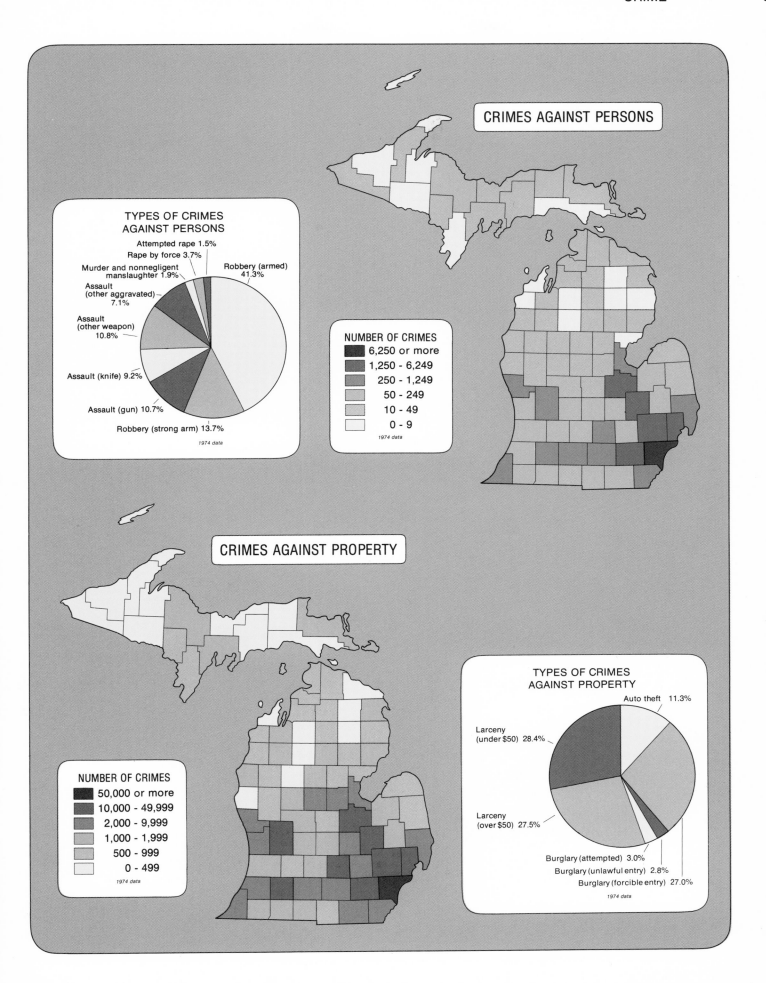

CRIMES AGAINST PERSONS

TYPES OF CRIMES
AGAINST PERSONS

Attempted rape 1.5%
Rape by force 3.7%
Murder and nonnegligent
manslaughter 1.9%
Assault
(other aggravated)
7.1%
Assault
(other weapon)
10.8%
Assault (knife) 9.2%
Assault (gun) 10.7%
Robbery (strong arm) 13.7%
Robbery (armed)
41.3%

1974 data

NUMBER OF CRIMES
6,250 or more
1,250 - 6,249
250 - 1,249
50 - 249
10 - 49
0 - 9

1974 data

CRIMES AGAINST PROPERTY

NUMBER OF CRIMES
50,000 or more
10,000 - 49,999
2,000 - 9,999
1,000 - 1,999
500 - 999
0 - 499

1974 data

TYPES OF CRIMES
AGAINST PROPERTY

Auto theft 11.3%
Larceny
(under $50) 28.4%
Larceny
(over $50) 27.5%
Burglary (attempted) 3.0%
Burglary (unlawful entry) 2.8%
Burglary (forcible entry) 27.0%

1974 data

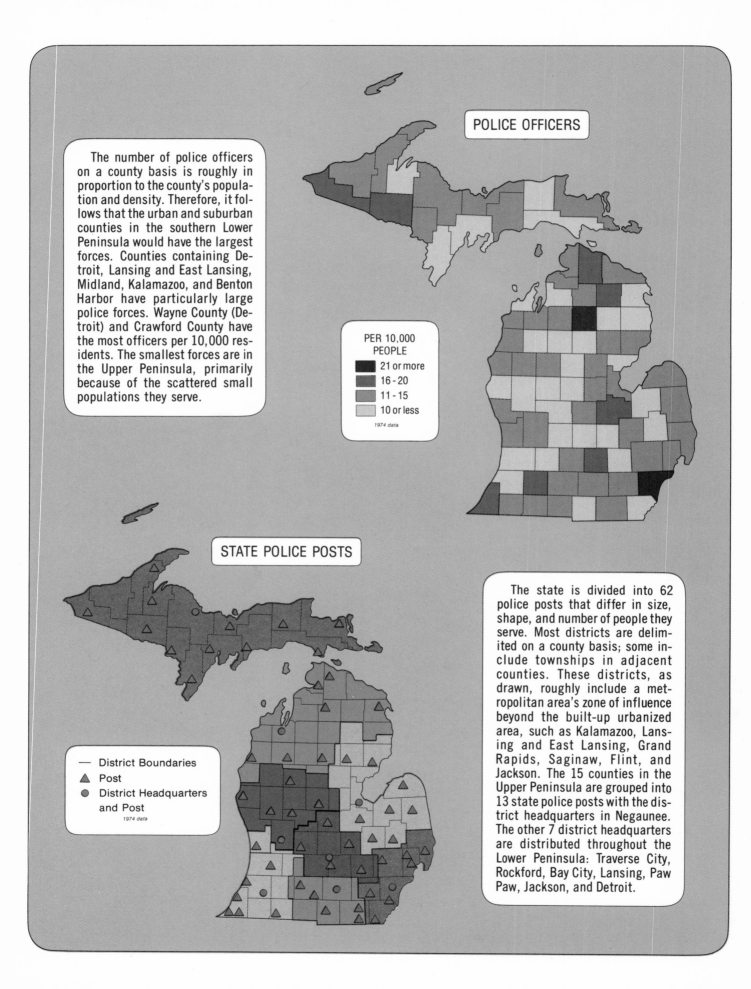

POLICE OFFICERS

The number of police officers on a county basis is roughly in proportion to the county's population and density. Therefore, it follows that the urban and suburban counties in the southern Lower Peninsula would have the largest forces. Counties containing Detroit, Lansing and East Lansing, Midland, Kalamazoo, and Benton Harbor have particularly large police forces. Wayne County (Detroit) and Crawford County have the most officers per 10,000 residents. The smallest forces are in the Upper Peninsula, primarily because of the scattered small populations they serve.

PER 10,000
PEOPLE
■ 21 or more
■ 16 - 20
■ 11 - 15
□ 10 or less

1974 data

STATE POLICE POSTS

— District Boundaries
▲ Post
● District Headquarters
   and Post

1974 data

The state is divided into 62 police posts that differ in size, shape, and number of people they serve. Most districts are delimited on a county basis; some include townships in adjacent counties. These districts, as drawn, roughly include a metropolitan area's zone of influence beyond the built-up urbanized area, such as Kalamazoo, Lansing and East Lansing, Grand Rapids, Saginaw, Flint, and Jackson. The 15 counties in the Upper Peninsula are grouped into 13 state police posts with the district headquarters in Negaunee. The other 7 district headquarters are distributed throughout the Lower Peninsula: Traverse City, Rockford, Bay City, Lansing, Paw Paw, Jackson, and Detroit.

HISTORY AND CULTURE

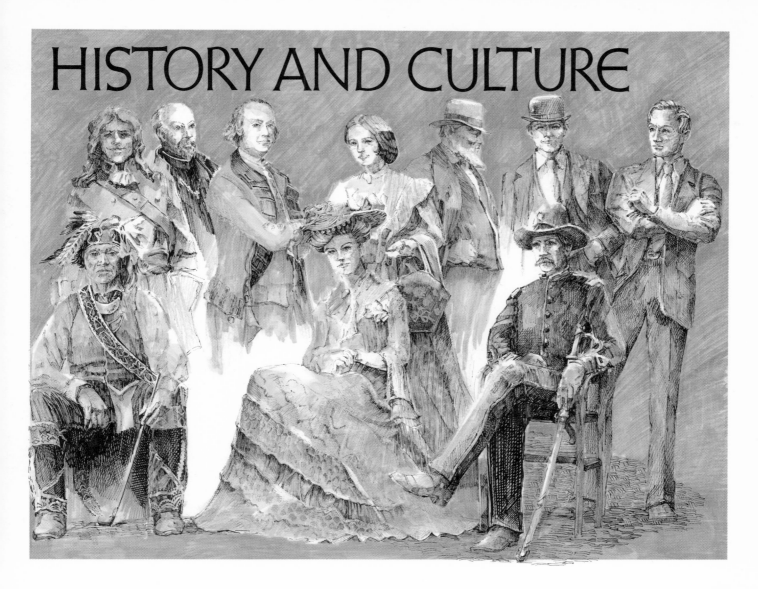

Although this section of the atlas is devoted to Michigan's history, the maps in the other sections are also indispensable to an understanding of the state's development. For example, some show the warmer climate and more fertile soil south of the present Muskegon–Bay City line, which held four-fifths of Michigan's sixteenth-century Indians; some show the ponds and swamps that were the home of the beaver, whose pelts lured French, English, and Americans to trade in Michigan; some show the election results or religious clusters that may have roots in an early settlement of immigrants; and some show Michigan's historic sites, where the tourist becomes the historian, even as one who studies this atlas must do.

Michigan shared parts of its history with other states, just as it shared resources, but it had many qualities that were rare or unequaled among its neighbors. It shared beaver with other Great Lakes states, but its Mackinac became the fur-trading center for the entire region. It borrowed a style of lumbering from Maine, but added the Shay engine before passing the process on to Oregon. Both Michigan and Wisconsin were settled by antislavery New Englanders who had paused first in New York State. Both vied for the honor of founding the Republican Party, but Michigan produced no politician of the La Follette tradition. It shared with others the midwestern hardwood, steel, and rubber industries, but no state matched Michigan's leadership in automobile production.

The Indians and the French

Michigan's many lakes, including the world's first, third, fourth, and tenth largest natural freshwater lakes, supplied the Indians with fish and animals for food and clothing and the means to travel easily by canoe, which they preferred to the arduous land travel through the forests. Of the estimated 15,000 Indians who were living in Michigan when the French came—mostly Chippewa, Ottawa, or Potawatomi—a vast majority lived in the openings and along the river valleys of southern Michigan. There they fished, killed deer and other game, captured beaver, boiled maple sap into sugar, gathered blueberries in the marshes, and set fires to burn off the brown grass in spring to lure game from the forest. Perhaps the Indian thus helped to create the "oak openings" and prairies that dotted southern Michigan. Some erected earthworks for religious worship; most of them built round-topped bark wigwams for their homes. The buffalo-skin tepee, the flowing feather headdress, the Spaniard's horse that made the Plains Indians so colorful were not for them.

When French missionaries, explorers, and traders entered what is now Michigan after 1615, they came as guests of the native people. Indians built and paddled the visitors' canoes, guided them through the maze of waterways, protected them against the environment, and foraged for game to feed them on sagamité soup. Indians also exchanged beaver and other pelts, which were abundant, for the guns, powder, knives, and blankets that lifted them out of the Stone Age into the dawn of the Industrial Revolution. They listened to a Recollet or Jesuit who offered salvation. Some accepted baptism into the Christian faith. They even acquiesced in the peace-keeping role of the king's garrisons at Michilimackinac, Saint Joseph, and Detroit. Explorers who sought a water route to the silks and teas of China never found the great rivers by which to reach the Pacific, but missionaries and traders were amply rewarded for their plunge into the wilderness.

Fur trading was so profitable for the few Frenchmen who engaged in it that British traders from Hudson's Bay and from Albany on the Hudson River were attracted to the Great Lakes area to secure a share. British penetration prompted French colonial governor Antoine de la Mothe Cadillac to found Detroit in 1701. Farmers accompanied Cadillac to Detroit, but their numbers remained small. A few could supply the entire needs of soldiers, priests, and traders for grain, vegetables, and meat. They could not profitably ship their surpluses down the Saint Lawrence to markets in France. Whereas the Atlantic seaboard prospered with the British colonists' search for religious diversity, self-government, and economic opportunity, Michigan languished for lack of these incentives. The French defense of its inland fur empire against those encroaching settlers provoked four costly wars with Britain. In losing the fourth, France surrendered its forts at Detroit, Saint Joseph, and Mackinac to the British (who chose to spell the latter as Mackinaw to approximate the "Mackinah" pronunciation of the Indians and the French).

After the British had garrisoned the western forts, but before the 1763 peace treaty was signed, Indian followers of Pontiac and others attacked in hopes of restoring their friends, the French, who had encouraged trade and had opposed the westward migration of American settlers who drove away game. Forts Saint Joseph and Michilimackinac fell to them; Detroit was besieged for a summer. With the close of the Seven Years War the Indians learned to accept the British, who soon learned to protect the Indians and their fur empire against encroaching settlers. They took the place of the French in the hearts of the Indians.

The Revolutionary War and After

In the Revolutionary War what is now Michigan remained loyal to King George III, as did the province of which it was a part, Quebec. From Detroit and other posts, the British supplied guns and ammunition to war parties that harried the Kentucky settlements and returned with scalps and prisoners. To take Detroit and remove the source of those attacks, Colonel George Rogers Clark led Kentuckians against British forts in the Ohio Valley, but he lacked the men and supplies to invade Michigan. Fearing a surprise attack by Clark, the British built a new fort, Lernoult, on higher ground at Detroit and replaced Fort Michilimackinac on the south shore of the Straits of Mackinac with a more secure Fort Mackinac on the bluff of Mackinac Island.

Tiring of a war they could not win, the British granted independence to the 13 colonies and set boundaries running through Lakes Erie, Huron, and Superior. Because Indians and traders objected that American settlers would destroy their way of life, British flags flew above the forts until 1796 when General Anthony Wayne's 1794 victory at Fallen Timbers forced the British to abandon Michigan, leaving little of themselves behind. Except for some Scots who had come as traders, a few Episcopal clergyman, two forts, and a very few place names, Michigan remained a French and Indian land.

Under Thomas Jefferson's Northwest Ordinance, which promised public education and prohibited slavery, Michigan lived first as a part of the Northwest Territory, then as a corner of Indiana Territory, and from 1805 to 1837 as Michigan Territory that grew to extend almost to the Black Hills of the Dakotas. A year after Wayne's 1794 victory, Ottawa, Chippewa, and Potawatomi gathered at Greenville, Ohio, and sold to the Americans some land at Mackinac and a strip along the Detroit River. In the next half century Americans exchanged cash and the promise of annual payments for all of the Indians' lands here except for a few "reservations." In the 1830s the federal government moved many of southern Michigan's Indians to Kansas and Oklahoma, but those who remained and those who returned have restored their numbers in the state.

County Divisions

Before 1825, a growing population prompted the first division of the original Wayne County into smaller governing units. New counties appeared on the map to match settlements carved in the forest. Each new county seat served a new community of people. Typically, a county was four townships high and four townships wide, 24 miles square (576 square miles or 922 square kilometers). Each built a courthouse that was often the grandest structure in the county.

In naming the counties, legislatures have recorded Michigan's history. Ottawa, Chippewa, Huron, and Menominee remembered the peoples who had occupied the peninsulas; Kalamazoo and Gogebic retained something of Indian culture; Marquette and Baraga honored missionaries who had brought Christianity. French place names survive in Saint Joseph and Presque Isle; French pioneers are recalled in Cadillac and Charlevoix. Wayne and Saint Clair remember generals who helped to open the West. Monroe honors one president, Jackson another. Cass was Michigan Territory's illustrious governor; Barry, Berrien, Calhoun, Eaton, Ingham, Livingston, and Van Buren were his associates in Jackson's cabinet. Mason was the state's first governor and Luce a later one. Clinton was named for the New Yorker who built the Erie Canal. Schoolcraft and Houghton helped to open the Upper Peninsula. And several names recall Irish counties such as Clare, Antrim, and Wexford from which the families of many Michigan legislators fled after the potato famine.

The Mid–Nineteenth Century

Americans usually moved directly west along lines of latitude, seeking both the shortest distance to cheap land and a familiar climate where familiar crops would grow in known ways. For many years westward-moving Americans preferred to settle in the Ohio Valley, whose waterways would carry their surplus grain, pork, and whiskey to market in New Orleans, the South, and even Europe. People from Maryland and Virginia settled southern Ohio, Indiana, and Illinois; Pennsylvanians filled central Ohio; those from Connecticut occupied Ohio's Western Reserve. Opening of the Erie Canal across New York state in 1825 changed the flow of settlers. Michigan became attractive because it could now ship its wool and wheat to the East and to Europe by cheap water transportation through Lake Erie, the canal, and down the Hudson. Upstate New York was seized by what it called "the Michigan fever." New England Yankees, many of them after living for a generation in upstate New York, swarmed into southern Michigan, filling its lower counties with Methodist, Baptist, Presbyterian, and Congregational churches. With sufficient population to be eligible for statehood, Michigan entered the Union in 1837 as the twenty-sixth state. Under the leadership of its youthful Democratic governor, Stevens T. Mason, it projected three state-owned canals and three state-owned railroads that promised to make Michigan prosperous as the Erie Canal had made New York.

Yankee zeal for education, for temperance in alcohol, and for an end to slavery set Michigan apart. In the 1840s Michigan pioneered state support for elementary schools, made them free to all in 1869 and, after the Kalamazoo Case, extended tax support to high schools. By the 1860s the University of Michigan was a leader among state universities, the Normal (now Eastern Michigan University) was one of the nation's oldest colleges of education, and the Agricultural College (now Michigan State University) was the prototype for the land-grant colleges endowed by the Morrill Land Act that President Lincoln signed in 1862.

Yankee devotion to freedom made Michigan a haven for escaping slaves who walked by night among the southerners of Ohio, Indiana, and Illinois into the daylight between the lakes. Quakers and others along the way provided food, clothing, and shelter, but the tracks of the Underground Railroad that led to Michigan were made by the shoes of fleeing blacks.

Antislavery sentiment founded the Republican Party in Michigan in 1854, "under the oaks" in Jackson. The party controlled the governor's chair and legislative chambers for most of a century. The first Republican legislature, that of 1855, petitioned Congress for a land grant to Michigan's agricultural college, enacted one of the first state prohibition laws, protected slaves who escaped to Michigan, and authorized church colleges to confer bachelor's degrees. Albion, Kalamazoo, Hillsdale, Olivet, and Adrian colleges were followed, in later years, by such colleges as Alma, Calvin, Hope, Aquinas, and Suomi and by the University of Detroit.

The Civil War and After

In the spring of 1861 Michigan responded with exceptional haste to President Lincoln's call for volunteers to recapture the seceded South. Its men fought on the major battlefields of the Civil War, winning their share of medals and honors, sacrificing their share of lives. In Reconstruction, its Zachariah Chandler was the foremost United States senator in defending those whom the war had freed. In the years after that war Michigan politics were dominated by the Republicans, who could take credit for freeing the slaves, for saving the Union, and for enacting high tariffs that protected Michigan's lumber, iron, copper, wool, salt, beet sugar, and chemicals from foreign competitors. As protector of industry and agriculture, the state earned the gratitude of both owner and worker.

Even before the Civil War men were mining iron on the Marquette Range, extracting copper on the Keweenaw Peninsula, and sawing pine in the Saginaw and Muskegon valleys. After the war production in these industries rose rapidly, cresting in various years between the 1880s and the 1920s. Miners from England's Cornwall came to dig deep shafts and bring out metallic copper for the button, clock, and kettle industries of Connecticut. Others from Pennsylvania and Europe brought up iron ore and watched it go down Lake Superior, through the new locks of the Soo Canal (1855), and on to steel plants that stretched from Lake Erie to Pittsburgh and later from Gary to Chicago.

Loggers from Maine, French Canada, and the Baltic stood on deep snow to saw down white and red pine. Decades later summer tourists saw the tall stumps above the snowless ground and believed stories of lumberjacks who had been giants or even Paul Bunyans. Teamsters skidded and hauled logs to the riverbank rollways, rivermen drove them downstream to mills where sawyers cut them into lumber that went by lake and rail to become houses, false-front stores, barns, fences, and boardwalks for Chicago and the treeless plains beyond.

Those were boom years for northern Michigan and for its hundreds of thriving lumber and mining towns. Mansions were built for people who made fortunes, opera houses were erected, libraries were opened, churches multiplied, and some surprisingly fine hotels sprang up for distinguished visitors and summer resorters. But by 1900 the north country was growing more slowly.

It could offer few jobs to newcomers. Its fur trade had faded after the 1830s, its good soil was all in farms, most of its copper and iron mines had been dug and many were running out of ore. Only remnants of its virgin pine forests survived in a stump-filled region. Michigan, which had supplied its raw materials for the profit of other states, was left with little evidence from its developing years.

Michigan was only beginning to found processing industries so that it too could reap the return from finished product. Converted lumber mills began turning hardwood forests into fine furniture; Grand Rapids became a national leader in that industry. Grain went to Battle Creek, where Dr. John Kellogg, famed for his sanitarium, turned it into breakfast food that made Battle Creek the dry-cereal capital of the world. Paper manufacture flourished along the Kalamazoo River. Detroit made cigars, stoves, and marine engines. Drugs and chemicals, buggies and bicycles were incipient industries. Canneries sprang up near the orchards that grew much of the nation's cherry, peach, and apple crops along the west shore, where Lake Michigan waters moderated the cold winds of winter, the hot winds of summer. After the turn of the century, farmers began to plant beets that were manufactured into Michigan sugar, cucumbers that were fermented into pickles, and peppermint whose leaves were distilled into oil beside Michigan peat fields. Later they grew potatoes that were sliced into chips. In time, many of these crops and industries would draw people from outside the state, notably the migrants of Mexican ancestry from the Southwest who worked in the orchards and vegetable fields. But in the 1890s these new industries were scarcely sufficient to absorb the young people growing to adulthood; they were not large enough to encourage immigration. The Michigan fever had ended.

The Twentieth Century

Then came the automobile, hesitantly at first but soon with a rush. Ransom E. Olds mass-produced the subject of the popular song, "My Merry Oldsmobile," sold the firm to General Motors, and built REO. Henry Ford assembled the Model T on a moving line and sold it so cheaply that his own workers could afford to buy it. William Durant merged Olds, Buick, and Leland's Cadillac into General Motors, to which he later added Chevrolet. Walter Chrysler acquired Dodge and introduced Plymouth. The availability of Michigan's hardwood for elegant bodies, iron for chassis, marine engines—built for lake shipping—for power, and of Ohio's rubber tires to smooth the bumps gave genius an opportunity to excel. Entrepreneurs and engineers, designers and toolmakers, foundrymen and assemblers all learned the art of auto production and taught it to thousands who joined them. Michigan became a reservoir of these automotive skills for the entire world.

By 1929 half of the nation's auto laborers worked in Michigan, and much of the other half were in branch plants of its "Big Three" auto companies. Ford's "five-dollar-day" had, since 1914, become almost standard in the industry. Other Michigan employers were forced to offer comparable rewards. People converged on southeast Michigan from the whole Great Lakes country, from the lower Middle West, from the upper South and the Gulf states. With them they brought their churches, their accents, their customs, their social attitudes to enrich the life of Detroit, Pontiac, Flint, and Lansing. As an automobile state, Michigan paved more highways early, paved them with wider lanes, and initiated roadside parks. In the 1950s it built more than its share of interstate freeways and spanned the Straits of Mackinac with the nation's longest suspension bridge. Going into the fourth quarter of the twentieth century, it was still an auto state, still a growing state.

By 1912 Michigan was not only known for its mining, furniture, fruit, and automobiles, but it was one of the leading Republican states. In all of the years since the party's founding at Jackson in 1854, the state had chosen only one governor who was not a Republican. It had elected farmers and lawyers, lumbermen, railroad builders, and industrialists. One of the latter was shoe manufacturer Hazen S. Pingree who, as mayor of Detroit in the depression of 1893, befriended the unemployed by developing community gardens and the employed people by forcing the car lines to reduce fares. One of the first leaders in the national Progressive movement, he served as governor at the close of the decade. His campaign to tax railroads, to enforce conservation laws, to place a levy on incomes, and to replace party conventions with direct primaries were all a bit ahead of their time. But the times caught up.

One of Pingree's protégés, conservationist and editor Chase Osborn of Sault Sainte Marie, became governor in 1910 at the height of the Progressive period. He increased railroad taxes, pushed the workmen's accident compensation law through the legislature, and spoke for the group of Midwest governors who persuaded Theodore Roosevelt to run again for president in 1912. Denied the nomination, Roosevelt ran as a Progressive, split the Republican Party, and insured the election of Democrats like President Woodrow Wilson and Governor Woodbridge Ferris. The founder and president of what is now Ferris State College, Ferris worked with a divided legislature that led the state to adopt initiative, referendum, and recall to strengthen the popular voice in government and statewide prohibition to improve the quality of life.

In World War I Michigan sent its full share of troops to France, many of them after training at Camp Custer near Battle Creek, and it produced a substantial share of the trucks, tanks, and airplane engines that armed the nation. Workers swarmed to Michigan's war production industries and stayed on to build cars for peacetime—cars that everyone seemed eager to buy. From the southern Middle West, people invaded Michigan's lakes, streams, and woods to fish, hunt, swim, and enjoy cool nights.

In those prosperous years, Michigan's governors introduced businesslike and business-oriented administrations that won the hearts of the vast majority of the voters. Even Democrats were converted, choosing Henry Ford in senatorial and presidential primaries. In that decade Michigan was as Republican as any state.

The Great Depression

In 1929 the Great Depression settled over America, a depression in which Michigan suffered more than did almost any other part of the country. Its autos were almost the first item that unemployed and underemployed families ceased to buy. No purchase was as postponable. So complete was the economic collapse that in February 1933 Michigan's banks were closed, thus precipitating a national crisis. Under Mayor Frank Murphy, Detroit provided relief to more of its families than did almost any other city. In 1932 Murphy organized the nation's mayors (they still meet) to demand federal relief for the unemployed from President Herbert Hoover and Congress. Father Charles E. Coughlin reinforced that plea in his Sunday afternoon radio sermons from the Shrine of the Little Flower in Royal Oak. To the largest audiences of any speaker on radio, he offered the alternatives of "Roosevelt or Ruin." Together, Coughlin and Murphy helped elect Franklin D. Roosevelt in 1932, the first Democrat to receive Michigan's full presidential electoral vote since before the Civil War.

Beginning in 1933 Roosevelt's New Deal made the federal government a pervasive force in Michigan. The Civilian Conservation Corps sent young men into camps where they planted trees, built forest trails, and developed recreation sites while making a better life for themselves, their families, and generations to come. Federal cash and work relief through the Works Project Administration (WPA) cared for desperate families like those whom Louise V. Armstrong served in Manistee and wrote about in her book, *We Too Are the People*. WPA set many people to raking leaves or building sidewalks, but it asked others to paint murals in post offices, to produce plays, to research and write the state's best travel guidebook, *Michigan, A Guide to the Wolverine State*. Other New Deal offices encouraged farmers to conserve soil and workers to form labor unions. In 1937 the CIO's United Auto Workers led its members in sit-down strikes that occupied many an auto factory while management and nonunion members went home. Governor Murphy played a decisive role in curbing violence and in assuring collective bargaining under the Wagner Act. In that bargaining, blacks and women participated as never before simply because they were fellow workers and therefore members of the new unions.

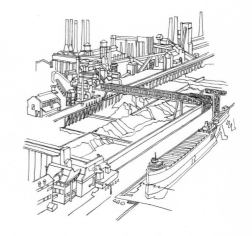

World War II brought recovery from the Great Depression and the exodus of young people into the armed services for training, followed by dispersal to the battlefields of Africa, Europe, and the islands of the Pacific. War production drew thousands of men and women from the Middle West and South to work in Michigan's converted auto plants. New communities, like that at the Willow Run bomber plant, sprang to life. Residential neighborhoods of older cities became crowded with newcomers. At the height of the influx, 1943, a deadly race riot broke out in Detroit, but black and white community leaders rose to the crisis; the summer passed. By 1944 there were few new arrivals seeking homes; peace prevailed then and for a quarter century until, in the midst of the Vietnam war boom, overcrowding again shattered the city's calm. But only for a summer.

Michigan—Since World War II

Since World War II Michigan has prospered more than other states in good times, suffered more than most in recession. Its farms, mines, and factories tended to rise and fall with the business cycle, but the auto industry rose faster and fell further. It paid generous wages for overtime and large dividends when production was up and margins were high; it laid off workers and pared dividends when sales dropped. When the nation's economy had a cold, Michigan's had pneumonia; but when the nation's hope rose, Michigan's optimism knew no bounds.

Michigan's economic and social needs were protected and furthered in Washington by senators, congressmen, and occasional cabinet members. But in World War II and the years immediately following, none were more influential in national policy than Detroit's Frank Murphy and Grand Rapids's Arthur Vandenberg. From opposite sides of the state, they came from opposite poles within their own political parties. To the U.S. Supreme Court in 1940 Murphy carried his experience as recorders court judge, as mayor of depression-blighted Detroit, as governor of strike-torn Michigan, and as Roosevelt's attorney general. He became the foremost spokesman for the rights of the oppressed: American Japanese in relocation camps, blacks in southern towns, Indians and minorities, and the poor everywhere. He served as liberal conscience to the Supreme Court and to his party. Vandenberg carried to the United States Senate in 1928 his long experience as newspaper editor, as arbiter of public issues. As a senator he spoke for the conservative wing of his party in the 1930s and for the internationalist wing in the postwar years. With eloquence and close reasoning, he led the Senate in its bipartisan foreign policy cooperation with President Harry S. Truman. His speeches, his amendments, his logic, his mustering of votes were decisive in America's entrance into the United Nations and in the passing of legislation that gave Truman doctrine, Marshall Plan, and NATO military and economic aid to many countries in Europe and Asia.

In Michigan government a Murphy protégé, G. Mennen Williams, served an unprecedented succession of six terms, 1949-61, in the governor's chair. His elections reflected the political support offered by the new CIO unions, which drew much of their liberalism from the formulations of labor leader Walter Reuther. In time, Williams was surrounded by liberal Democrats like himself within state administration, the legislature, and even city councils. Together

they represented workers as wage earners, as consumers, and as citizens. One of their number, Philip Hart, became United States senator, speaking for liberals into the mid-1970s.

Just as the Michigan Democratic Party spoke especially for auto labor, so did the Michigan Republican Party often speak for auto management. In President Dwight Eisenhower's cabinet, General Motors president Charles E. Wilson was one of the most influential policy makers. In his insistence on building missiles and planes rather than tanks and trucks, he sought more firepower for less money, "more bang for a buck." The postmaster general and party chairman was a Flint General Motors dealer, Arthur Summerfield, whose prime goal was economy and efficiency. In the next decade American Motors president George Romney fostered better schools for Detroit, led Republican liberals in Michigan's 1961 Constitutional Convention, governed the state for six years, and served as President Richard Nixon's secretary of housing and urban development. Both parties in those years reflected the divisions within the car industry, between management and labor, between company and company.

In the 1970s the center of political gravity has shifted. A Republican senator, Robert Griffin, the Republican governor, William Milliken, and Michigan's only White House occupant, Gerald Ford, speak, as did Arthur Vandenberg, for their Lake Michigan shore as much as for southeast Michigan's automobile empire. One of their strengths may lie in a capacity to reconcile the rivalries within the mass-production industry that Michigan gave to the world.

Madison Kuhn

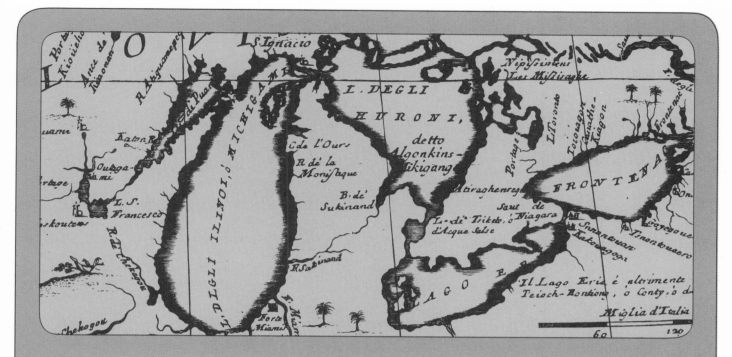

This portion of Vincenzo Coronelli's 1696 **Atlante Veneto** map was based on fragmentary reports from French explorers. It defined with remarkable accuracy those shorelines that the French had studied, but erred in those that they had seen from a distance or learned of only by conversation. "Michigami," which had also ap-peared on Coronelli's 1688 French map, represented one explorer's hearing of the Indian name for the lake. Later visitors detected other sounds in the Indian pronunciation. By 1805 it was known as Lake Michigan, and Congress had given the lake's name to the new territory.

In 1718 Guillaume Delisle introduced the "Plaine elevee" on a map of "Louisiana." The long plateau was an exaggeration of vague reports from explorers of uplands dotting a low interior—uplands that stretch from the Irish Hills to Caberfae and the Boyne Highlands. However inaccurate the snakelike ridge of Delisle's map, it was repeated with infinite variation by cartographers for more than a century. The errors so common in nineteenth century maps are an unintended tribute to the skills of cartographic pioneers like Coronelli and Delisle.

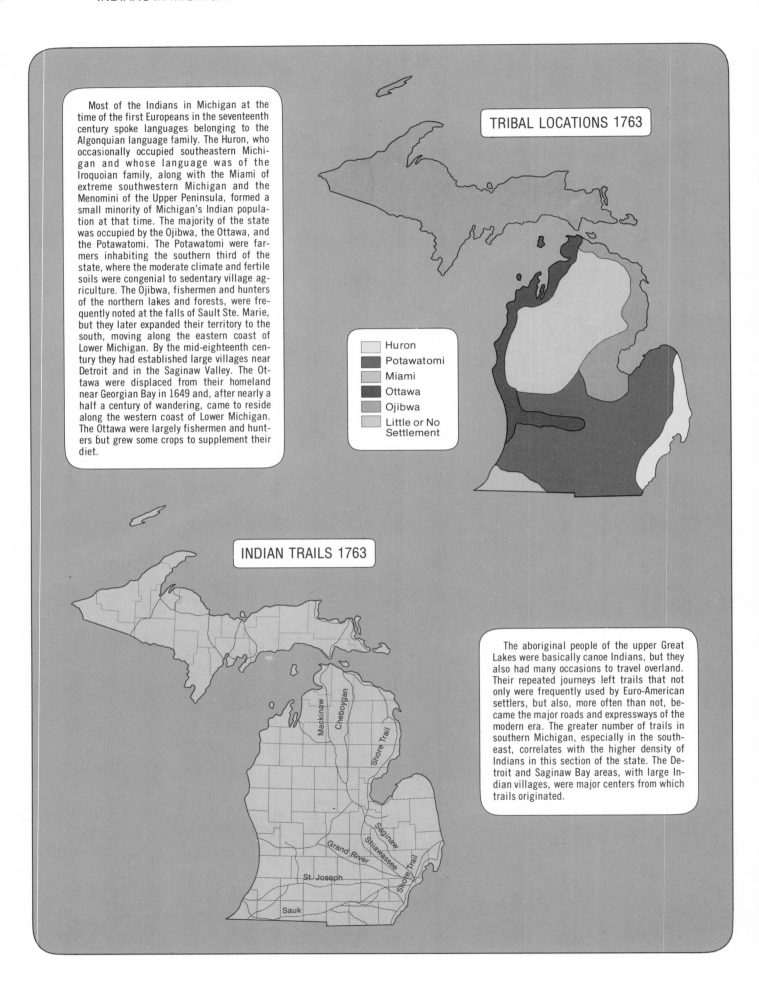

Most of the Indians in Michigan at the time of the first Europeans in the seventeenth century spoke languages belonging to the Algonquian language family. The Huron, who occasionally occupied southeastern Michigan and whose language was of the Iroquoian family, along with the Miami of extreme southwestern Michigan and the Menomini of the Upper Peninsula, formed a small minority of Michigan's Indian population at that time. The majority of the state was occupied by the Ojibwa, the Ottawa, and the Potawatomi. The Potawatomi were farmers inhabiting the southern third of the state, where the moderate climate and fertile soils were congenial to sedentary village agriculture. The Ojibwa, fishermen and hunters of the northern lakes and forests, were frequently noted at the falls of Sault Ste. Marie, but they later expanded their territory to the south, moving along the eastern coast of Lower Michigan. By the mid-eighteenth century they had established large villages near Detroit and in the Saginaw Valley. The Ottawa were displaced from their homeland near Georgian Bay in 1649 and, after nearly a half a century of wandering, came to reside along the western coast of Lower Michigan. The Ottawa were largely fishermen and hunters but grew some crops to supplement their diet.

TRIBAL LOCATIONS 1763

Huron
Potawatomi
Miami
Ottawa
Ojibwa
Little or No Settlement

INDIAN TRAILS 1763

The aboriginal people of the upper Great Lakes were basically canoe Indians, but they also had many occasions to travel overland. Their repeated journeys left trails that not only were frequently used by Euro-American settlers, but also, more often than not, became the major roads and expressways of the modern era. The greater number of trails in southern Michigan, especially in the southeast, correlates with the higher density of Indians in this section of the state. The Detroit and Saginaw Bay areas, with large Indian villages, were major centers from which trails originated.

Mackinaw
Cheboygan
Shore Trail
Saginaw
Shiawassee
Grand River
Shore Trail
St. Joseph
Sauk

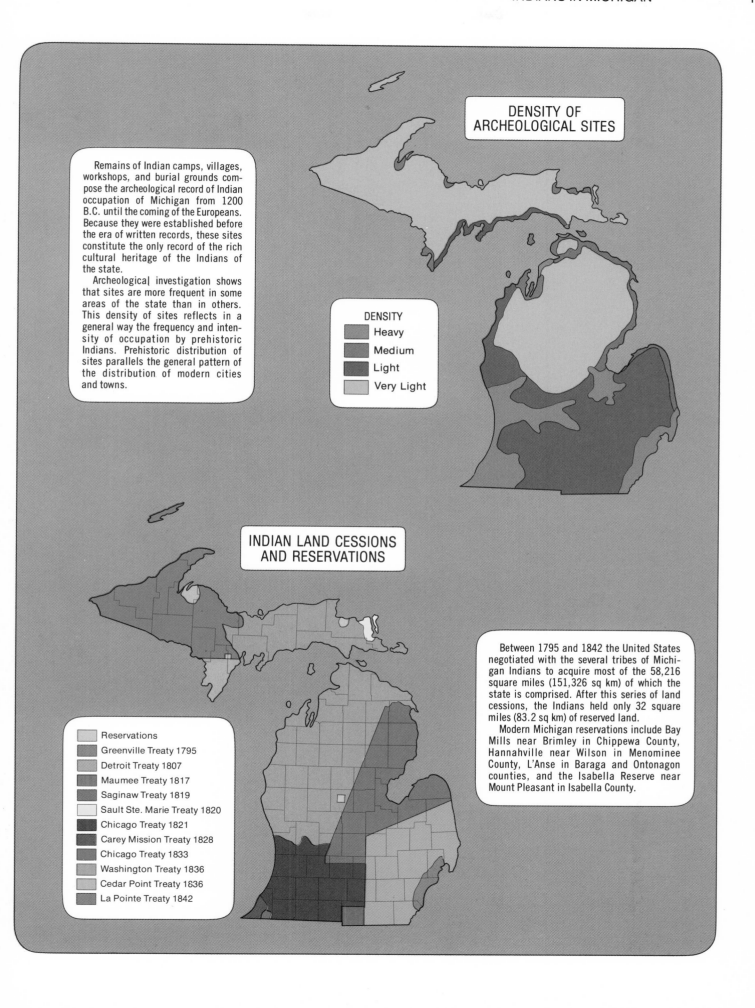

DENSITY OF ARCHEOLOGICAL SITES

Remains of Indian camps, villages, workshops, and burial grounds compose the archeological record of Indian occupation of Michigan from 1200 B.C. until the coming of the Europeans. Because they were established before the era of written records, these sites constitute the only record of the rich cultural heritage of the Indians of the state.

Archeological investigation shows that sites are more frequent in some areas of the state than in others. This density of sites reflects in a general way the frequency and intensity of occupation by prehistoric Indians. Prehistoric distribution of sites parallels the general pattern of the distribution of modern cities and towns.

DENSITY

- Heavy
- Medium
- Light
- Very Light

INDIAN LAND CESSIONS AND RESERVATIONS

Between 1795 and 1842 the United States negotiated with the several tribes of Michigan Indians to acquire most of the 58,216 square miles (151,326 sq km) of which the state is comprised. After this series of land cessions, the Indians held only 32 square miles (83.2 sq km) of reserved land.

Modern Michigan reservations include Bay Mills near Brimley in Chippewa County, Hannahville near Wilson in Menominee County, L'Anse in Baraga and Ontonagon counties, and the Isabella Reserve near Mount Pleasant in Isabella County.

- Reservations
- Greenville Treaty 1795
- Detroit Treaty 1807
- Maumee Treaty 1817
- Saginaw Treaty 1819
- Sault Ste. Marie Treaty 1820
- Chicago Treaty 1821
- Carey Mission Treaty 1828
- Chicago Treaty 1833
- Washington Treaty 1836
- Cedar Point Treaty 1836
- La Pointe Treaty 1842

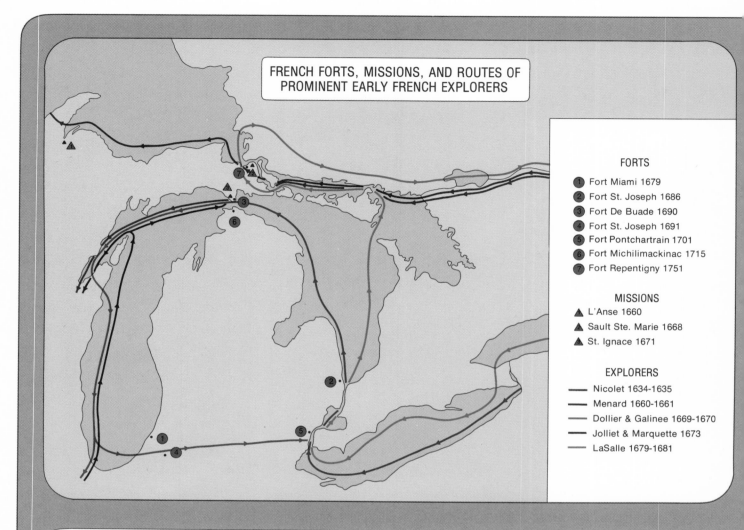

FRENCH FORTS, MISSIONS, AND ROUTES OF
PROMINENT EARLY FRENCH EXPLORERS

FORTS

1. Fort Miami 1679
2. Fort St. Joseph 1686
3. Fort De Buade 1690
4. Fort St. Joseph 1691
5. Fort Pontchartrain 1701
6. Fort Michilimackinac 1715
7. Fort Repentigny 1751

MISSIONS

▲ L'Anse 1660
▲ Sault Ste. Marie 1668
▲ St. Ignace 1671

EXPLORERS

— Nicolet 1634-1635
— Menard 1660-1661
— Dollier & Galinee 1669-1670
— Jolliet & Marquette 1673
— LaSalle 1679-1681

Before the Pilgrims landed at Plymouth Rock, the French had penetrated the heart of America to proclaim Christian salvation to the Indians and to search out a water route to the tea, silks, and spices of China and its neighbors. They stayed in the Great Lakes area to trade for furs and to cultivate ribbon farms along the rivers, all under the Bourbon flag of the Sun King, Louis XIV, and his successors.

Samuel de Champlain founded Quebec in 1608, the year after Jamestown's settlement, and spent the winter of 1615–16 at a Recollet mission at the head of Lake Huron's Georgian Bay. His canoes, and many that followed, were paddled by Indians up the Ottawa River, through Lake Nipissing, and down the French River to Georgian Bay because the Iroquois controlled the Niagara route. Champlain dispatched Jean Nicolet in 1634 to find a river flowing from the west at whose headwaters one might portage to another river that would flow into the Pacific. This would open a French-controlled water route to China to rival those of Spain, Portugal, and the Italian cities. Nicolet abandoned the search a bit beyond Lake Michigan's Green Bay, but he reported a mighty river to the west.

By 1660 Pierre Radisson and Médard Groseilliers had brought out of Lake Superior a flotilla of canoes laden with furs, and Father René Menard, a Jesuit, was preaching to Ottawas on Keweenaw Bay. A decade later, in 1671, agents of Louis XIV raised his flag at Sault Ste. Marie. Soon Father Jacques Marquette was working among the Indians and joined Louis Jolliet to descend the Mississippi. Robert La Salle followed the Mississippi to its mouth, but it emptied into a gulf off the Atlantic, not off the Pacific as he had hoped.

Losing hope of finding a water route to China, the French might have abandoned the Great Lakes but for the zeal of traders and missionaries at St. Ignace (named for Jesuit founder St. Ignatius Loyola), the Sault, Fort St. Joseph (on the site of Niles), and many other rivermouths where Indians fished, raised corn, hunted, and developed temporary settlements.

In 1760, when France's flag was replaced by Britain's Union Jack, there were only a few hundred French at Detroit and not many more at missions, trading posts, and the forts of Michilimackinac and St. Joseph. But the French and their culture dominated life in the third of a century of British rule and were only slowly engulfed by the tide of Americans that rose slowly after 1796 and swelled to a flood after 1825.

True settlement began at the strait (**étroit**) where Cadillac founded Detroit in 1701. In addition to the usual soldiers, traders, and missionaries, he brought settlers to whom he assigned narrow ribbon farms that gave each family access to river transportation and as much land in the interior as it might choose to clear and plant. (These holdings are shown below as they looked in 1810.) When the Americans came they imposed rectangular surveys that made roads run north-south or east-west. But from Grosse Pointe to Monroe the margins of ribbon farms survive in roads that run at various angles but always perpendicular to the river.

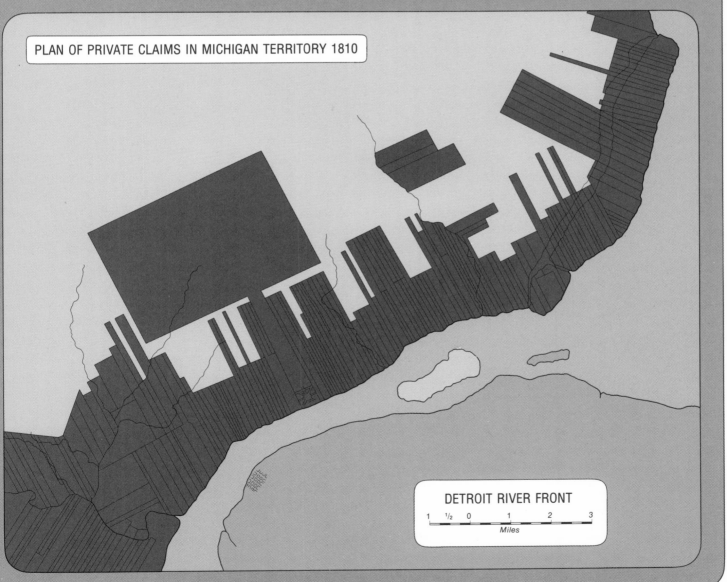

PLAN OF PRIVATE CLAIMS IN MICHIGAN TERRITORY 1810

DETROIT RIVER FRONT

1 ½ 0 1 2 3

Miles

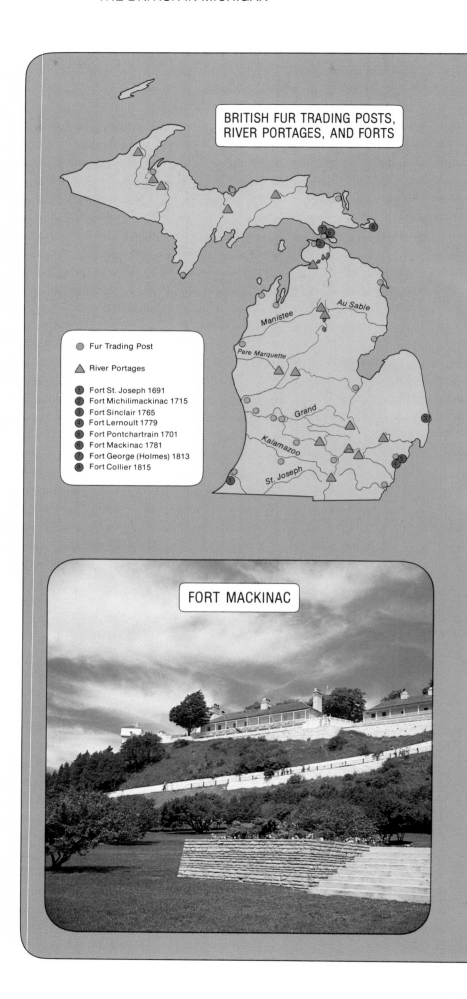

BRITISH FUR TRADING POSTS, RIVER PORTAGES, AND FORTS

Au Sable

Manistee

Pere Marquette

Grand

Kalamazoo

St. Joseph

● Fur Trading Post

▲ River Portages

① Fort St. Joseph 1691
② Fort Michilimackinac 1715
③ Fort Sinclair 1765
④ Fort Lernoult 1779
⑤ Fort Pontchartrain 1701
⑥ Fort Mackinac 1781
⑦ Fort George (Holmes) 1813
⑧ Fort Collier 1815

FORT MACKINAC

As conquered peoples, Michigan's Indians and French distrusted the British garrisons that arrived after early victories in the Seven Years War. In 1763 that distrust led Indians to capture Ft. St. Joseph (at what is now Niles) and Ft. Michilimackinac (in present Mackinaw City) and, for a summer under Chief Pontiac, to besiege the fort at Detroit.

After the close of that war, Indians and French alike learned to accept the British as allies against westward-moving American settlers who might drive out the game and substitute Protestant clergy for Catholic. In the Revolutionary War the British encouraged Indian war parties to attack Americans lest they cross the Ohio River into Quebec Province. When Colonel George Rogers Clark's Kentucky militiamen captured British posts near the Ohio River and threatened those in Michigan, the Detroit garrison added Ft. Lernoult and the Michilimackinac garrison moved from the south side of the straits to Mackinac Island. After the battle of Yorktown, title to the region passed to the United States, but Britain delayed the surrender of Michigan's forts until 1796.

For almost 40 years the British had ruled Michigan without greatly changing its way of life. Fur trading, farming, religion, and place names remained Indian and French. The two cultures that had shared Michigan for more than a century would survive well into the American period.

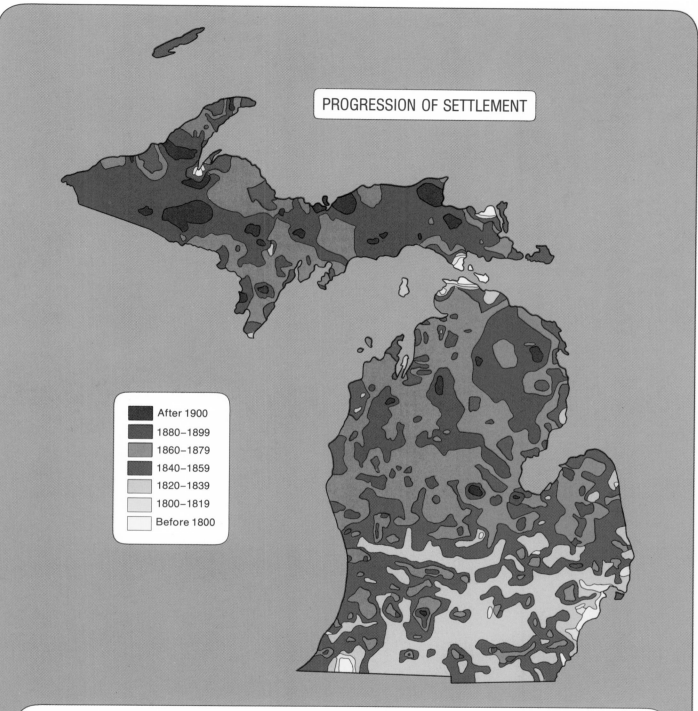

PROGRESSION OF SETTLEMENT

After 1900
1880–1899
1860–1879
1840–1859
1820–1839
1800–1819
Before 1800

The map above has been drawn from a computer analysis of the founding dates of some 1,400 settlements, ranging from French posts and missions to stations along Michigan's youngest railroads and resort communities around many of the state's thousands of inland lakes. It depicts the flow of settlers after the Erie Canal opened eastern markets to Michigan's surplus wheat and wool in 1825. Settlement fingered out along the Chicago, Territorial, Grand River, Saginaw, and Gratiot roads until the lower tiers of counties—the wrist and palm of the Lower Peninsula "mitten"—were filled with farm families. Along every road and river, wherever there was water power for flour and lumber mills, speculators located townsites and promised homes,

churches, stores, schools, hotels, and even opera houses. A few towns exceeded even the wildest of hopes, but many never consisted of more than a school, a church, a post office, and a general store. Even those amenities were disappearing by the mid-twentieth century.

In the north people settled at lake fishing ports and the mouths of rivers where mills sawed the pine logs that rivermen drove downstream with the floods of spring. Others clustered their homes about the towers above copper and iron mines of the western Upper Peninsula. Along every new railroad towns sprang up at lonesome whistle stops, even as today new communities are born at interstate highway exits.

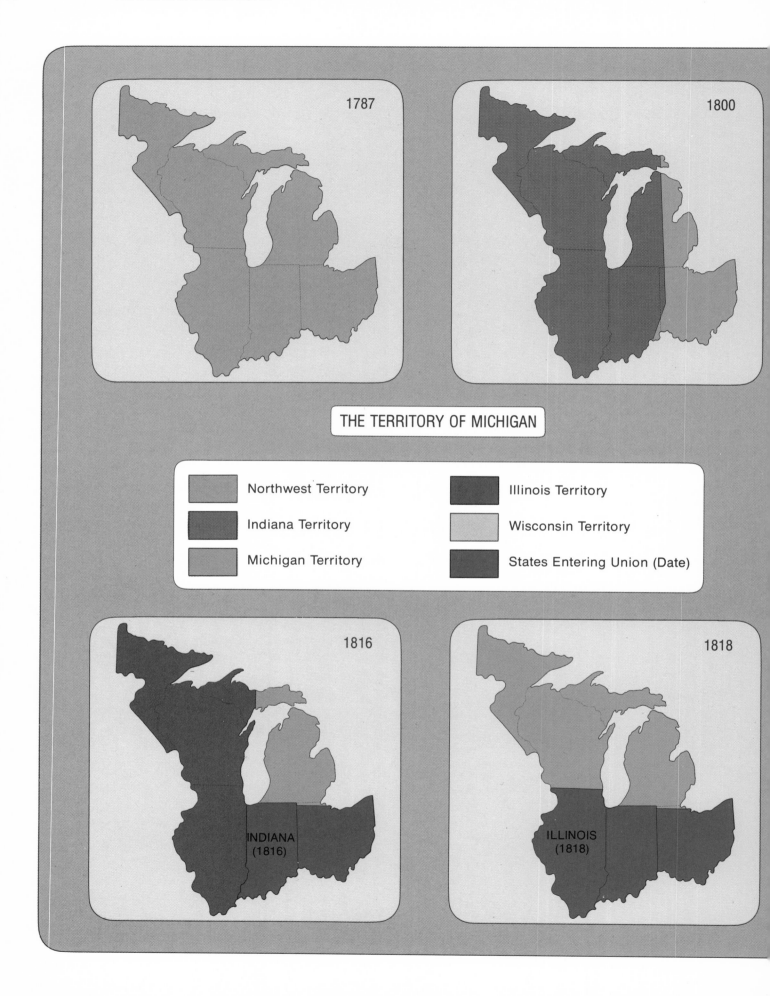

1787

1800

THE TERRITORY OF MICHIGAN

Northwest Territory

Indiana Territory

Michigan Territory

Illinois Territory

Wisconsin Territory

States Entering Union (Date)

1816

INDIANA
(1816)

1818

ILLINOIS
(1818)

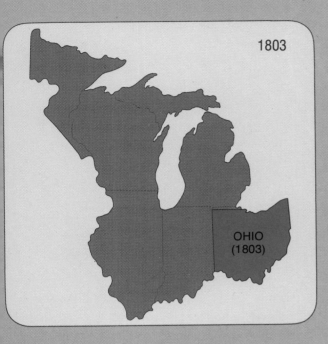

1803

OHIO
(1803)

1805

In 1787 Thomas Jefferson's Northwest Ordinance chartered a government for the American portion of what had been Britain's Province of Quebec. The ordinance encouraged public education, forbad slavery, and promised the equality of statehood as soon as the territory contained enough people. When Ohio was on the eve of statehood, the western half of what is now Michigan joined the new Indiana Territory, and after Ohio became a state in 1803 all of Michigan was governed from Indiana. Two years later Congress created Michigan Territory with Detroit as its capital and William Hull as its governor. As the Ohio Valley filled with people, Indiana and Illinois joined the Union, leaving to Michigan the residue of the Northwest Territory. To this Congress added the northern end of the Louisiana Purchase, stretching Michigan Territory over 1,000 miles (1,600 km) from the Detroit River to the Missouri River in the Dakotas.

With the opening of New York's Erie Canal in 1825, settlers crowded into southern Michigan, confident that they could send wheat and wool to market via Lake Erie and the canal. By 1837 Michigan's original peninsula had more than twice the 60,000 people required for statehood, and it had surrendered to the new Wisconsin Territory all of the land to the west of Lake Michigan. But Congress insisted that Michigan must give up the Toledo Strip to Ohio and accept as compensation the northern peninsula along Lake Superior's shore. Reluctantly, Michigan acquiesced to become the twenty-sixth state on January 26, 1837. With its two peninsulas separated by the Straits of Mackinac, it was one of the widest states in the union, a constant challenge to mapmakers.

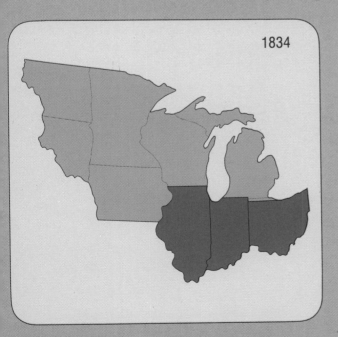

1834

1837

MICHIGAN
(1837)

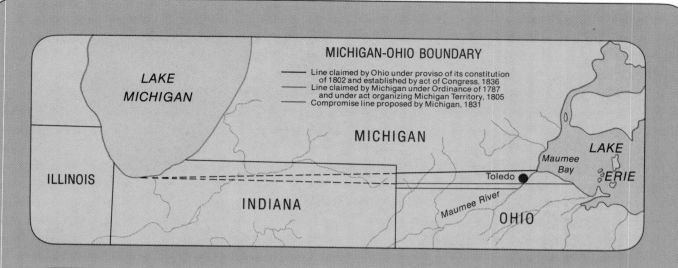

MICHIGAN-OHIO BOUNDARY

Line claimed by Ohio under proviso of its constitution
of 1802 and established by act of Congress, 1836
Line claimed by Michigan under Ordinance of 1787
and under act organizing Michigan Territory, 1805
Compromise line proposed by Michigan, 1831

Because of its unwillingness to accept Ohio's version of the common boundary, Michigan's admission to the Union was delayed until 1837, years after its Lower Peninsula had accumulated the requisite 60,000 people. The Northwest Ordinance had specified a line due east from the southern tip of Lake Michigan, but by 1803 Ohio, on the eve of statehood, recognized that it would lose the strategic mouth of the Maumee River. In their constitution Ohioans thus defined a northern boundary that followed a diagonal line from Lake Michigan to the north cape of Maumee Bay. This action assured possession of the new lakeport that would grow up at the mouth of the Maumee.

When Michigan was ready for statehood in the 1830s, it saw the value of that lakeport, Toledo, at the northern terminus of a new canal planned from the Ohio River. Relying upon the Ordinance of 1787, Michigan claimed the "Toledo Strip." In response Ohio created a new county. Michigan's Territorial Council threatened any intruding Ohio officials with fine and imprisonment, and Governor Mason led militia into the strip to oust Ohioans. An almost bloodless "Toledo War" followed, with Michigan retaining possession. But Ohio had senators and representatives in Congress, whereas Michigan lacked a vote. Congress awarded the Toledo area to Ohio and compensated Michigan with all of the Upper Peninsula, giving it some of America's richest iron and copper country as well as picturesque shores along Lakes Michigan and Superior.

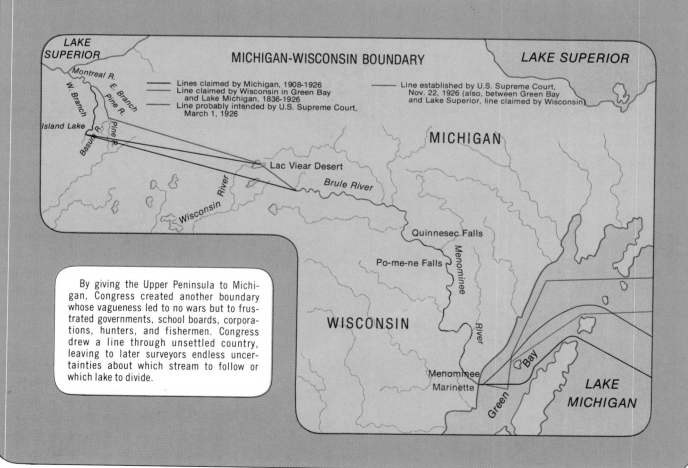

MICHIGAN-WISCONSIN BOUNDARY

Lines claimed by Michigan, 1908-1926
Line claimed by Wisconsin in Green Bay
and Lake Michigan, 1836-1926
Line probably intended by U.S. Supreme Court,
March 1, 1926

Line established by U.S. Supreme Court,
Nov. 22, 1926 (also, between Green Bay
and Lake Superior, line claimed by Wisconsin)

By giving the Upper Peninsula to Michigan, Congress created another boundary whose vagueness led to no wars but to frustrated governments, school boards, corporations, hunters, and fishermen. Congress drew a line through unsettled country, leaving to later surveyors endless uncertainties about which stream to follow or which lake to divide.

H.S. Tanner's map indicates county boundaries and names as they existed in 1841. Certain place names are spelled differently than today. The pattern of railroads, roads, and canals is clearly portrayed.

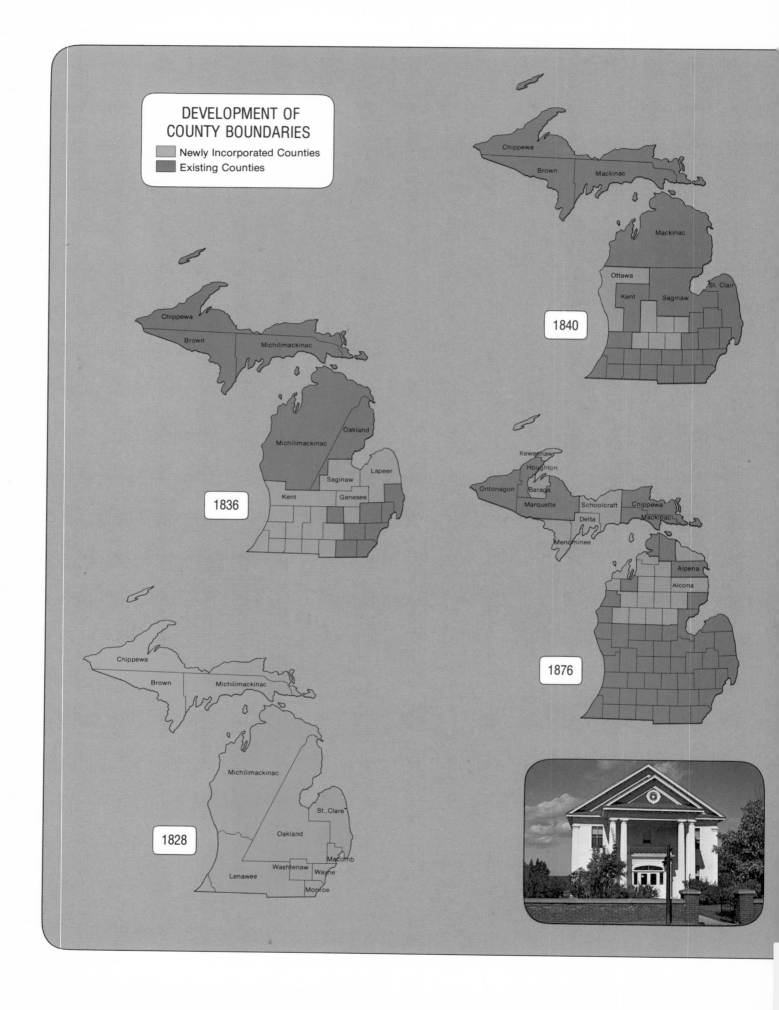

DEVELOPMENT OF
COUNTY BOUNDARIES
Newly Incorporated Counties
Existing Counties

1828

1836

1840

1876

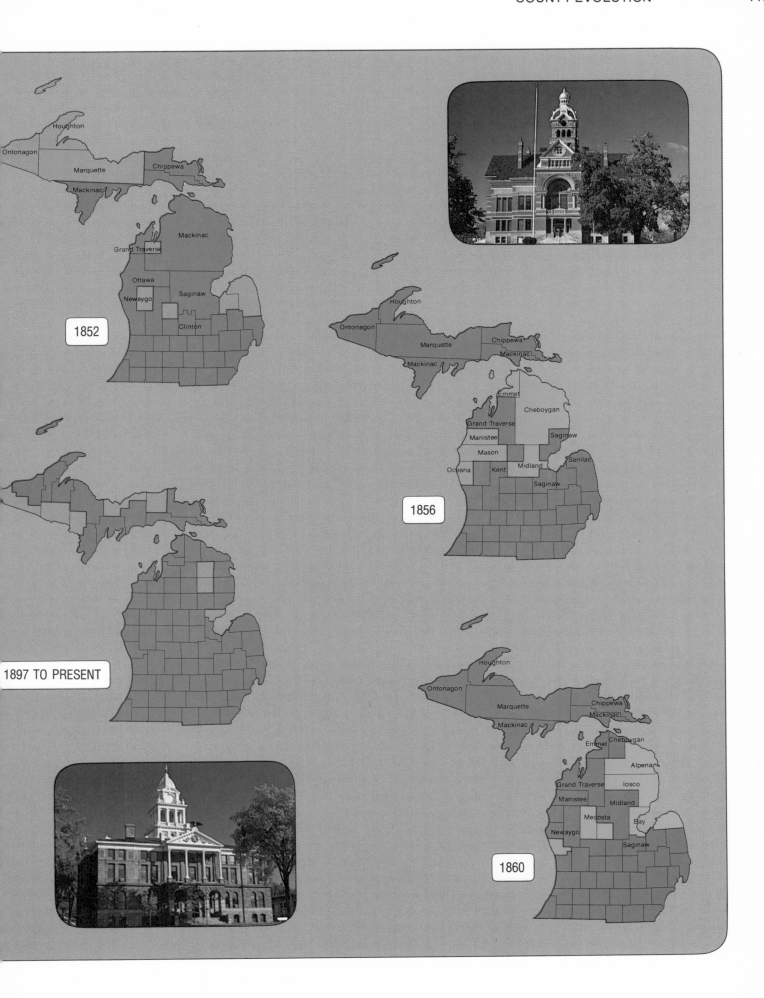

1852

1856

1897 TO PRESENT

1860

IMMIGRATION

Der Staat „Michigan", Vereinigte Staaten von Nord = Amerika.

Endesunterzeichneter, von seiner Regierung angestellter Emigrations= Commissär für Europa, ertheilt unentgeltlich Auskunft über obigen Staat. Auch übersendet derselbe Jedem auf Verlangen portofrei eine Broschüre über den Staat mit Special=Karte, sowie Probenummern des von ihm herausge= gebenen „Michigan Wegweiser". Man adressire:

M. H. Allardt, Hamburg.

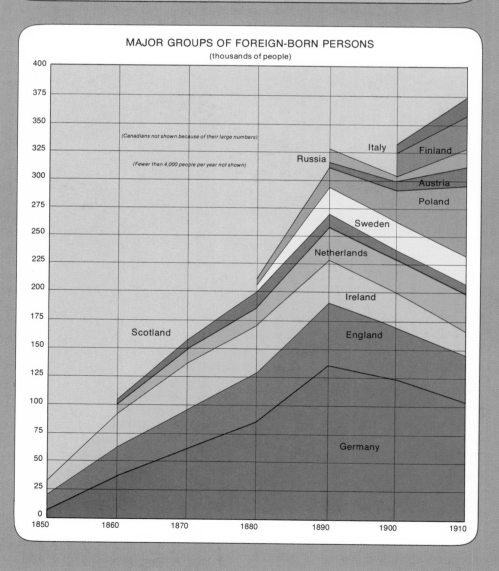

MAJOR GROUPS OF FOREIGN-BORN PERSONS
(thousands of people)

(Canadians not shown because of their large numbers)

(Fewer than 4,000 people per year not shown)

Michigan's population has always been predominantly native-born, even in 1701 when Indians vastly outnumbered the French. But the 1840s saw the beginning of those great waves of European immigration that have so enriched Michigan's culture. Englishmen and Scots, many coming by way of Canada, entered the state in a steady stream, founding Episcopal and Presbyterian churches and reinforcing British traditions among the American-born. Potato failures and abortive political and religious revolutions brought the Irish, Dutch, and Germans in great numbers who founded Catholic, Reformed, and Lutheran churches and built railroads, farms, machines, and furniture. After the Civil War, Scandinavians joined men from Maine and Canada in logging Michigan's pine and sawing it into lumber. They stayed to farm the "cutover" land left behind.

Before 1880 many of the immigrants came from the shores of the North Sea. After 1880 eastern and southern Europeans came in mounting numbers. Polish immigrants from the three countries among which their nation was divided farmed in eastern Michigan as far north as Posen, joined the furniture industry in Grand Rapids, and entered auto factories as they expanded into the southeastern counties. People from what is now Finland moved to the mining country to farm, work at surface jobs, and finally enter the mines. Italians, Austrians, Hungarians, and Russians found homes in the cities, entering industry and business. Immigrants bolstered the membership of the Catholic churches that the French had founded; brought Orthodox churches and Jewish congregations; enriched the cultural mix; fostered lodges, political clubs, schools, and restaurants; and built closely knit ethnic islands that eased the trauma of assimilation into an unfamiliar society.

World War I sharply reduced the influx of Europeans and, after the war, federal immigration laws prevented a return of that era when America welcomed the world. People from Canada and Mexico continued to come when employment was assured, but their numbers never matched the prewar European totals. Some years the gates reopened slightly to admit refugees from a new force of oppression in Europe or the Americas or Asia, reminding Michigan of the times when many peoples were adding their customs, celebrations, dress, and religious beliefs to a basically Anglo-Saxon society. Melting pot or tossed salad, Michigan continued to be an ever new and interesting place in which to live.

By 1850 Michigan was a transplanted New England; the majority of its people were Yankees or their descendants. People from Vermont, Massachusetts, and their neighbors had settled upstate New York. In search of cheaper land, more profitable storekeeping, or better jobs, they or their children moved farther west to Michigan once the Erie Canal across New York state offered an inexpensive outlet for wheat, wool, or lumber. They moved directly west because that was the shortest route to frontier opportunity and would keep them in a latitude where crops and climate would be familiar.

When a census was taken in 1850 it was discovered that a sixth of Michigan's people had been born in New England, a third in New York, presumably of New England stock, and a third in Michigan, mostly children of the New England-to-New York migrants seized with the "Michigan fever" in the 1830s. These immigrants had overwhelmed the Indians, French, and British, replacing their customs with Yankee ones.

Whether born near Boston, Buffalo, or Pontiac, they preserved a New England pattern of life. They used the word "pails" rather than "buckets" and transplanted the institutions that they had reluctantly left behind. Because of the rectangular federal land surveys, their roads could no longer wind and their farmers could not reside in towns, but they erected schools near the heart of townships, founded Congregational, Presbyterian, Baptist, and Methodist churches, created colleges in the image of Yale and Harvard, formed temperance clubs to stamp out the demon rum, and fostered antislavery societies that helped found the Republican Party in Jackson, Michigan, in 1854.

After the Civil War, people from Ohio and western Pennsylvania came to the iron and copper mines, to the lumber camps, and to factory towns. By 1910 the New York–New England-born were outnumbered by Midwesterners, some of whom were the families of men who had left farm or town to work in the exciting new automobile industry. In later years they would be joined in the auto plants by people from the upper South and finally from the Gulf states. Meanwhile rural Michigan would come to depend upon Latino peoples from the Southwest who tended and harvested fruits and vegetables. Whatever the source, each group added its churches, societies, accents, and crafts to Michigan's cultural heritage.

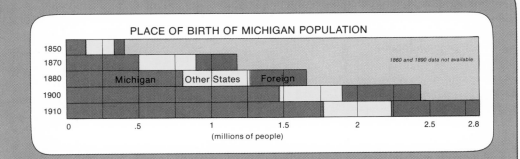

PLACE OF BIRTH OF MICHIGAN POPULATION

1860 and 1890 data not available

Michigan Other States Foreign

(millions of people)

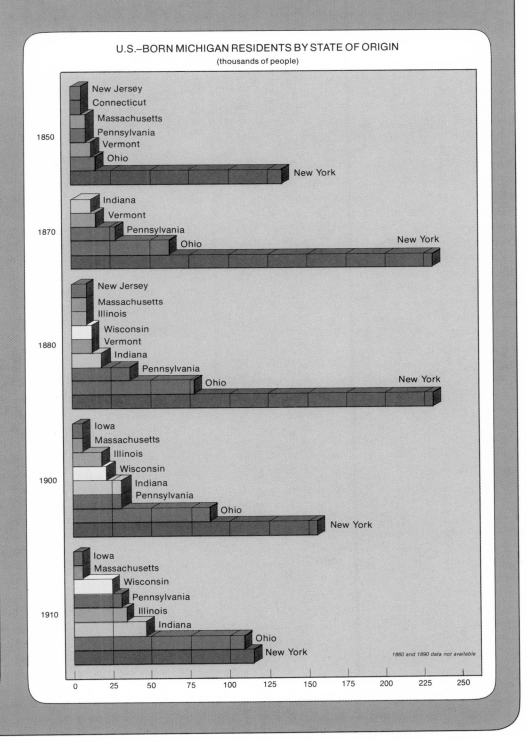

U.S.–BORN MICHIGAN RESIDENTS BY STATE OF ORIGIN

(thousands of people)

1850
New Jersey
Connecticut
Massachusetts
Pennsylvania
Vermont
Ohio
New York

1870
Indiana
Vermont
Pennsylvania
Ohio
New York

1880
New Jersey
Massachusetts
Illinois
Wisconsin
Vermont
Indiana
Pennsylvania
Ohio
New York

1900
Iowa
Massachusetts
Illinois
Wisconsin
Indiana
Pennsylvania
Ohio
New York

1910
Iowa
Massachusetts
Wisconsin
Pennsylvania
Illinois
Indiana
Ohio
New York

1860 and 1890 data not available

President Lincoln's call for volunteers in April 1861 met a ready response in Michigan where the Republican Party had been founded to resist the expansion of slavery. Local militia companies like the Detroit Light Guard and the Jackson Greys became nuclei for volunteer regiments that were soon on their way to Washington. Caught up in the cry of "on to Richmond," the Michigan First Infantry fought at Bull Run in July; the Second and Third arrived to cover the retreat. At the second Bull Run, Shiloh, Antietam, Gettysburg, and other battles, Michigan regiments suffered heavy casualties. In July 1863 George Pickett's Confederate charge was halted at Gettysburg by the Michigan Cavalry Brigade under General George Custer of Monroe. That same month a half-dozen Michigan regiments joined Ulysses S. Grant's successful siege of Vicksburg. In the following year a dozen Michigan regiments followed William Sherman to the sea and almost double that number fought with Grant in Virginia. Squeezed between Grant and Sherman, Robert E. Lee surrendered at Appomattox in April 1865. A month later the Fourth Michigan Cavalry captured the fleeing Confederate President, Jefferson Davis. For a generation Michigan veterans would "vote the way they shot."

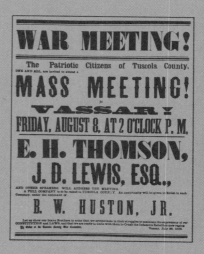

SHERMAN'S MARCH

MAJOR BATTLES AND CAMPAIGNS INVOLVING MICHIGAN REGIMENTS

1. Bull Run
2. Shiloh
3. Bull Run
4. Antietam
5. Gettysburg
6. Vicksburg
7. Chattanooga
8. Shenandoah
9. Wilderness
10. Spotsylvania
11. Sherman's March
12. Appomattox

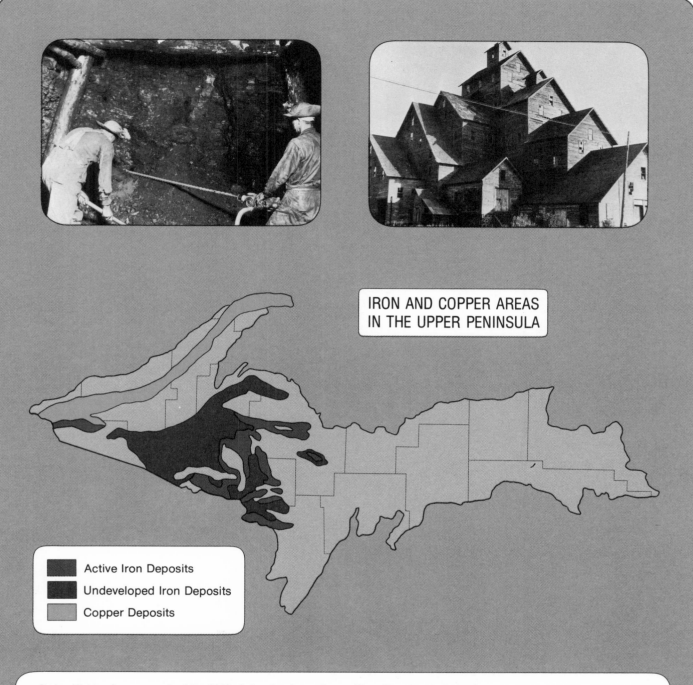

IRON AND COPPER AREAS
IN THE UPPER PENINSULA

■ Active Iron Deposits
■ Undeveloped Iron Deposits
■ Copper Deposits

During Michigan's copper rush of the 1840s fortunate miners who combed the surface of the Keweenaw Peninsula, dug shallow pits, and finally sent shafts a mile or more into the rock beneath shaft houses like the one above Quincy Mine near Hancock were rewarded with nuggets of pure metal. Deep mining was the work of Cornish miners who brought their skills, sledges, drills, and blasting powder from the declining pits of Cornwall to the prospering shafts of the Lake Superior shore. Their families brought a way of life that included the pasty, a potato-and-meat turnover that the miner heated at noon on his shovel held over his candle.

Keweenaw's copper was shipped south on the lakes to New England to become clocks and kettles for the world. In time, the mines themselves came under the control of New England investors. For half a century Michigan led the nation in copper production before surrendering to the West. The miners stayed on, even after most of the mines were shut down. Copper had settled the Keweenaw, a peninsula that, if it had waited for farmers, would have remained a virtual wilderness.

Michigan's iron ore supplied a local charcoal smelting industry until the 1855 Soo Lock opened a cheap water route to the Lake Erie shore and Pittsburgh. Iron ore from shaft mines on the Marquette, Gogebic, and Menominee ranges joined Appalachian coal to make steel in the mills along the shores of the lower lakes. Many of the mine workers came from Pennsylvania, Cornwall, Italy, and Finland. They made Michigan a national leader in mining ore during the brief interval between the decline of Pennsylvania mining and the opening of Minnesota's Mesabi range, sources now eclipsed by Labrador. They also left behind a society at the western end of the Upper Peninsula.

PEAK LUMBER PRODUCTION BY RIVER VALLEY

1910 Manistique
1893 Cheboygan
1889 Menominee
1884 Manistee
1884 Muskegon
1882 Saginaw
1880 N.E. Shore (Au Gres, Au Sable, Thunder Bay)
1872 Cass
1871 Black (Port Huron)

0 1 2 3 4 5 6 7 8 9 10 11 12 13 14 15
(millions of board feet)

Jefferson Carson   James Inglis & Sons   Sextus N. Wilcox

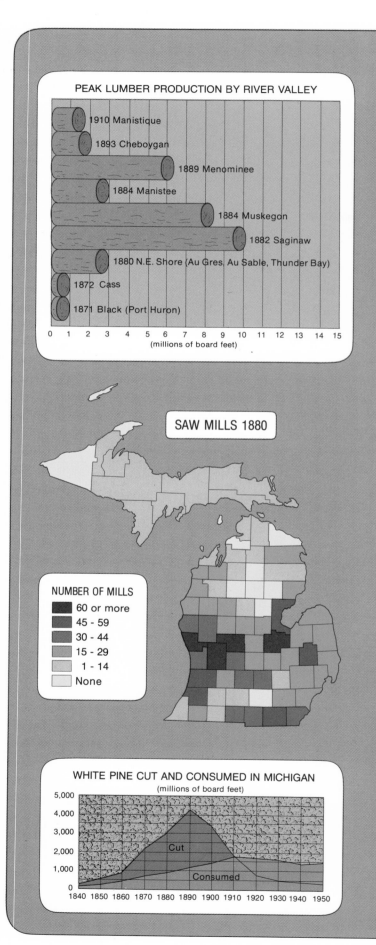

SAW MILLS 1880

NUMBER OF MILLS
- 60 or more
- 45 - 59
- 30 - 44
- 15 - 29
- 1 - 14
- None

Beginning with the first settlements in Michigan by white man, waterpowered mills sawed oak and maple for local use, but after 1840 the state became an exporter of pine. Loggers cut white and red pine in northern forests and hammered the owner's logmark—some are shown here—into the ends of each timber. Registered in county court-houses, the first logmarks were usually one or two simple initials, but latecomers introduced variations to avoid dupli-cation. In winter teamsters moved the logs by sleigh down icy roads to rollways on a riverbank a few miles away. During the spring flood rivermen rolled the logs into the water and drove them downstream to logbooms at rivermouth towns like Saginaw, Muskegon, Alpena, and Menominee. There the pine was sorted by logmark, sawed into lumber for each owner, and shipped by the lakes or by rail to Chicago and the almost treeless Midwestern prairies beyond. Pine logging became a year-round occupation after "big wheels" permitted horses to drag logs across snowless ground and narrow-gauge railroads replaced rivers when they were low in summer or iced over in winter. After 1910 Michigan became a net importer of lumber, but its pine and hardwood had helped to create a furniture industry in Grand Rapids, an auto industry in southeast Michigan, and a net-work of railroads, milltowns, and supply points across the north country.

Oliver Iron Mining Co.

Augustus Paddock

W.S. Prettyman

WHITE PINE CUT AND CONSUMED IN MICHIGAN
(millions of board feet)

5,000
4,000
3,000
2,000
1,000
0

Cut

Consumed

1840 1850 1860 1870 1880 1890 1900 1910 1920 1930 1940 1950

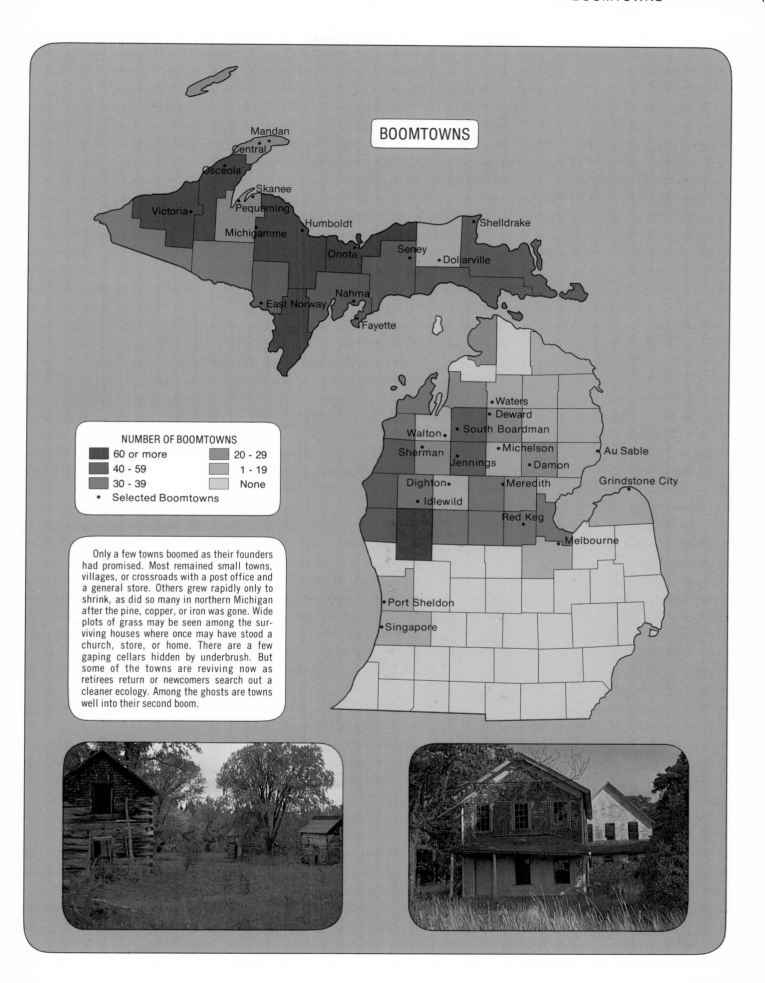

BOOMTOWNS

NUMBER OF BOOMTOWNS
- 60 or more
- 40 - 59
- 30 - 39
- 20 - 29
- 1 - 19
- None
- • Selected Boomtowns

Only a few towns boomed as their founders had promised. Most remained small towns, villages, or crossroads with a post office and a general store. Others grew rapidly only to shrink, as did so many in northern Michigan after the pine, copper, or iron was gone. Wide plots of grass may be seen among the surviving houses where once may have stood a church, store, or home. There are a few gaping cellars hidden by underbrush. But some of the towns are reviving now as retirees return or newcomers search out a cleaner ecology. Among the ghosts are towns well into their second boom.

Map labels (Upper Peninsula): Mandan, Central, Osceola, Skanee, Victoria, Pequaming, Michigamme, Humboldt, Shelldrake, Onota, Seney, Dollarville, East Norway, Nahma, Fayette

Map labels (Lower Peninsula): Waters, Deward, Walton, South Boardman, Sherman, Michelson, Au Sable, Jennings, Damon, Dighton, Meredith, Grindstone City, Idlewild, Red Keg, Melbourne, Port Sheldon, Singapore

*William Hull
1805 - 1813

*Lewis Cass
1813 - 1831

*George Porter
1831 - 1834

*Stevens Mason
1834 - 1840

William Woodbridge
1840 - 1841

John Barry
1842 - 1846
1850 - 1851

Alpheus Felch
1846 - 1847

Epaphroditus P
1848 - 185

*Territorial governor

George Romney
1963 - 1968

John Swainson
1961 - 1962

G. Mennen Williams
1949 - 1960

Kim Sigler
1947 - 1948

Harry Kelly
1943 - 1946

GOVERNORS OF MICHIGAN
1805 TO PRESENT

William Milliken
1969 -

Each Dot Denotes
Hometown of
a Governor

Murray Van Wagoner
1941 - 1942

Luren Dickinson
1939 - 1940

Frank Murphy
1937 - 1938

Frank Fitzgerald
1935 - 1936
1939 (Died)

William Comstock
1933 - 1934

Wilber Brucker
1931 - 1932

Fred Green
1927 - 1930

Alexander Groe
1921-1926

McClelland
61 - 1853

Andrew Parsons
1853 - 1854

Kinsley Bingham
1855 - 1858

Moses Wisner
1859 - 1860

Austin Blair
1861 - 1864

Henry Crapo
1865 - 1868

Henry Baldwin
1869 - 1872

John Bagley
1873 - 1876

Charles Croswell
1877 - 1880

David Jerome
1881 - 1882

Josiah Begole
1883 - 1884

Russell Alger
1885 - 1886

Cyrus Luce
1887 - 1890

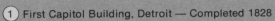

① First Capitol Building, Detroit — Completed 1828
② Second Capitol Building, Lansing — First Used 1848
③ Present Capitol Building, Lansing — Completed 1879

bert Sleeper
917 - 1920

Woodbridge Ferris
1913 - 1916

Chase Osborn
1911 - 1912

Fred Warner
1905 - 1910

Aaron Bliss
1901 - 1904

Hazen Pingree
1897 - 1900

John Rich
1893 - 1896

Edwin Winans
1891 - 1892

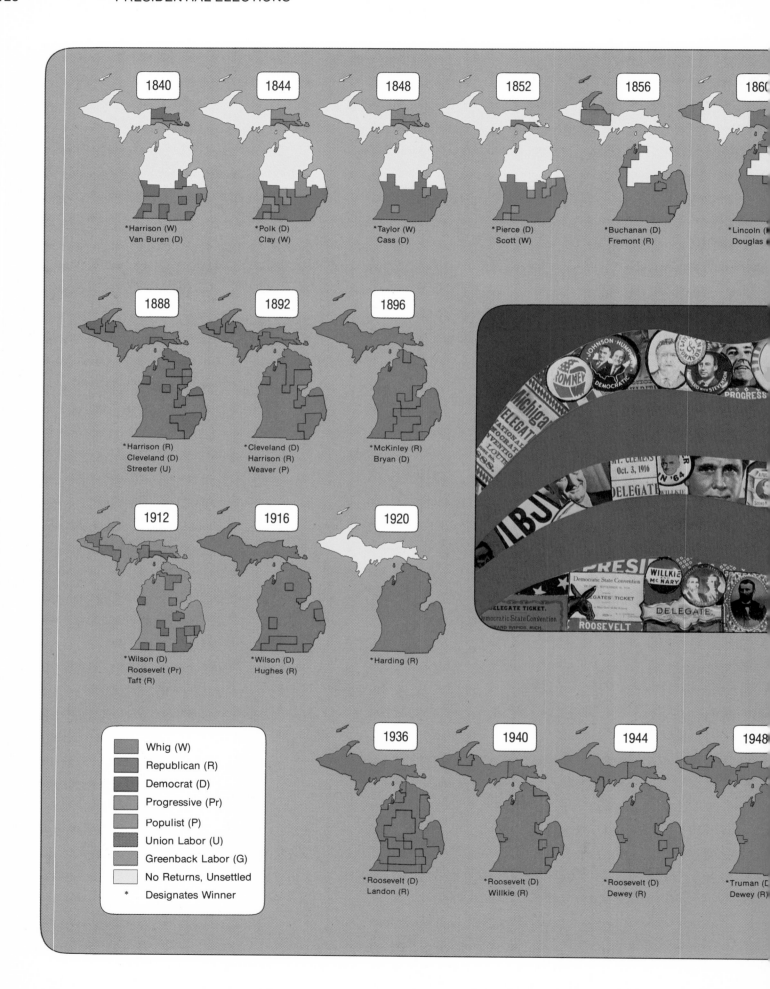

1840
*Harrison (W)
Van Buren (D)

1844
*Polk (D)
Clay (W)

1848
*Taylor (W)
Cass (D)

1852
*Pierce (D)
Scott (W)

1856
*Buchanan (D)
Fremont (R)

1860
*Lincoln (R)
Douglas

1888
*Harrison (R)
Cleveland (D)
Streeter (U)

1892
*Cleveland (D)
Harrison (R)
Weaver (P)

1896
*McKinley (R)
Bryan (D)

1912
*Wilson (D)
Roosevelt (Pr)
Taft (R)

1916
*Wilson (D)
Hughes (R)

1920
*Harding (R)

Whig (W)
Republican (R)
Democrat (D)
Progressive (Pr)
Populist (P)
Union Labor (U)
Greenback Labor (G)
No Returns, Unsettled
*   Designates Winner

1936
*Roosevelt (D)
Landon (R)

1940
*Roosevelt (D)
Willkie (R)

1944
*Roosevelt (D)
Dewey (R)

1948
*Truman (D)
Dewey (R)

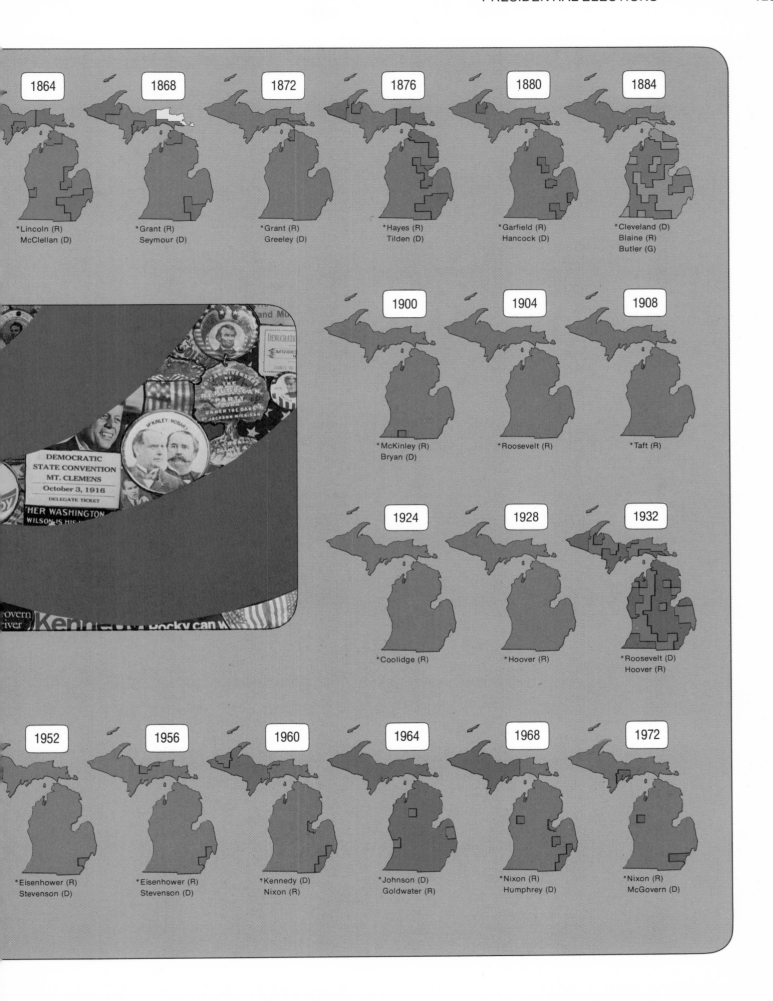

1864 | *Lincoln (R) / McClellan (D)

1868 | *Grant (R) / Seymour (D)

1872 | *Grant (R) / Greeley (D)

1876 | *Hayes (R) / Tilden (D)

1880 | *Garfield (R) / Hancock (D)

1884 | *Cleveland (D) / Blaine (R) / Butler (G)

1900 | *McKinley (R) / Bryan (D)

1904 | *Roosevelt (R)

1908 | *Taft (R)

1924 | *Coolidge (R)

1928 | *Hoover (R)

1932 | *Roosevelt (D) / Hoover (R)

1952 | *Eisenhower (R) / Stevenson (D)

1956 | *Eisenhower (R) / Stevenson (D)

1960 | *Kennedy (D) / Nixon (R)

1964 | *Johnson (D) / Goldwater (R)

1968 | *Nixon (R) / Humphrey (D)

1972 | *Nixon (R) / McGovern (D)

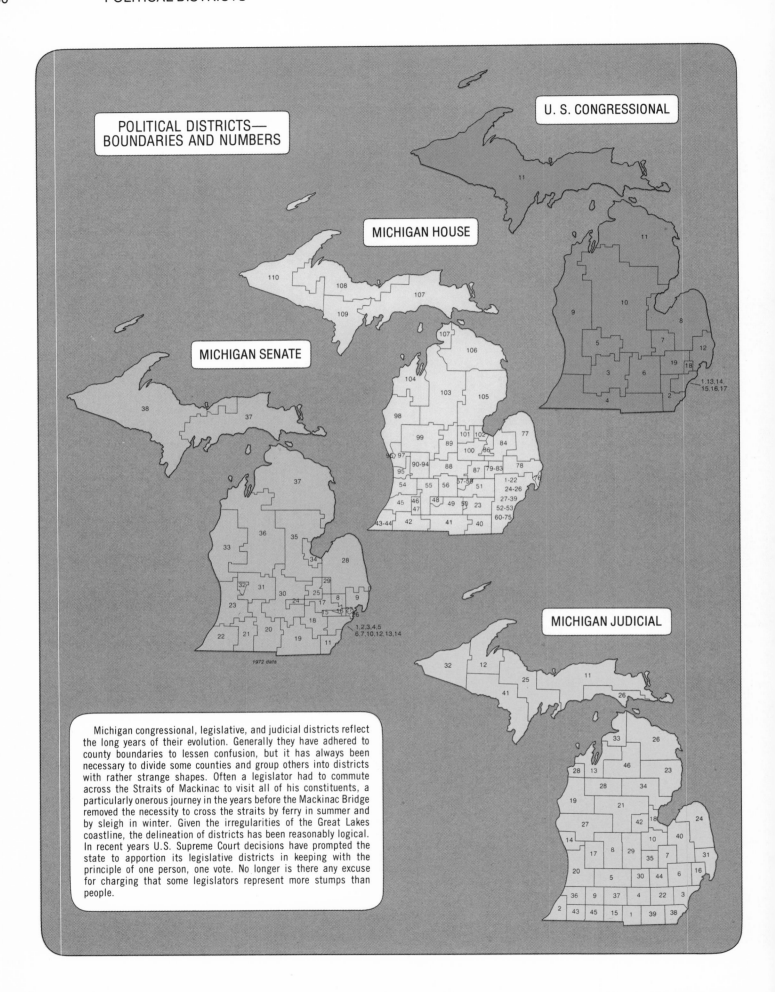

POLITICAL DISTRICTS—
BOUNDARIES AND NUMBERS

U. S. CONGRESSIONAL

MICHIGAN HOUSE

MICHIGAN SENATE

MICHIGAN JUDICIAL

1972 data

Michigan congressional, legislative, and judicial districts reflect the long years of their evolution. Generally they have adhered to county boundaries to lessen confusion, but it has always been necessary to divide some counties and group others into districts with rather strange shapes. Often a legislator had to commute across the Straits of Mackinac to visit all of his constituents, a particularly onerous journey in the years before the Mackinac Bridge removed the necessity to cross the straits by ferry in summer and by sleigh in winter. Given the irregularities of the Great Lakes coastline, the delineation of districts has been reasonably logical. In recent years U.S. Supreme Court decisions have prompted the state to apportion its legislative districts in keeping with the principle of one person, one vote. No longer is there any excuse for charging that some legislators represent more stumps than people.

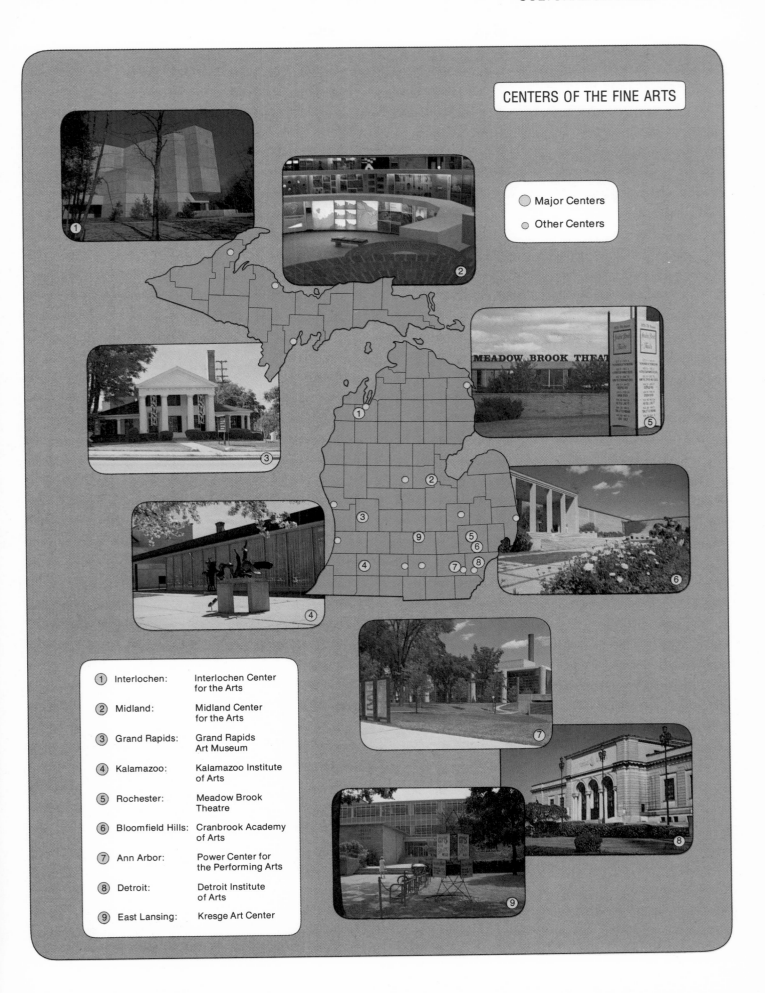

CENTERS OF THE FINE ARTS

⬤ Major Centers
◦ Other Centers

① Interlochen: Interlochen Center
                    for the Arts

② Midland: Midland Center
                    for the Arts

③ Grand Rapids: Grand Rapids
                    Art Museum

④ Kalamazoo: Kalamazoo Institute
                    of Arts

⑤ Rochester: Meadow Brook
                    Theatre

⑥ Bloomfield Hills: Cranbrook Academy
                    of Arts

⑦ Ann Arbor: Power Center for
                    the Performing Arts

⑧ Detroit: Detroit Institute
                    of Arts

⑨ East Lansing: Kresge Art Center

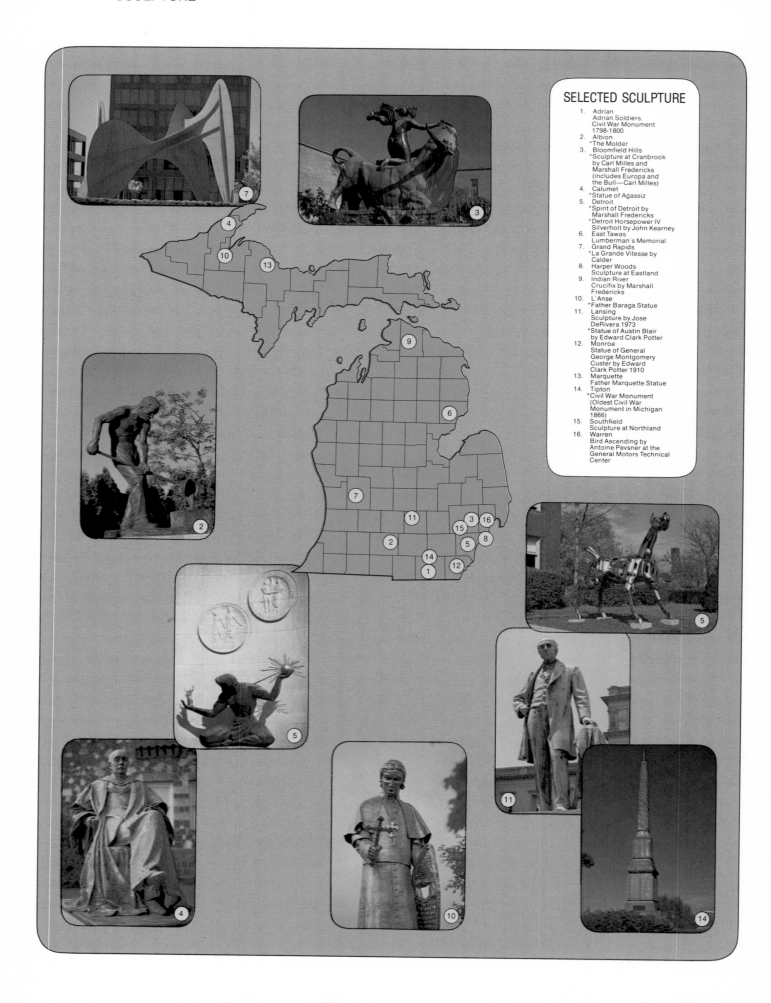

SELECTED SCULPTURE

1. Adrian
   Adrian Soldiers,
   Civil War Monument
   1798-1800
2. Albion
   *The Molder
3. Bloomfield Hills
   *Sculpture at Cranbrook
   by Carl Milles and
   Marshall Fredericks
   (includes Europa and
   the Bull—Carl Milles)
4. Calumet
   *Statue of Agassiz
5. Detroit
   *Spirit of Detroit by
   Marshall Fredericks
   *Detroit Horsepower IV
   Silverholt by John Kearney
6. East Tawas
   Lumberman's Memorial
7. Grand Rapids
   *La Grande Vitesse by
   Calder
8. Harper Woods
   Sculpture at Eastland
9. Indian River
   Crucifix by Marshall
   Fredericks
10. L'Anse
   *Father Baraga Statue
11. Lansing
   Sculpture by Jose
   DeRivera 1973
   *Statue of Austin Blair
   by Edward Clark Potter
12. Monroe
   Statue of General
   George Montgomery
   Custer by Edward
   Clark Potter 1910
13. Marquette
   Father Marquette Statue
14. Tipton
   *Civil War Monument
   (Oldest Civil War
   Monument in Michigan
   1866)
15. Southfield
   Sculpture at Northland
16. Warren
   Bird Ascending by
   Antoine Pevsner at the
   General Motors Technical
   Center

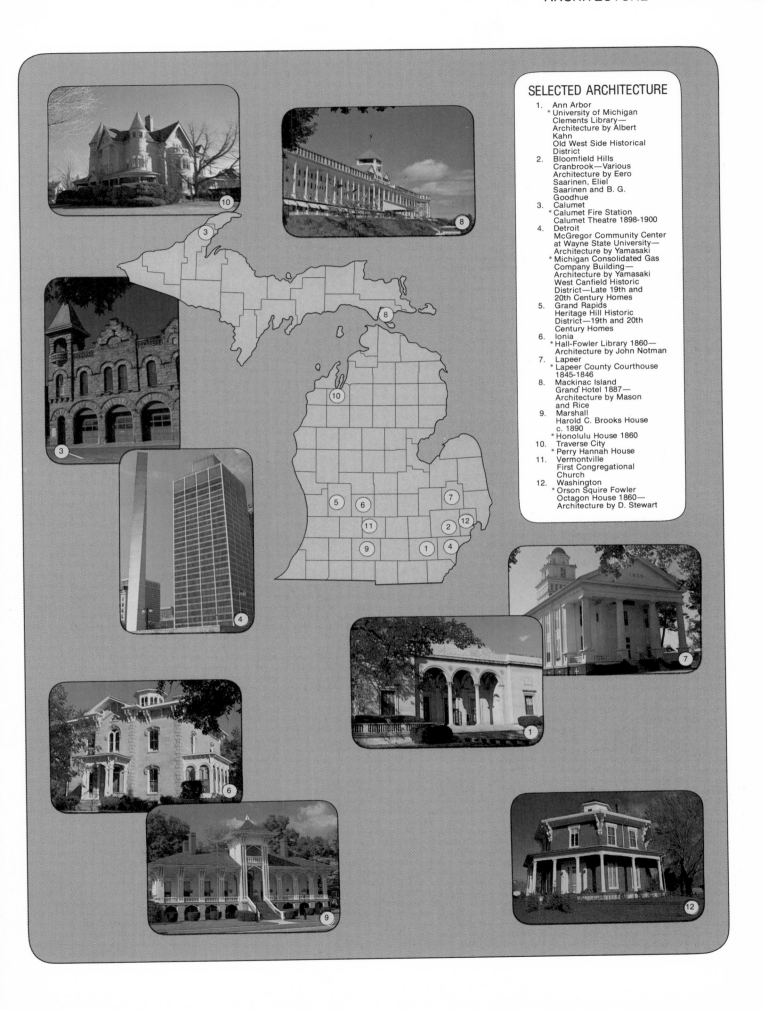

SELECTED ARCHITECTURE

1. Ann Arbor
   * University of Michigan Clements Library—Architecture by Albert Kahn
   Old West Side Historical District
2. Bloomfield Hills
   Cranbrook—Various Architecture by Eero Saarinen, Eliel Saarinen and B. G. Goodhue
3. Calumet
   * Calumet Fire Station
   Calumet Theatre 1898-1900
4. Detroit
   McGregor Community Center at Wayne State University—Architecture by Yamasaki
   * Michigan Consolidated Gas Company Building—Architecture by Yamasaki
   West Canfield Historic District—Late 19th and 20th Century Homes
5. Grand Rapids
   Heritage Hill Historic District—19th and 20th Century Homes
6. Ionia
   * Hall-Fowler Library 1860—Architecture by John Notman
7. Lapeer
   * Lapeer County Courthouse 1845-1846
8. Mackinac Island
   Grand Hotel 1887—Architecture by Mason and Rice
9. Marshall
   Harold C. Brooks House c. 1890
   * Honolulu House 1860
10. Traverse City
    * Perry Hannah House
11. Vermontville
    First Congregational Church
12. Washington
    * Orson Squire Fowler Octagon House 1860—Architecture by D. Stewart

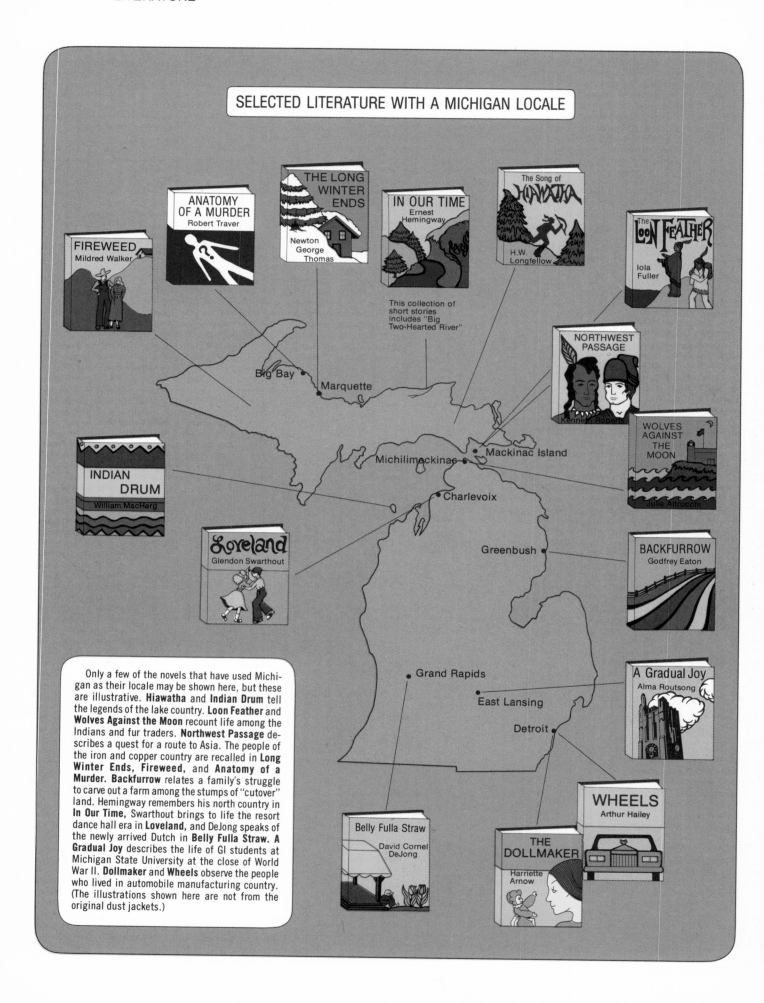

SELECTED LITERATURE WITH A MICHIGAN LOCALE

FIREWEED
Mildred Walker

ANATOMY
OF A MURDER
Robert Traver

THE LONG
WINTER
ENDS
Newton George Thomas

IN OUR TIME
Ernest Hemingway

This collection of short stories includes "Big Two-Hearted River"

The Song of
HIAWATHA
H.W. Longfellow

The LOON FEATHER
Iola Fuller

NORTHWEST PASSAGE
Kenneth Roberts

INDIAN DRUM
William MacHarg

WOLVES AGAINST THE MOON
Julia Altrocchi

Loveland
Glendon Swarthout

BACKFURROW
Godfrey Eaton

A Gradual Joy
Alma Routsong

WHEELS
Arthur Hailey

Belly Fulla Straw
David Cornel DeJong

THE DOLLMAKER
Harriette Arnow

Big Bay
Marquette
Michilimackinac
Mackinac Island
Charlevoix
Greenbush
Grand Rapids
East Lansing
Detroit

Only a few of the novels that have used Michigan as their locale may be shown here, but these are illustrative. **Hiawatha** and **Indian Drum** tell the legends of the lake country. **Loon Feather** and **Wolves Against the Moon** recount life among the Indians and fur traders. **Northwest Passage** describes a quest for a route to Asia. The people of the iron and copper country are recalled in **Long Winter Ends, Fireweed,** and **Anatomy of a Murder. Backfurrow** relates a family's struggle to carve out a farm among the stumps of "cutover" land. Hemingway remembers his north country in **In Our Time,** Swarthout brings to life the resort dance hall era in **Loveland,** and DeJong speaks of the newly arrived Dutch in **Belly Fulla Straw. A Gradual Joy** describes the life of GI students at Michigan State University at the close of World War II. **Dollmaker** and **Wheels** observe the people who lived in automobile manufacturing country. (The illustrations shown here are not from the original dust jackets.)

ECONOMY

Michigan, one of the leading industrial states in the United States, has many assets for economic development. Its central location on the Great Lakes and in the Midwest provides transportation and trade advantages. Its diverse natural resources include iron ore, petroleum, natural gas, fertile soil, abundant water, and forests. Most important, however, is its heterogeneous population with a comparatively high level of education and trade skills that provides the labor supply and managerial ability for the state's variety of industries. Michigan's people have pioneered in a number of economic enterprises, notably the automotive industry that now dominates the state's economy and makes Michigan the national leader in automobile production. Headquarters for the major vehicle companies are centered in Detroit and vicinity, and this area sets the trend for the future development of the industry throughout the country and world.

Michigan can be ranked in comparison with the other 49 states to give an idea of its significance in the nation and also to indicate the diversity of the state's economy. Some of these rankings are shown on the following page. Manufacturing, recreation and tourism, and agriculture are the three leaders in value of goods produced.

Change in the Twentieth Century

The economy of Michigan has changed radically in the current century. In 1900 agriculture and forestry/ lumbering were the leading sectors of the economy, and the processing of forest and agricultural products was the major manufacturing activity. The period of dominance by manufacturing in Michigan really began with the introduction of the automobile and numerous other kinds of mechanical products. Since 1900 rapid changes in Michigan's economy have been brought about by a large increase in the growth of the total population, especially in the cities of the southern third of the state; an increased demand for various products as well as a growing labor supply; a marked improvement in transportation systems, particularly the all-weather highway network; the influx of numerous skilled and unskilled migrants from Europe, Latin America, and the southern states of the United States (primarily blacks); the availability of new and enlarged power sources—petroleum, natural gas, and hydro and thermal electricity; and the increased availability of capital to invest in manufacturing enterprises.

As a net result of these changes, manufacturing has emerged as the major source of employment, the prin-

cipal user of raw materials, the most important contributor to the value added to Michigan products, and the dominant force in the total economy of the state. Michigan's growing urban population and residents of heavily industrial nearby states and of Ontario, Canada have made increasingly greater use of the state's numerous recreational assets. A significant tourism industry has thus developed. Agriculture has also benefited from population growth and has expanded and mechanized greatly. More recently, service industries and professional and government employment have grown rapidly and now play a major role in the state's economy.

Another change has been the rapid development of labor unions since 1930. First developed in large numbers in assembly-line manufacturing, they have spread to most branches of the labor force, including professional groups such as teachers. Total membership in 121 unions in the state was nearly 1.4 million in 1974. Another 126,000 people are members in 61 employee associations. The United Auto Workers Union, with more than a half million members, is by far the leading labor organization, reflecting the importance of vehicle manufacturing in the state. The union movement is strongest in the highly urbanized and industrialized southeastern part of the state.

Major Bases of Michigan's Economy

Michigan has always possessed a number of advantages for the development of its economy. The degree of significance of any given factor has varied over time. The natural resources of soil and forests were most significant when agriculture and lumbering dominated the state's industries. As manufacturing became more significant, the labor force and power resources became the most important assets. A skilled labor supply is even more critical in the present postindustrial period because the professions, services, and government have begun to dominate employment.

Michigan's 3.5 million laborers represent a variety of ethnic backgrounds and abilities. During the early twentieth century large numbers of Europeans migrated to the state and brought diverse skills. Some now dominate the labor supply of certain regions, such as the Poles in Hamtramck, the Finns in the Upper Peninsula, and the Dutch in Grand Rapids and Holland. Southern blacks were first attracted to Michigan by the jobs that mass production in the automobile factories provided between 1920 and 1940 and then by the work available in plants manufacturing war materials from 1940 to 1945. Blacks now are a major component of Detroit's labor supply, especially for the vehicle industry. Between 1920 and 1970 many itinerant agricultural laborers from Mexico, Cuba, and Puerto Rico entered the state to work in the labor-intensive fruit and vegetable regions. Scientific, professional, and managerial personnel have been drawn to the state from all over the country and world. In 1970 Michigan employed about 4 percent of those possessing the doctorate degree in the United States. Thus, in total, the skilled and unskilled manpower of Michigan is its economy's greatest asset.

Michigan's central location both in the eastern Midwest and on the Great Lakes is a second asset to its economy. Transportation on Lakes Michigan, Superior, Huron, and Erie and the connecting waterways has greatly facilitated cheap movement of both manufactured products and heavy raw materials such as iron ore, coal, petroleum, and limestone for the industrial areas of the state. A large volume of easily accessible fresh water is a boon to many communities and is the basis for a major part of the state's recreation as well as for limited commercial fishing. Since the opening of the Saint Lawrence Seaway in 1959, Michigan has had direct access to all foreign ports of the world. Michigan's location also makes easily available the markets of the large urban population centers of the Midwest and Northeast. In addition to water links, excellent highway, railway, and air networks connect Michigan with raw materials as well as with markets for finished products.

Much of the state's energy needs must be fulfilled by importing resources from other states or countries, but Michigan does possess petroleum and natural gas fields and develops considerable amounts of hydro and thermal electric power within its borders. An embryonic nuclear power industry is being developed with ten operating and planned units scattered in various parts of the state. With 3,700 wells producing 24 million barrels of petroleum, Michigan ranks seventeenth in the United States and supplies 5 percent of its needs for both petroleum and natural gas. Major production areas are scattered in the southern, central, and northern portions of the Lower Peninsula. Michigan currently has the largest oil boom in the United States outside of Alaska's North Slope. The Niagaran reef formation of the northern Lower Peninsula, estimated to hold 500 to 600 million barrels of reserves, is being extensively explored. Negligible amounts of Michigan's coal are being mined because of its poor quality, and high costs prohibit the mining of the state's large quantities of oil shale.

Other minerals are of consequence for the state's economy. Michigan produced about 15 million long tons of iron ore in the western Upper Peninsula in 1975. It is a low-quality ore that must be concentrated before shipment south from Marquette and Escanaba, largely by lake carriers. Copper mining has caused boom and bust periods in the Keweenaw Peninsula. After a number of poor years that left desolate many areas of that part of the state, new refining and mining processes now show promise. At Rogers City and Petoskey, limestone is quarried for use as a flux material in the iron and steel industry. Vast salt beds along both shores of the Lower Peninsula provide an important raw material for the state's chemical industry and provide table and road salt as well.

Manufacturing

Michigan produced $66.2 billion of the $1,397.4 billion total U.S. gross national product in 1974. Manufacturing is a dominant sector of Michigan's economy, and value added by manufacture accounts for nearly 40 percent of the gross state product.

Transport equipment, primarily automobiles and trucks, produces more than half of the value of Michigan manufactured products. Automobile assembly plants are concentrated in Detroit and vicinity, but automobiles and trucks are also produced in Pontiac, Flint, Lansing, and Kalamazoo. The next most important manufacturing category is the production of machinery, including electric machinery, which accounts for about one-fifth of the goods produced. Some of this manufacturing is also related to the vehicle industry, but a wide variety of machines is produced. Factories making machines are also concentrated in the greater Detroit area, with secondary concentrations in the other cities of the southern third of the state.

The next category in importance, primary and fabricated metal industries, is closely related to the first two and is often found in association with the automotive industry. A good example is the Ford Motor Company's integrated industrial complex at River Rouge, where iron ore is converted to iron and steel products that in turn become parts used in the automobile assembly plant—all taking place in the River Rouge area.

Production of chemicals and allied products, located in salt- and brine-producing areas such as Midland – Saginaw – Bay City, Muskegon, and around Detroit, accounts for about 5 percent of the manufactured goods in Michigan. Chemicals are also produced as by-products of petroleum refining and iron and steel manufacturing. The latter relationship helps concentrate this industry in the southeast.

Three other categories account for about 1.5 to 2 percent each of the value of products by industry groups, namely, food and kindred products, apparel and related products, and lumber and wood products. The locations of these industries are widespread but have some relation to the distribution of the raw material sources or market areas. Some industries are concentrated in one regional center, such as furniture in Grand Rapids, paper in Kalamazoo, breakfast cereals in Battle Creek, and baby food in Fremont.

Recreation and Tourism

This rapidly growing sector has replaced agriculture in second place in the state's economy. Public and private recreational facilities and establishments are widespread throughout the state. In some counties, particularly in the northern Lower Peninsula and the Upper Peninsula, the recreation and tourist industry is the leading source of employment and income. The outdoor recreational assets of Michigan are considerable both in summer and winter. Lakes, including the Great Lakes, and hills are widely distributed throughout the state as a result of continental glaciation. Forests and streams are also plentiful. Michigan's excellent highway system is a major factor in making recreation areas accessible to the large urban populations. Recreation and tourism are so important to Michigan that they are covered in a separate section of this atlas.

Agriculture

Even though the relative significance of agriculture has steadily declined during the current century, farming is still important in most Michigan counties. The total land in farms peaked at 18.5 million acres (7.4 million hectares) in 1935 and had declined to 12.3 million (4.92 million hectares) by 1975. Farm population as a percentage of the total population was 22.8 in 1920, compared to only 3.4 in 1970. Agriculture produces 4 percent of the value of Michigan's goods, and farm employment accounts for only 1.5 percent of the state's total employment.

The agriculture of Michigan varies from intensive, highly productive types, such as the navy bean production in the Saginaw Valley, to marginal farming in the infertile, sandy regions of northern Michigan. The best agricultural areas, as is true in manufacturing, are found south of the Muskegon–Bay City line, where soil, topographic, and growing-season conditions are all more favorable. This area also includes the urban population centers that are the major markets for farm produce.

Dairying, with corn, grain, and hay as crops, is the dominant farming type in Michigan. It is best developed in the interior parts of the southern Lower Peninsula but is found throughout the state. The lower summer temperatures and shorter growing season in northern Michigan are less favorable for corn, but hybrid varieties that mature in fewer days allow this crop to be grown in northern areas that have appropriate slope and soil conditions.

Specialized crops are a feature of many parts of Michigan and help greatly in raising the value of the state's farming. Fruit—particularly cherries, peaches, apples, plums, and blueberries—is grown just inland from Lake Michigan from Berrien County to Grand Traverse Bay. Here the colder temperatures that are due to the water temperatures of Lake Michigan retard the blooming of the trees in the spring until frost is unlikely, and the warming influence of lake water in the fall lengthens the growing season and lessens the danger of early killing frosts. The predominantly sandy soil also promotes fruit growth. Another crop specialization is the navy bean production on the fertile, flat, lake-bottom soils of the Saginaw Valley. Michigan leads the nation in the growing of dry edible beans. Potatoes are a major crop on the sandy, loam soils of Montcalm County. Large amounts of vegetables are produced on the muck soils scattered throughout Michigan in poorly drained areas left behind by glaciation. Excess water is drawn off these areas by drainage ditches and tiles.

In general, Michigan's agricultural patterns are not as consistent as those in the corn-belt prairie states. The state, nevertheless, ranks tenth in the nation in harvested acres of principal crops. Some of the recent trends in Michigan agriculture are a decrease in number of farms (26 percent from 1963 to 1973), a sharp increase in yields, much larger farms, less land in farms, fewer farms and farmers, more part-time and corporate farmers, greater mechanization, more use of fertilizer, increased specialization, better-educated farmers, and in general a much more scientific basis of operation.

Land-Use Patterns and Trends

Trends in land use in Michigan are evident from the table in the margin: urban land is increasing, farm land is decreasing rapidly, and forest and recreation land is increasing. The current major land-use patterns are closely related to the dominant economic activities in various parts of Michigan. Urban land is found primarily in the southern third of the state, particularly in the southeast. Future change to urban land uses will also occur largely in this area. It is estimated that an average of 50,000 acres (20,000 hectares) of rural land per year are converted to urban and suburban land in Michigan. The major intensive agricultural areas are also found south of the Muskegon–Bay City line. Land in farms varies from more than 81 percent in Huron County to about 7 percent in Houghton County. Forest and recreation lands are located primarily in the northern Lower Peninsula and the Upper Peninsula. The fastest change from agriculture to other uses is in these areas, most of it being converted to forest and recreation land.

Services, the Professions, and Government

Michigan is typical of the rest of the United States in terms of the growing importance of government, the professions, and other services to its economy, a trend characteristic of postindustrial societies. In Michigan nearly half of those employed are in these service categories. The proportion of employment in services and government has grown steadily since 1910 and even more rapidly since 1960. More than a half million people are now employed in federal, state, and local government in Michigan.

The relative importance of services and government is directly related to the total numbers of people in various parts of the state. Sales tax collection figures are one indicator of where the service industries and government employment are concentrated. About 48 percent of the state sales tax revenue is collected in Macomb, Oakland, and Wayne counties, which is consistent with the fact that 45 percent of the state's total population resides in these counties. Government is the leading employer in such cities as Ann Arbor, Lansing, and Detroit. Being the seat of state government, Ingham County has a striking number of government employees, as does Washtenaw County because of the dominance of the University of Michigan and its related medical complexes.

Service sectors are particularly important in the nonmanufacturing and sparsely populated areas of the northern Lower Peninsula and the Upper Peninsula. Military employment is also concentrated in the less-developed parts of the state. The Sawyer (Marquette County), Kincheloe (Chippewa), and Wurtsmith (Iosco) Air Force bases are dominant factors in the total employment and economy of their respective counties. Thus there is great concern in these areas when phasing out a particular air base is proposed as an economy move by the federal government.

The professional/managerial category includes government and university employees. Washtenaw County, with 33.8 percent of its labor force in this category, leads the state largely as a result of the University of Michigan and the related professions. Midland County, the home of Dow Chemical Company, also has about a third of its employed in this classification. In the Detroit area Oakland County leads with 31.0 percent, because many of the professionals and managers employed in government, industry, and education in the city of Detroit reside in this county.

Economic Regionalization

Southern Michigan. The intensity and total volume of economic development reach a maximum in Wayne, Oakland, and Macomb counties and decrease generally westward and northward. Exceptions to this trend are other major urban areas. The Detroit area has a diversity of industry, wholesale and retail trade, and government and service activities. The transportation industry, especially the manufacturing of automobiles and related parts, dominates

MAJOR CATEGORIES OF LAND USE
IN MICHIGAN (PERCENTAGES)

	1960	1970	1985 (projected)
Urban and suburban land	4.3	6.3	8.2
Farm land	40.5	32.6	24.7
Forest and recreation land	49.3	54.8	66.6
Other rural land	5.6	6.3	5.5

southeast Michigan economically. The headquarters of General Motors, Chrysler, and American Motors are in Detroit, and Ford's is in Dearborn. Basic iron and steel industries, petroleum refineries, chemical industries, a variety of machinery making, and food processing are also of major importance in the Detroit area. Detroit's domination of Michigan's population, labor, capital, and markets results in the concentrated industrial development there.

Secondary economic nodes are (1) Grand Rapids–Holland–Muskegon, (2) Kalamazoo–Battle Creek, (3) Lansing–Jackson–Flint, and (4) Bay City–Saginaw–Midland. Each of these centers has specializations—for example, chemicals in Midland, automobiles in Lansing and Flint, and furniture in Grand Rapids. Numerous smaller cities add to the concentration of manufacturing (especially the making of vehicle parts), trade, and service south of the Muskegon–Bay City line. This area also has the most intensive agriculture (dairy, cash grains, and horticultural crops) and the best-developed air, road, and railway transportation network. The southern third of Michigan thus stands out in terms of economic importance and compares favorably with other intensely developed regions both nearby in the Midwest and in other parts of the country.

Central and Northern Lower Peninsula. Economic intensity declines very rapidly north of the Muskegon–Bay City line. Recreation and other service industries dominate the economic activity of this part of Michigan. Some general agriculture is scattered throughout the area, and specialized fruit farming is located in the Traverse City and Hart–Shelby areas. Petroleum and natural gas are locally important, and forests provide the base for some wood processing and manufacturing industry. Because of the lakes, rivers, forests, and rugged glacial topography, recreation and its related service industries supply much of the income of the population of the area.

Upper Peninsula. The Upper Peninsula is a marginal part of the state economically. Mining, forestry, and recreation are the major bases of the scattered industrial and urban development. Iron mining dominates the economic activity of the western Upper Peninsula, and forestry, recreation, and limited agriculture dominate in the east. The Soo Locks, the bridge to Canada, and the Mackinac Bridge are economically important as links in the transportation system and as tourist attractions. The Tahquamenon Falls north of Newberry and Mackinac Island are also significant to the Upper Peninsula's recreation industry.

In total, Michigan's economy is diverse but highly dependent upon the automotive and related industries. The severe impact on the state by the economic recession with resulting low sales of automobiles in the early to mid 1970s illustrates this dependence. As the postindustrial period evolves, it is likely that Michigan's economic dependence on the automotive industry will decrease and that retail, government, and recreation activities will increase.

Lawrence M. Sommers

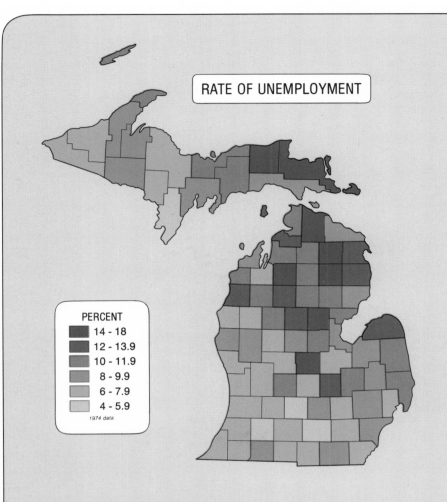

RATE OF UNEMPLOYMENT

PERCENT
14 - 18
12 - 13.9
10 - 11.9
8 - 9.9
6 - 7.9
4 - 5.9

1974 data

Michigan's labor force is engaged in a variety of occupations ranging from agriculture, forestry, mining, fishing, and manufacturing to recreation, transportation, and government services. The employment and unemployment levels at the county level reflect expanding economic conditions as well as recession periods at both the state and national levels.

The unemployment rate is a measure of the number of people looking for work. In 1974 Michigan had an average annual unemployment rate of 8.5 percent, but there was substantial variation in the unemployment levels among counties. The highest rates were mostly in the Upper Peninsula and the northern Lower Peninsula: Cheboygan County had a rate of 18 percent, followed by Chippewa, Montmorency, and Oscoda counties with 17 percent, and Gladwin and Kalkaska counties with 16 percent. On the other hand, the lowest percentages were in the urban counties in the southwest and south central parts of the state and in selected counties in the western Upper Peninsula whose economies are based on mining. In Menominee County the unemployment rate was 5 percent, followed by Clinton, Dickinson, Eaton, Gogebic, Jackson, and Kalamazoo counties with 6 percent. Wayne County (Detroit) had a 10 percent figure, which indicates a poor year in the automobile industry.

Unemployment varies from county to county and from year to year. From 1956 to 1975 the number of people in the civilian labor force gradually increased, largely because of the population increase in Michigan. The unemployment level was highest during the national recession years of 1958, 1961, and 1975. For the most part, the number of unemployed has remained relatively constant even as more workers have been added to the state's labor force.

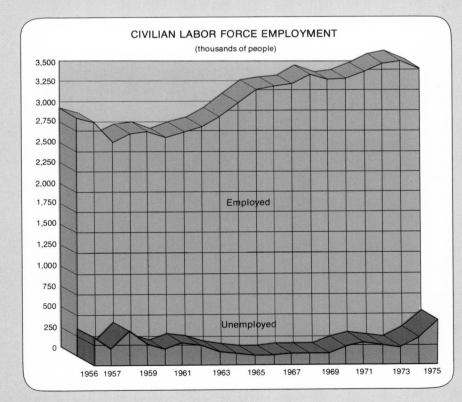

CIVILIAN LABOR FORCE EMPLOYMENT

(thousands of people)

3,500
3,250
3,000
2,750
2,500
2,250
2,000
1,750
1,500
1,250
1,000
750
500
250
0

Employed

Unemployed

1956 1957   1959   1961   1963   1965   1967   1969   1971   1973   1975

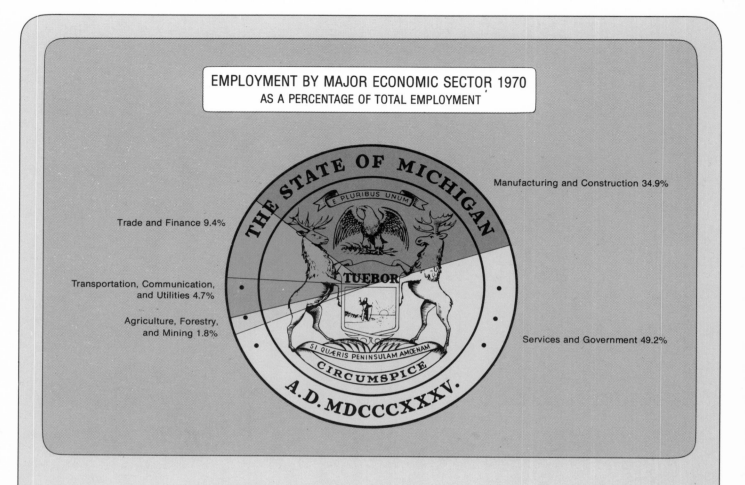

EMPLOYMENT BY MAJOR ECONOMIC SECTOR 1970
AS A PERCENTAGE OF TOTAL EMPLOYMENT

Trade and Finance 9.4%

Manufacturing and Construction 34.9%

Transportation, Communication, and Utilities 4.7%

Agriculture, Forestry, and Mining 1.8%

Services and Government 49.2%

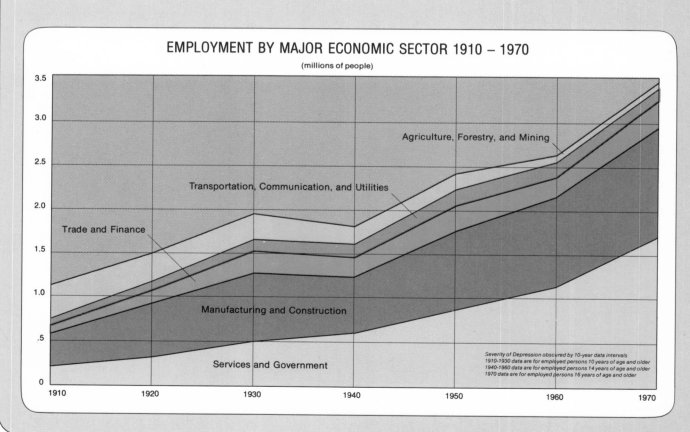

EMPLOYMENT BY MAJOR ECONOMIC SECTOR 1910 – 1970
(millions of people)

Agriculture, Forestry, and Mining

Transportation, Communication, and Utilities

Trade and Finance

Manufacturing and Construction

Services and Government

Severity of Depression obscured by 10-year data intervals
1910-1930 data are for employed persons 10 years of age and older
1940-1960 data are for employed persons 14 years of age and older
1970 data are for employed persons 16 years of age and older

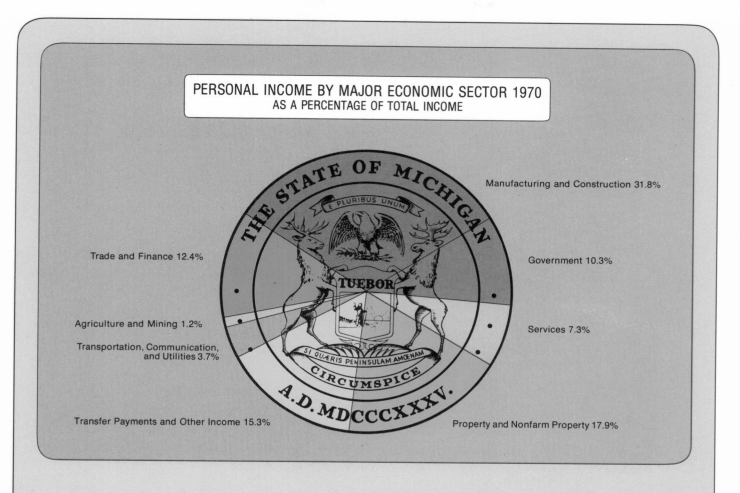

PERSONAL INCOME BY MAJOR ECONOMIC SECTOR 1970
AS A PERCENTAGE OF TOTAL INCOME

Manufacturing and Construction 31.8%

Trade and Finance 12.4%

Government 10.3%

Agriculture and Mining 1.2%

Services 7.3%

Transportation, Communication, and Utilities 3.7%

Transfer Payments and Other Income 15.3%

Property and Nonfarm Property 17.9%

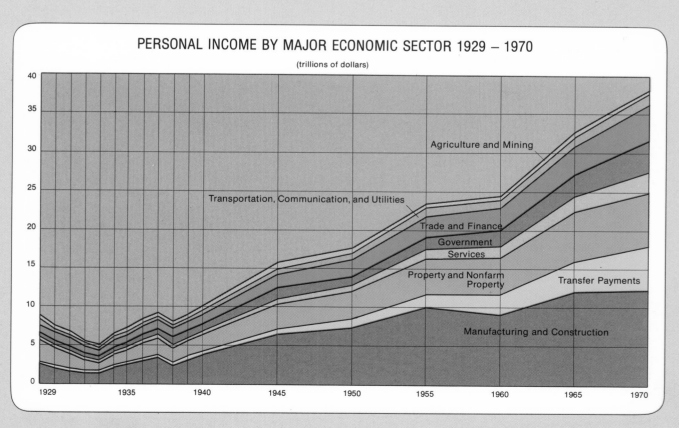

PERSONAL INCOME BY MAJOR ECONOMIC SECTOR 1929 – 1970
(trillions of dollars)

Agriculture and Mining

Transportation, Communication, and Utilities

Trade and Finance

Government

Services

Property and Nonfarm Property

Transfer Payments

Manufacturing and Construction

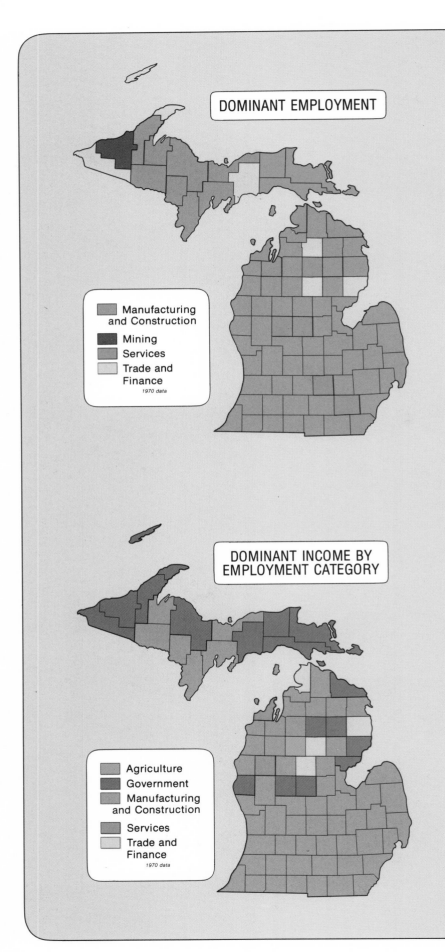

DOMINANT EMPLOYMENT

Manufacturing and Construction
Mining
Services
Trade and Finance
1970 data

DOMINANT INCOME BY EMPLOYMENT CATEGORY

Agriculture
Government
Manufacturing and Construction
Services
Trade and Finance
1970 data

The relative importance of the dominant economic activities within the state's 83 counties can be indicated by evaluating them in terms of the number of people they employ and the amount of income they produce. In 1970, 63 Michigan counties had more workers in the manufacturing and construction employment category than in the mining, services (including government), trade and finance, or agriculture categories. These counties were primarily in the Lower Peninsula and had large urban and suburban populations. Manufacturing plants produce a variety of industrial items in the Lower Peninsula's small towns as well as in the larger cities. Mining is the dominant employment category only in the Upper Peninsula's Ontonagon County. Services, which include government, education, tourism, and recreation, are dominant in counties around Traverse City and the Mackinac Bridge and in counties having universities, such as Washtenaw, Ingham, and Isabella. Ingham County with the state capital complexes also employs thousands of people in various services. Trade and finance and wholesale and retail trade employ the most people in scattered counties where regional shopping centers cater to the needs of local residents.

The significance of manufacturing and construction is further evident by mapping the dominant income by employment. In 1970 the dominant income in 59 of the 83 counties, mostly south of the Bay City–to–Muskegon line, was for employees in manufacturing and construction. North of this line the income categories were mixed. In 15 counties, particularly in the Upper Peninsula, the dominant income was in the government category. Such income includes not only revenue from federal, state, and local sources but also social security benefits and unemployment compensation. Agriculture was the most important source of income only in Missaukee County. Trade and finance were dominant in scattered rural and sparsely populated counties.

Military installations and facilities are dispersed throughout the state. They include nearly 60 Coast Guard units (lighthouses, cutters, and stations), air force bases, an army tank command in Detroit, a naval air facility in Mt. Clemens, 61 National Guard armories, and various Reserve Officers Training Corps units on Michigan college and university campuses.

According to 1975 data, most military personnel work at the four air force bases, namely Sawyer (3,502), Wurtsmith (2,751), Kincheloe (2,684), and Selfridge (175). There are 280 employed at the tank command center and 272 at the naval air facility. The numerous Coast Guard units, often several at the same location, are stationed along Lakes Huron, Michigan, and Superior to assist commercial and recreational users of the Great Lakes. National Guard armories are distributed roughly in proportion to the state's population density, with the largest number in the Lower Peninsula. Army ROTC units are at Michigan State University; Central, Eastern, and Western Michigan universities; the University of Michigan; Michigan Technological University; Lake Superior State College; and the University of Detroit. The University of Michigan campus also has a navy ROTC unit and an air force unit, and Michigan State and Michigan Technological universities each have air force commands.

Local, state, and federal government is one of the most rapidly increasing categories of employment. It includes people in various civil service offices, legislators and assistants, park employees, university professors and administrators, highway engineers, planners, foresters, and hospital employees. The sizable supporting staffs (secretaries and clerks) are also part of the government labor force. In 1972 the percentage of workers employed in government ranged from 9 percent in Cass, Kent, and Monroe counties to 46 percent in Luce County. The highest percentages were in counties with several state complexes such as the capital, universities, hospitals, and various governmental facilities and offices. The fewest government workers on a relative basis were found in counties with a dominant manufacturing and construction or agricultural base. In Wayne County (Detroit) 13 percent of the population was employed in government services.

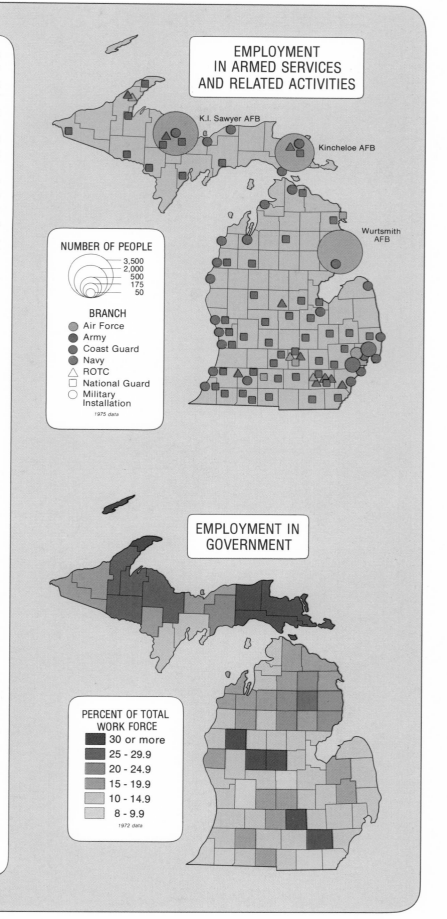

EMPLOYMENT
IN ARMED SERVICES
AND RELATED ACTIVITIES

K.I. Sawyer AFB

Kincheloe AFB

Wurtsmith AFB

NUMBER OF PEOPLE

3,500
2,000
500
175
50

BRANCH
Air Force
Army
Coast Guard
Navy
△ ROTC
☐ National Guard
○ Military Installation

1975 data

EMPLOYMENT IN
GOVERNMENT

PERCENT OF TOTAL
WORK FORCE
30 or more
25 - 29.9
20 - 24.9
15 - 19.9
10 - 14.9
8 - 9.9

1972 data

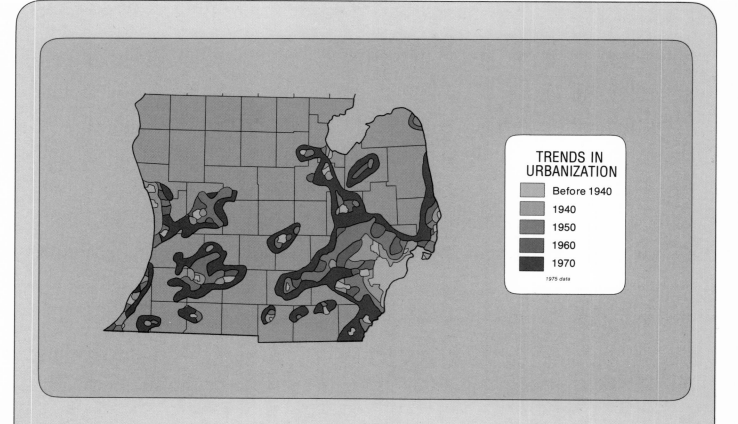

TRENDS IN
URBANIZATION

Before 1940
1940
1950
1960
1970

1975 data

Roughly half (50.7 percent) of the state's total area of 56,817 square miles (147,156 sq km) is forest and almost another third (31.9 percent) is agricultural land. The large number of acres these uses account for contain few people. The various land uses for transportation, such as highways, streets, airports, and railroads, constitute only 3 percent of the state's total area, yet this land carries millions of dollars of commerce daily and enables thousands of people to travel to and from work, shopping, and recreation. Three-fourths of all people in Michigan live in cities that cover less than 3 percent of the state's land area, which illustrates the high densities of population and clusters of urban settlement on relatively small amounts of land.

Recreational land uses—parks, playgrounds, campgrounds, scenic areas—are significant in the state's economy and play a large role in the leisure time of Michiganians and those from other states and Canada. Yet the total amount of land used for recreation is 2.5 percent of the state's total area (excluding forests). The area covered by the state's inland lakes and rivers is roughly the same percent, 2.4.

In the past several decades three changes in the state's urban development patterns have occurred: an increase in the number of urban centers in the southern half of the state; an expansion of suburban areas, not only around new and old cities but also into the surrounding countryside; and a gradual coalescing of urban development into broad bands that fairly closely parallel the interstate highways linking major cities. Urban and suburban sprawl is gradually filling in the open spaces between such cities as Saginaw and Flint, Grand Rapids and Lansing, and Jackson and Battle Creek and engulfing former small trade centers on or near the major interstate highways that traverse southern lower Michigan.

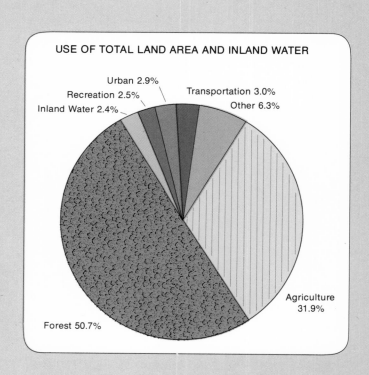

USE OF TOTAL LAND AREA AND INLAND WATER

Urban 2.9%
Recreation 2.5%
Transportation 3.0%
Inland Water 2.4%
Other 6.3%
Agriculture 31.9%
Forest 50.7%

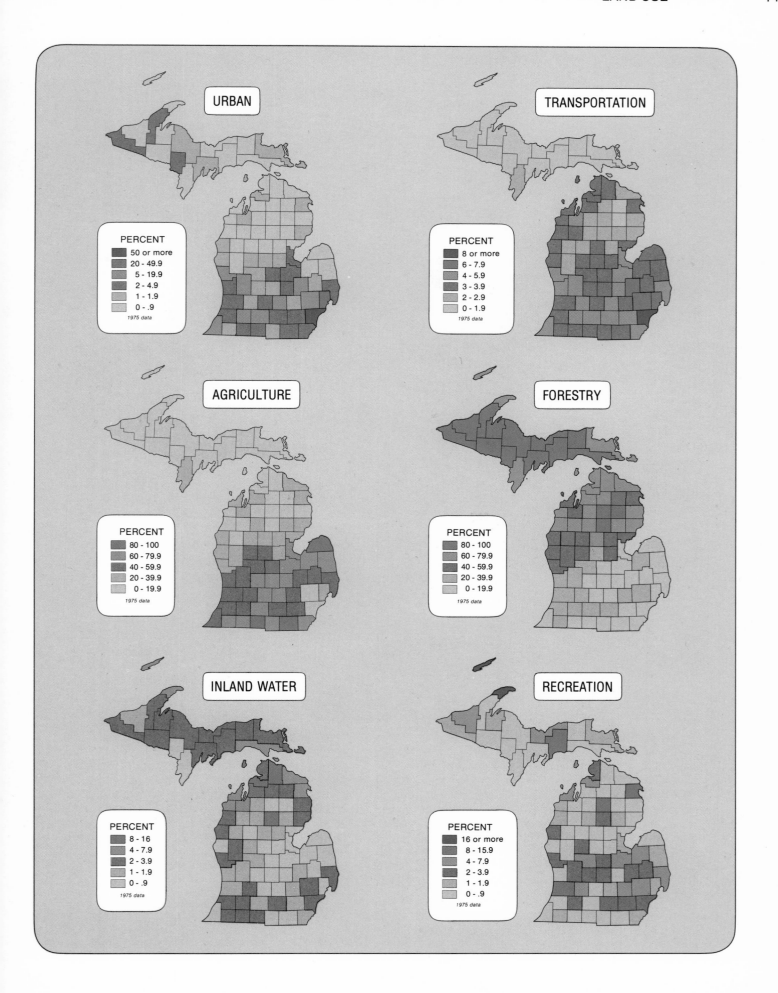

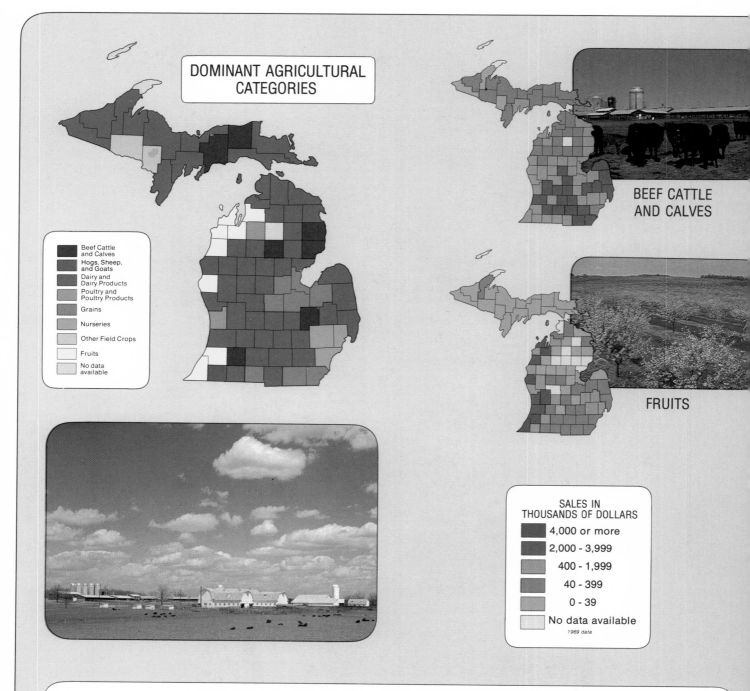

DOMINANT AGRICULTURAL CATEGORIES

Beef Cattle and Calves
Hogs, Sheep, and Goats
Dairy and Dairy Products
Poultry and Poultry Products
Grains
Nurseries
Other Field Crops
Fruits
No data available

BEEF CATTLE AND CALVES

FRUITS

SALES IN THOUSANDS OF DOLLARS

4,000 or more
2,000 - 3,999
400 - 1,999
40 - 399
0 - 39
No data available

1969 data

The state's overall agricultural diversity is shown by its variety of major livestock and crop products. Most counties have a mixture of crop and livestock production. The dominant agricultural category in terms of farm product sales by county in 1969 was dairy products. On a dollar basis the leading categories in farm product sales in 1969 were dairy products ($219 million), grains ($132 million), and beef cattle and calves ($108 million). Next in importance, although much less in total dollar sales, were fruits ($70 million); hogs, sheep, and goats ($50 million); poultry and poultry products ($48 million); vegetables ($39 million); and nursery products ($37 million).

Sales of dairy products exceeded sales in all other crop and livestock categories in 50 counties located throughout the Upper Peninsula and Lower Peninsula. Beef cattle and calves were most important in both peninsulas in a few scattered counties that usually were adjacent to dairy areas. Beef cattle production is also related to the availability of corn or soybeans as fattening agents. Fruits were the most important in those counties bordering Lake Michigan where sandy soils and lake-influenced climate conditions favor their production.

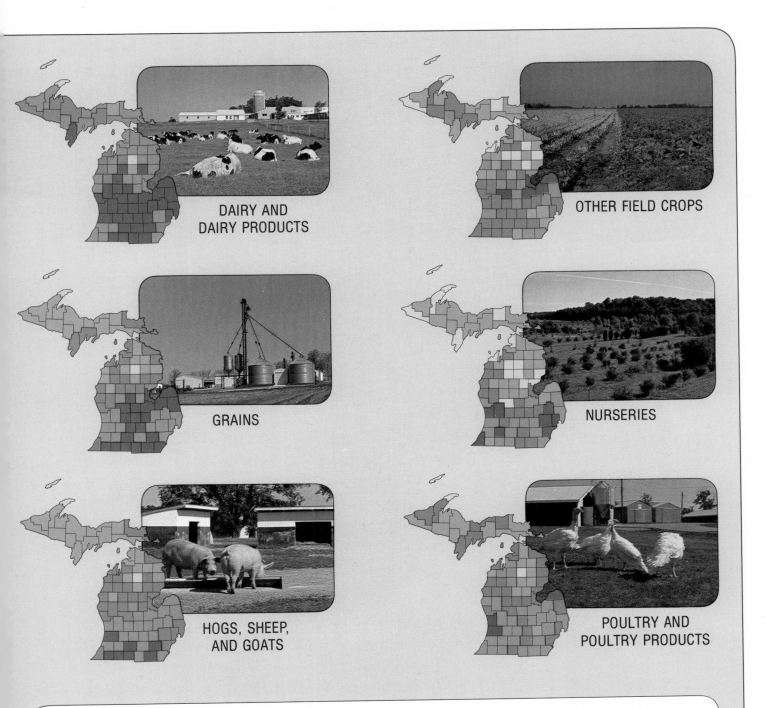

DAIRY AND
DAIRY PRODUCTS

OTHER FIELD CROPS

GRAINS

NURSERIES

HOGS, SHEEP,
AND GOATS

POULTRY AND
POULTRY PRODUCTS

Hogs and especially sheep and goats are relatively unimportant in Michigan in comparison to dairy products and beef cattle. Cass is the only county where this category predominates in agricultural sales, and its dominance is based in large part on hog production.

The map showing the importance of grains highlights the soybean growing areas of Michigan, primarily the Saginaw Valley and the Thumb region.

The distribution of nursery stock and products shows a strong correlation with urban areas where the major markets are found. Thus, the three Detroit-area counties of Wayne, Oakland, and Macomb dominate this category. Secondary concentrations can be found in other heavily urbanized counties in the southern Lower Peninsula.

Because the mass production of poultry in Michigan is found in the Holland-Zeeland area, poultry and poultry products constitute the dominant agricultural sales category in Ottawa County. Most of the people who raise poultry are of Dutch ancestry.

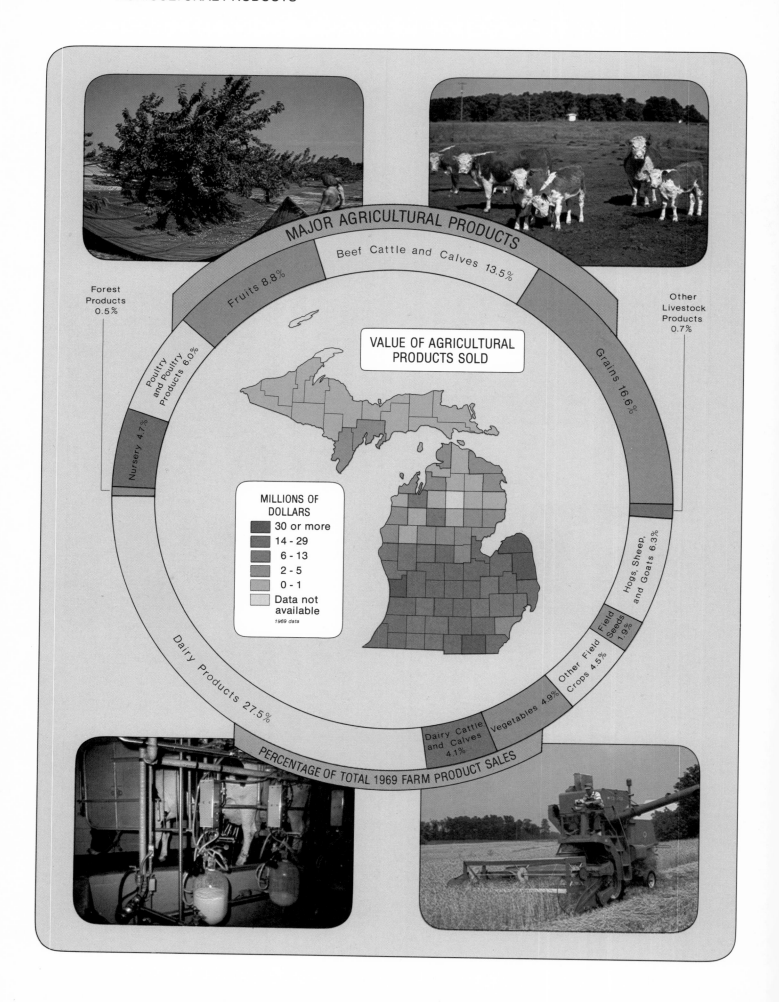

MAJOR AGRICULTURAL PRODUCTS

VALUE OF AGRICULTURAL PRODUCTS SOLD

Beef Cattle and Calves 13.5%

Fruits 8.8%

Forest Products 0.5%

Other Livestock Products 0.7%

Grains 16.6%

Poultry and Poultry Products 6.0%

Nursery 4.7%

Hogs, Sheep, and Goats 6.3%

Field Seeds 1.9%

Other Field Crops 4.5%

Vegetables 4.9%

Dairy Cattle and Calves 4.1%

Dairy Products 27.5%

PERCENTAGE OF TOTAL 1969 FARM PRODUCT SALES

MILLIONS OF DOLLARS

30 or more
14 - 29
6 - 13
2 - 5
0 - 1
Data not available

1969 data

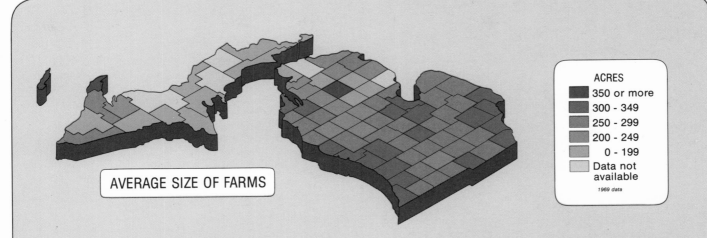

AVERAGE SIZE OF FARMS

ACRES
- 350 or more
- 300 - 349
- 250 - 299
- 200 - 249
- 0 - 199
- Data not available

1969 data

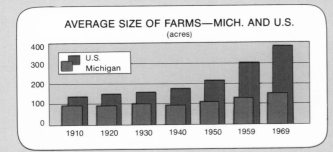

AVERAGE SIZE OF FARMS—MICH. AND U.S.
(acres)

U.S.
Michigan

400
300
200
100
0

1910 1920 1930 1940 1950 1959 1969

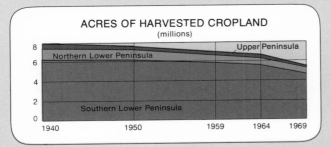

ACRES OF HARVESTED CROPLAND
(millions)

8
6
4
2
0

Upper Peninsula
Northern Lower Peninsula
Southern Lower Peninsula

1940 1950 1959 1964 1969

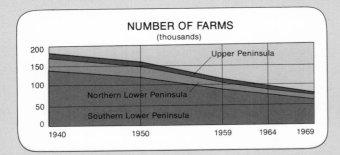

NUMBER OF FARMS
(thousands)

200
150
100
50
0

Upper Peninsula
Northern Lower Peninsula
Southern Lower Peninsula

1940 1950 1959 1964 1969

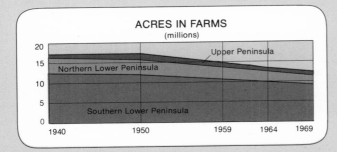

ACRES IN FARMS
(millions)

20
15
10
5
0

Upper Peninsula
Northern Lower Peninsula
Southern Lower Peninsula

1940 1950 1959 1964 1969

The state's 77,946 farms in 1969 comprised 11,900,689 acres (4,819,779 ha). The average size per farm was 153 acres (62 ha). As a result of the various products raised and the different types of agricultural operations, the range of farm sizes per county is great. The highest averages are in three Upper Peninsula counties, Luce (479 acres or 194 ha), Marquette (430 acres or 174 ha), and Schoolcraft (418 acres or 169 ha). Most farms in the sparsely populated and heavily forested Upper Peninsula average more than 300 acres (121.5 ha) or roughly half a section. The soils there are generally of poor quality, and the farms contain considerable nonarable areas of forested wetlands. Farms in the Lower Peninsula are much smaller as a result of the better soils and climate and more intensive types of farming. It takes less acreage for a successful farm, and often agriculture is competing with urban and suburban development. The averages are lowest in the counties of Ottawa (117 acres or 47.4 ha), Berrien (124 acres or 50.2 ha), Macomb (126 acres or 51 ha), and Wayne (127 acres or 51.4 ha). Farms along the Lake Michigan shoreline generally are less than 200 acres (81 ha).

Michigan's farms have increased in size and decreased in number in the last 35 years; both trends are evident also at the national level. In 1940 the average farm size in Michigan was 96 acres (39 ha) compared to 153 acres (62 ha) in 1969. The number of farms has declined from 188,000 to nearly 78,000 in the same period. At the same time there has been a drop in Michigan's total acreage in farmland from 18 million to 12 million acres (7.3 million to 4.9 million ha) and in acres of cropland harvested from 78 million to 5.5 million acres (3.1 million to 2.2 million ha). The decreases in farm numbers, acres in farms, and acreages in cropland have occurred throughout the state. Some regional patterns are noticeable, such as a sharper decline in the number of farms in the Upper Peninsula and a rather constant pattern of cropland acreages in the southern Lower Peninsula.

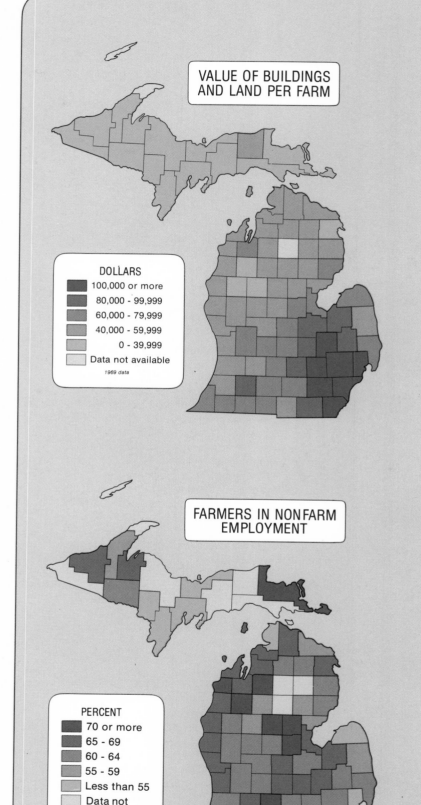

VALUE OF BUILDINGS AND LAND PER FARM

DOLLARS
- 100,000 or more
- 80,000 - 99,999
- 60,000 - 79,999
- 40,000 - 59,999
- 0 - 39,999
- Data not available

1969 data

FARMERS IN NONFARM EMPLOYMENT

PERCENT
- 70 or more
- 65 - 69
- 60 - 64
- 55 - 59
- Less than 55
- Data not available

1969 data

The total value of farms in Michigan in 1969 was $3.8 billion, an average of $49,821 per farm. The value of machinery and equipment on farms totaled $716 million, an average of $9,185 per farm. Sales of farm products in the state totaled $829 million, nearly 60 percent coming from livestock and other products. The average farm in Michigan sold nearly $10,600 worth of farm products in 1969.

Farm real estate or the average value of buildings and land per farm ranged widely among counties from $185,000 in Oakland County and $178,000 in Wayne County to only $19,000 in Houghton County. Most counties had farms in the $40,000–$80,000 range. All Upper Peninsula counties except Luce had averages of less than $40,000. On the other hand, all counties in the southeast quarter had averages that exceeded $100,000. These farms were usually smaller in size and had intensive activities such as dairying or the production of corn, vegetables, or nursery stock. Encroaching urban land has contributed to the high real estate values of farms in this area. Soil qualities are better in the southern Lower Peninsula than in the northern part of the state.

Farm values have increased over time, especially from 1959 to 1969. Michigan averages have always been slightly below the national figures, in part because of the varying quality of farmland and lower agricultural productivity per farm, especially in the northern two-thirds of the state. In these areas many of the farms are marginal, and nonfarm employment tends to be high.

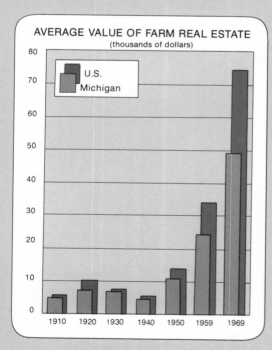

AVERAGE VALUE OF FARM REAL ESTATE
(thousands of dollars)

U.S.
Michigan

1910 1920 1930 1940 1950 1959 1969

In 1969, 595,000 tons of commercial fertilizers were used in Michigan at a cost of more than $53 million. Such fertilizers were applied on roughly 3.5 million (1.4 million ha) of the state's 8.5 million acres (3.4 million ha) of cropland and averaged more than 400 pounds (181 kg) per acre. The figures on the accompanying map and those below pertain only to the acreage on which commercial fertilizer is used. The amounts applied per acre were highest in the Upper Peninsula and northwest part of the Lower Peninsula to offset poor soils. Counties with the highest averages were Dickinson (627 pounds or 284.4 kg), Iron (626 pounds or 283.9 kg), Manistee (600 pounds or 272.1 kg), and Luce (539 pounds or 244.4 kg). The average applications were somewhat less in the major general farming areas of the Lower Peninsula and in the more specialized fruit and vegetable counties along the Lake Michigan shore.

Feeding Michigan's growing population depends on food products raised within the state as well as on importing a variety of commodities produced elsewhere such as wheat, soybeans, hogs, cattle, and eggs. Michigan is a major supplier of dry edible beans for the United States and raises more beets than it needs. Farms in the state produce more than half the milk, corn, and potatoes consumed by Michigan residents.

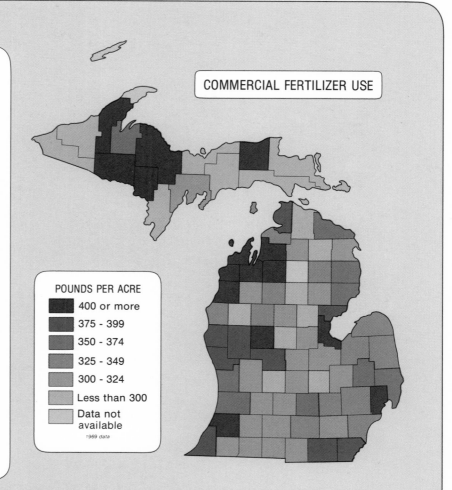

COMMERCIAL FERTILIZER USE

POUNDS PER ACRE

- 400 or more
- 375 - 399
- 350 - 374
- 325 - 349
- 300 - 324
- Less than 300
- Data not available

1969 data

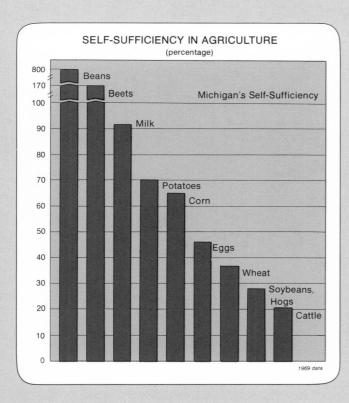

SELF-SUFFICIENCY IN AGRICULTURE
(percentage)

Beans
Beets
Michigan's Self-Sufficiency
Milk
Potatoes
Corn
Eggs
Wheat
Soybeans, Hogs
Cattle

1969 data

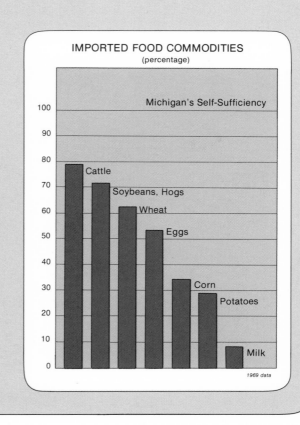

IMPORTED FOOD COMMODITIES
(percentage)

Michigan's Self-Sufficiency
Cattle
Soybeans, Hogs
Wheat
Eggs
Corn
Potatoes
Milk

1969 data

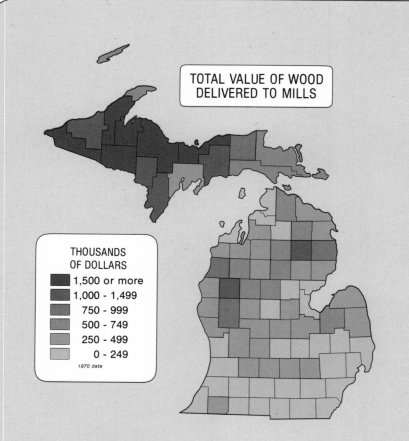

TOTAL VALUE OF WOOD
DELIVERED TO MILLS

THOUSANDS
OF DOLLARS

■ 1,500 or more
■ 1,000 - 1,499
■ 750 - 999
■ 500 - 749
■ 250 - 499
□ 0 - 249

1970 data

The largest acreage in forests is in the Upper Peninsula, and not surprisingly counties in this area had the highest values for wood delivered to mills in 1970. Six counties, Marquette, Baraga, Gogebic, Iron, Houghton, and Alger, each had sales of more than $1.5 million; four others in the Upper Peninsula averaged more than $1 million. Commercial forestry is the major economic activity throughout most of the sparsely populated Upper Peninsula. Marquette County led the state in sales of wood with more than $3.1 million in 1970, followed by Baraga County with $2.8 million and Gogebic County with $2.6 million. At the other extreme, the prosperous livestock and cash grain areas in the Lower Peninsula and the counties with large urban and suburban land areas had little commercial forest land. The total value of wood delivered to mills was less than $50,000 in Macomb, Monroe, and Bay counties. Both forestry and agriculture are important to the economies of the counties in the center of the Lower Peninsula.

The species of trees providing raw material for pulpwood in Michigan have varied considerably over the last 30 years. The major change is the increase in the importance of aspen and, to a lesser extent, hardwoods and hardwood residue. The cyclical variations in the total amount of pulpwood produced reflect economic conditions in the country: in the recession years of 1958 and 1961 the amount produced decreased; an increasing total production reflects the demands of a growing population.

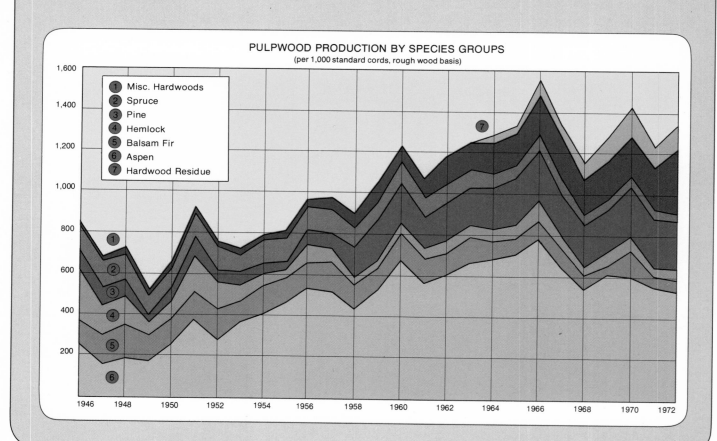

PULPWOOD PRODUCTION BY SPECIES GROUPS
(per 1,000 standard cords, rough wood basis)

① Misc. Hardwoods
② Spruce
③ Pine
④ Hemlock
⑤ Balsam Fir
⑥ Aspen
⑦ Hardwood Residue

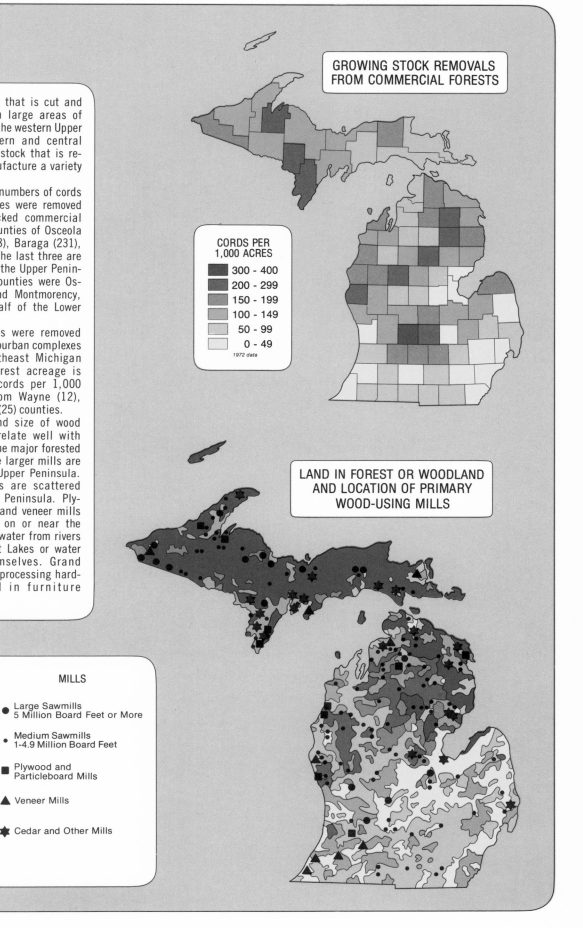

Most growing stock that is cut and marketed comes from large areas of commercial forests in the western Upper Peninsula and northern and central Lower Peninsula. The stock that is removed is used to manufacture a variety of industrial products.

In 1972 the largest numbers of cords of logs per 1,000 acres were removed from Michigan's stocked commercial forest lands in the counties of Osceola (287), Menominee (238), Baraga (231), and Dickinson (227). The last three are in the western half of the Upper Peninsula. Other leading counties were Oscoda, Roscommon, and Montmorency, all in the northern half of the Lower Peninsula.

Fewer cords of logs were removed from the urban and suburban complexes in southern and southeast Michigan where commercial forest acreage is limited. The fewest cords per 1,000 acres were taken from Wayne (12), Macomb (18), and Bay (25) counties.

The distribution and size of wood processing mills correlate well with their accessibility to the major forested areas of the state. The larger mills are predominantly in the Upper Peninsula. Medium-size sawmills are scattered throughout the Lower Peninsula. Plywood, particle board, and veneer mills are generally located on or near the coasts with access to water from rivers flowing into the Great Lakes or water from the lakes themselves. Grand Rapids is a center for processing hardwood that is used in furniture manufacturing.

GROWING STOCK REMOVALS FROM COMMERCIAL FORESTS

CORDS PER 1,000 ACRES

- 300 - 400
- 200 - 299
- 150 - 199
- 100 - 149
- 50 - 99
- 0 - 49

1972 data

LAND IN FOREST OR WOODLAND AND LOCATION OF PRIMARY WOOD-USING MILLS

PERCENT OF LAND IN FOREST OR WOODLAND

- 95 - 100
- 70 - 94
- 40 - 69
- 15 - 39
- 5 - 14
- 0 - 4

1972 data

MILLS

- ● Large Sawmills 5 Million Board Feet or More
- • Medium Sawmills 1-4.9 Million Board Feet
- ■ Plywood and Particleboard Mills
- ▲ Veneer Mills
- ✦ Cedar and Other Mills

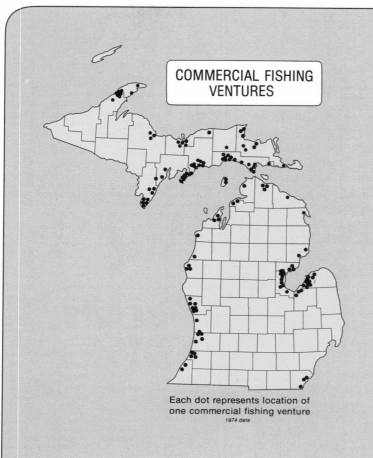

COMMERCIAL FISHING VENTURES

Each dot represents location of one commercial fishing venture
1974 data

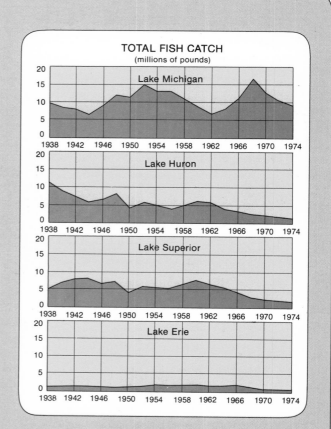

TOTAL FISH CATCH
(millions of pounds)

Lake Michigan

Lake Huron

Lake Superior

Lake Erie

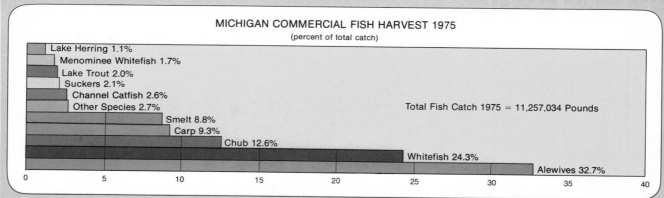

MICHIGAN COMMERCIAL FISH HARVEST 1975
(percent of total catch)

Lake Herring 1.1%
Menominee Whitefish 1.7%
Lake Trout 2.0%
Suckers 2.1%
Channel Catfish 2.6%
Other Species 2.7%
Smelt 8.8%
Carp 9.3%
Chub 12.6%
Whitefish 24.3%
Alewives 32.7%

Total Fish Catch 1975 = 11,257,034 Pounds

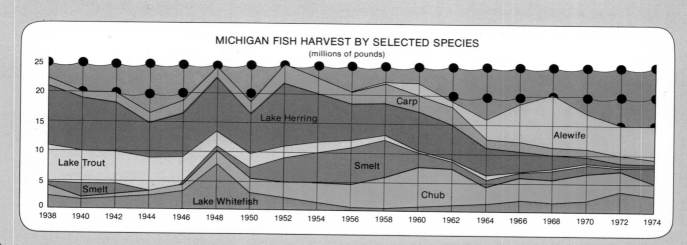

MICHIGAN FISH HARVEST BY SELECTED SPECIES
(millions of pounds)

Lake Trout

Smelt

Lake Herring

Carp

Alewife

Smelt

Chub

Lake Whitefish

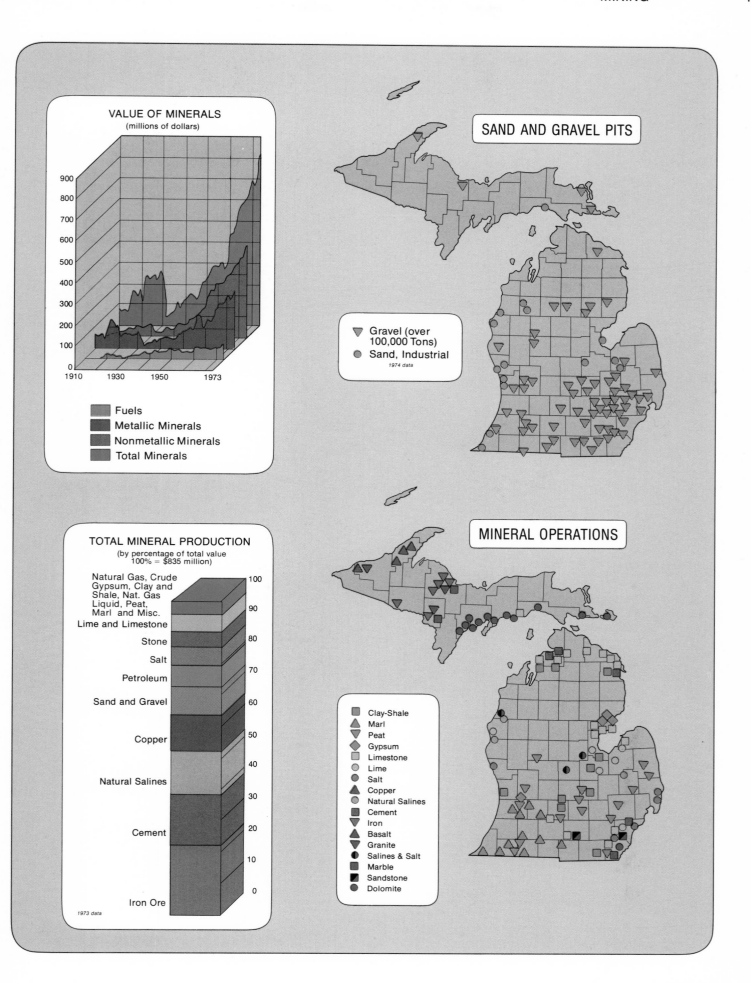

VALUE OF MINERALS
(millions of dollars)

900
800
700
600
500
400
300
200
100
0
1910   1930   1950   1973

Fuels
Metallic Minerals
Nonmetallic Minerals
Total Minerals

SAND AND GRAVEL PITS

▽ Gravel (over 100,000 Tons)
● Sand, Industrial
1974 data

TOTAL MINERAL PRODUCTION
(by percentage of total value
100% = $835 million)

Natural Gas, Crude
Gypsum, Clay and
Shale, Nat. Gas
Liquid, Peat,
Marl and Misc.   100
Lime and Limestone   90
Stone   80
Salt   70
Petroleum
Sand and Gravel   60
Copper   50
                                  40
Natural Salines   30
Cement   20
                                  10
                                  0
Iron Ore

1973 data

MINERAL OPERATIONS

■ Clay-Shale
▲ Marl
▽ Peat
◆ Gypsum
□ Limestone
○ Lime
● Salt
▲ Copper
● Natural Salines
▣ Cement
▼ Iron
▲ Basalt
▽ Granite
◑ Salines & Salt
■ Marble
◨ Sandstone
● Dolomite

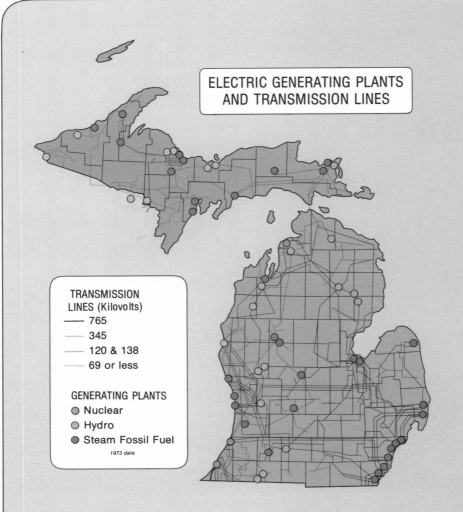

ELECTRIC GENERATING PLANTS
AND TRANSMISSION LINES

TRANSMISSION
LINES (Kilovolts)
——— 765
——— 345
——— 120 & 138
——— 69 or less

GENERATING PLANTS
● Nuclear
● Hydro
● Steam Fossil Fuel

1973 data

Michigan residents and industries receive energy by a series of pipelines and electric generating stations and substations. High-power transmission lines criss-cross the state. The network is densest in the southern Lower Peninsula, correlating with population and industrial concentration. The cluster of plants and stations along western Lake Erie (Detroit-Toledo area) is especially large.

Petroleum supplied 38 percent of the prime energy consumed in terms of heat content in 1972. Energy supplied by natural gas is second and by coal and coke is third. There is relatively little dependence on hydroelectric power or nuclear generation today, even though use of nuclear energy is expected to increase in the future. The major change since 1950 in the energy mix is a greater reliance on natural gas and less dependence on coal. Dependence on oil has remained roughly the same as on gas and coal.

Michigan consumes more energy than it produces. In 1972 the state consumed 2,999 trillion BTUs (British Thermal Units) but produced only 130 trillion BTUs. The dependence on sources outside the state and nation has grown. In 1947 the state produced 12 percent of what it used; in 1972 it was able to produce only 4 percent. Over the 25-year period shown below, the state's energy production has remained relatively constant. However, consumption has increased sharply with rising domestic, commercial, and industrial demands.

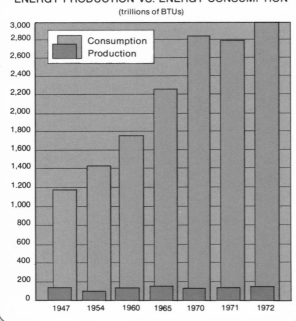

ENERGY PRODUCTION VS. ENERGY CONSUMPTION
(trillions of BTUs)

Consumption
Production

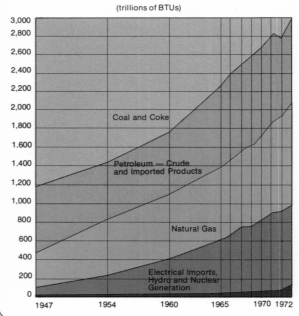

HEAT CONTENT OF PRIMARY ENERGY CONSUMED
(trillions of BTUs)

Coal and Coke

Petroleum — Crude
and Imported Products

Natural Gas

Electrical Imports,
Hydro and Nuclear
Generation

Even though Michigan ranked only seventeenth in U.S. oil production in 1973, it has several regions in which oil is locally an important energy and employment producer. Of the 14 million barrels produced in 1973 almost half came from only four counties, namely Otsego (2.5 million), Kalkaska and Hillsdale (1.6 million each), and Ingham (1.4 million). These were the only counties that produced more than 1 million barrels. The state's spotty production patterns are further illustrated by the fact that 35 counties produce no oil. Production is concentrated in the central northern part of the Lower Peninsula, in the south central part of the state, and in St. Clair County. As a result of the limited production, the industrial, commercial, and residential users of Michigan depend on petroleum from other states, Canada, and various other foreign sources.

Natural gas fields are frequently adjacent to petroleum areas. Like petroleum, major gas fields are concentrated particularly in central portions of the Lower Peninsula. Of the 43.7 million cubic feet (MCF) (1.24 million cu m) of gas produced in 1973, more than half came from the counties of Kalkaska (9.3 MCF or .26 million cu m), St. Clair (6.7 MCF or .19 million cu m), Ingham (4.7 MCF or .13 million cu m), and Hillsdale (4.4 MCF or .12 million cu m). Altogether nearly 95 percent came from these four counties and from Grand Traverse, Calhoun, Otsego, and Macomb counties.

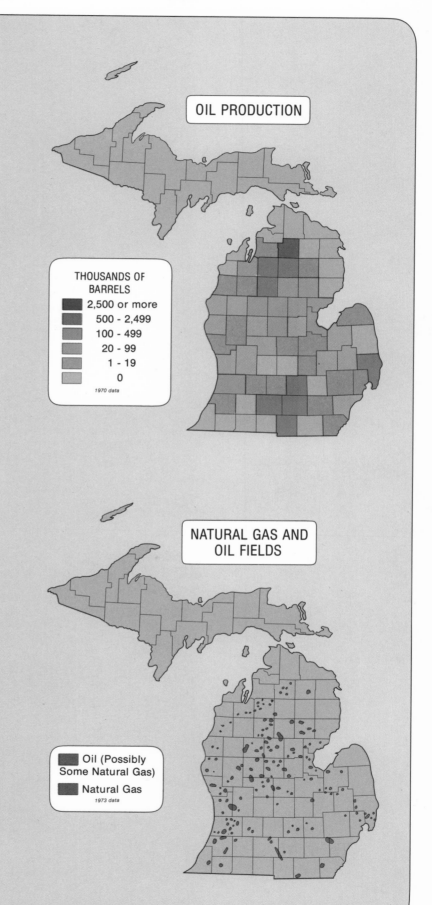

OIL PRODUCTION

THOUSANDS OF BARRELS
- 2,500 or more
- 500 - 2,499
- 100 - 499
- 20 - 99
- 1 - 19
- 0

1970 data

NATURAL GAS AND OIL FIELDS

- Oil (Possibly Some Natural Gas)
- Natural Gas

1973 data

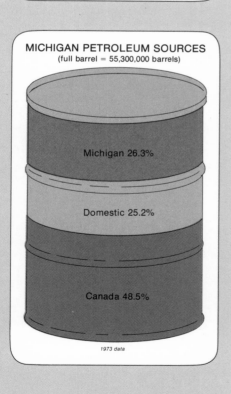

MICHIGAN PETROLEUM SOURCES
(full barrel = 55,300,000 barrels)

Michigan 26.3%

Domestic 25.2%

Canada 48.5%

1973 data

VALUE ADDED BY MANUFACTURING

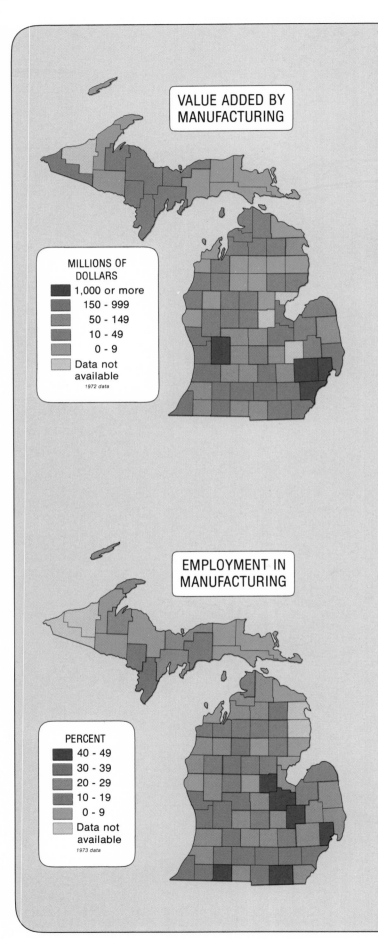

MILLIONS OF DOLLARS

- 1,000 or more
- 150 - 999
- 50 - 149
- 10 - 49
- 0 - 9
- Data not available

1972 data

EMPLOYMENT IN MANUFACTURING

PERCENT

- 40 - 49
- 30 - 39
- 20 - 29
- 10 - 19
- 0 - 9
- Data not available

1973 data

INDUSTRIAL EMPLOYMENT
(as a percent of total employment)

The importance of manufacturing in Michigan is revealed by the income generated and employment levels. The United States Census of Manufacturing uses the term "value added by manufacturing" to indicate how much processing and fabricating contributes to the value of raw materials. It is derived by subtracting from the value of shipments (including resales) the cost of materials, parts, components, supplies, fuels, goods purchased for resale, and contract work and adjusting for the net change in finished and unfinished product inventories during the year. In 1972 the total value added by manufacturing for the state exceeded $23 billion. Not unexpectedly the three counties in the Detroit area—Wayne, Oakland, and Macomb with $7.6, $2.0, and $1.7 billion respectively—had the highest values. The only other county with more than $1 billion was Kent County (Grand Rapids). Other urban areas in the southern half of the Lower Peninsula had sizable manufacturing operations and sales, such as Muskegon, Bay City, Saginaw, Lansing, Jackson, Kalamazoo, Ann Arbor, and Battle Creek. The lowest values were in the northern Lower Peninsula and the Upper Peninsula. There was less than $1 million each in values added by manufacturing in Missaukee, Keweenaw, and Lake counties. For several counties data on the value added were not available because they would disclose information about a single or small number of operators.

The distribution of the percent of the labor force in manufacturing is almost a mirror image of the value-added pattern. Higher percents would be expected in counties where there is less diversity in economic activities such as agriculture, mining, or government services. The highest percent in 1973 was in Midland County (48 percent), followed by Macomb (44 percent), Genesee (43 percent), St. Joseph (42 percent), and Osceola and Saginaw (40 percent). The largest urban counties, as expected, had more than 30 percent of their labor force in manufacturing. Less than 10 percent were in this occupational category in most Upper Peninsula and northern Lower Peninsula counties. Chippewa (3 percent) and Leelanau (5 percent) had the lowest percentages.

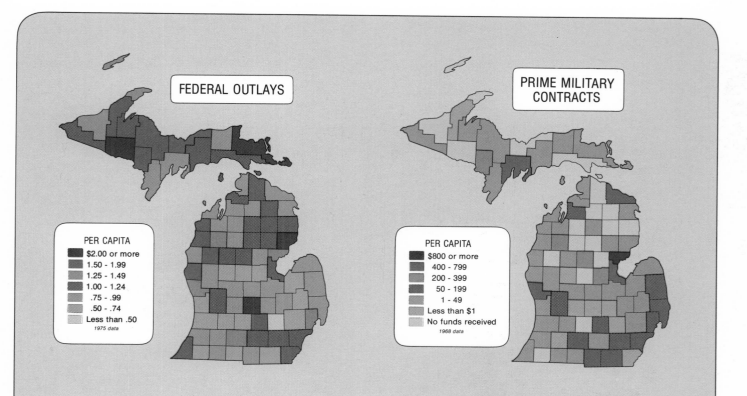

FEDERAL OUTLAYS

PER CAPITA
- $2.00 or more
- 1.50 - 1.99
- 1.25 - 1.49
- 1.00 - 1.24
- .75 - .99
- .50 - .74
- Less than .50

1975 data

PRIME MILITARY CONTRACTS

PER CAPITA
- $800 or more
- 400 - 799
- 200 - 399
- 50 - 199
- 1 - 49
- Less than $1
- No funds received

1968 data

Each year the federal treasury spends or allocates dollars to counties and local governments for a variety of programs. In fiscal year 1975 more than $9.5 million went to the state's 83 counties, a per capita average of $1.06. Monies for agriculture, transportation, housing, education, welfare, and environment were awarded to each county in varying amounts. The greatest dollar amounts were received by the most populous counties: Wayne obtained $2.8 million; Macomb, $923,000; Oakland, $676,000; Ingham, $471,000; and Kent, $436,000. Six counties received less than $10,000 each, Keweenaw and Luce counties receiving the least—$2,899 and $6,458 respectively. The per capita amounts varied widely within the state from $2.48 in Iosco County, $2.20 in Iron County, and $2.17 in Chippewa County to $0.63 in Lapeer, $0.62 in Ottawa, and $0.49 in Livingston counties. The figures reflect the number of federal programs operating in the county and the degree of participation of local governments.

In 1968, the peak year of military spending in the Vietnam War, 65 counties received more than $635 million in prime military contracts from the federal government. More than $197 million went to various firms in Wayne County (Detroit). Three other counties received more than $50 million each: Monroe, $76 million; Muskegon, $74 million; and Bay, $55 million. Eight others received more than $10 million each to manufacture equipment for the armed services. When these supply contracts are computed on a per capita basis, the leading counties are Arenac, $912 per capita; Muskegon, $472; Delta, $401; and Dickinson, $348. Midland, Clare, and Wexford counties all received more than $200 per capita. Some of the densely populated counties received much less, as illustrated by Wayne County's $74 per capita, Oakland's $20, and Ingham's $56. In nine counties the contracts received amounted to less than $1.00 per person. Eighteen counties, mostly in the Upper Peninsula and northern Lower Peninsula, received no prime military contracts.

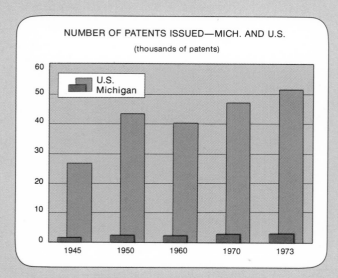

NUMBER OF PATENTS ISSUED—MICH. AND U.S.

(thousands of patents)

- U.S.
- Michigan

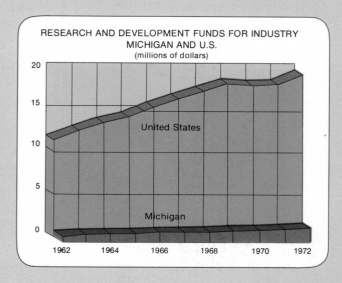

RESEARCH AND DEVELOPMENT FUNDS FOR INDUSTRY MICHIGAN AND U.S.

(millions of dollars)

United States

Michigan

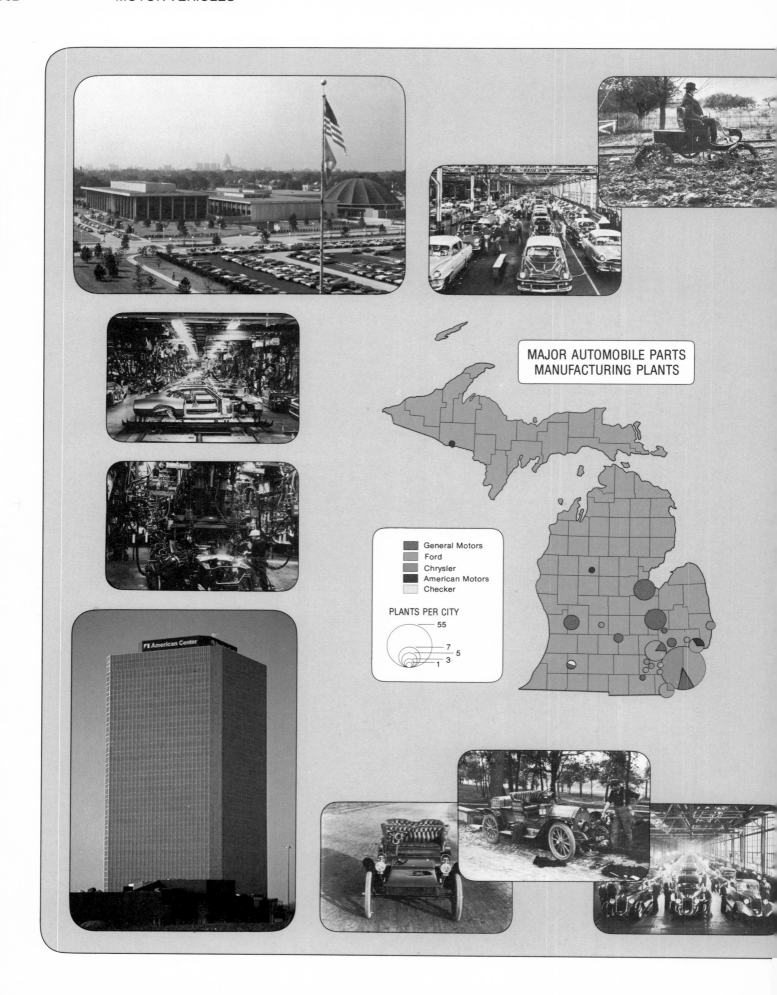

MAJOR AUTOMOBILE PARTS
MANUFACTURING PLANTS

General Motors
Ford
Chrysler
American Motors
Checker

PLANTS PER CITY

55
7
5
3
1

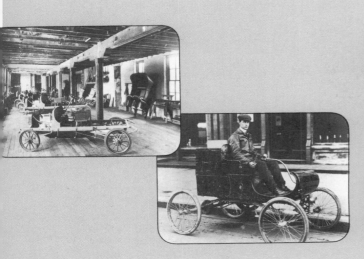

CAR AND TRUCK PRODUCTION IN THE U.S.
(millions of cars and trucks)

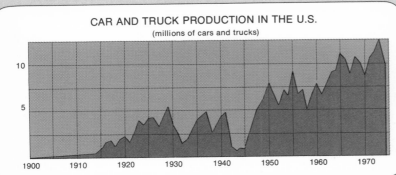

EMPLOYMENT IN THE AUTOMOBILE INDUSTRY IN THE U.S.
(thousands of employees)

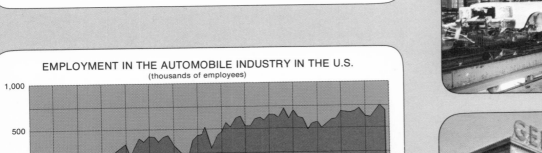

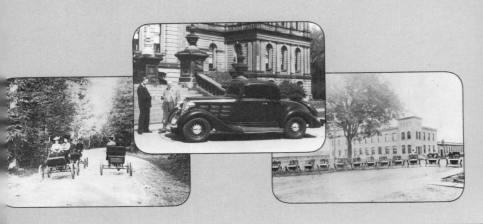

PRODUCTION BY THE "BIG THREE" AUTOMOBILE COMPANIES
(millions of vehicles)

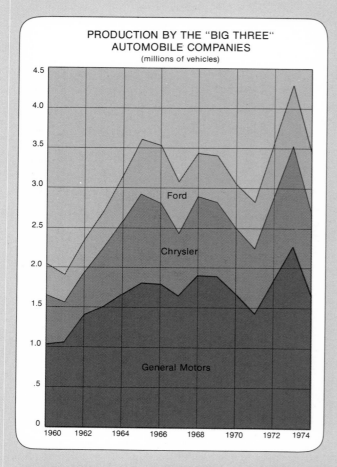

In 1974 Michigan produced more than 3.4 million motor vehicles. Nearly half or 1.6 million were produced by General Motors, 29 percent by Chrysler, and 23 percent by the Ford Motor Company. The largest concentration of these auto assembly plants is in the Detroit area. Fifty-seven percent of all cars are produced in the Motor City alone. This figure rises to nearly 80 percent when the production in Detroit's suburbs is included: Willow Run (10 percent), Pontiac (7 percent), and Wixom (5 percent). General Motors, Chrysler, and American Motors all have their corporate headquarters in Detroit; Ford's is in Dearborn. Outside the Detroit area, three other automobile cities are important: Lansing (12 percent of all cars made), Flint (8 percent), and Kalamazoo (2 percent). Checker cabs are produced in Kalamazoo. Automobile manufacturing is one of the most densely concentrated industries in the state.

The proportion of vehicles produced by the "Big Three" automobile companies in Michigan has been roughly the same from 1960 to 1974. General Motors has always clearly been the leader. Volume has changed from year to year in relation to increasing population and national economic trends. The peak year was 1973 when 9.6 million cars and 2.9 million trucks and buses were manufactured nationally; the 1974 recession year figures were 7.3 and 2.7 million respectively. The number produced rebounded again in 1975-76.

AUTOMOBILE PRODUCTION AND LOCATION OF ASSEMBLY PLANTS

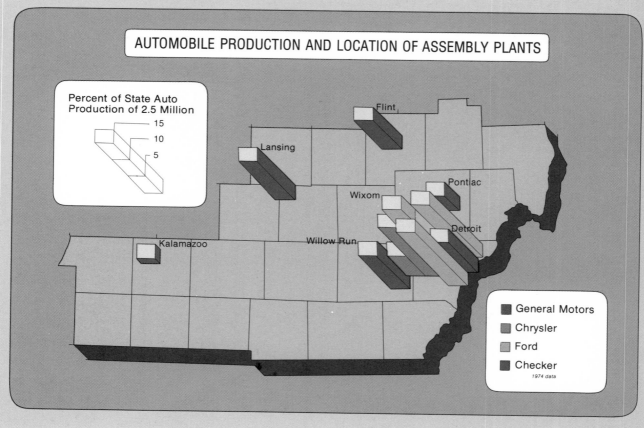

Percent of State Auto Production of 2.5 Million

- General Motors
- Chrysler
- Ford
- Checker

1974 data

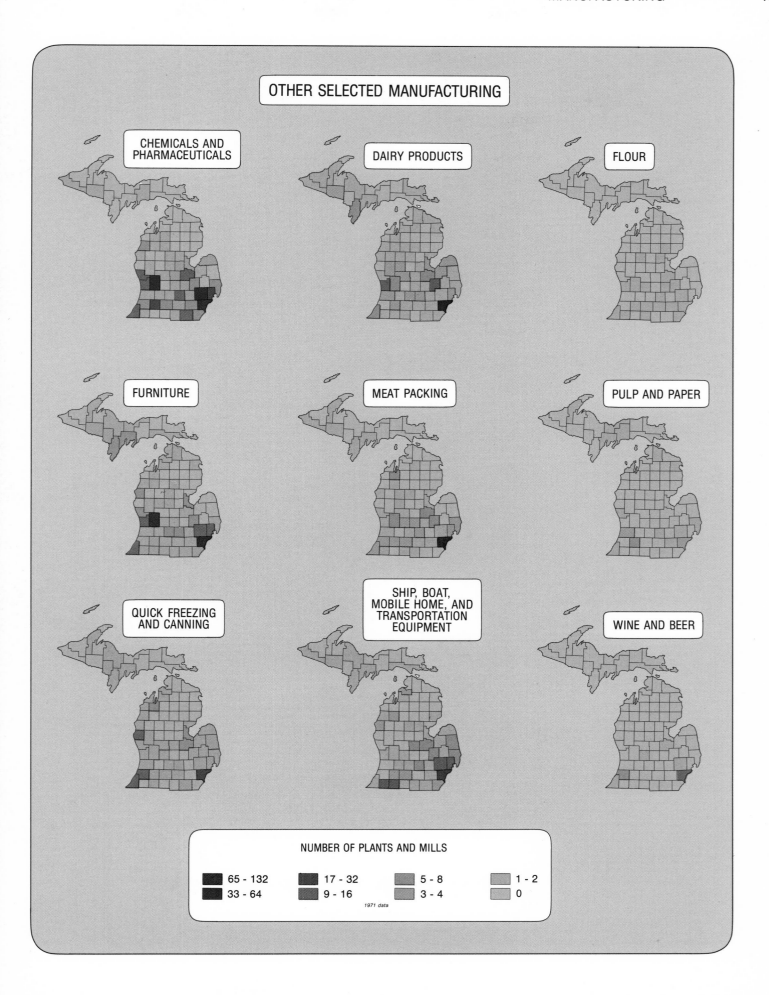

OTHER SELECTED MANUFACTURING

CHEMICALS AND PHARMACEUTICALS

DAIRY PRODUCTS

FLOUR

FURNITURE

MEAT PACKING

PULP AND PAPER

QUICK FREEZING AND CANNING

SHIP, BOAT, MOBILE HOME, AND TRANSPORTATION EQUIPMENT

WINE AND BEER

NUMBER OF PLANTS AND MILLS

65 - 132
33 - 64
17 - 32
9 - 16
5 - 8
3 - 4
1 - 2
0

1971 data

The outline of the state of Michigan appears frequently as a logo in the advertising for many companies and organizations located in Michigan.

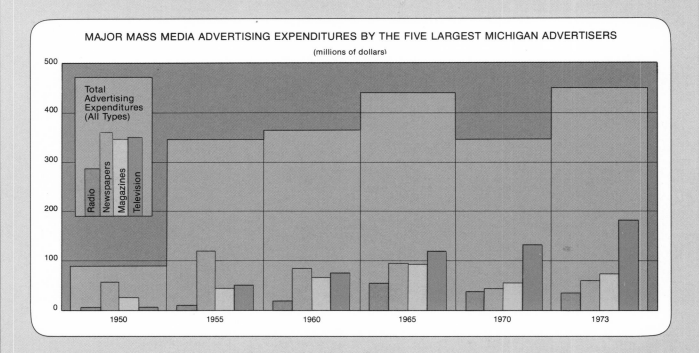

MAJOR MASS MEDIA ADVERTISING EXPENDITURES BY THE FIVE LARGEST MICHIGAN ADVERTISERS

(millions of dollars)

Advertising budgets for all kinds of enterprises have grown rapidly since 1950. Newspapers led among mass media used for advertising up to the early 1960s, but since 1965 television has outdistanced radio, newspapers, and magazines. By 1973 the advertising dollars brought in by television were more than double those brought in by magazines, the next most used media. Despite the increasing use of television for advertising, radio has shown a gradual increase in importance. Radio is used primarily for local advertising, whereas television is used more to advertise on a regional or national scale. Magazines also are used for products distributed on the national level.

Four of the five largest advertisers in Michigan are automobile manufacturers whose headquarters are in the state, namely General Motors, Ford Motor Company, Chrysler Company, and American Motors. The Kellogg Company, specializing in cereal production and located in Battle Creek, advertises nationwide and sells its products worldwide. There is a strong correlation in Michigan between the source of money spent on advertising and the densely populated, urbanized, and industrialized southern areas, particularly the Detroit area where automobiles and automobile parts manufacturing are concentrated. The automobile companies emphasize nationwide advertising, and thus most of their advertising fits best into the television and magazine formats. Automobile companies often become identified with certain television programs and advertise their products year after year in association with a program or a star performer.

Michigan corporations spend a little over 1 percent of sales for advertising or slightly more than $1 billion. Eighty-six advertising agencies have their headquarters in Michigan, and the state's 11,066 advertisers give it a rank of eighth among the states.

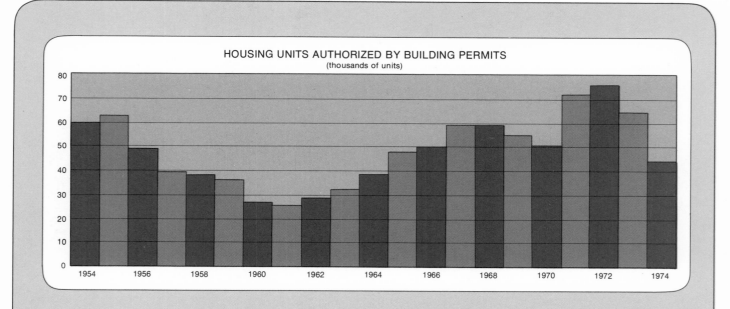

HOUSING UNITS AUTHORIZED BY BUILDING PERMITS
(thousands of units)

NEW HOUSING STARTS

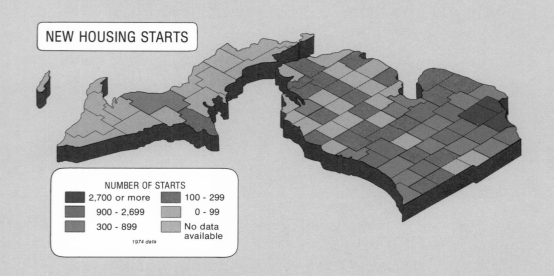

NUMBER OF STARTS

- 2,700 or more
- 900 - 2,699
- 300 - 899
- 100 - 299
- 0 - 99
- No data available

1974 data

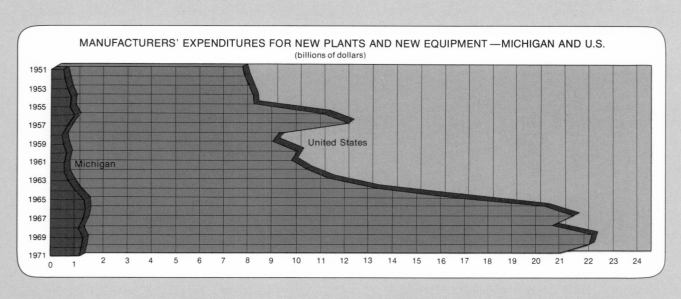

MANUFACTURERS' EXPENDITURES FOR NEW PLANTS AND NEW EQUIPMENT —MICHIGAN AND U.S.
(billions of dollars)

Michigan

United States

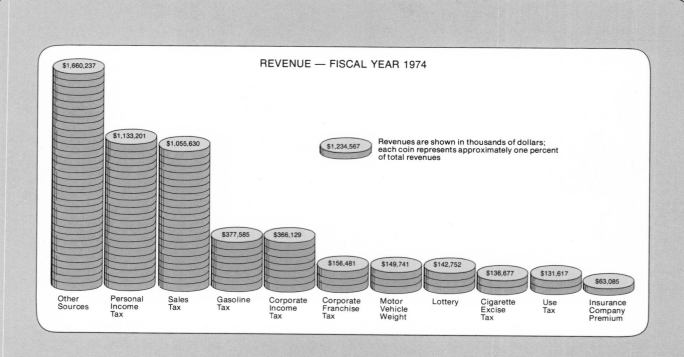

REVENUE — FISCAL YEAR 1974

$1,660,237

$1,133,201

$1,055,630

$1,234,567   Revenues are shown in thousands of dollars; each coin represents approximately one percent of total revenues

$377,585

$366,129

$156,481

$149,741

$142,752

$136,677

$131,617

$63,085

Other Sources | Personal Income Tax | Sales Tax | Gasoline Tax | Corporate Income Tax | Corporate Franchise Tax | Motor Vehicle Weight | Lottery | Cigarette Excise Tax | Use Tax | Insurance Company Premium

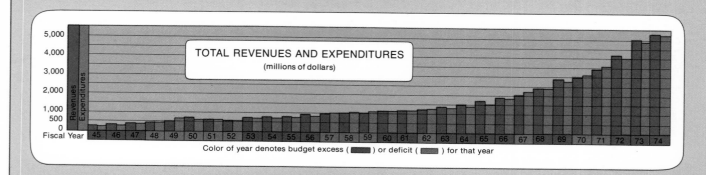

TOTAL REVENUES AND EXPENDITURES
(millions of dollars)

5,000
4,000
3,000
2,000
1,000
500
0

Revenues   Expenditures

Fiscal Year 45 46 47 48 49 50 51 52 53 54 55 56 57 58 59 60 61 62 63 64 65 66 67 68 69 70 71 72 73 74

Color of year denotes budget excess ( ) or deficit ( ) for that year

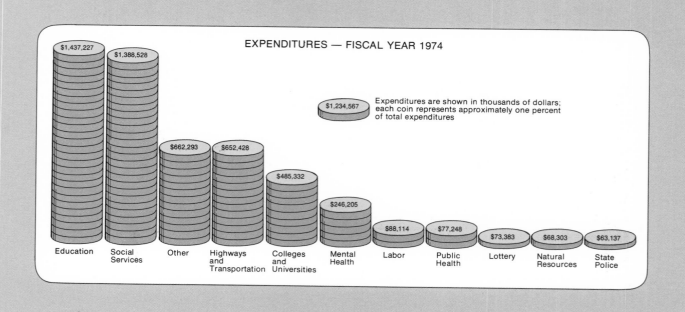

EXPENDITURES — FISCAL YEAR 1974

$1,437,227

$1,388,528

$1,234,567   Expenditures are shown in thousands of dollars; each coin represents approximately one percent of total expenditures

$662,293

$652,428

$485,332

$246,205

$88,114

$77,248

$73,383

$68,303

$63,137

Education | Social Services | Other | Highways and Transportation | Colleges and Universities | Mental Health | Labor | Public Health | Lottery | Natural Resources | State Police

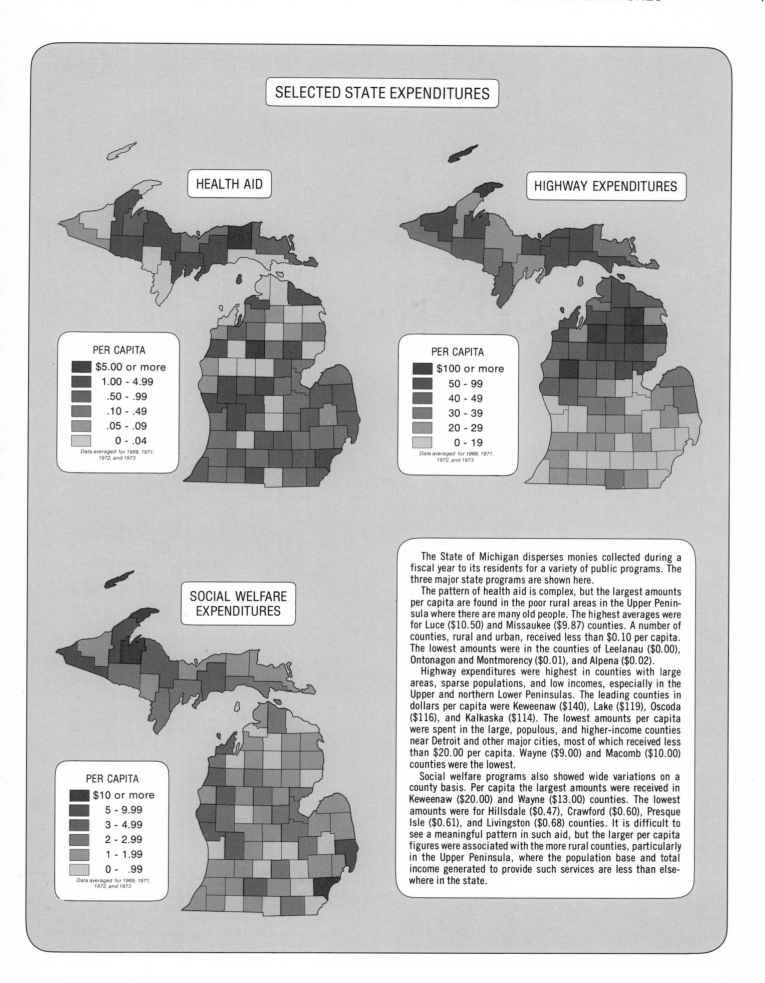

SELECTED STATE EXPENDITURES

HEALTH AID

PER CAPITA
- $5.00 or more
- 1.00 - 4.99
- .50 - .99
- .10 - .49
- .05 - .09
- 0 - .04

Data averaged for 1969, 1971, 1972, and 1973

HIGHWAY EXPENDITURES

PER CAPITA
- $100 or more
- 50 - 99
- 40 - 49
- 30 - 39
- 20 - 29
- 0 - 19

Data averaged for 1969, 1971, 1972, and 1973

SOCIAL WELFARE EXPENDITURES

PER CAPITA
- $10 or more
- 5 - 9.99
- 3 - 4.99
- 2 - 2.99
- 1 - 1.99
- 0 - .99

Data averaged for 1969, 1971, 1972, and 1973

The State of Michigan disperses monies collected during a fiscal year to its residents for a variety of public programs. The three major state programs are shown here.

The pattern of health aid is complex, but the largest amounts per capita are found in the poor rural areas in the Upper Peninsula where there are many old people. The highest averages were for Luce ($10.50) and Missaukee ($9.87) counties. A number of counties, rural and urban, received less than $0.10 per capita. The lowest amounts were in the counties of Leelanau ($0.00), Ontonagon and Montmorency ($0.01), and Alpena ($0.02).

Highway expenditures were highest in counties with large areas, sparse populations, and low incomes, especially in the Upper and northern Lower Peninsulas. The leading counties in dollars per capita were Keweenaw ($140), Lake ($119), Oscoda ($116), and Kalkaska ($114). The lowest amounts per capita were spent in the large, populous, and higher-income counties near Detroit and other major cities, most of which received less than $20.00 per capita. Wayne ($9.00) and Macomb ($10.00) counties were the lowest.

Social welfare programs also showed wide variations on a county basis. Per capita the largest amounts were received in Keweenaw ($20.00) and Wayne ($13.00) counties. The lowest amounts were for Hillsdale ($0.47), Crawford ($0.60), Presque Isle ($0.61), and Livingston ($0.68) counties. It is difficult to see a meaningful pattern in such aid, but the larger per capita figures were associated with the more rural counties, particularly in the Upper Peninsula, where the population base and total income generated to provide such services are less than elsewhere in the state.

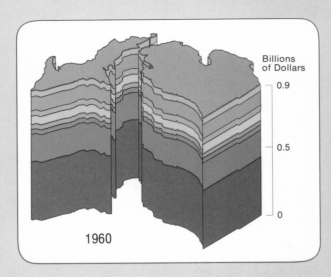

1960

MANUFACTURED EXPORTS

- Other Manufactured Products
- Chemical and Allied Products
- Food and Kindred Products
- Primary Metal Products
- Electrical Equipment
- Fabricated Metal Products
- Nonelectrical Machinery
- Transportation Equipment

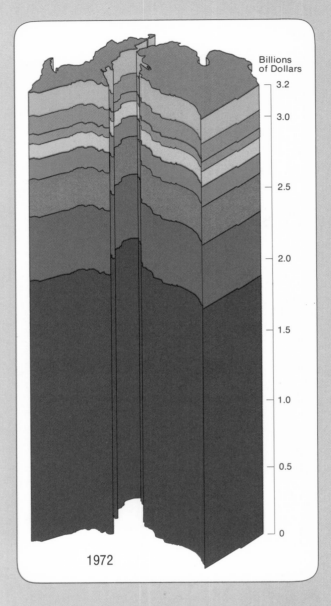

1972

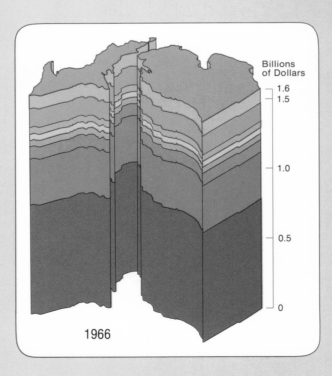

1966

Michigan as a key industrial and agricultural state exports millions of dollars worth of products to all parts of the nation and the world. From 1960 to 1972 the dollar volume of these exports has more than tripled from $936 million to $3.2 billion. The volume of products and the dollar amounts normally increase annually. Not unexpectedly the greatest exports in dollars (almost 55 percent) in 1972 included transportation equipment (autos, trucks, buses, and cabs). This dominant industrial category in the state's economy has consistently exceeded all other exports in dollar value from 1960 to 1972. Other leading products exported include nonelectrical machinery, fabricated metals, electrical equipment, primary metals, chemicals and allied products, and food and kindred products. Although there have been some shifts in the rankings in the dollar volume of these exports, it is noteworthy that industrial products usually constitute at least 90 percent of the total.

RECREATION

Society began only recently to understand and acknowledge the importance of recreation. The work ethic previously fostered the attitude that satisfying recreation needs of individuals was not worthy of serious attention by government and professionals. In addition, many people feel everyone is knowledgeable about such a common human activity as recreation and that related data gathering, planning, and policy development are therefore unnecessary. Actually our knowledge of the scope, mechanism, and impact of recreation is often extremely limited and frequently founded on emotion — for example, people's divergent attitudes toward such activities as professional sport, hunting, snowmobiling, and wilderness experiences. This is unfortunate because recreation is one of our most complex behavioral patterns involving psychological processes and spatial movements that are often difficult to fully understand and hard to predict. Consequently few people comprehend the full extent of recreation's present and future significance.

Michigan has a unique recreation system. No other political unit of comparable size encompasses recreation resources of such diversity and magnitude and so readily available to the great majority of a large population. As a result, Michigan residents participate exten-sively in a wide range of recreational activities, and many people from surrounding states and provinces travel to the state to enjoy its amenities. Recreation is thus of great economic importance; in fact, it may be thought of as embracing or being the source of a greater part of the Michigan economy than any other human activity. Many products and services are used exclusively for recreation; others involve recreation only periodically. Even our automobile industry depends to a great extent on the recreational benefits of owning and traveling by car. A multitude of other industries and small businesses provide employment in producing recreation goods and services.

Recreation is also the major use of land in Michigan. Besides the areas used exclusively for recreation, large portions of Michigan's agricultural lands, forest lands, and wetlands are used extensively for hunting, snow-mobiling, and other activities. Substantial portions of urban areas — from backyards and school yards to parks and shopping centers — also provide a wide range of recreation opportunities.

The most important benefits of recreation are less tangible. The relief it can provide from stress, boredom, or loneliness is of great value to mental health, especially in this era of industrialization and urbanization.

171

EXAMPLES OF RECREATIONAL PRODUCTS
Sporting goods
Boats
Cottages
Musical goods
Art supplies
Books and magazines
Beverages
Recreational clothing
Automobiles

EXAMPLES OF RECREATION SERVICES
Resort vacations
Camping facilities
Fish management
Theater programs
Professional sports
City recreation programs
Pool rooms
TV programs

Recreational activities that involve exercise are of growing importance to basic physical health as more people spend more time in sedentary occupations and traveling by mechanically driven transportation. Many activities also provide social benefits, such as bringing together people from different backgrounds or geographic areas. Some have great educational and cultural significance, especially reading, arts and crafts, performing arts, nature study, or travel. Environmental education is frequently associated with recreation, and much traditional learning, particularly for the handicapped or underprivileged, is enhanced when made part of a recreational experience.

Recreation involves both monetary and social costs. Substantial federal, state, and local tax monies are expended for highways, parks, libraries, and other publicly owned components of the recreation system. Recreation also absorbs a large portion of private budgets, sometimes with detrimental effects. Recreation-oriented activities are directly or indirectly responsible for many deaths and injuries each year, particularly in highway accidents and water-related mishaps. Disputes concerning the desirable use of both public and private lands that involve recreation are increasing. Managers of recreation lands frequently face conflicts between groups such as motorcyclists and hikers or snowmobilers and cross-country skiers who wish to use the same resource. Some resources are used to excess of their social or biological carrying capacities with consequent depreciation of the experiences or resources. Measures to regulate use, such as limits on the numbers of users, reduced seasons, and higher entrance fees, may distribute opportunities more equitably but also result in fewer recreational possibilities for some segments of society.

Recreation is, therefore, an extremely significant aspect of life in Michigan. Unfortunately it is difficult to assemble a series of maps that adequately represent recreation because it is such a complex phenomenon and the recording of pertinent statistics is only in its infancy. It is particularly difficult to obtain statewide data on many types of commercial recreation, on recreation at home, and on much of the activity that takes place in urban parks. Information on the maps largely represents recreation that takes place in nonurban environments, although the participants are mostly urban residents.

MICHIGAN'S RECREATION SYSTEM

The state's recreation system consists of three basic components: populations, transportation, and recreation resources.

Populations

The size, age structure, income, and education of an area's population affect the quantity and nature of recreation participation. Because more than three-quarters of Michigan's people are concentrated in the southeastern quarter of the state and because the nearby belt of urban centers in Ontario, Ohio, Indiana, and Illinois are a source of many recreation participants, pressure on recreation resources is greatest in the southern part of Michigan and decreases in a northerly direction. Moreover, Michigan's population is undergoing a number of changes that affect recreation participation. The state's population continues to grow. The increasing proportion of teenagers and those in their early twenties is producing a surge of participation in the kinds of activities popular with young people. Longevity and better health are resulting in greater use of recreation resources that appeal to older people. Free time for recreation is continuing to increase for many workers as union contracts specify shorter work weeks and longer vacations. In spite of inflation and economic setbacks, discretionary income (the part remaining after the essentials are purchased) continues to grow, and a large proportion of it is spent on recreation. Personal mobility, a major factor in most recreation, is closely tied to automobile ownership, which also partly depends on discretionary income. Although depressed by the 1974 oil crisis and higher prices, sales of automobiles and recreational vehicles are increasing again. The collective effect of these factors is a continuing increase in total participation in most public and commercial recreation.

Transportation

Michigan's excellent system of toll-free highways has made most recreation resources readily accessible to a majority of residents and many visitors. Before the construction of interstate highways and the Mackinac Bridge, it took at least two days of continuous driving to reach the western part of the Upper Peninsula. The interstate highways planned for the Upper Peninsula and along the western side of the Lower Peninsula will increase recreation participation in those areas.

Other forms of transportation play a relatively minor role in travel to recreation resources except in urban areas. In some cities, particularly Detroit, buses are an important component of the recreation system, especially for low-income groups. Service on weekends and holidays, however, is often reduced or eliminated, and many facilities are not served by any type of public transportation.

Recreation Resources

The resource components of the Michigan recreation system range from largely undeveloped areas such as Isle Royale National Park with its moose, wolves, and other wildlife to highly developed commercial facilities in downtown Detroit.

Water Resources. Since most nonurban recreation is water related, Michigan's most valuable recreation resource is its thousands of miles of lake and river shoreline. It has more shoreline on major water bodies than any state except Alaska and possibly Florida. The state also has jurisdiction over 41 percent of the Great Lakes surface, an area equal to 66 percent of its land area. Two features of the Great Lakes shoreline are especially valuable for recreation: sand beaches suitable for swimming and associated activities and sheltered bay waters particularly favorable for boating and fishing. Michigan has hundreds of miles of fine sand beaches, some of which are wide and gently sloping and thus particularly valuable for use by large numbers of people. Many of Michigan's state parks include beaches of this type. The state also has hundreds of lakes and reservoirs and thousands of miles of streams and rivers, most of which have considerable recreational value even in the southern agricultural and urban areas.

Geological Resources. Michigan's geologic history—the glacial era in particular—has strongly influenced its recreation resources. As the vast glacial lobes retreated, they built up great belts of morainic hills that in many cases trapped water as permanent lakes. In some places huge masses of ice were left behind and formed pothole lakes. Important locations for recreation such as the Irish Hills, the lakes of southwestern Michigan, and the ski resorts in the northwestern part of the Lower Peninsula are located in hilly morainic areas. These rolling landscapes are also esthetically appealing, especially when covered with mixtures of natural vegetation and agricultural crops. They are particularly attractive during the fall color season.

Climate. Climate plays a major role in many recreation activities. A location's latitude, altitude, and position relative to the Great Lakes all contribute to its climate. The summer migration of urban dwellers northward to second homes, resorts, and campgrounds is at least partly stimulated by a desire to reach cooler, less humid conditions. In winter the more northerly areas have better snow for skiing or snowmobiling, and lake ice is safer for ice fishing and other activities. Michigan's humid continental climate can be frustrating to those who prefer continuous sunny weather for recreation; clouds cover the sky more than 50 percent of the time, although rainfall is quite moderate.

Vegetation. Michigan's diverse vegetation is another important recreation resource. Deciduous forests in the south and various combinations of deciduous and coniferous trees farther north create appealing landscapes. Maples in particular provide splashes of vivid color in the fall. Young hardwoods and

MAIN WATER RESOURCES

Great Lakes shoreline	3,251 miles (5,201 km)
Great Lakes surface	38,575 square miles (100,295 sq km)
Inland lakes of more than five acres	7,500
Reservoirs	More than 5,000
Rivers and streams	38,350 (61,360 km)

Gathering Petoskey stones

Mushroom hunting

THE MULTIPLE-USE SUSTAINED-YIELD
ACT REQUIRES MANAGEMENT IN PERPETUITY
FOR THREE OF THE FOLLOWING FIVE USES

Recreation
Grazing
Timber
Water supply
Fish and wildlife

shrubs are food for deer, especially in the recently cutover areas. Michigan is one of the best areas in the nation for mushroom lovers because of its varied vegetative types and consequent wide range of fungi species. Wild blueberry and raspberry gathering also involves substantial numbers of people.

Fauna. Michigan's variety of water bodies, landforms, soils, climate, and vegetation produce a diverse and interesting natural fauna. However, human occupance and modern game and fish management practices have played a major part in determining the nature and extent of today's animal, bird, and fish populations. One of Michigan's most important animals is the white-tailed deer, which is popular with both sightseers and hunters. Cottontail rabbit, ruffed grouse, and squirrels are hunted extensively, and the pheasant, an introduced species, is an important quarry in much of the southern third of the state. Waterfowl viewing and hunting are facilitated by the state's extensive wetlands and shallow Great Lakes bays. Michigan fish range from warmwater species such as sunfish and catfish to cold-water fish like the brook and lake trout. Fish populations have been severely affected by water pollution, changes in land use, the sea lamprey's invasion of the Great Lakes, and in some cases overfishing. In recent decades, however, pollution control, habitat improvement, hatchery programs, and the introduction of exotic species such as the coho salmon have substantially increased fishing opportunities.

Ownership and Administration of Recreation Resources

Access to resources is the key to most nonurban recreational enjoyment. Recreationally valuable lands are owned, controlled, or administered by many individuals, private entrepreneurs, organizations, and government agencies. Accessibility and the scope of recreational developments depend on the purposes and policies of the owners or administrators.

Recreation Resources Administered by the Federal Government. The Forest Service, U.S. Department of Agriculture, provides more recreational opportunities in Michigan than any other federal agency. There are three national forests in the state: the Huron-Manistee in northern lower Michigan, the Hiawatha in the central and eastern Upper Peninsula, and the Ottawa in the extreme northwest. The 2.7 million acres (1.09 million hectares) of federally owned land within the national forest boundaries are a public recreation resource of immense value. Recreation, however, is only one purpose of these lands; the Forest Service administers them on a multiple-use basis. Since the national forests in Michigan contain so many excellent resources and are within a day's drive for more than 20 million people, recreation developments are extensive and participation is great, but much usage is difficult to measure since it is dispersed.

The National Park Service, U.S. Department of the Interior, the federal agency that makes the next largest direct contribution to recreation in the state, has three areas under its jurisdiction. Isle Royale National Park, consisting of a 210-square-mile (81-square-kilometer) main island and 200 surrounding small islands, is situated in Lake Superior some 56 miles (90 kilometers) from Copper Harbor. Its remote location protects the park's wilderness, including the only remaining moose-wolf ecosystem in Michigan. Some 15,000 people visit the park annually and enjoy its two commercial lodges, 24 small campgrounds, and 168 miles (268 kilometers) of trails. There are no roads in the park, and visitors travel on foot or by water.

A more recent addition to the national park system is Pictured Rocks National Lakeshore which lies along Lake Superior in the middle of the Upper Peninsula. It preserves 35 miles (56 kilometers) of magnificent shoreline ranging from high, deeply eroded, multicolored sandstone cliffs to a large expanse of huge sand dunes. The federal government has acquired 26,000 acres (10,530 hectares); an even larger buffer zone of privately owned forest land around the lakeshore will be managed by its owners for timber on a sustained-yield basis. Development by the National Park Service has been limited because of lack of congressional appropriations, but other agencies previously developed some roads, parking areas, and campsites in the area, so public use is extensive.

The newest National Park Service area is Sleeping Bear Dunes National Lakeshore near Traverse City. It consists of spectacular sand dunes, 64 miles (103 kilometers) of Lake Michigan shoreline, rolling landscapes with magnificent views of famous Glen Lake, and interesting, scientifically valuable ecosystems. The total area authorized for acquisition is almost 61,000 acres (24,700 hectares), of which one-third is North and South Manitou Islands. Land acquisition and development have been slowed by limited appropriations. Since the surrounding land was already well developed with farms, permanent residences, and seasonal homes, it was not possible to acquire a large contiguous area. Therefore, the national lakeshore has irregular boundaries, and many purchased parcels within the park itself are still occupied by previous owners on a life-lease basis.

The Fish and Wildlife Service, U.S. Department of the Interior, has 111,400 acres (45,117 hectares) of land in Michigan. The largest unit is the 98,000-acre (39,690-hectare) Seney National Wildlife Refuge, a block of predominantly wetland in the center of the Upper Peninsula that is valuable as a waterfowl breeding site and migratory resting area. A variety of recreational activities is permitted including picnicking, camping, and hunting for small and large game, but the majority of the more than 100,000 people who visit the refuge annually come to see the wildlife and exhibits. The Fish and Wildlife Service has another 8,900 acres (3,600 hectares) in southeastern Michigan known as the Shiawassee National Wildlife Refuge.

The only other federal government facilities of major significance to recreation in Michigan are the U.S. Army Corps of Engineers' navigational locks at Sault Sainte Marie and the various Great Lakes harbors built by the corps. The locks are one of the state's top sightseeing attractions, and the harbors are important to recreational boating and fishing. The federal government also provides funding and technical assistance particularly through the Bureau of Outdoor Recreation and various urban recreation programs.

Recreation Resources Administered by State Government. Michigan is fortunate that its legislators and voters saw the need for a strong state resources program many years ago. Today the Michigan Department of Natural Resources administers more than 4.25 million acres (1.7 million hectares) of forests, parks, and wildlife lands. More than 3.75 million acres (1.5 million hectares) are state forest, the largest state forest acreage in the nation. These lands are managed on a multiple-use basis and provide generally the same types of recreational opportunities as the national forests.

The most concentrated and measurable recreational use of state land takes place in the 92 parks and recreation areas of the state park system. Most units are located on water bodies; 43 have Great Lakes shoreline and 40 are situated on inland lakes or streams. The state park system not only preserves some of Michigan's finest scenery and many significant ecosystems but also contains environments suitable for intensive recreation. Of the 85 currently developed parks, 80 percent offer swimming facilities and 87 percent have campgrounds with a combined total of 15,000 campsites. Mackinac Island State Park and nearby Michilimackinac State Park are administered by a separate state commission.

The Department of Natural Resources also administers 262,400 acres (106,272 hectares) of state game and wildlife areas, most of which are in southern Michigan since the northern game areas were merged with the state forests in 1946. The Wildlife Division is responsible for these tracts and for wildlife management on other state lands. The Fish Division operates fish hatcheries and rearing facilities and undertakes other fish management projects. The wildlife, fish, and other supporting divisions make a major contribution to recreation by enhancing hunting, fishing, and nature observation on both public and private lands through their management and technical assistance programs. The Waterways Division develops and administers

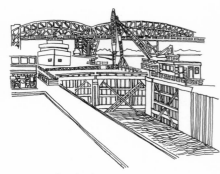

Soo Locks

SELECTED STATE PARK STATISTICS

Total area	218,200 acres (88,400 ha)
Porcupine Mountains S.P.	58,300 acres (23,510 ha)
Tahquamenon Falls S.P.	18,900 acres (7,650 ha)
Waterloo Recreation Area	16,000 acres (6,480 ha)

STATE HIGHWAY DEPARTMENT
RESOURCES

State freeways	1,600 miles (2,560 km)
Other state highways	9,300 miles (14,880 km)
Freeway rest areas	45
Roadside parks	104 with 1,700 picnic tables
Picnic sites	1,800

NUMBER OF LOCAL PARK FACILITIES

2,100 softball diamonds
1,900 tennis courts
160 refrigerated ice rinks
710 ordinary rinks
140 swimming pools
460 recreation centers

LOCAL PARKS: AREA

Total area	115,600 acres (46,818 ha)
County parks	37,000 acres (14,985 ha)
Township parks	6,000 acres (2,430 ha)
City parks	52,000 acres (21,060 ha)
Huron-Clinton parks	20,000 acres (8,100 ha)

PERCENT OF POPULATION
PARTICIPATING IN
RECREATIONAL ACTIVITIES

	MICH.	U.S.
Picnicking	54	47
Swimming (in lakes, rivers, and streams)	48	34
Fishing	31	24
Camping	22	16
Canoeing	12	3
Hunting	10	3
Horseback riding	9	5

AMOUNT OF PARTICIPATION
IN RECREATIONAL ACTIVITIES
(Millions of User-Days per Year
in Michigan)

Swimming (in lakes, rivers, and streams)	90
Driving for pleasure	Unknown
Walking for pleasure	Unknown
Outdoor sports	57
Bicycle trips	56
Fishing	47
Picnicking	44
Indoor sports	44

access sites and marinas on inland waters and, often in cooperation with the Corps of Engineers and local government authorities, on the Great Lakes. The Department of Natural Resources also makes many indirect contributions to recreation including statewide recreation planning, administration of federal grants, provision of technical assistance to local government park agencies, and enforcement of the state's pollution, waste disposal, and land-use controls.

Many other state agencies contribute to recreation in Michigan. State freeways and other state-operated highways are not only the main transportation links in the recreation system but, together with adjoining lands, become recreation resources themselves as people drive on them for pleasure. The five-mile-long (eight-kilometer) Mackinac Bridge is a major sightseeing attraction. A series of state historic sites and museums are administered by the Secretary of State.

Recreation Resources Administered by Local Governments. Although most recreation on public land takes place in parks and community centers administered by local governments, their collective role in the state's recreation system is not well documented. Local government systems provide picnicking, playgrounds, boating, swimming, sports facilities, hiking, urban beautification, formal gardens, zoos, cultural activities, arts and crafts, and open space where people can stroll, jog, play frisbee, sit in the sun, or sleep on the grass. No statewide information concerning the amount of activity that takes place in local government systems is available, but it is probably at least ten times larger than the combined total for state and federal lands. Local governments also provide many opportunities at facilities not designed for recreation; county and township roads, for example, are used extensively for pleasure driving.

Private Recreation Resources. Even less is known about the extent and contribution of privately owned recreation resources. The Michigan Travel Commission estimates that at least 34,600 businesses and more than 346,000 employees of commercial firms are involved in providing recreation-related goods and services for overnight tourists, such as transportation, lodging, food and drink, souvenirs, and entertainment. Data on private, noncommercial recreation resources are generally lacking. Michigan has more than 170,000 seasonal or second homes, but it is currently impossible to tell what proportion of these properties is used primarily for recreation. Much of the state's 12 million acres (4.9 million hectares) of farmland is used for recreation either by the owner, the owner's friends, tolerated trespassers, or various kinds of paying users such as hunters. Similarly, forest industries, public utilities, and individuals own more than 9 million acres (3.7 hectares) of commercially productive forest land and millions of acres of nonagricultural open lands that are also used extensively for recreation.

PARTICIPATION IN RECREATION

Data on the amount of participation in recreation that takes place in the state have only appeared relatively recently and are still fragmentary. As one would expect, Michigan has generally higher participation rates than the rest of the nation. The percentages in the margin show the proportions of Michigan and U.S. citizens who participated at least once a year in activities. Picnicking is the most important outdoor activity away from home in terms of the proportion of Michigan residents that participate. However, picnicking is fifth in terms of the total number of participant-days spent on an activity. A slightly smaller proportion of the population goes swimming in lakes, streams, and rivers, but people swim more often; as a result, swimming is first in total participation with an estimated 90 million user-days a year. Driving for pleasure and walking are probably the two next most important activities, but data for Michigan are not available. Total participation for 20 popular activities is estimated to be in excess of 600 million participant-days—a tremendous pressure even on Michigan's excellent resources since much of this activity is concentrated on a relatively few heavily used areas of private, local government, and state land in the southern Lower Peninsula.

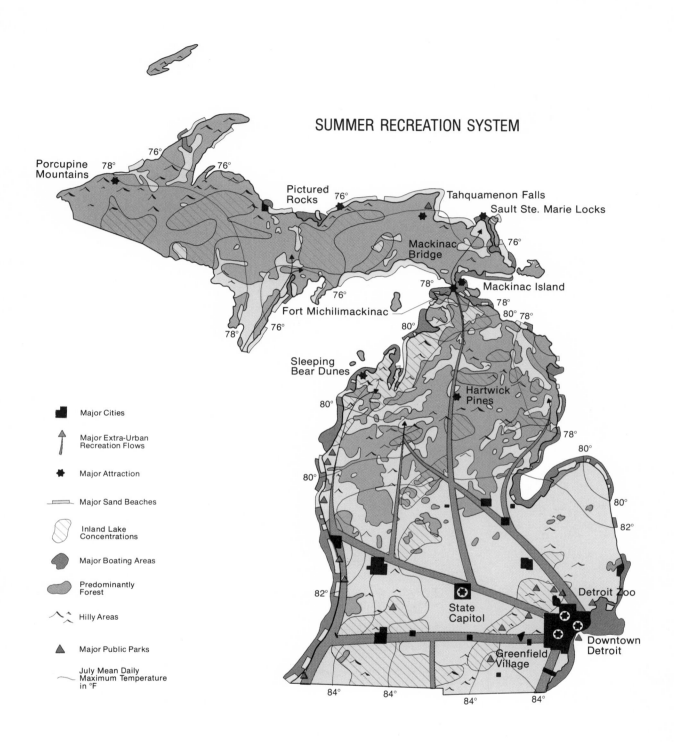

SUMMER RECREATION SYSTEM

Porcupine Mountains 78° 76° 76°

Pictured Rocks 76°

Tahquamenon Falls

Sault Ste. Marie Locks 76°

Mackinac Bridge

Mackinac Island

78°

78°

80° 78°

Fort Michilimackinac 76°

76°

80°

Sleeping Bear Dunes

Hartwick Pines

80°

78°

80°

78°

80°

80°

80°

82°

82°

State Capitol

Detroit Zoo

84° 84° 84° 84°

Greenfield Village

Downtown Detroit

◼ Major Cities

↑ Major Extra-Urban Recreation Flows

✦ Major Attraction

▭ Major Sand Beaches

Inland Lake Concentrations

Major Boating Areas

Predominantly Forest

⌃⌃ Hilly Areas

▲ Major Public Parks

July Mean Daily Maximum Temperature in °F

Recreation Patterns

Summer Patterns

The majority of recreation away from home takes place during June, July, and August. Families take their vacations then, and weekends are used for one-, two-, or three-day excursions. Some people visit urban attractions such as the Detroit Zoo, Greenfield Village, or the State Capitol in Lansing; others travel to the beaches, lakes, and forests. The flow of people along transpor-

tation linkages to groupings of recreation resources creates six distinct regions.

The Saginaw Lobe "Recreation Suburb" Region. A horseshoe-shaped region of hills, lakes, and woods that runs southwest from near Flint to the Indiana border and then turns northeast through Grand Rapids to Clare traces the outline of the retreating Saginaw Lobe of the last Ice Age glacier. This region is used heavily for weekend and evening recreation by residents of adjacent urban areas. It contains many major parks such as Kensington Metropolitan Park and the Waterloo and

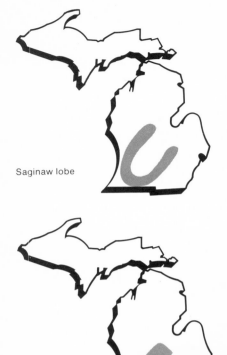

Saginaw lobe

Lakeless plain

MAJOR STATE PARKS WITH BEACHES
IN THE WESTERN CORRIDOR

Warren Dunes
Hoffmaster
Muskegon
Silver Lake
Ludington
Containing a total of 10,000 acres
(4,050 ha) and 21 miles (34 km) of
Lake Michigan shoreline

Southern lakeshore

Northern woodland

Yankee Springs state recreation areas. The lakes in these parks and other lakes and ponds in the region are intensively used for swimming, boating, water skiing, fishing, and sailing. Many are surrounded by houses; some of these homes are still only used seasonally, but dozens of former cottages have been converted to year-round residences, and new permanent homes are also being constructed. The region is becoming a great recreation-oriented suburb from which many people travel each day to jobs in surrounding cities.

The Lakeless Plain Region. Enclosed by the horseshoe-shaped "recreation suburb" is a region with more limited recreation resources. It is primarily agricultural land that was once the relatively flat bed of Lake Saginaw that existed in front of the retreating glacier. This "lakeless" region of Michigan has few major recreation developments. Rivers, streams, and city parks are the main public recreation resources. Plans to construct a series of large man-made lakes similar to the new Sleepy Hollow State Park have been abandoned because of environmental problems and high costs.

The Southern Lakeshore Day-Use Region. Outside the "recreation suburb" horseshoe is a third region comprising two narrow corridors along the Great Lakes. One follows Lake Michigan from the Indiana boundary to Ludington. Much of this corridor is high-quality shoreline and is part of what is claimed to be the world's largest freshwater beach. There are a number of beach-oriented resort communities such as New Buffalo and Saugatuck, several large parks such as Warren Dunes State Park, extensive boating facilities, and seasonally good fishing. It is the warmest, most developed, and most heavily used portion of the state's Lake Michigan shoreline.

The eastern corridor lies along Lake Erie, the Detroit River, Lake Saint Clair, Lake Huron, and Saginaw Bay. Its shorelines have fewer stretches of good sand beach and cannot be compared to Michigan's "Riviera" to the west. However, it does have extensive boating facilities and substantial fishing opportunities. Lake Saint Clair, together with adjacent portions of the Detroit River, is one of the busiest recreational boating areas in the world. The eastern corridor also contains nine heavily used parks—Metropolitan Beach, administered by the Huron-Clinton Metropolitan Authority, and Sterling, Algonac, Lakeport, Sanilac, Port Crescent, Sleeper, Bay City, and Tawas state parks. A great variety of commercial recreation facilities including marinas, amusement parks, and restaurants have also been attracted to this corridor.

These two shoreline corridors and their adjacent waters are close enough to population centers for many people to enjoy their amenities during one-day excursions. Some portions, however, have numerous recreation-oriented permanent residences or seasonal homes. In addition, tourists stop for overnight or longer visits, especially along the Lake Michigan shore to which many come from Indiana and Illinois.

The Northern Woodland Weekend and Vacation Region. The interior portions of the northern half of the Lower Peninsula constitute a fourth recreation region. A combination of resources, including lakes, streams, fish, forested landscape (much of which is public land), and cooler, less humid weather, attracts cottagers, campers, fishermen, and canoeists to this traditional "northwoods" area of the state. It is too far from the southern urban areas for one-day visits, so most of the recreation usage is by those who come for a weekend or longer period. Year-round recreational use of this area is increasing as automobile travel becomes easier and more retired persons have the resources necessary to convert a seasonal home or build a permanent residence.

The Northern Lakeshore Weekend and Vacation Region. The fifth region, the Lake Michigan and Lake Huron shoreline corridors of the northern Lower Peninsula, has some excellent sand beaches but not of the size and quality found in southwestern Michigan. Fishing is good, especially in some bays. Grand Traverse Bay, the Charlevoix area, and the Straits of Mackinac are important boating areas. Four of the state's major tourist attractions—Sleeping Bear Dunes, the Mackinac Bridge, Mackinac Island, and Fort Michilimackinac

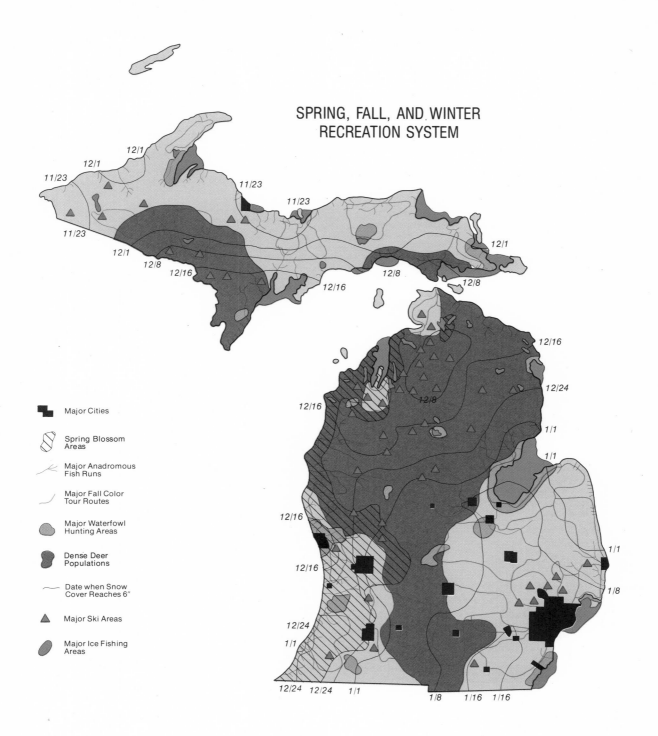

SPRING, FALL, AND WINTER
RECREATION SYSTEM

Major Cities

Spring Blossom
Areas

Major Anadromous
Fish Runs

Major Fall Color
Tour Routes

Major Waterfowl
Hunting Areas

Dense Deer
Populations

Date when Snow
Cover Reaches 6"

Major Ski Areas

Major Ice Fishing
Areas

—lie in this region as do five important resort centers. Although many permanent residents and seasonal home owners enjoy recreation in this zone, a large proportion of the recreational use consists of overnight trips by sportsmen and tourists. Many reach the region while touring on U.S. Highways 31 and 23; others take the circle route around Lake Michigan; and some visit it while on their way to Sault Sainte Marie or Canada.

The Upper Peninsula Vacation Region. The sixth region is the Upper Peninsula. Many of its attributes are similar to the northern Lower Peninsula; it is mostly forest and has several sizable inland lake areas and some excellent sand beaches, especially along the Lake Michigan shore. Its unique attractions include the navigation locks at Sault Sainte Marie, Tahquamenon Falls, the Pictured Rocks, the Keweenaw Peninsula, and the Porcupine Mountains. This region, however, is 250 miles (400 kilometers) from major population centers; its main attractions are considerable distances apart; it is not now served by modern four-lane highways (except for a short

Northern lakeshore

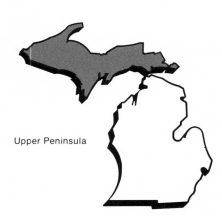

Upper Peninsula

stretch of I-75); it has few resort communities like those in region five; its climate is somewhat cooler; and it has a shorter "summer" season. Recreation use, therefore, tends to be less than elsewhere in the state.

Spring, Fall, and Winter Patterns

During the other nine months of the year, recreation away from the major cities does not fall into regional patterns. It tends to exhibit patterns based on single activities rather than groupings of activities and generally involves only one-day or weekend trips.

Visiting Michigan's fruit belt for a few hours or a day to see the trees in flower is an important spring activity. This takes place primarily in a 300-mile (480-kilometer) strip of orchards along the Lake Michigan shoreline. In the autumn similar excursions are made to see the fall colors, but not to any distinct region; appealing colors appear in rural landscapes throughout the state. Fishing for coho salmon and other anadromous fish, especially in portions of Lake Michigan and adjacent rivers in the northwestern Lower Peninsula, is also concentrated in the fall. Waterfowl hunting is dispersed throughout the wetlands of the state, but areas along the shorelines of Lake Erie, Lake Saint Clair, and Saginaw Bay are heavily used. Deer are hunted nearly everywhere except urban areas, but the central portion of the northern Lower Peninsula is especially popular.

People take part in many winter activities throughout the state. Snowmobiling occurs almost everywhere, but during winters with reasonable snow conditions much of it takes place on open lands close to southern urban centers. Many people ice fish close to home, even on lakes adjacent to urban areas. Only downhill skiing exhibits a distinct geographical pattern. In southern Michigan much skiing is done close to home on small hills near major cities, but most serious skiers try to spend as much time as possible at the cluster of ski resorts in the hilly, colder, and more snowy northwestern part of the Lower Peninsula where there are more than a dozen heavily used winter resorts, making it one of the nation's major ski areas.

Michigan's recreation system, therefore, exhibits some distinct distributions of resources and corresponding patterns of participation; the northwestern portion of the Lower Peninsula is particularly favorably endowed. Many resources are of such magnitude and so widely distributed that participation in extraurban recreation is uniquely diversified and widespread for such a populous, industrial state. Careful research, planning, and management will preserve this unique system of recreation resources for the future.

Michael Chubb

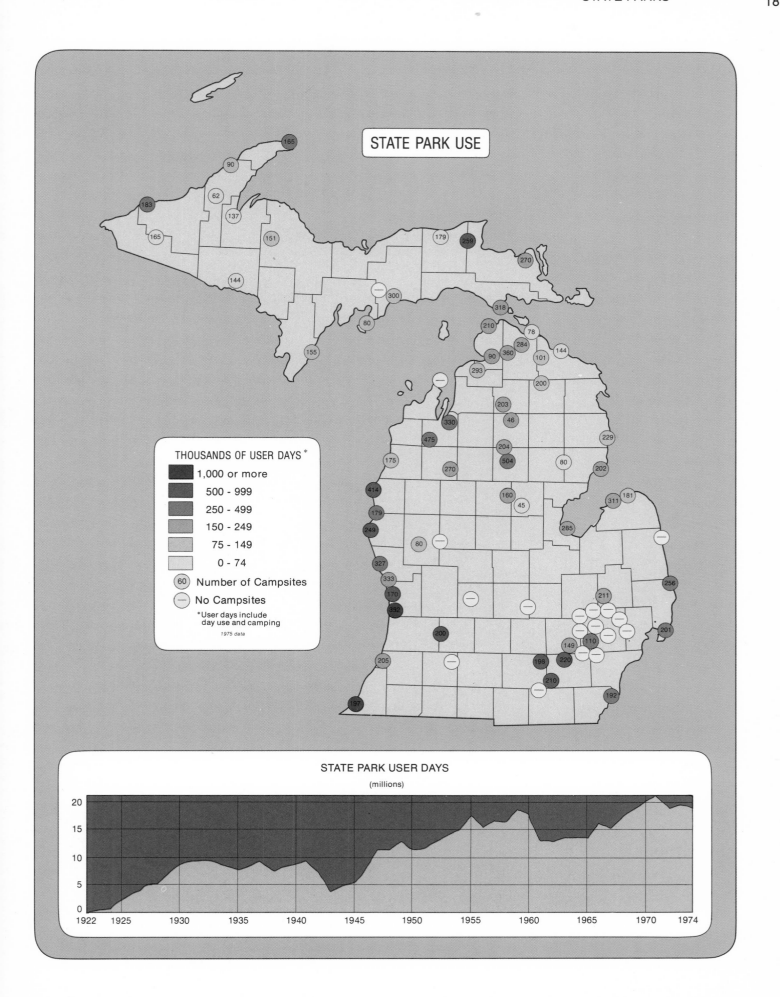

STATE PARK USE

THOUSANDS OF USER DAYS *

1,000 or more
500 - 999
250 - 499
150 - 249
75 - 149
0 - 74

60 Number of Campsites

— No Campsites

*User days include
day use and camping

1975 data

STATE PARK USER DAYS

(millions)

20
15
10
5
0

1922 1925 1930 1935 1940 1945 1950 1955 1960 1965 1970 1974

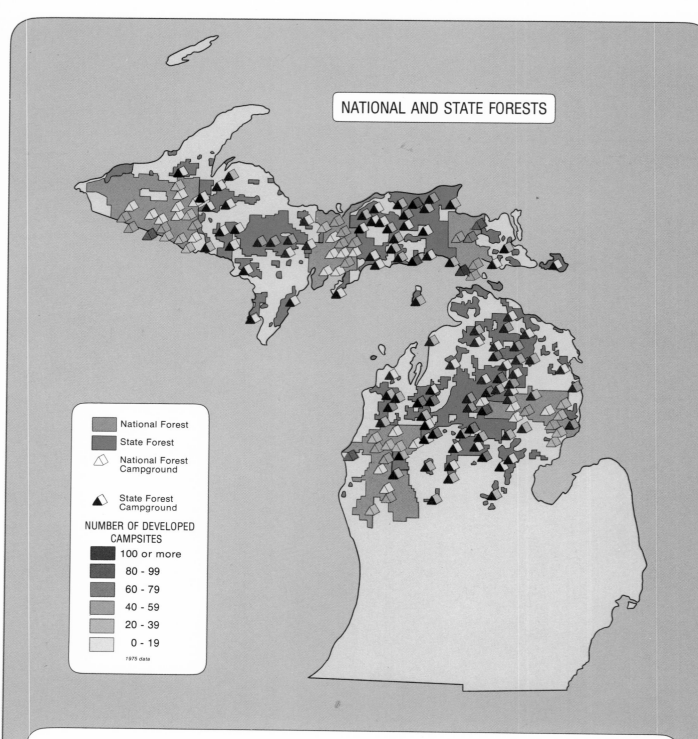

NATIONAL AND STATE FORESTS

National Forest

State Forest

National Forest Campground

State Forest Campground

NUMBER OF DEVELOPED CAMPSITES

100 or more

80 - 99

60 - 79

40 - 59

20 - 39

0 - 19

1975 data

National and state forests cover 6.5 million acres (2.6 million ha) or 17 percent of the state's land area. Much of this public acreage is not mature woodland. The original forest was practically all harvested during the lumbering era and in many cases severely damaged by fires that followed. Some areas were cleared for farming but proved too rocky or sandy or were climatically unsuitable; many such areas have been reforested and are now plantations in various stages of development. A majority of the forests will require many years of careful management to return to full production. Currently the public forests provide a diversified but changing environment for recreation. Stream conditions for fish will continue to improve and more vistas of mature forests will develop. However, deer and elk browse will continue to decrease, production of berries and some kinds of mushrooms will decline, and many aesthetically pleasing views will disappear.

Current recreational use of national and state forests is substantial. Summer use tends to be concentrated in and around developed campgrounds, beaches, and picnic areas, at certain special locations such as the Lumberman's Monument, and on popular fishing and canoeing rivers. Deer hunting in the fall is widely dispersed, but winter use focuses on marked snowmobile trails and forest lands that are adjacent to downhill skiing developments.

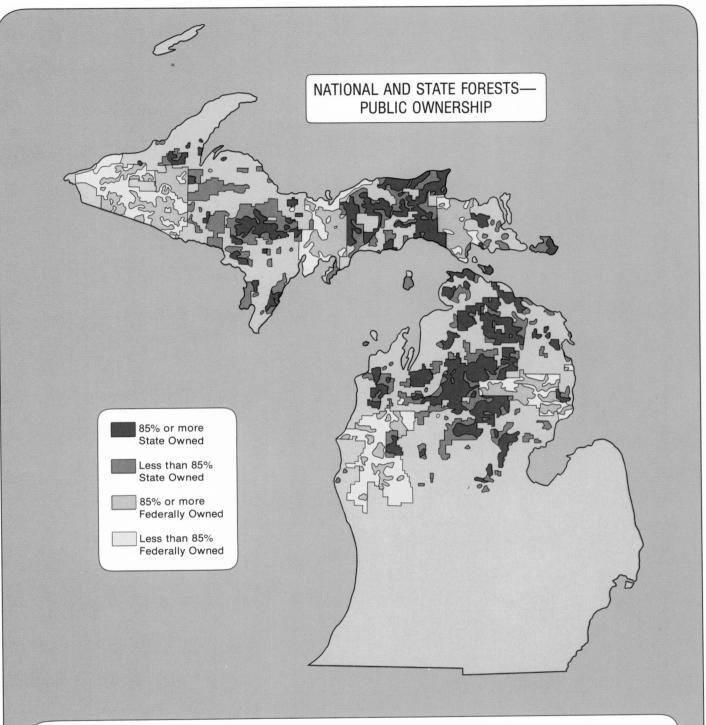

NATIONAL AND STATE FORESTS—
PUBLIC OWNERSHIP

85% or more
State Owned

Less than 85%
State Owned

85% or more
Federally Owned

Less than 85%
Federally Owned

Mixed public and private ownership is a significant characteristic of Michigan's public forests. As the map shows, only a portion of these forests is at least 85 percent in public ownership. Most of the publicly owned lands were acquired when owners failed to pay local government taxes after the valuable timber had been cut or during the land depression of the 1920s and 1930s. Subsequent forest purchases by federal and state government were usually of low value; most of the better parcels—especially those with lake and stream frontage—remained in private hands. Now many cottage sites, hunting and fishing cabins, and rural residences are scattered through the public forests, particularly in the northern Lower Peninsula. Owners of such private holdings are becoming less tolerant of public use, and more of these lands are being fenced and posted against trespassing. Conflicts are increasing as more people participate in motorcycling, snowmobiling, hunting, and other dispersed activities. On the other hand, some private holdings are enhanced by protection from encroaching development and by the recreation opportunities provided by the surrounding public forest, whereas recreation on public lands is often depreciated because of adjacent private developments. Rapidly increasing land values are severely reducing the ability of the forest agencies to solve conflicts and improve public recreation opportunities by purchasing key private lands, such as those lying along important trails, fishing streams, and canoe routes.

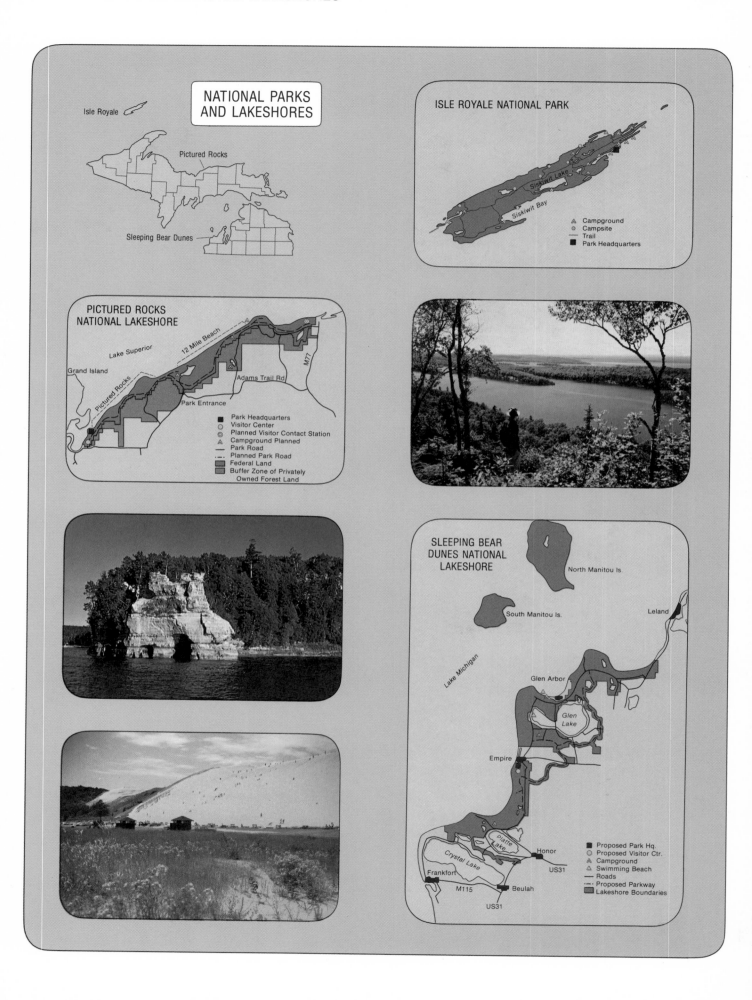

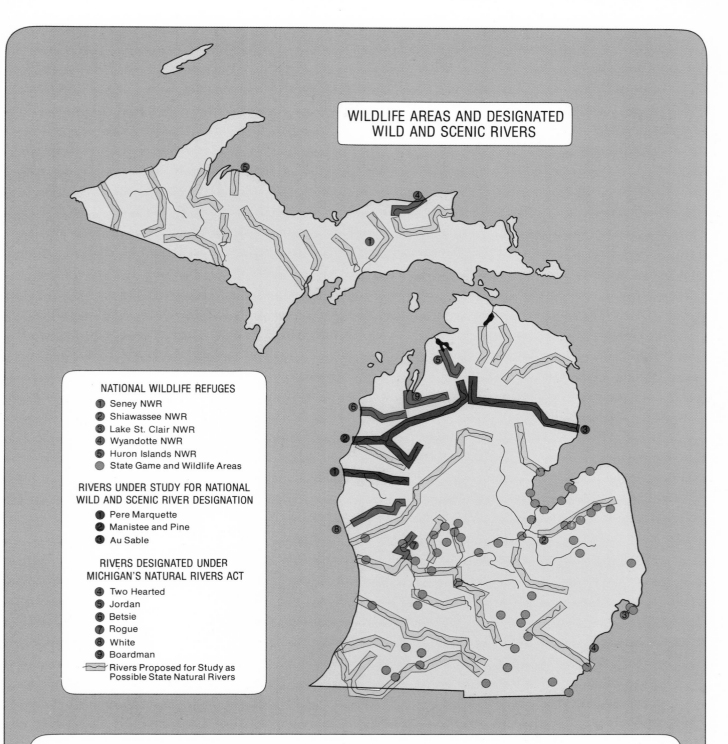

WILDLIFE AREAS AND DESIGNATED WILD AND SCENIC RIVERS

NATIONAL WILDLIFE REFUGES
① Seney NWR
② Shiawassee NWR
③ Lake St. Clair NWR
④ Wyandotte NWR
⑤ Huron Islands NWR
⬤ State Game and Wildlife Areas

RIVERS UNDER STUDY FOR NATIONAL WILD AND SCENIC RIVER DESIGNATION
① Pere Marquette
② Manistee and Pine
③ Au Sable

RIVERS DESIGNATED UNDER MICHIGAN'S NATURAL RIVERS ACT
④ Two Hearted
⑤ Jordan
⑥ Betsie
⑦ Rogue
⑧ White
⑨ Boardman
〜 Rivers Proposed for Study as Possible State Natural Rivers

Large areas of the national and state forests are important wildlife habitats. Michigan has numerous other public areas managed primarily for wildlife purposes. The federal Fish and Wildlife Service operates a large national wildlife refuge at Seney in Schoolcraft County and another along the Shiawassee River near Saginaw. In the southern part of the state the Michigan Department of Natural Resources has more than 50 state game and wildlife areas which are important both as wildlife habitats and recreation sites. Most of these lands, although purchased with revenues received from state hunting license fees and the federal tax on firearms and ammunition, are used extensively by fishermen, hikers, bird watchers, snowmobilers, and cross-country skiers as well as by hunters.

A relatively new approach to resource preservation and the provision of recreation opportunities is the designation of rivers as national or state rivers under federal or state wild and scenic river legislation. Designation is intended to preserve a river's natural features by cooperative action of public agencies, organizations, and individuals. The federal program anticipates future government purchase of river frontage. The state program, in contrast, is based on restricting development of private lands along designated rivers by encouraging the adoption of township or county zoning ordinances, or, failing that, adoption of zoning rules by the Michigan Natural Resources Commission.

WATERFALLS

① Gorge Falls on the Black River
② Laughing Whitefish Falls
③ Upper Tahquamenon Falls
④ Munising Falls
⑤ Sable River Falls
⑥ Nanabezho Falls

FALL COLORS

Late September

Late September - Early October

Early October

Middle October

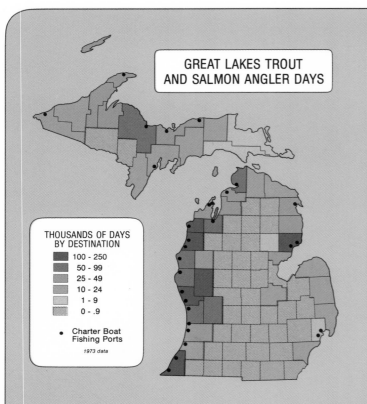

GREAT LAKES TROUT AND SALMON ANGLER DAYS

THOUSANDS OF DAYS
BY DESTINATION

100 - 250
50 - 99
25 - 49
10 - 24
1 - 9
0 - .9

• Charter Boat
  Fishing Ports

1973 data

Close to 3 million people go fishing in Michigan every year. Angling is third among the 20 recreation activities for which Michigan data are available. This high participation rate is possible because of the extensive fish habitat available in the state's inland and Great Lakes waters, the improvements in water quality resulting from pollution abatement measures, and the fish management activities of the Michigan Department of Natural Resources and other agencies.

A spectacular change in Great Lakes fishing has taken place in the past decade. Previously, invasion of the Great Lakes by the parasitic sea lamprey, introduction and a population explosion of alewife, overfishing by commercial fishermen, pollution, and other environmental changes severely reduced game fish catches. Control of the sea lamprey and restocking with hatchery-reared fish have begun to restore the lake trout numbers, but natural reproduction has not yet been reestablished satisfactorily. Yellow perch, another native species that became scarce, are also recovering and are now caught in fair numbers again along both the Lake Michigan and Lake Huron shorelines. Perch is a particularly valuable species because it can be caught at many locations from the shore, from piers, or from small boats. Thus it provides much recreation for those who do not have access to larger boats and special tackle used for deep-water fishing. The introduction of the coho and chinook salmon has had a major impact; millions of hatchery-produced salmon are now being planted annually in Michigan waters, and fish weighing more than 20 pounds are frequently caught.

Boats crowd Great Lakes bays and estuaries as fishermen enjoy salmon and trout fishing.

A Department of Natural Resources truck transports fish from hatcheries to planting sites.

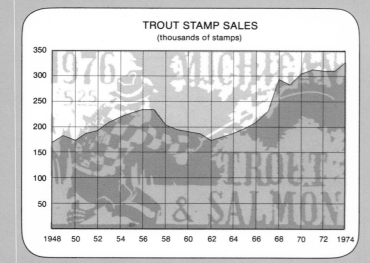

TROUT STAMP SALES
(thousands of stamps)

350
300
250
200
150
100
50

1948 50 52 54 56 58 60 62 64 66 68 70 72 1974

People fishing for trout or salmon in Michigan are required to buy a state trout and salmon stamp. Sales of these stamps increased substantially after 1967 reflecting the growing success of the Great Lakes trout and salmon stocking programs. Currently about 34 percent of the time spent fishing is on the Great Lakes, 53 percent is on inland lakes, and 13 percent is on rivers and streams. However, the Great Lakes provide about 60 percent of the weight of fish caught. A major portion of the lake trout and salmon fishing takes place along the Lake Michigan shoreline of the Lower Peninsula where ports with numerous charter boats are located. Trout and salmon catches are also improving in Lakes Huron and Superior. Pollution abatement has made it feasible to stock waters in southern Michigan, so coho and chinook salmon are now being caught in the Detroit River close to downtown Detroit and in the Grand River at Grand Rapids.

The state's extensive river systems and numerous inland lakes form a large and varied habitat for fish. Unfortunately, land clearance, logging, agriculture, road building, and waste disposal have all depreciated that habitat. Many waters, especially in southern Michigan, were badly damaged by removal of vegetation, accelerated erosion, and diminished summer flow. Silt, nutrients from fertilizers and sewage, and lower water levels speeded up lake aging. Natural fish populations were often eliminated completely or changed so that only small, less desirable fish and the introduced foreign carp remained. Some progress has been made in reversing these trends, but the distribution of fish and fishing participation is still much affected by habitat problems.

The patterns of participation in fishing on inland waters are based on habitat conditions, management programs, and human population distribution. A four-county area—Macomb, Oakland, St. Clair, and Wayne—has the highest amount of participation because of large populations and the extensive fishing opportunities now offered by Lake St. Clair, the St. Clair and Detroit rivers, and numerous lakes in Oakland County. The other major fishing area is in the southwest corner of the state where there are numerous lakes in several counties, improved fishing on rivers such as the Grand and St. Joseph, and comparatively large resident populations. In contrast, the lakeless counties in the center of the state have low total participation levels in spite of the proximity of population centers such as Saginaw, Flint, and Lansing. Total fishing on inland waters is medium to low elsewhere in the state, except for Roscommon County.

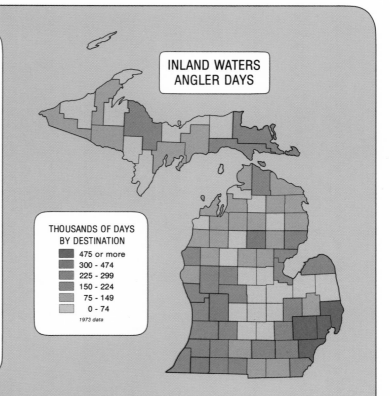

INLAND WATERS ANGLER DAYS

THOUSANDS OF DAYS BY DESTINATION

- 475 or more
- 300 - 474
- 225 - 299
- 150 - 224
- 75 - 149
- 0 - 74

1973 data

Pollution reduction, shoreline, and hatchery programs are restoring fishing in Detroit.

A Department of Natural Resources biological survey unit samples a fish population with electro-fishing gear.

During earlier decades, state inland fisheries management concentrated on cold-water species, particularly brook, brown, and rainbow trout, and most management efforts occurred in the northern counties. More recently, the Department of Natural Resources has increased its efforts to improve warmwater fishing, especially in the southern part of the state. Water pollution abatement projects and new management skills have aided this work. In 1970 a Metrofishing Program was started in the Detroit area, which stocks major waters with fish, develops fishing ponds for use, provides access to piers and shorelines, offers fishing instruction, and encourages marinas, bait stores, and charter boats. As a result 4.5 million people have a fishery developing on their doorstep that includes coho, chinook, and kokanee salmon; brook trout; walleye; tiger muskellunge; northern pike; largemouth bass; and yellow perch.

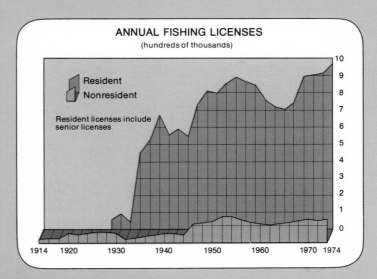

ANNUAL FISHING LICENSES
(hundreds of thousands)

Resident
Nonresident

Resident licenses include senior licenses

1914 1920 1930 1940 1950 1960 1970 1974

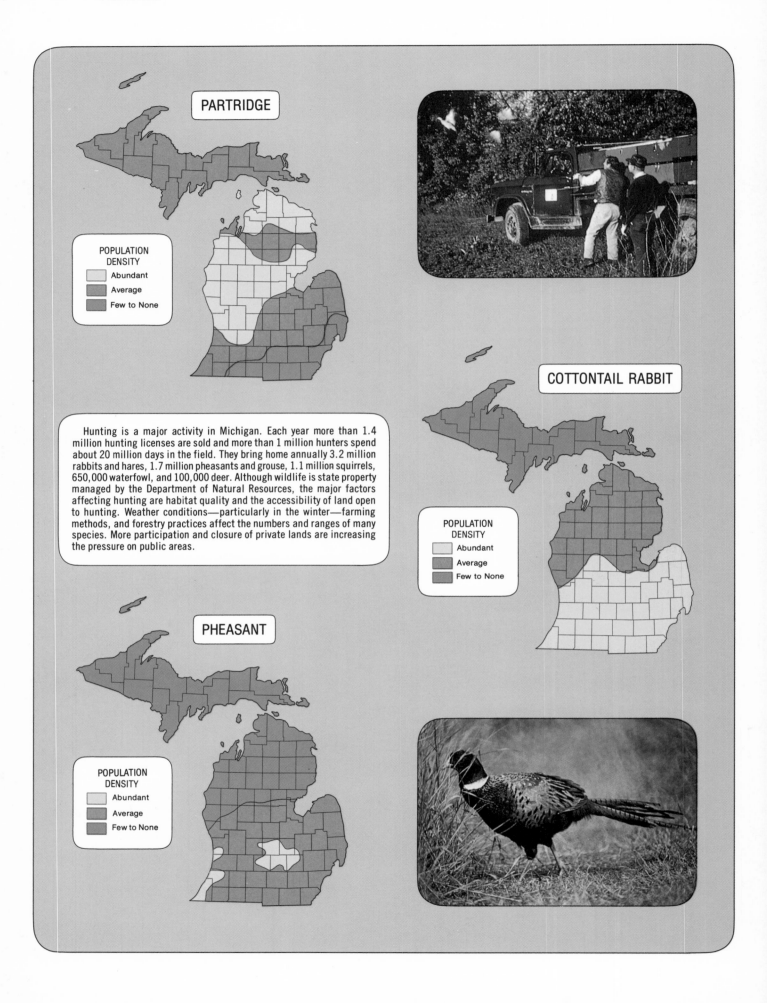

PARTRIDGE

POPULATION
DENSITY
Abundant
Average
Few to None

Hunting is a major activity in Michigan. Each year more than 1.4 million hunting licenses are sold and more than 1 million hunters spend about 20 million days in the field. They bring home annually 3.2 million rabbits and hares, 1.7 million pheasants and grouse, 1.1 million squirrels, 650,000 waterfowl, and 100,000 deer. Although wildlife is state property managed by the Department of Natural Resources, the major factors affecting hunting are habitat quality and the accessibility of land open to hunting. Weather conditions—particularly in the winter—farming methods, and forestry practices affect the numbers and ranges of many species. More participation and closure of private lands are increasing the pressure on public areas.

COTTONTAIL RABBIT

POPULATION
DENSITY
Abundant
Average
Few to None

PHEASANT

POPULATION
DENSITY
Abundant
Average
Few to None

About 120,000 people go waterfowl hunting in Michigan each year. The state offers numerous opportunities for this activity because of its extensive wetlands and location on waterfowl migration routes. More than 25 species of ducks and geese are hunted. Most are migratory species, so management involves cooperation among Michigan, other states, the federal government, and Canadian authorities under terms of the federal migratory bird protection acts. The majority of the birds use the Mississippi Valley Flyway (which includes several subsidiary routes through Michigan) when traveling between southern wintering areas and summer breeding grounds in the northern states and Canada. Waterfowl hunting is managed by protecting and enhancing suitable wetland habitats and by regulating hunting seasons and bag limits. Hunting for ducks involves a point system in which the least numerous species are assigned the highest number of points. Since hunters may not exceed a specified maximum number of points, they are encouraged to identify ducks carefully and shoot the more abundant species. As the map shows, duck hunting is concentrated in southeast Michigan.

DUCK HUNTER DAYS

THOUSANDS OF DAYS
BY DESTINATION

- 25 - 50
- 15 - 24
- 10 - 14
- 5 - 9
- 2.5 - 4
- 0 - 2.4

1973 data

**COTTONTAIL RABBIT
HUNTER DAYS**

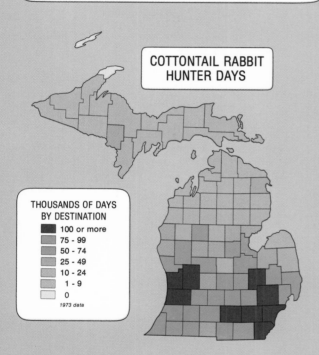

THOUSANDS OF DAYS
BY DESTINATION

- 100 or more
- 75 - 99
- 50 - 74
- 25 - 49
- 10 - 24
- 1 - 9
- 0

1973 data

**SNOWSHOE HARE
HUNTER DAYS**

THOUSANDS OF DAYS
BY DESTINATION

- 25 - 50
- 15 - 24
- 10 - 14
- 5 - 9
- .5 - 4
- 0 - .4

1973 data

The cottontail rabbit is Michigan's most important game species both in terms of the number of animals killed and the hours spent hunting. Over 400,000 hunters harvest about 2.5 million rabbits each year. The species is particularly valuable because cottontails are most numerous in the southern third of the state where the largest number of hunters live. Rabbit hunting is concentrated in the counties containing or adjacent to the major urban centers, especially the Detroit and Grand Rapids areas. Hunting success is greatest in southwestern Michigan where the habitat is better and hunting pressures lower. In the northern part of the state rabbits are scarce. However, these areas are the habitat of the snowshoe hare which changes to a white color in winter. Snowshoe hare hunting appears to be affected by human population distribution, the counties around Traverse City, Charlevoix, Alpena, Mackinaw City, and similar urban centers providing the most hunting. Rabbit and hare hunting is the longest game season, running from October to March.

PRIMARY WOODCOCK AREAS

CONGREGATING AREAS OF CANADIAN GEESE

PERMANENT WETLANDS IMPORTANT TO WATERFOWL

Although large tracts of wetland have been drained or filled, the state still has many shallow lakes, swamps, and marshes that are valuable waterfowl habitats. Much wetland borders Great Lakes bays and estuaries, but there are also many significant inland areas. Wetlands are year-around habitats for some waterfowl species and seasonal feeding, resting, or breeding places for others. They also act as spawning and nursery areas for fish, provide food and shelter for many other kinds of wildlife, trap silt and excess nutrients, store surplus water, recharge ground water, and maintain stream flow during dry periods. Wetlands are highly productive biologically and of great value to hunting, fishing, bird-watching, photography, canoeing, and many other forms of recreation.

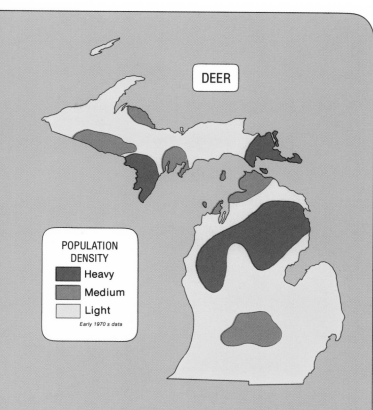

DEER

Deer hunting is significant in Michigan because of the magnitude of participation and the continuing debates concerning deer management practices. The number of hunters has more than tripled since 1940. At the same time, much of the state's cut and burned forest land has regrown and produces less deer browse. Currently some 750,000 hunters bring home about 100,000 animals each year, which is about 10 percent of the deer population. Deer are more numerous and larger in size in the southern third of the state. A surprising amount of hunting takes place in heavily populated southern counties.

POPULATION
DENSITY

Heavy
Medium
Light

Early 1970 s data

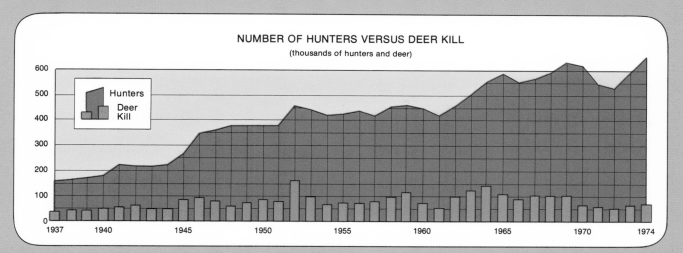

NUMBER OF HUNTERS VERSUS DEER KILL
(thousands of hunters and deer)

Hunters
Deer
Kill

1937 1940 1945 1950 1955 1960 1965 1970 1974

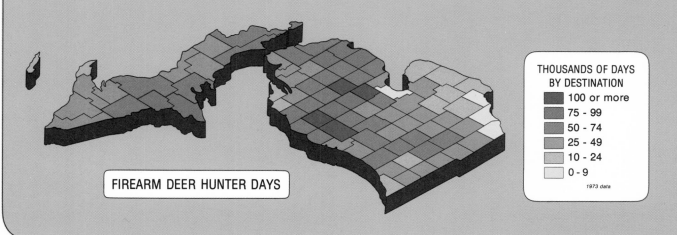

FIREARM DEER HUNTER DAYS

THOUSANDS OF DAYS
BY DESTINATION

100 or more
75 - 99
50 - 74
25 - 49
10 - 24
0 - 9

1973 data

SNOWMOBILING

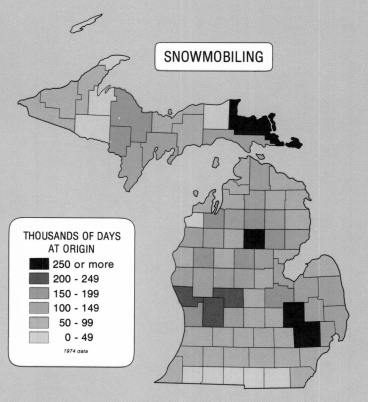

The northern two-thirds of the state has the best snow conditions, the majority of the public land open to snowmobiling, and most of the snowmobile trails. Snowmobiling, however, is concentrated in a broad band of counties across the middle of the Lower Peninsula because most snowmobilers do not travel far from home. Many southern Michigan residents snowmobile on nearby agricultural or unused lands and travel north only occasionally. About half of the snowmobiling takes place on private lands and one-fourth on federal or state lands.

The map shows the number of snowmobiler days spent by residents of each county. The southern three tiers of counties have low values in spite of substantial populations because snow conditions are generally poorer, and it is some distance to better conditions and large expanses of public land. Just to the north is a belt of counties with higher values. Grand Rapids–Muskegon and Oakland–Saginaw have especially high values because of their large populations and proximity to better snow conditions and land available for snowmobiling.

THOUSANDS OF DAYS AT ORIGIN

- 250 or more
- 200 - 249
- 150 - 199
- 100 - 149
- 50 - 99
- 0 - 49

1974 data

PRINCIPAL DOWNHILL SKI AREAS

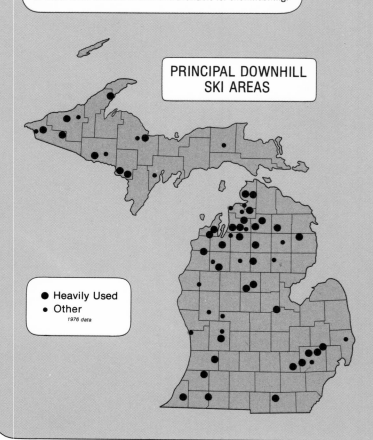

- ● Heavily Used
- • Other

1976 data

Although Michigan has no high mountains, it is one of the nation's major skiing areas. Reliable winter snow conditions and hilly terrain offer reasonable skiing within weekend driving distance of large populations. The 70 downhill ski facilities in the state have a total of more than 400 lifts and tows servicing some 700 ski runs. Most of the major ski areas improve snow conditions by using snow-making machines. The southern third of the state has 14 percent of the runs and 37 percent of the lifts and tows; again, most are located in the glacial hills west of Detroit where use is intensive even on weekday evenings. The northern half of lower Michigan contains 56 percent of the runs and 48 percent of the lifts and tows. It includes the major weekend ski resorts offering dining, lodging, and entertainment. Facilities in the Upper Peninsula are oriented primarily toward the Chicago and southeastern Wisconsin market.

RECREATIONAL BOATING PARTICIPATION AND HARBORS

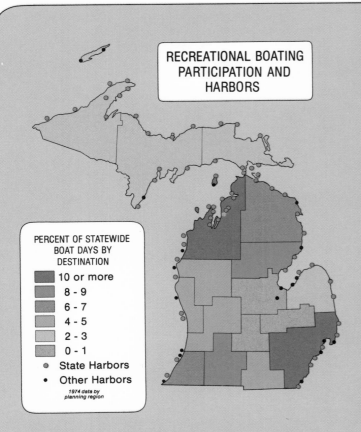

PERCENT OF STATEWIDE BOAT DAYS BY DESTINATION

10 or more
8 - 9
6 - 7
4 - 5
2 - 3
0 - 1
● State Harbors
• Other Harbors

1974 data by planning region

The state's more than 3,000 miles of Great Lakes shoreline, over 11,000 inland lakes and ponds, and many miles of rivers are excellent for boating. However, boating on these waters would be severely limited without public access facilities provided by various federal, state, and local agencies, especially the Department of Natural Resources. More than 500 water access points were developed between 1939 and 1968 with the aid of state fishing license fees and federal fishing tackle tax funds, the number and quality of new sites gradually increasing in recent years. On the Great Lakes a major program of harbor, marina, and launching ramp construction uses a portion of the state gasoline taxes supplemented in many cases by federal and local funds. There are now more than 60 state harbors spaced every 15 to 30 miles along the Great Lakes shorelines, many with extensive public marina facilities. Commercial marinas are particularly important on intensively used waterways. Great Lakes boating facilities are concentrated in four main regions, namely, the Detroit area, the southern portion of the Lake Michigan shoreline, the Traverse City–Charlevoix region, and the Straits of Mackinac area. Although many of the owners of Michigan's more than half million registered boats travel considerable distances during summer vacations and the Great Lakes fishing season, more than half of all boating takes place within a one-hour drive from home. In fact, residents of the lower third of the state are responsible for almost 80 percent of the boating participation, and 60 percent of all Michigan boating actually takes place within this region.

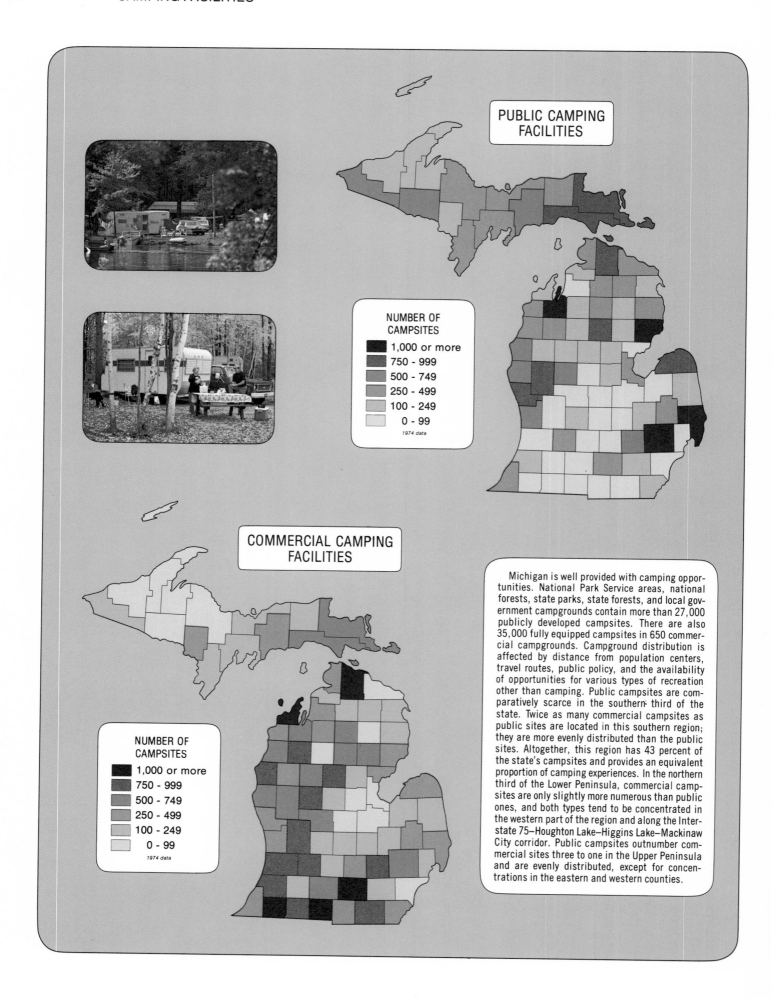

PUBLIC CAMPING
FACILITIES

NUMBER OF
CAMPSITES

1,000 or more
750 - 999
500 - 749
250 - 499
100 - 249
0 - 99

1974 data

COMMERCIAL CAMPING
FACILITIES

NUMBER OF
CAMPSITES

1,000 or more
750 - 999
500 - 749
250 - 499
100 - 249
0 - 99

1974 data

Michigan is well provided with camping opportunities. National Park Service areas, national forests, state parks, state forests, and local government campgrounds contain more than 27,000 publicly developed campsites. There are also 35,000 fully equipped campsites in 650 commercial campgrounds. Campground distribution is affected by distance from population centers, travel routes, public policy, and the availability of opportunities for various types of recreation other than camping. Public campsites are comparatively scarce in the southern third of the state. Twice as many commercial campsites as public sites are located in this southern region; they are more evenly distributed than the public sites. Altogether, this region has 43 percent of the state's campsites and provides an equivalent proportion of camping experiences. In the northern third of the Lower Peninsula, commercial campsites are only slightly more numerous than public ones, and both types tend to be concentrated in the western part of the region and along the Interstate 75–Houghton Lake–Higgins Lake–Mackinaw City corridor. Public campsites outnumber commercial sites three to one in the Upper Peninsula and are evenly distributed, except for concentrations in the eastern and western counties.

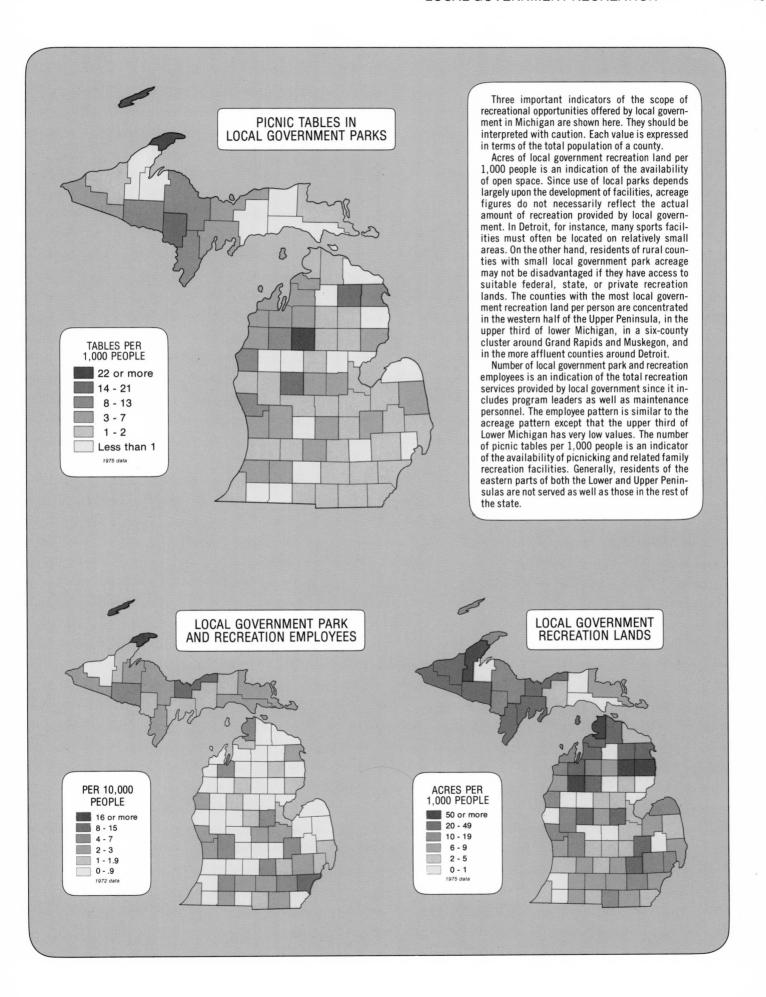

PICNIC TABLES IN
LOCAL GOVERNMENT PARKS

TABLES PER
1,000 PEOPLE

22 or more
14 - 21
8 - 13
3 - 7
1 - 2
Less than 1

1975 data

Three important indicators of the scope of recreational opportunities offered by local government in Michigan are shown here. They should be interpreted with caution. Each value is expressed in terms of the total population of a county.

Acres of local government recreation land per 1,000 people is an indication of the availability of open space. Since use of local parks depends largely upon the development of facilities, acreage figures do not necessarily reflect the actual amount of recreation provided by local government. In Detroit, for instance, many sports facilities must often be located on relatively small areas. On the other hand, residents of rural counties with small local government park acreage may not be disadvantaged if they have access to suitable federal, state, or private recreation lands. The counties with the most local government recreation land per person are concentrated in the western half of the Upper Peninsula, in the upper third of lower Michigan, in a six-county cluster around Grand Rapids and Muskegon, and in the more affluent counties around Detroit.

Number of local government park and recreation employees is an indication of the total recreation services provided by local government since it includes program leaders as well as maintenance personnel. The employee pattern is similar to the acreage pattern except that the upper third of Lower Michigan has very low values. The number of picnic tables per 1,000 people is an indicator of the availability of picnicking and related family recreation facilities. Generally, residents of the eastern parts of both the Lower and Upper Peninsulas are not served as well as those in the rest of the state.

LOCAL GOVERNMENT PARK
AND RECREATION EMPLOYEES

PER 10,000
PEOPLE

16 or more
8 - 15
4 - 7
2 - 3
1 - 1.9
0 - .9

1972 data

LOCAL GOVERNMENT
RECREATION LANDS

ACRES PER
1,000 PEOPLE

50 or more
20 - 49
10 - 19
6 - 9
2 - 5
0 - 1

1975 data

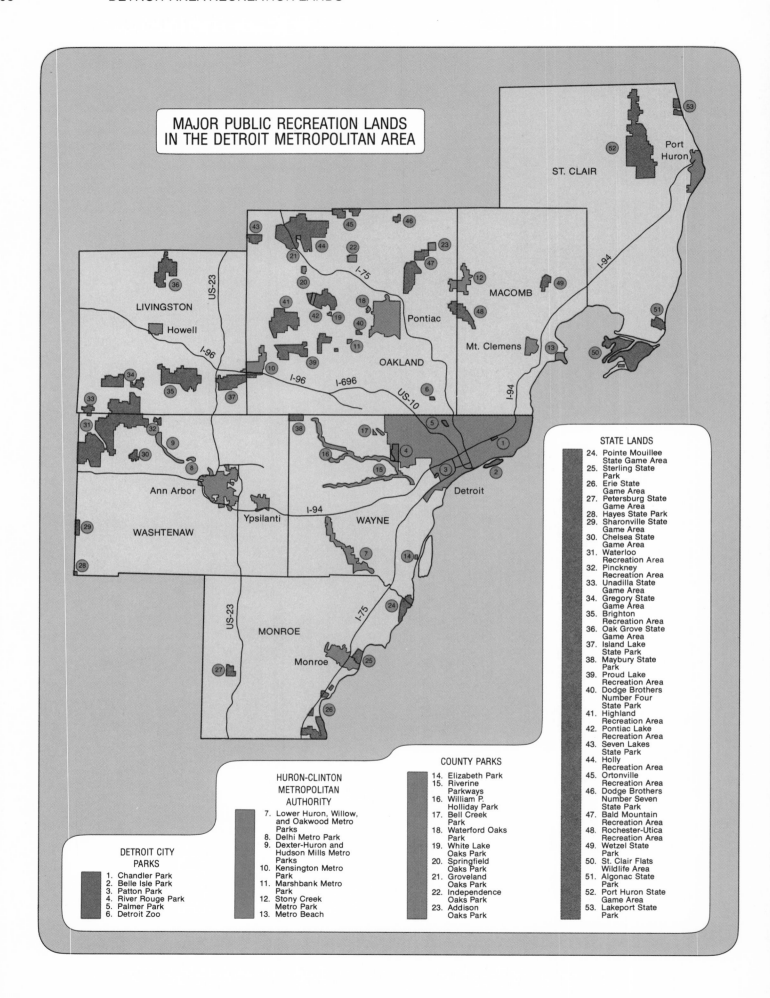

MAJOR PUBLIC RECREATION LANDS
IN THE DETROIT METROPOLITAN AREA

ST. CLAIR
Port Huron

LIVINGSTON
Howell

MACOMB
Pontiac
Mt. Clemens

OAKLAND

WASHTENAW
Ann Arbor
Ypsilanti

WAYNE
Detroit

MONROE
Monroe

DETROIT CITY PARKS

1. Chandler Park
2. Belle Isle Park
3. Patton Park
4. River Rouge Park
5. Palmer Park
6. Detroit Zoo

HURON-CLINTON METROPOLITAN AUTHORITY

7. Lower Huron, Willow, and Oakwood Metro Parks
8. Delhi Metro Park
9. Dexter-Huron and Hudson Mills Metro Parks
10. Kensington Metro Park
11. Marshbank Metro Park
12. Stony Creek Metro Park
13. Metro Beach

COUNTY PARKS

14. Elizabeth Park
15. Riverine Parkways
16. William P. Holliday Park
17. Bell Creek Park
18. Waterford Oaks Park
19. White Lake Oaks Park
20. Springfield Oaks Park
21. Groveland Oaks Park
22. Independence Oaks Park
23. Addison Oaks Park

STATE LANDS

24. Pointe Mouillee State Game Area
25. Sterling State Park
26. Erie State Game Area
27. Petersburg State Game Area
28. Hayes State Park
29. Sharonville State Game Area
30. Chelsea State Game Area
31. Waterloo Recreation Area
32. Pinckney Recreation Area
33. Unadilla State Game Area
34. Gregory State Game Area
35. Brighton Recreation Area
36. Oak Grove State Game Area
37. Island Lake State Park
38. Maybury State Park
39. Proud Lake Recreation Area
40. Dodge Brothers Number Four State Park
41. Highland Recreation Area
42. Pontiac Lake Recreation Area
43. Seven Lakes State Park
44. Holly Recreation Area
45. Ortonville Recreation Area
46. Dodge Brothers Number Seven State Park
47. Bald Mountain Recreation Area
48. Rochester-Utica Recreation Area
49. Wetzel State Park
50. St. Clair Flats Wildlife Area
51. Algonac State Park
52. Port Huron State Game Area
53. Lakeport State Park

The map to the left shows that Detroit is almost surrounded by a belt of public recreation land consisting primarily of state parks, recreation areas, and game areas. The Huron-Clinton Metropolitan Authority also has three parks in this belt as well as heavily used Metropolitan Beach on Lake St. Clair and several parks along the Huron River. Oakland County parks and Wayne County parks along the Rouge River are the other main components of the belt. Metropolitan area residents use these lands intensively for picnicking, swimming, sunbathing, fishing, and other activities. Most of these parks can be reached only by private automobile and are therefore largely inaccessible to many disadvantaged citizens. The scope and distribution of city-provided recreation opportunities are thus of great significance to the disadvantaged and those who wish to devote less of their recreation time to travel.

DETROIT CITY PARKS

REDFORD GOLF COURSE

Southfield (39)

PALMER PARK

Lodge

Woodward

Gratiot

Ford (I-94)

ELIZA HOWELL PARK

Grand River

I-75

CHANDLER PARK

Jeffries

I-96

RIVER ROUGE PARK

I-75

Ford (I-94)

Michigan

I-96
I-75

BELLE ISLE PARK

GENERAL PATTON PARK

Fisher

Detroit River

Rouge River

Playfields, Playgrounds, and Playlots

Other Parks and Facilities

Recreation Centers

Major Parks

The 5,840-acre (2,370 ha) City of Detroit park system consists of 59 parks, 43 sports fields, 116 playgrounds, 98 playlots, 13 boulevards, 16 greenbelts, 22 parkways, and 24 miscellaneous areas. Most larger parks are some distance from the city's core. Belle Isle Park is one of the largest. Located in the Detroit River, it provides some relief from urban heat on hot summer nights and views of Great Lakes shipping, in addition to usual park facilities. During the summer, the Detroit Recreation Department provides regular programs for thousands of young people at 500 different sites. Activities include sports, crafts, story telling, and games. Softball and volleyball for teenagers take place regularly at most sports fields. Events such as youth fitness, day camps, model building, band concerts, field trips, and other special programs are organized. Mobile recreation equipment provides opportunities at 600 additional locations. Winter recreation programs for all ages are offered at 30 city recreation centers and at many schools.

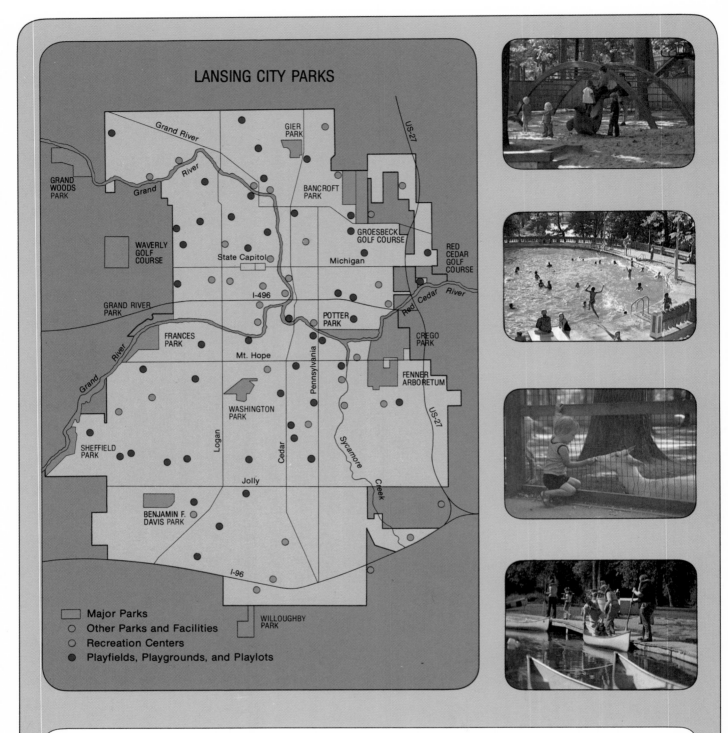

LANSING CITY PARKS

Lansing's first park was acquired in 1878; now the system consists of more than 100 tracts totaling more than 2,500 acres (1,050 ha). Facilities include 5 recreation centers, 50 ball fields, 4 golf courses, 2 swimming pools, a zoo, and a nature center. The city enjoys a good ratio of park acreage to population, but a large proportion of the land is virtually inaccessible to many citizens who do not have the use of a car. Most major parks are outside the central city and two-thirds of the acreage is close to or even beyond the city limits. As the map shows, some neighborhoods are not only considerable distances from the larger parks, they also lack walk-in access to playfields, swimming pools, and recreation centers. Lansing's first two modern recreation centers were built only recently and several more are needed. In spite of these problems, participation in city recreation programs is high. More than 45,000 individuals actively take part in various sports, crafts, clubs, and special activities for a total of more than 500,000 user-occasions. Use of summer playground programs, softball leagues, and young people's drop-in centers contribute half of this total. Spectators at sports and other Department of Parks and Recreation events account for an additional half million user-occasions. Use of the park system for unorganized activities such as walking, playing games, bicycling, picnicking, fishing, and visits to the zoo and arboretum nature center probably adds several million more user-occasions.

TOURIST ATTRACTIONS

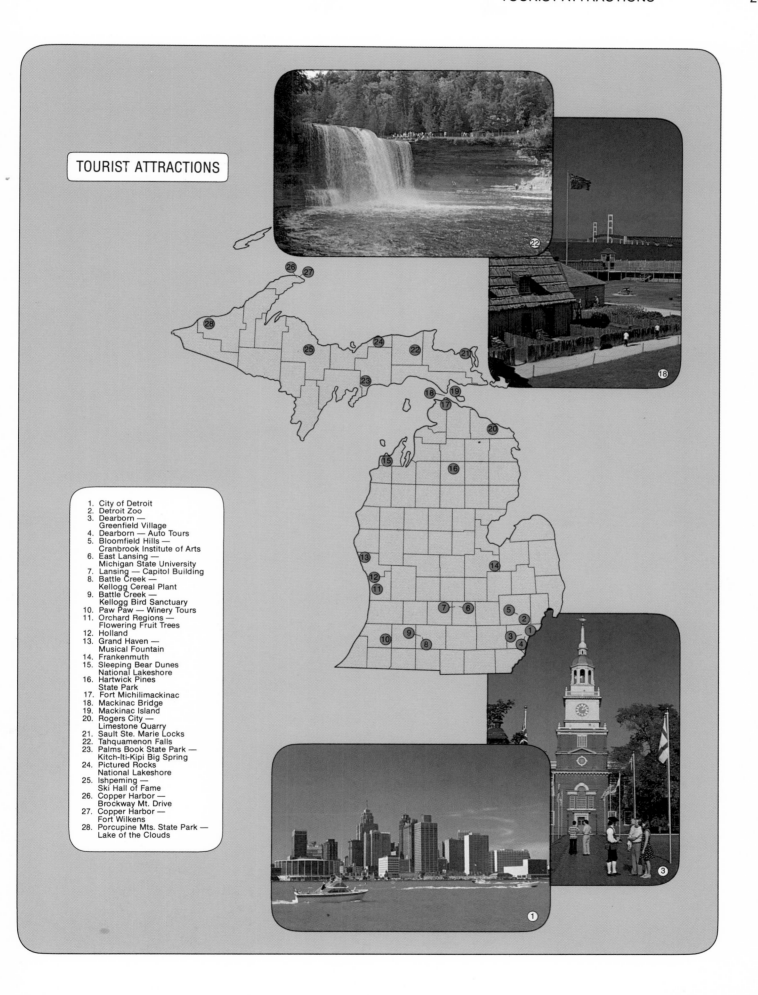

1. City of Detroit
2. Detroit Zoo
3. Dearborn —
   Greenfield Village
4. Dearborn — Auto Tours
5. Bloomfield Hills —
   Cranbrook Institute of Arts
6. East Lansing —
   Michigan State University
7. Lansing — Capitol Building
8. Battle Creek —
   Kellogg Cereal Plant
9. Battle Creek —
   Kellogg Bird Sanctuary
10. Paw Paw — Winery Tours
11. Orchard Regions —
    Flowering Fruit Trees
12. Holland
13. Grand Haven —
    Musical Fountain
14. Frankenmuth
15. Sleeping Bear Dunes
    National Lakeshore
16. Hartwick Pines
    State Park
17. Fort Michilimackinac
18. Mackinac Bridge
19. Mackinac Island
20. Rogers City —
    Limestone Quarry
21. Sault Ste. Marie Locks
22. Tahquamenon Falls
23. Palms Book State Park —
    Kitch-Iti-Kipi Big Spring
24. Pictured Rocks
    National Lakeshore
25. Ishpeming —
    Ski Hall of Fame
26. Copper Harbor —
    Brockway Mt. Drive
27. Copper Harbor —
    Fort Wilkens
28. Porcupine Mts. State Park —
    Lake of the Clouds

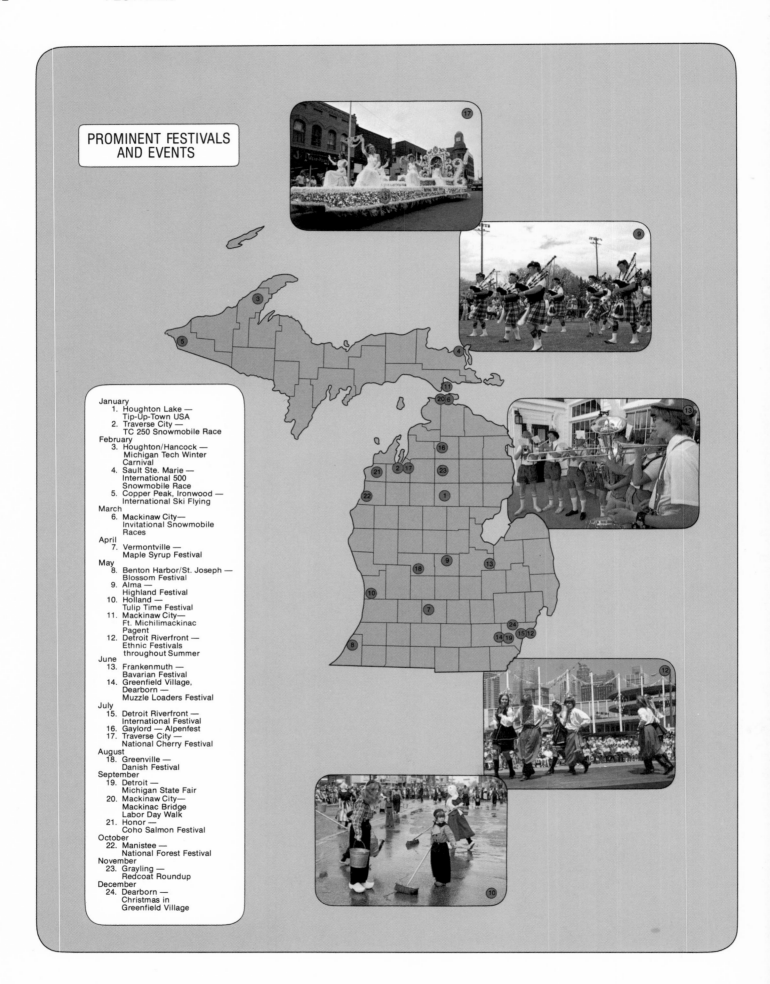

PROMINENT FESTIVALS AND EVENTS

January
1. Houghton Lake —
   Tip-Up-Town USA
2. Traverse City —
   TC 250 Snowmobile Race

February
3. Houghton/Hancock —
   Michigan Tech Winter
   Carnival
4. Sault Ste. Marie —
   International 500
   Snowmobile Race
5. Copper Peak, Ironwood —
   International Ski Flying

March
6. Mackinaw City—
   Invitational Snowmobile
   Races

April
7. Vermontville —
   Maple Syrup Festival

May
8. Benton Harbor/St. Joseph —
   Blossom Festival
9. Alma —
   Highland Festival
10. Holland —
    Tulip Time Festival
11. Mackinaw City—
    Ft. Michilimackinac
    Pagent
12. Detroit Riverfront —
    Ethnic Festivals
    throughout Summer

June
13. Frankenmuth —
    Bavarian Festival
14. Greenfield Village,
    Dearborn —
    Muzzle Loaders Festival

July
15. Detroit Riverfront —
    International Festival
16. Gaylord — Alpenfest
17. Traverse City —
    National Cherry Festival

August
18. Greenville —
    Danish Festival

September
19. Detroit —
    Michigan State Fair
20. Mackinaw City—
    Mackinac Bridge
    Labor Day Walk
21. Honor —
    Coho Salmon Festival

October
22. Manistee —
    National Forest Festival

November
23. Grayling —
    Redcoat Roundup

December
24. Dearborn —
    Christmas in
    Greenfield Village

TRANSPORTATION AND COMMUNICATION

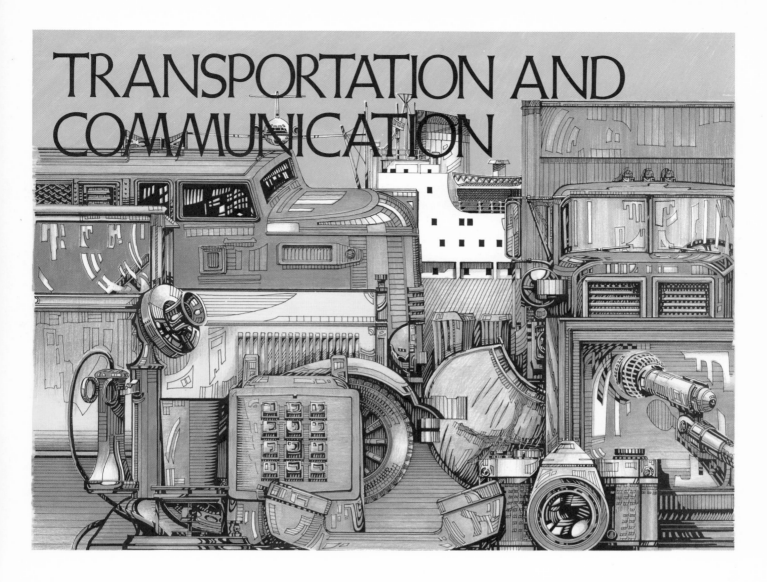

Imagine, if you will, the area we call Michigan as it might have been 200 or 300 years ago. Contact among the people inhabiting the area would have been made by walking, canoeing, or riding animals. There may have been some signaling with fire or drums over short distances, but to get a message from what is now Coldwater in the south to Marquette in the north would have required several days. Today it can be done in a matter of a few seconds via electronic media. To travel by air would require only an hour or two; by auto, about ten hours. The flood of messages and modes of transport among which present-day inhabitants of Michigan may choose is staggering in comparison to the alternatives available to the inhabitants of 300 or even 100 years ago.

Evolution of Transportation

During the period of exploration and discovery in Michigan (1618–1760), the French voyageurs and missionaries moved by canoe up the Saint Lawrence and Ottawa rivers, portaging into Lakes Huron and Superior before the southern peninsula was traversed and settled. The French explorers sought an empire, an all-water passage to the Orient, and conversion of the Indians. Fur trade was the only commercial development and was amply served by canoes, long boats, and bateaux that could be portaged around the difficult connecting passages between bodies of water.

The period of settlement and primary development in Michigan (1701-1890) began with the establishment of posts at Sault Sainte Marie, Saint Ignace, and Mackinac before Antoine Cadillac founded Detroit at the strategic straits controlling the lakes. Sailing ships, log booms and rafts, and steamships displaced the canoe and bateaux and raised demands for canals to connect the lakes. The burgeoning growth of copper and iron ore in the Upper Peninsula underwrote the success of Harvey's Soo Canal (1855), and soon new types of vessels such as lakers and whale-backs emerged on the Great Lakes.

During this same period railroads were extended inland from the eastern ports, starting with the Baltimore and Ohio in 1830. At first they acted as canal feeders, but soon they swept canals aside. By the mid-1850s they hauled more than 50 percent of the nation's freight and by 1890 more than 90 percent of both its freight and passengers. Railroads shifted the major line of national development to the south and west of Michigan. The first sizable rail project completed in Michigan was the Michigan Central Railroad in 1852, and it reached to Chicago. Railroads came to terms with the Great Lakes,

establishing both feeder and car ferry services. As a consequence, Michigan never became as totally dependent upon railroads or as devoid of waterway services as the rest of the midcontinent.

With the period of massive industrialization in Michigan (1890–1950) came a decline in the relative importance of agriculture, forestry, and minerals and an increase in urbanization and manufacturing. Other modes of transportation emerged to challenge the railroads. Originating in the western Pennsylvania oil fields, pipelines soon paralleled the railroads to long-haul markets. Energy-short Michigan was served by pipelines extending first from Illinois, then from the Southwest, and later from Colorado-Wyoming and prairie Canada fields.

Ransom E. Olds established the first automobile factory in 1899 and was soon producing the lightweight, low-cost, curved-dash Olds Runabout. Henry Ford's unique contribution was the discovery of the mass market, i.e., a car within every man's means (the Model T sold for as little as $360), and he paid sufficient wages—a minimum of $5 a day—to enable the working man to buy one. William Durant and Walter Chrysler were skilled in industrial organization and established General Motors (1910) and Chrysler Corporation (1925) to challenge Ford's leadership. After hundreds of companies had formed and failed over the years, the so-called "Big Three," all based in Detroit, dominated the industry.

The automobile required better roads than the mud holes that continually filled the state and nation in the spring. In 1909 Michigan was the first state to complete a paved road, and from that modest beginning more than 3 million miles (4.8 million kilometers) of improved roads have been extended across the United States. Within a single lifetime the country became a highway-oriented nation, the automobile being responsible for more than 90 percent of the passenger miles, and trucks carrying a higher value of goods than all other modes of transportation combined. Buses were the chief mass transit carrier. Until 1950 Detroit was the unchallenged center of motor vehicle production.

Rail-based mass transit never took a strong hold in the motor state and city, and the electric trolley quickly disappeared from the urban scene. Commuter rail services, however, have survived in Detroit.

Air passenger service was initiated on the east and west coasts, but air freight services between Detroit and Chicago were started in Michigan by the Ford Motor Company. Of the nearly 10 million passengers who now depart and arrive each year in Michigan by certified route air carriers, nearly 80 percent are served by Detroit Metropolitan Airport alone.

Transportation in a Postindustrial Age

After 1950 Michigan entered the postindustrial period, characterized by the growing dominance of service occupations, increased urbanization, and expansion of personal incomes. These changes have resulted in an accelerating shift to premium modes of transportation such as the automobile, truck, and air carrier. Between 1950 and 1970 Michigan's expenditures for transportation more than doubled. In 1951 the state, under its own authority, completed the Mackinac Bridge and the International Bridge to Canada over the Soo to provide new links with the isolated Upper Peninsula. The Saint Lawrence Seaway was opened in 1959 and provided Michigan with direct access to international markets and services. In the same period cars increased faster than population and second and third cars became commonplace.

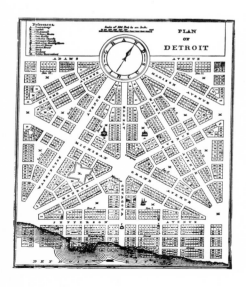

With most of its major highways in place, Michigan will have to shift its expenditures to maintaining and improving existing roads, achieving a balance among kinds of transportation, and integrating existing transportation into a system. In the cities, automotive congestion and pollution are increasing and alternatives for mass transit lag. The streets of Detroit, laid out according to L'Enfant's hub and spoke, present a special problem requiring major alterations, and funds are scarce.

The prospect of greater rural isolation is increasing with the massive abandonment of the railroads (1,200 miles or 1,920 kilometers) proposed under the Regional Railroad Restructuring Act. All rail ferry services across Lake Michigan are eligible for abandonment. Commerce on the Saint Lawrence Seaway, after 15 years of growth, has declined with recession, fuel shortages, and increased railway and truck container competition. Automobile sales declined in 1974 and 1975 to the lowest level since the early 1960s, although 1976 saw a major resurgence of the automotive industry.

Change continues to characterize Michigan's transportation. Using existing infrastructures and lower capital measures, the state appears to be moving toward acquiring more viable rail lines and cross-lake services and toward arranging substitute service. In the winter of 1976 the Soo Locks were kept open year-round, suggesting eventual year-round operation on the seaway. The automotive industry has made a major transition to smaller, cleaner, and more energy-efficient cars. Although the problems have grown more complex, it seems that transportation will continue to serve Michigan's economy.

Evolution of Mass Communication

Michigan has been a leader in the introduction and use of mass media. As in all parts of the world, the newspaper is the oldest form of mass media in the state that allows widespread, rapid dissemination of news with potential for storage and retrieval for future use. Michigan's oldest existing newspaper is the *Detroit Free Press*. It began as a weekly in 1831 and became the first daily in the state in 1835 as the *Michigan Intelligencer*. Improvements in postal and telegraph service in the 1850s aided newspaper development. By 1850 Detroit had three daily papers, and by 1885 a total of 253 newspapers had been started there. By that time, every sizable city normally had two newspapers, one Republican and one Democratic. Outside Detroit, the *Kalamazoo Gazette*, founded in 1837, is the state's oldest existing newspaper.

A German language newspaper, the *Allegemeine Zeitung*, was first published in Detroit in 1844. A large influx to Detroit of well-educated Germans resulted in the publication of several additional German language newspapers there during the 1850s. At the peak of publication of foreign language newspapers, there were 43 in Michigan representing 9 languages other than English. At one time or another 17 different languages have been represented among these publications. Such newspapers provided a continuing bond among people within each of the ethnic groups in the state, helping to preserve some aspects of the culture of the diverse groups who settled here.

Michigan's oldest periodical, the *Michigan Farmer*, was first published in 1843. The first religious periodical, the Baptist *Michigan Christian Herald*, was started in Detroit as a monthly in 1842. Within a year it had 1,000 subscribers, and in 1845 it became a weekly. Today there are many periodicals in the state for different vocational and civic interests.

On November 30, 1847 the first telegraph message in Michigan was sent on wires strung along the Michigan Central Railroad tracks between Detroit and Ypsilanti. By 1860 telegraph lines connected most Michigan cities, but it was not until after the Civil War that telegraph service was available in the Upper Peninsula.

The telephone, the communication link considered virtually a necessity today, first appeared in Michigan in 1877. Business houses in Detroit were the first subscribers. By 1893 long distance service between Detroit and Chicago became available. The nearly 6 million telephones in the state today are connected by enough underground cable to go around the earth 1,185 times at the equator and enough aerial wire to go around the earth 7 and a half times. That length of cable and wire is about 125 times the average distance of the moon from the earth.

Rural Free Delivery (RFD) of mail in Michigan started in Climax in 1896, two years after the first appropriations in the Congress of $30,000 for experimental service. The first three routes were started in West Virginia, amidst

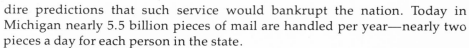

dire predictions that such service would bankrupt the nation. Today in Michigan nearly 5.5 billion pieces of mail are handled per year—nearly two pieces a day for each person in the state.

Michigan's first radio station was WWJ, Detroit. Operated by the *Detroit News*, it broadcast its first scheduled program on August 31, 1920. It vies with KDKA, Pittsburgh for the honor of being the first broadcasting station in the world. WWJ-TV was also the first television station in Michigan, going on the air in 1947. There are now 266 radio and 30 TV stations in Michigan. In comparison with the printed word, these electronic media permit instantaneous transmission of information, but the problems of storing such information for retrieval in the future are greater. Phone-a-vision and two-way interactive cable television are technological developments that indicate continuing progress in overcoming limitations of distance and time.

Advertising, one of the many functions served by the various communication media, has existed in some form since the exchange of goods and services first occurred. Today in Michigan it's a multimillion dollar business: in 1973 the state's expenditure for advertising was $1.1 billion, compared to $25.1 billion expended nationally. Three Michigan-based companies—General Motors, Ford Motor Company, and Chrysler Corporation—are among the top 20 leaders in the nation in advertising expenditures. General Motors ranks second with $225 million; Ford, eighteenth with $91 million; and Chrysler, fifteenth with $98.2 million. Kellogg Company, with expenditures of $60.8 million, ranked thirty-ninth, and American Motors, with a $32.9 million expenditure, ranked seventy-first. The 1972 Census of Business listed 334 advertising service establishments in Michigan with receipts of $610 million. The state's 86 advertising agency headquarters and 11,066 advertisers give it a rank of eighth among U.S. states. Michigan corporations spend about 1.1 percent of sales for advertising.

Communication in the Future

The increasing energy at our disposal through continually developing technology is dependent upon and contributes to our capabilities for communication and transportation. Already technology produces a veritable flood of messages for people throughout Michigan that can be transmitted to and received from most parts of the world within minutes—even to and from the moon and Mars. Two-way audio-video communication to many distant points by Michigan businesses and individuals is already technically possible. Dramatic changes also have taken place in the technology of printing: handset type, hand presses, and later the linotype machines have given way to photocomposition controlled by electronic computers and high-speed presses that can print 60,000 pages per hour. The future promises even more amazing developments, particularly in storing and retrieving information more efficiently and easily by means of video and audio cassettes.

The problem 200 years ago was one of getting information to places beyond walking distance. Today and in the future the problem is going to be how to sift, sort, and choose from the mass of available messages that deal with every subject imaginable. In all of this we must, individually and collectively, continually ask whether we are using our potential for both communication and transportation as effectively as possible to contribute to our well-being.

John L. Hazard
Lawrence Sarbaugh

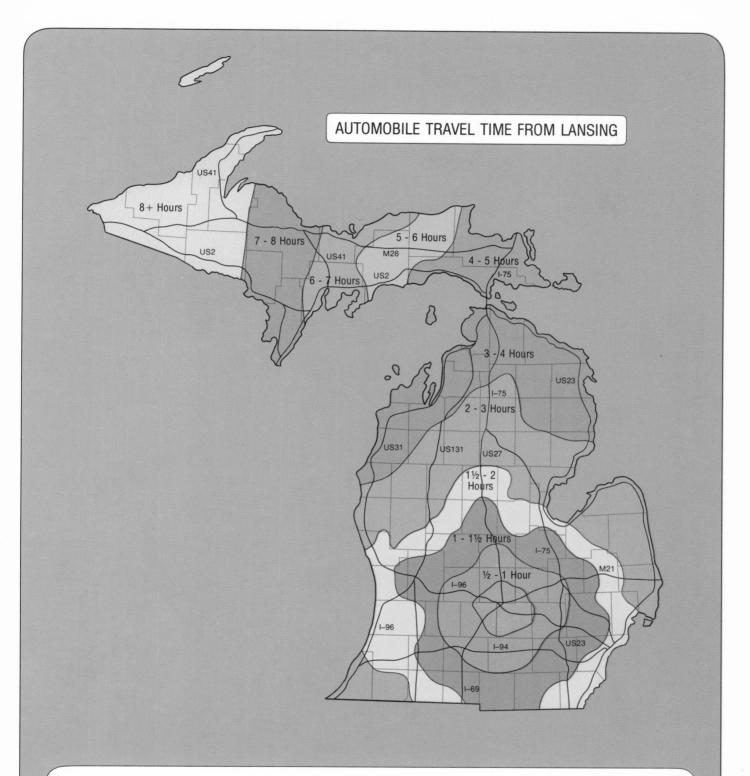

AUTOMOBILE TRAVEL TIME FROM LANSING

8+ Hours

7 - 8 Hours

6 - 7 Hours

5 - 6 Hours

4 - 5 Hours

3 - 4 Hours

2 - 3 Hours

1½ - 2 Hours

1 - 1½ Hours

½ - 1 Hour

US41
US2
US41
M28
US2
I-75
US23
I-75
US31
US131
US27
I-75
M21
I-96
I-96
I-94
US23
I-69

The accessibility of various parts of Michigan is illustrated by this map of automobile travel time from Lansing, the state capital. The driving times were calculated using the 55 mile-per-hour speed limit and major highways and expressways whenever possible. The fact that the only automobile access point between the state's two peninsulas is the Mackinac Bridge accounts for the lengthy travel times to reach the western Upper Peninsula.

The elongated time zones northward from Lansing indicate the savings in time by traveling on U.S. 27 and Interstate 75. A similar elongated pattern occurs adjacent to Interstate 96. Most of the larger population centers in the state are within two hours' driving time from the state capital. It takes almost as long to drive from Lansing to the western extremes of the Upper Peninsula as it does to drive from Lansing to St. Louis or Cincinnati.

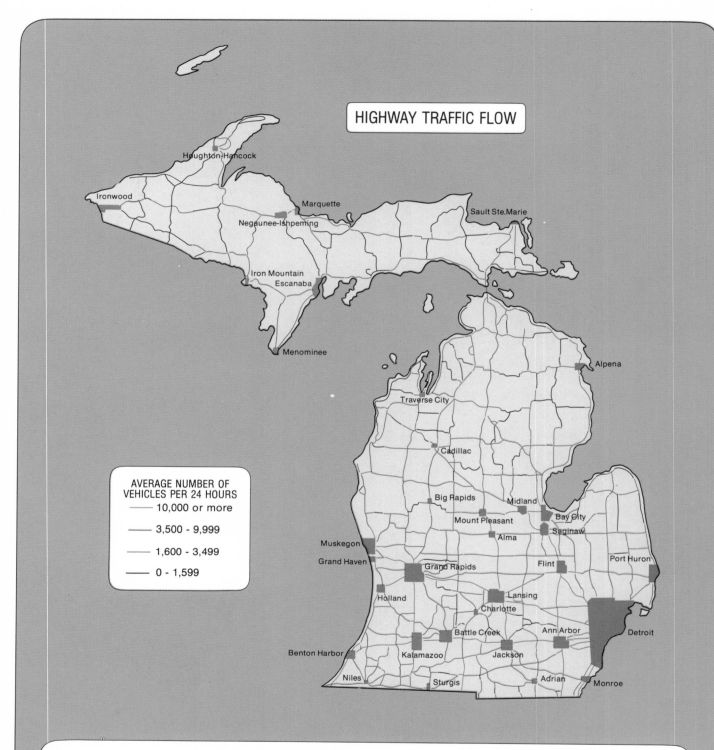

HIGHWAY TRAFFIC FLOW

AVERAGE NUMBER OF
VEHICLES PER 24 HOURS
— 10,000 or more
— 3,500 - 9,999
— 1,600 - 3,499
— 0 - 1,599

Houghton-Hancock

Ironwood

Marquette

Negaunee-Ishpeming

Sault Ste.Marie

Iron Mountain
Escanaba

Menominee

Alpena

Traverse City

Cadillac

Big Rapids   Midland

Mount Pleasant   Bay City

Muskegon   Alma   Saginaw

Grand Haven

Flint   Port Huron

Grand Rapids

Holland

Lansing

Charlotte

Battle Creek   Ann Arbor   Detroit

Benton Harbor

Kalamazoo   Jackson

Niles

Sturgis   Adrian   Monroe

Highways account for close to 90 percent of the intercity passenger movement. Both the state population distribution and the use of the highway system are illustrated on this map of highway traffic flow. For the most part the highest traffic densities are found on those highways connecting the major population centers in the southern Lower Peninsula; particularly apparent are Interstate Highways 94, 96, and 75. The short lengths of heavy traffic flow radiating from some of the smaller population centers generally indicate daily commuter traffic patterns. As would be expected, there is a strong relationship between the size of a city's population and the density and length of traffic flows radiating from that city. Compare, for instance, the heavier traffic surrounding Grand Rapids (population 197,649) with that of smaller Jackson (population 45,484). Some of the smallest traffic flows in the southern Lower Peninsula are on highways that closely parallel the newer interstate highways, which suggests that the interstates are drawing traffic away from older and narrower roads.

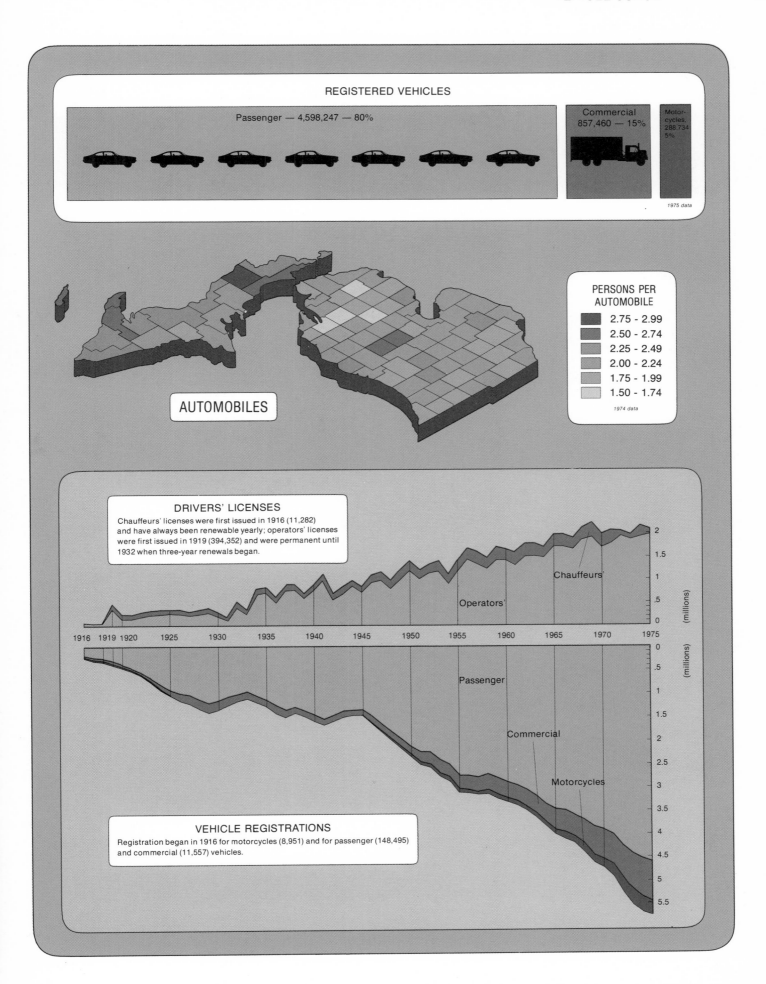

REGISTERED VEHICLES

Passenger — 4,598,247 — 80%

Commercial
857,460 — 15%

Motor-
cycles,
288,734
5%

1975 data

AUTOMOBILES

PERSONS PER
AUTOMOBILE

2.75 - 2.99
2.50 - 2.74
2.25 - 2.49
2.00 - 2.24
1.75 - 1.99
1.50 - 1.74

1974 data

DRIVERS' LICENSES

Chauffeurs' licenses were first issued in 1916 (11,282)
and have always been renewable yearly; operators' licenses
were first issued in 1919 (394,352) and were permanent until
1932 when three-year renewals began.

Chauffeurs'

Operators'

1916 1919 1920 1925 1930 1935 1940 1945 1950 1955 1960 1965 1970 1975

(millions)

2
1.5
1
.5
0

(millions)

0
.5
1
1.5
2
2.5
3
3.5
4
4.5
5
5.5

Passenger

Commercial

Motorcycles

VEHICLE REGISTRATIONS

Registration began in 1916 for motorcycles (8,951) and for passenger (148,495)
and commercial (11,557) vehicles.

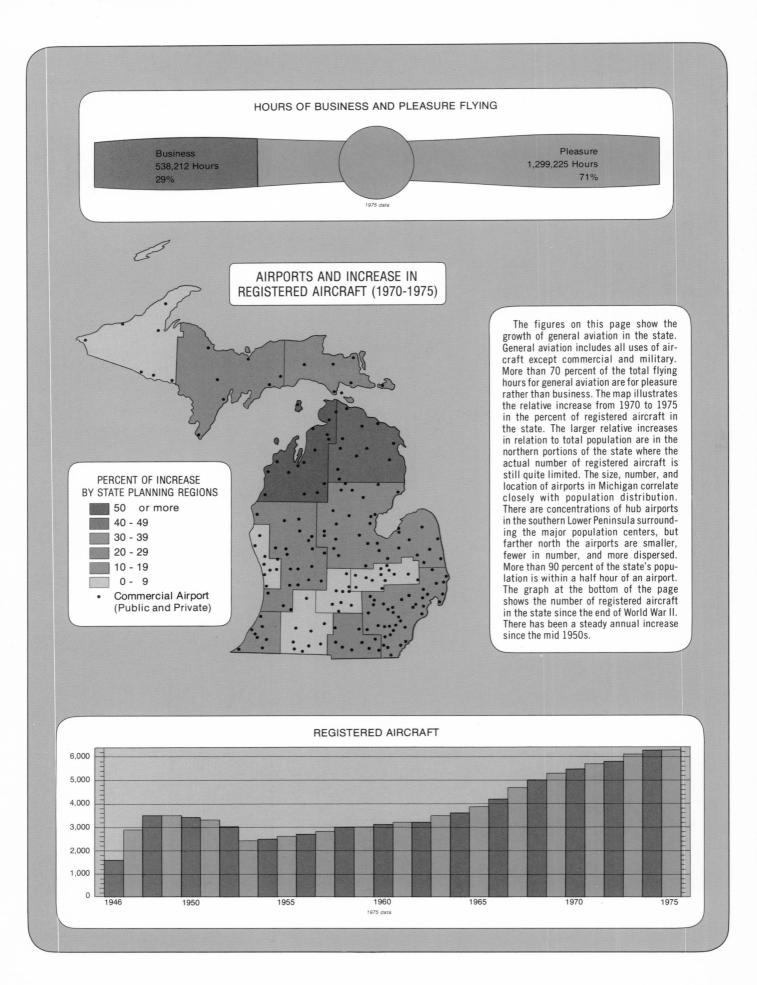

HOURS OF BUSINESS AND PLEASURE FLYING

Business
538,212 Hours
29%

Pleasure
1,299,225 Hours
71%

1975 data

AIRPORTS AND INCREASE IN
REGISTERED AIRCRAFT (1970-1975)

The figures on this page show the growth of general aviation in the state. General aviation includes all uses of aircraft except commercial and military. More than 70 percent of the total flying hours for general aviation are for pleasure rather than business. The map illustrates the relative increase from 1970 to 1975 in the percent of registered aircraft in the state. The larger relative increases in relation to total population are in the northern portions of the state where the actual number of registered aircraft is still quite limited. The size, number, and location of airports in Michigan correlate closely with population distribution. There are concentrations of hub airports in the southern Lower Peninsula surrounding the major population centers, but farther north the airports are smaller, fewer in number, and more dispersed. More than 90 percent of the state's population is within a half hour of an airport. The graph at the bottom of the page shows the number of registered aircraft in the state since the end of World War II. There has been a steady annual increase since the mid 1950s.

PERCENT OF INCREASE
BY STATE PLANNING REGIONS

50   or more
40 - 49
30 - 39
20 - 29
10 - 19
0 - 9

•   Commercial Airport
(Public and Private)

REGISTERED AIRCRAFT

6,000

5,000

4,000

3,000

2,000

1,000

0

1946   1950   1955   1960   1965   1970   1975

1975 data

CARGO AND PASSENGERS
Arriving and Departing

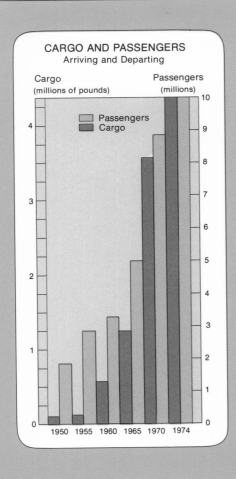

Cargo
(millions of pounds)

Passengers
(millions)

Passengers
Cargo

1950 1955 1960 1965 1970 1974

AIR CARRIER ROUTES

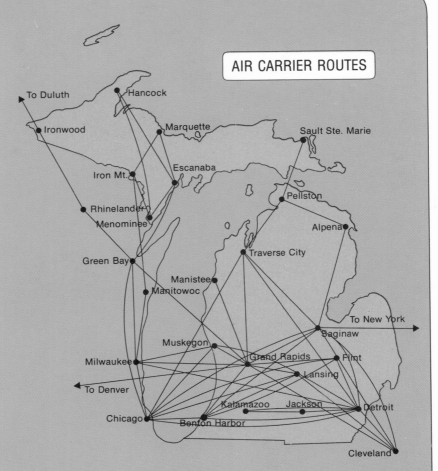

To Duluth
Hancock
Ironwood
Marquette
Sault Ste. Marie
Iron Mt.
Escanaba
Pellston
Rhinelander
Menominee
Alpena
Green Bay
Traverse City
Manistee
Manitowoc
To New York
Muskegon
Saginaw
Milwaukee
Grand Rapids
Flint
Lansing
To Denver
Kalamazoo
Jackson
Detroit
Chicago
Benton Harbor
Cleveland

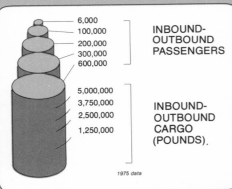

6,000
100,000
200,000
300,000
600,000

INBOUND-
OUTBOUND
PASSENGERS

5,000,000
3,750,000
2,500,000
1,250,000

INBOUND-
OUTBOUND
CARGO
(POUNDS).

1975 data

Commercial air carriers conduct about 10 percent of the nation's intercity passenger mileage. The air carriers serving Michigan concentrate their services in the major population centers in the southern Lower Peninsula. The interstate trunk routes are oriented east-west, connecting the state with Chicago, Cleveland, and Milwaukee. The intrastate feeder routes are, for the most part, oriented north-south, connecting the large cities in the northern portion of the state with those southern Michigan cities on the interstate air routes.

AIR PASSENGERS AND CARGO

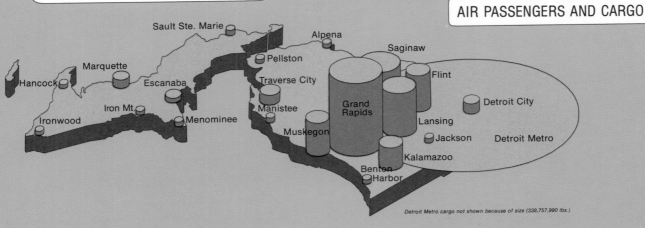

Sault Ste. Marie
Alpena
Saginaw
Hancock
Marquette
Pellston
Flint
Escanaba
Traverse City
Iron Mt.
Manistee
Grand Rapids
Detroit City
Ironwood
Menominee
Lansing
Muskegon
Jackson
Detroit Metro
Kalamazoo
Benton Harbor

Detroit Metro cargo not shown because of size (338,757,990 lbs.)

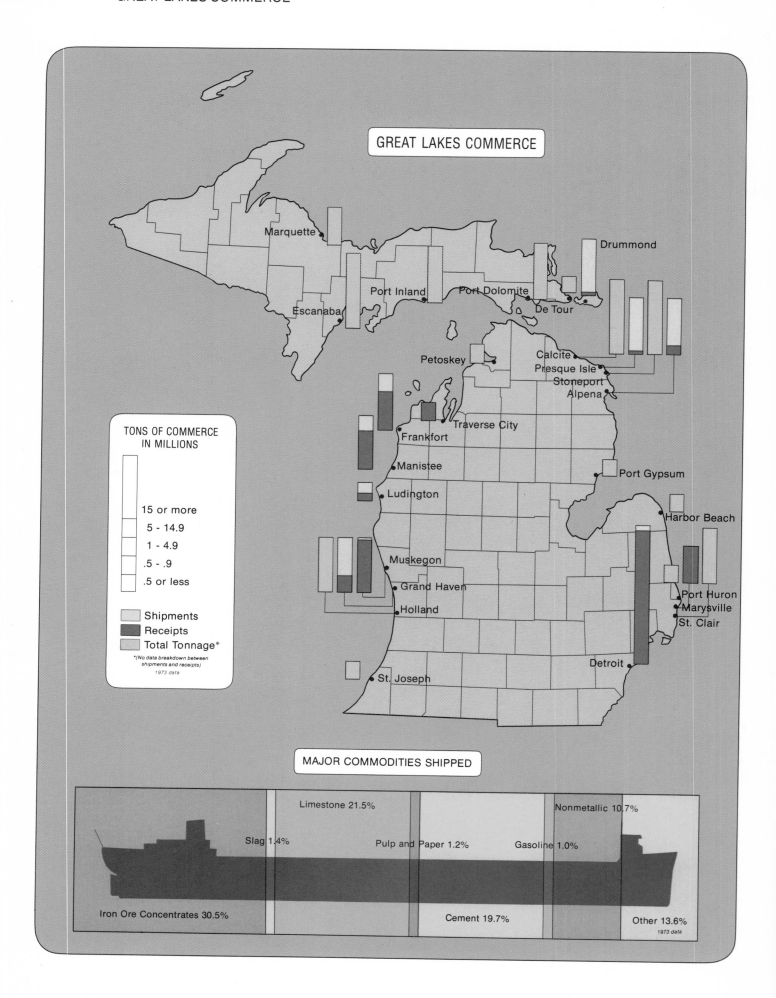

GREAT LAKES COMMERCE

Marquette
Drummond
Port Inland
Port Dolomite
De Tour
Escanaba
Petoskey
Calcite
Presque Isle
Stoneport
Alpena
Traverse City
Frankfort
Manistee
Port Gypsum
Ludington
Harbor Beach
Muskegon
Grand Haven
Port Huron
Marysville
Holland
St. Clair
Detroit
St. Joseph

TONS OF COMMERCE
IN MILLIONS

15 or more
5 - 14.9
1 - 4.9
.5 - .9
.5 or less

Shipments
Receipts
Total Tonnage*

*(No data breakdown between
shipments and receipts)
1973 data

MAJOR COMMODITIES SHIPPED

Limestone 21.5%
Nonmetallic 10.7%
Slag 1.4%
Pulp and Paper 1.2%
Gasoline 1.0%
Iron Ore Concentrates 30.5%
Cement 19.7%
Other 13.6%
1973 data

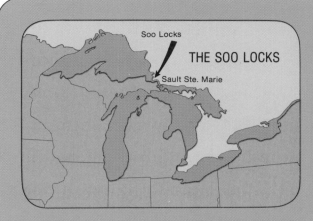

THE SOO LOCKS

Soo Locks

Sault Ste. Marie

OPERATION OF THE LOCKS

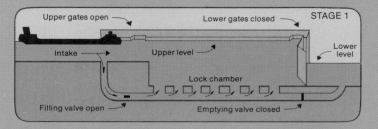

Upper gates open | Lower gates closed | STAGE 1
Intake | Upper level | Lower level
Lock chamber
Filling valve open | Emptying valve closed

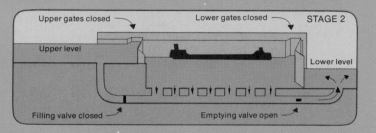

Upper gates closed | Lower gates closed | STAGE 2
Upper level | Lower level
Filling valve closed | Emptying valve open

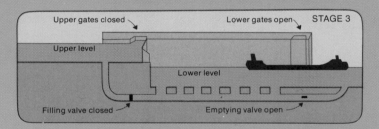

Upper gates closed | Lower gates open | STAGE 3
Upper level | Lower level
Filling valve closed | Emptying valve open

CARGO SHIPPED THROUGH THE LOCKS

(millions of tons)

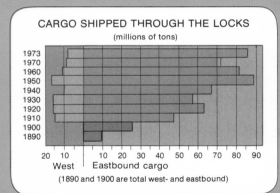

1973
1970
1960
1950
1940
1930
1920
1910
1900
1890

20 10 | 10 20 30 40 50 60 70 80 90
West | Eastbound cargo

(1890 and 1900 are total west- and eastbound)

The Great Lakes have given rise to a unique inland system of deepwater shipping serving Michigan. In 1959 the system was opened to deepwater ocean shipping via the St. Lawrence Seaway. Michigan's excellent and well-dispersed series of ports and harbors are now reached by both lake and ocean ships carrying more tonnage to and from Michigan than any other mode of transport. Much of the tonnage consists of industrial bulk materials because the Soo Locks provide access to Lake Superior and the iron ore and grain resources of the upper lake region. Coal is another bulk product of major significance passing through the Soo Locks. Foreign vessels bring in a variety of materials.

The Soo Locks stand four abreast and lift and lower a ship 17 to 19 feet, as illustrated in the diagram above. Tonnage passing through the locks, which at one time exceeded that of any canal in the world, has in recent years leveled at around 80 to 90 million tons annually. The overwhelming majority of the cargo moves eastbound through the locks.

Two recent innovations may add to the economy and capacity of the locks. In 1969 the substantially expanded Poe Lock was opened allowing the passage of superlakers of more than 50,000 tons capacity. A winter demonstration project in 1975 established that the Soo Locks could be kept open and free of ice 365 days a year. The experimental project may be the first step toward achieving year-round navigation on the whole Great Lakes–St. Lawrence system.

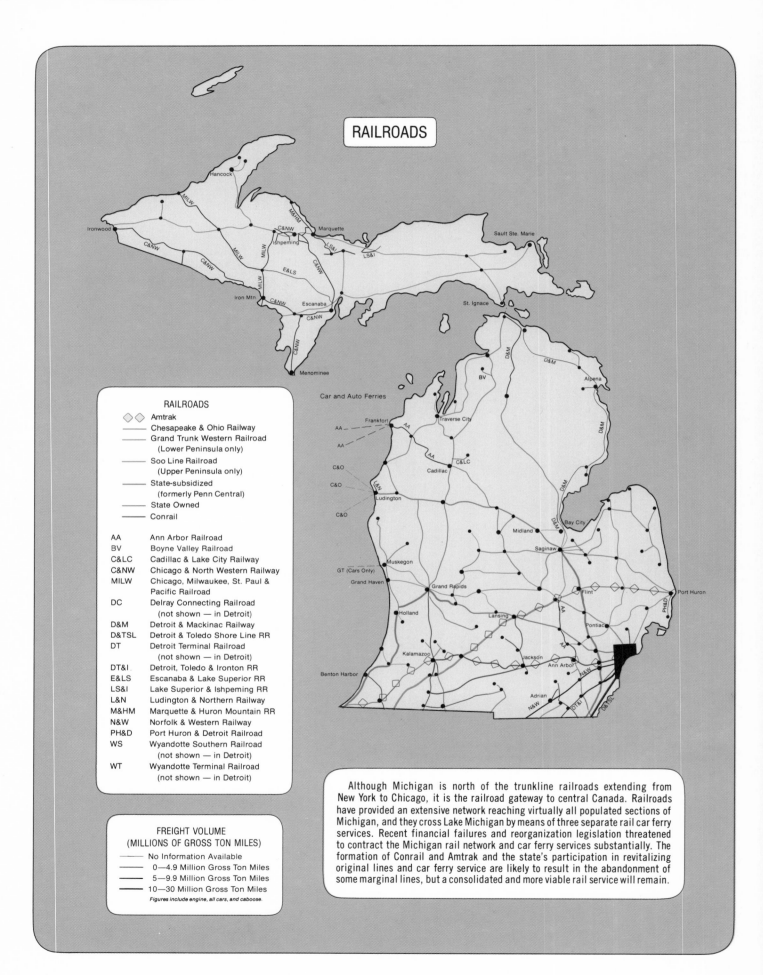

RAILROADS

RAILROADS

◇◇ Amtrak
—— Chesapeake & Ohio Railway
—— Grand Trunk Western Railroad
(Lower Peninsula only)
—— Soo Line Railroad
(Upper Peninsula only)
—— State-subsidized
(formerly Penn Central)
—— State Owned
—— Conrail

AA	Ann Arbor Railroad
BV	Boyne Valley Railroad
C&LC	Cadillac & Lake City Railway
C&NW	Chicago & North Western Railway
MILW	Chicago, Milwaukee, St. Paul & Pacific Railroad
DC	Delray Connecting Railroad (not shown — in Detroit)
D&M	Detroit & Mackinac Railway
D&TSL	Detroit & Toledo Shore Line RR
DT	Detroit Terminal Railroad (not shown — in Detroit)
DT&I	Detroit, Toledo & Ironton RR
E&LS	Escanaba & Lake Superior RR
LS&I	Lake Superior & Ishpeming RR
L&N	Ludington & Northern Railway
M&HM	Marquette & Huron Mountain RR
N&W	Norfolk & Western Railway
PH&D	Port Huron & Detroit Railroad
WS	Wyandotte Southern Railroad (not shown — in Detroit)
WT	Wyandotte Terminal Railroad (not shown — in Detroit)

FREIGHT VOLUME
(MILLIONS OF GROSS TON MILES)

—— No Information Available
—— 0—4.9 Million Gross Ton Miles
—— 5—9.9 Million Gross Ton Miles
—— 10—30 Million Gross Ton Miles
Figures include engine, all cars, and caboose.

Although Michigan is north of the trunkline railroads extending from New York to Chicago, it is the railroad gateway to central Canada. Railroads have provided an extensive network reaching virtually all populated sections of Michigan, and they cross Lake Michigan by means of three separate rail car ferry services. Recent financial failures and reorganization legislation threatened to contract the Michigan rail network and car ferry services substantially. The formation of Conrail and Amtrak and the state's participation in revitalizing original lines and car ferry service are likely to result in the abandonment of some marginal lines, but a consolidated and more viable rail service will remain.

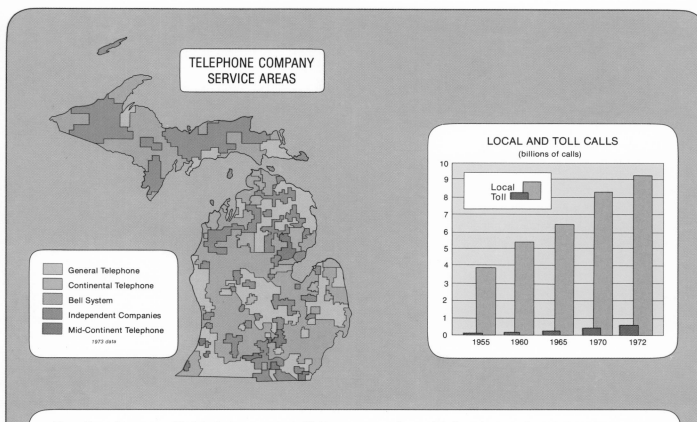

TELEPHONE COMPANY SERVICE AREAS

General Telephone
Continental Telephone
Bell System
Independent Companies
Mid-Continent Telephone

1973 data

LOCAL AND TOLL CALLS
(billions of calls)

Local
Toll

1955   1960   1965   1970   1972

The pattern of areas served by telephone companies in Michigan is very irregular. The Michigan Bell System serves the largest proportion of the state and dominates the urban portions of the Lower Peninsula. Next in importance is General Telephone, which functions more commonly in rural areas than Bell. Continental is the third most important company. Independent companies are scattered throughout the state, located primarily in more sparsely populated rural areas. Some independent companies serve very small populations, as in the case of tiny Hickory Corners, Michigan.

An area's mail volume closely correlates with its population size and the number and size of its business and government establishments. Thus southeast Michigan is the origin and destination of the largest quantity of mail in the state.

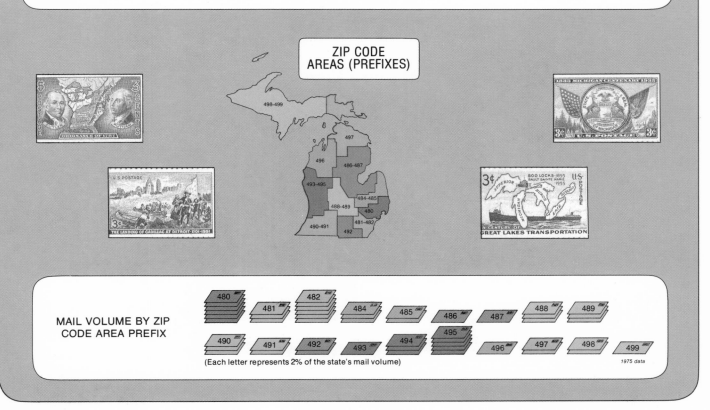

ZIP CODE AREAS (PREFIXES)

498-499
497
496
486-487
493-495
484-485
488-489
480
490-491
481-482
492

MAIL VOLUME BY ZIP CODE AREA PREFIX

480 481 482 484 485 486 487 488 489
490 491 492 493 494 495 496 497 498 499

(Each letter represents 2% of the state's mail volume)

1975 data

NETWORK AFFILIATIONS

ABC   American Broadcasting Company
CBS   Columbia Broadcasting System
MBS   Mutual Broadcasting System
MFN   Michigan Farm Radio Network
NBC   National Broadcasting Company
NPR   National Public Radio
*   Noncommercial Stations

LOCATION	CALL LETTERS	CHANNEL	POWER	NETWORK
Adrian	WABJ	1490	1 kw day	ABC
			250 w night	
	WABJ-FM	95.3	3 kw	
	WLEN(FM)	103.9	3 kw	MBS
	*WVAC(FM)	88.1	10 w	MBS
Albion	WALM	1260	1 kw day	
			500 w night	
	WUFN(FM)	96.7	3 kw	
Allendale	*WSRX(FM)	88.5	10 w	
Alma	WFYC	1280	1 kw day only	ABC
				MFN
	WFYC-FM	104.9	3 kw	
Alpena	WATZ	1450	1 kw day	NBC
			250 w night	
	WATZ-FM	93.5	3 kw	
	WHSB(FM)	107.7	98 kw	ABC
Ann Arbor	WAAM	1600	5 kw	ABC
	*WCBN-FM	89.5	10 w	
	WIQB(FM)	102.9	10 kw	ABC
	WPAG	1050	5 kw day only	ABC
	WPAG-FM	107.1	3 kw	
	*WUOM(FM)	91.7	230 kw	NPR
Auburn Heights	*WAHS(FM)	89.5	10 w	
Bad Axe	WLEW	1340	1 kw day	
			250 w night	
	WLEW-FM	92.1	3 kw	
Battle Creek	WBCK	930	5 kw day	NBC
			1 kw night	
	WDFP(FM)	95.3	3 kw	
	WKNR	1400	1 kw day	ABC
			250 w night	
	WKFR-FM	103.3	31 kw	
	WVOC	1500	1 kw day only	MBS
Bay City	WBCM	1440	1 kw day	ABC
			500 w night	
	WCHW-FM	91.3	10 w	
	WGER-FM	102.5	86 kw	
	WHNN(FM)	96.1	97 kw	
	WXOX	1250	1 kw day only	
Benton Harbor	WHFB	1060	5 kw day	ABC
			1 kw critical hrs.	
	WHFB-FM	99.9	9.2 kw	ABC
Berrien Springs	*WAUS(FM)	90.9	17 kw	NPR
Big Rapids	WBRN	1460	1 kw day only	
	WBRN-FM	100.9	3 kw	
Birmingham	WHNE	94.7	49 kw	
Bloomfield Hills	*WBFH(FM)	88.1	10 w	
Cadillac	WATT	1240	1 kw day	NBC
			250 w night	
	WITW(FM)	96.7	3 kw	
	WKJF(FM)	92.9	100 kw	
	WWAM	1370	5 kw day	CBS
			1 kw night	
Caro	WKYO	1360	500 w day only	MFN
	WKYO-FM	104.9	3 kw	
Charlevoix	WVOY	1270	5 kw	
Charlotte	WCER	1390	5 kw day only	ABC
				MBS
				MFN
	WCER-FM	92.7	3 kw	
Cheboygan	WCBY	1240	1 kw day	ABC
			250 w night	
	WCBY-FM	105.1	25 kw	
Clare	WCRM	990	250 w day only	
	WCRM-FM	95.3	3 kw	
Coldwater	WANG(FM)	98.5	50 kw	
	WTVB	1590	5 kw day	ABC
			1 kw night	
Dearborn	WNIC	1310	5 kw	
	WNIC-FM	100.3	50 kw	
Detroit	WABX(FM)	99.5	36 kw	
	WBFG(FM)	98.7	50 kw	
	WCAR	1130	50 kw day	
			10 kw night	
	WCAR-FM	92.3	10 kw	
	WDEE	1500	50 kw day	ABC
			5 kw night	MBS
	*WDET(FM)	101.9	79 kw	NPR
	WDRQ(FM)	93.1	20 kw	
	*WDTR(FM)	90.9	17 kw	
	WGPR(FM)	107.5	50 kw	
	WJLB	1400	1 kw day	
			250 w night	
	WJR	760	50 kw	CBS
	WJR-FM	96.3	50 kw	
	WJZZ-FM	105.9	34 kw	
	WLDM(FM)	95.5	165 kw horiz.	
			43 kw vert.	
	WMUZ(FM)	103.5	115 kw horiz.	
			89 kw vert.	
	WMZK-FM	97.9	50 kw	
	WOMC(FM)	104.3	190 kw	
	WQRS(FM)	105.1	50 kw	
	WRIF(FM)	101.1	27.2 kw	ABC
	WWJ	950	5 kw	NBC
	WWJ-FM	97.1	12 kw	
	WWWW(FM)	106.7	61 kw	ABC
	WXYZ	1270	5 kw	ABC
Dowagiac	WDOW	1440	1 kw day only	
	WDOW-FM	97.7	3 kw	
Drayton Plains	*WTSD(FM)	88.1	10 w	
East Lansing	WFMK(FM)	99.1	110 kw	ABC
	*WKAR	870	10 kw day only	NPR
	*WKAR-FM	90.5	125 kw	NPR
	WVIC	730	500 w day only	ABC
	WVIC-FM	94.9	20 kw	
Escanaba	WBDN	600	1 kw day only	ABC
	WDBC	680	10 kw day	CBS
			1 kw night	MFN
	WAMM	1420	500 w day only	
Flint	WCZN	1570	1 kw day only	MBS
	*WFBE(FM)	95.1	3.7 kw	NPR
	WFDF	910	5 kw day	NBC
			1 kw night	

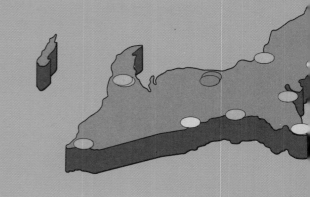

RADIO BROADCASTING STATIONS

NUMBER OF STATIONS BY MUNICIPALITY	
● 11 or more	● 2 - 3
● 7 - 10	○ 1
● 4 - 6	*1975 data*

LOCATION	CALL LETTERS	CHANNEL	POWER	NETWORK
Flint	WGMZ(FM)	107.9	50 kw	
	WKMF	1470	5 kw day	ABC
			1 kw night	
	WTAC	600	1 kw day	ABC
			500 w night	
	WTRX	1330	5 kw day	ABC
			1 kw night	
Fremont	WWCK(FM)	105.5	3 kw	ABC
	WSHN	1550	1 kw day only	
Garden City	WSHN-FM	100.1	3 kw	
Gaylord	WIID	1090	250 w day only	
	WATC	900	1 kw day only	NBC
Gladwin	WWRM(FM)	106.7	50 kw	
Grand Haven	WJEB	1350	1 kw day only	
	WGHN	1370	500 w day only	
	WGHN-FM	92.1	3 kw	
Grand Rapids	*WCSG(FM)	91.3	20 kw	
	WCUZ	1230	1 kw day	MBS
			250 w night	
	WFUR	1570	1 kw day only	
	WFUR-FM	102.9	40 kw	
	WGRD	1410	1 kw day only	
	WGRD-FM	97.9	19 kw	
	WJFM(FM)	93.7	470 kw horiz.	CBS
			64 kw vert.	
	WLAV	1340	1 kw day	ABC
			250 w night	
	WLAV-FM	96.9	28 kw	ABC
	WMAX	1480	5 kw day only	ABC
				NBC
	WOOD	1300	5 kw	NBC
	WOOD-FM	105.7	265 kw	
	*WVGR(FM)	104.1	107.5 kw	NPR
	WYON(FM)	101.3	50 kw	ABC
	WZZM-FM	95.7	50 kw	
Grayling	WGRY	1590	1 kw day only	
Greenville	WPLB	1380	1 kw day	
			500 w night	
	WPLB-FM	107.3	50 kw	
Hancock	WMPL	920	1 kw day only	NBC
	WMPL-FM	93.5	3 kw	NBC
Harrison	WKKM(FM)	92.1	3 kw	ABC
Hastings	WBCH	1220	250 w day only	ABC
	WBCH-FM	100.1	1.55 kw	
Highland Park	*WHPR(FM)	88.1	10 w	
Hillsdale	WCSR	1340	500 w day	
			250 w night	
	WCSR-FM	92.1	3 kw	
Holland	WHTC	1450	1 kw day	MBS
			250 w night	
	WHTC-FM	96.1	41 kw	
	WJBL	1260	5 kw day only	
	WJBL-FM	94.5	10 kw	
Houghton	*WGGL-FM	91.1	100 kw	NPR
	WHDF	1400	1 kw day	
			250 w night	
Houghton Lake	WHGR	1290	4 kw	ABC
	WJGS(FM)	98.5	100 kw	
Howell	WHMI	1350	500 w day only	ABC
Inkster	WCHB	1440	1 kw day	
			500 w night	
Interlochen	*WIAA(FM)	88.3	115 kw	NPR
Ionia	WION	1430	5 kw day only	ABC
Iron Mountain	WJNR-FM	103.9	560 w	
	WMIQ	1450	1 kw day	ABC
			250 w night	
Iron River	WIKB	1230	1 kw day	NBC
			250 w night	
Ironwood	WIMI(FM)	99.7	51 kw	
	WJMS	590	5 kw day	
			1 kw night	
Ishpeming	WJPD	1240	1 kw day	NBC
			250 w night	
	WJPD-FM	92.3	100 kw	

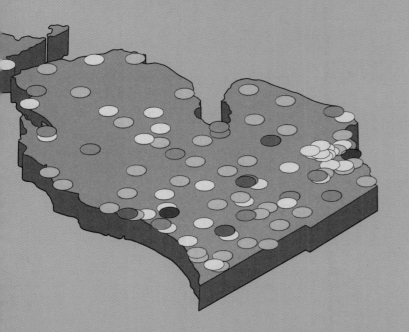

Radio stations are concentrated in the lower half of the Lower Peninsula, where the population density is greatest. Since 1960 FM stations have increased much more rapidly than AM stations, largely because of the high fidelity and stereophonic qualities of the FM signal. AM broadcast signals tend not to carry as far in Michigan as in other parts of the country because of the magnetic characteristics of the soil in the state. FM signals are line-of-sight signals and, given the magnetic qualities of the soil, FM signals sometimes carry greater distances than the AM signals in the same broadcast area. There is less broadcast interference among FM stations; therefore, more stations can be licensed.

LOCATION	CALL LETTERS	CHANNEL	POWER	NETWORK
Ishpeming	WJPD-FM	92.3	100 kw	
	WMQT(FM)	107.1	540 w	
	WUPY	970	5 kw day only	
Jackson	WHFI(FM)	94.1	50 kw	
	WIBM	1450	1 kw day	ABC
			250 w night	
	WJCO	1510	5 kw day only	
	WKHM	970	1 kw	MBS
	WKHM-FM	106.1	20 kw	MBS
Kalamazoo	*WIDR(FM)	89.1	10 w	ABC
	WKMI	1360	5 kw day	ABC
			1 kw night	
	WKPR	1420	1 kw day only	
	WKZO	590	5 kw	CBS
	*WMUK(FM)	102.1	50 kw	NPR
	WQLR(FM)	106.5	40 kw	
	WYYY	1470	500 w day only	MBS
Lansing	WILS	1320	5 kw day	
			1 kw night	
	WILS-FM	101.7	3 kw	
	WITL	1010	500 w day only	
	WITL-FM	100.7	55 kw	
	WJIM	1240	1 kw day	NBC
			250 w night	
	WJIM-FM	97.5	28 kw	
Lapeer	WMPC	1230	1 kw day	
			250 w night	
	WTHM	1530	5 kw day only	
	WTHM-FM	103.1	3 kw	
Ludington	WKLA	1450	1 kw day	ABC
			250 w night	
	WKLA-FM	106.3	3 kw	
Manistee	WMTE	1340	1 kw day	ABC
			250 w night	
	WMTE-FM	97.7	3 kw	
Manistique	WTIQ	1490	1 kw day	
			250 w night	
Marine City	WSMA	1590	1 kw day only	
Marquette	WDMJ	1320	1 kw	ABC
	WDMJ-FM	95.7	100 kw	
	*WNMU(FM)	90.1	100 kw	NPR
	WUUN(FM)	100.1	1.8 kw	
Marshall	WELL(FM)	104.9	3 kw	
Mason	*WUNN	1110	250 w day only	
Menominee	WAGN	1340	1 kw day	ABC
			250 w night	
Midland	WMPX	1490	1 kw day	MBS
			250 w night	
	WUGN(FM)	99.7	100 kw	
	(New FM)	93.5	3 kw	
Monroe	WHND	560	500 w day only	
	WVMO(FM)	98.3	3 kw	
Mount Clemens	WBRB	1430	500 w day only	ABC
	WBRB-FM	102.7	17 kw	ABC
Mount Pleasant	WCEN	1150	1 kw day	MBS
			500 w night	
	WCEN-FM	94.5	16 kw	
	*WCMU-FM	89.5	100 kw	NPR
	*WMHW-FM	91.5	32 w	
Munising	WGON	1400	1 kw day	
			250 w night	
	WQXO(FM)	98.3	1.8 kw	
Muskegon	WKBZ	850	1 kw	ABC
	WMUS	1090	1 kw day only	MBS
	WMUS-FM	106.9	31 kw	MBS
	WQWQ-FM	104.5	50 kw	ABC
	WTRU	1600	5 kw	
Muskegon Heights	WKJR	1520	10 kw	
	WKJR-FM	101.7	3 kw	
Newberry	WNBY	1450	1 kw day	
			250 w night	
Niles	WNIL	1290	500 w day only	MBS MFN
	WNIL-FM	95.3	3 kw	
Oak Park	*WOPR(FM)	90.3	18.5 kw	

LOCATION	CALL LETTERS	CHANNEL	POWER	NETWORK
Olivet	*WOCR(FM)	89.7	10 w	
Orchard Lake	*WBLD(FM)	89.3	10 w	
Otsego	WAOP	980	1 kw day only	ABC
Owosso	WOAP	1080	1 kw day only	
	WOAP-FM	103.9	2.8 kw	
Petoskey	WJML	1110	10 kw	ABC
	WJML-FM	98.9	100 kw	ABC
	WMBN	1340	1 kw day	NBC
			250 w night	
	WMBN-FM	96.7	1 kw	
Plymouth	*WSDP(FM)	89.3	10 w	
Pontiac	WPON	1460	1 kw day	
			500 w night	
Portage	WBUK	1560	1 kw day only	ABC
Port Huron	WHLS	1450	1 kw day	
			250 w night	
	*WORW(FM)	91.9	10 w	NPR
	WPHM	1380	5 kw	ABC
	WSAQ(FM)	107.1	3 kw	
	*WSGR-FM	91.3	10 w	
Rockford	WJPW	810	500 w day only	ABC
Rogers City	WHAK	960	5 kw day only	
Royal Oak	WEXL	1340	1 kw day	
			250 w night	
	*WOAK(FM)	89.3	10 w	NPR
Saginaw	WIOG(FM)	106.3	3 kw	
	WKCQ(FM)	98.1	50 kw	
	WKNX	1210	10 kw day only	ABC
	WSAM	1400	1 kw day	NBC
			250 w night	
	WSGW	790	5 kw day	CBS
			1 kw night	MFN
	WWWS(FM)	107.1	2 kw	Natl. Black
St. Ignace	WIDG	940	5 kw day only	
St. Johns	WRBJ	1580	1 kw day only	MBS MFN
	WRBJ-FM	92.1	3 kw	
St. Joseph	WIRX(FM)	107.1	3 kw	
	WSJM	1400	1 kw day	NBC
			250 w night	
Saline	WNRS	1290	500 w day only	MBS
Sandusky	WMIC	1560	1 kw	MFN
	WMIC-FM	97.7	3 kw	MFN
Sault Ste. Marie	WSMM(FM)	92.7	3 kw	
	WSOO	1230	1 kw	ABC
			250 w night	
Southfield	*WSHJ(FM)	88.3	125 w	
South Haven	WJOR	940	1 kw day only	ABC MFN
Spring Arbor	*WSAE(FM)	89.3	1 kw	
Sturgis	WSTR	1230	1 kw day	
			250 w night	
	WSTR-FM	99.3	850 w	
Tawas City	WDBI-FM	101.7	3 kw	
	WIOS	1480	1 kw day only	ABC
Three Rivers	WLKM	1510	500 w day only	MBS
	WLKM-FM	95.9	3 kw	
Traverse City	WCCW	1310	5 kw day only	ABC
	WCCW-FM	92.1	840 w	
	WLDR(FM)	101.9	50 kw horiz.	
			3 kw vert.	
	WTCM	1400	1 kw day	NBC
			250 w night	
	WTCM-FM	103.5	38 kw	
Warren	*WPHS(FM)	91.5	10 w	
West Branch	WBMB	1060	1 kw day only	
Whitehall	WLRC	1490	1 kw day	ABC
			250 w night	
	WLRQ(FM)	95.3	1.5 kw	
Wyoming	WYGR	1530	500 w day	ABC
			250 w night	
Ypsilanti	*WEMU(FM)	88.1	10 w	
	WSDS	1480	500 w day only	ABC
	WYFC	1520	250 w day only	ABC
Zeeland	WZND(FM)	99.3	3 kw	ABC

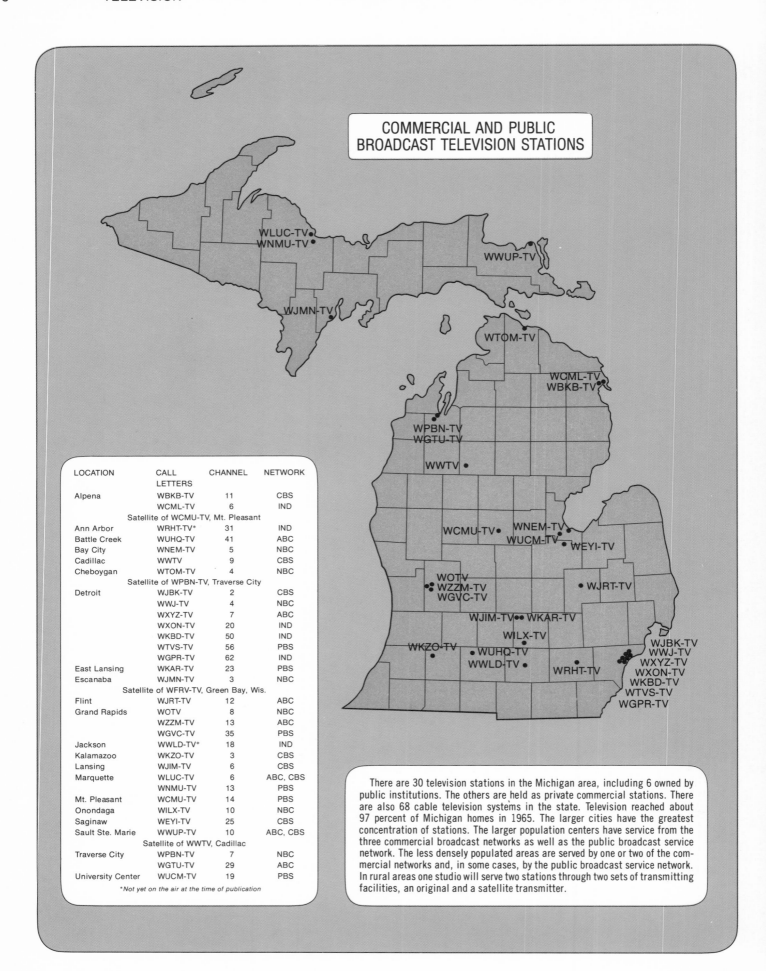

COMMERCIAL AND PUBLIC
BROADCAST TELEVISION STATIONS

LOCATION	CALL LETTERS	CHANNEL	NETWORK
Alpena	WBKB-TV	11	CBS
	WCML-TV	6	IND
Satellite of WCMU-TV, Mt. Pleasant			
Ann Arbor	WRHT-TV*	31	IND
Battle Creek	WUHQ-TV	41	ABC
Bay City	WNEM-TV	5	NBC
Cadillac	WWTV	9	CBS
Cheboygan	WTOM-TV	4	NBC
Satellite of WPBN-TV, Traverse City			
Detroit	WJBK-TV	2	CBS
	WWJ-TV	4	NBC
	WXYZ-TV	7	ABC
	WXON-TV	20	IND
	WKBD-TV	50	IND
	WTVS-TV	56	PBS
	WGPR-TV	62	IND
East Lansing	WKAR-TV	23	PBS
Escanaba	WJMN-TV	3	NBC
Satellite of WFRV-TV, Green Bay, Wis.			
Flint	WJRT-TV	12	ABC
Grand Rapids	WOTV	8	NBC
	WZZM-TV	13	ABC
	WGVC-TV	35	PBS
Jackson	WWLD-TV*	18	IND
Kalamazoo	WKZO-TV	3	CBS
Lansing	WJIM-TV	6	CBS
Marquette	WLUC-TV	6	ABC, CBS
	WNMU-TV	13	PBS
Mt. Pleasant	WCMU-TV	14	PBS
Onondaga	WILX-TV	10	NBC
Saginaw	WEYI-TV	25	CBS
Sault Ste. Marie	WWUP-TV	10	ABC, CBS
Satellite of WWTV, Cadillac			
Traverse City	WPBN-TV	7	NBC
	WGTU-TV	29	ABC
University Center	WUCM-TV	19	PBS

Not yet on the air at the time of publication

There are 30 television stations in the Michigan area, including 6 owned by public institutions. The others are held as private commercial stations. There are also 68 cable television systems in the state. Television reached about 97 percent of Michigan homes in 1965. The larger cities have the greatest concentration of stations. The larger population centers have service from the three commercial broadcast networks as well as the public broadcast service network. The less densely populated areas are served by one or two of the commercial networks and, in some cases, by the public broadcast service network. In rural areas one studio will serve two stations through two sets of transmitting facilities, an original and a satellite transmitter.

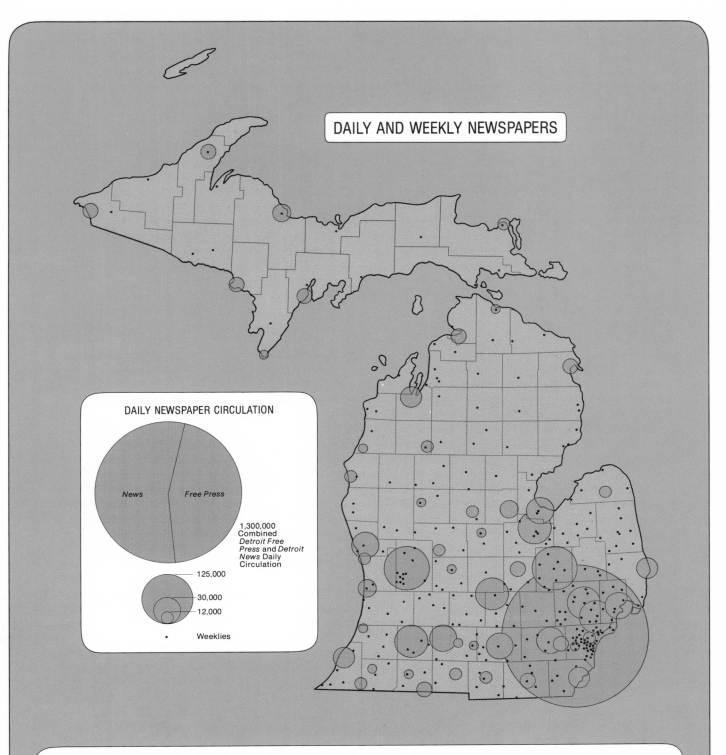

DAILY AND WEEKLY NEWSPAPERS

DAILY NEWSPAPER CIRCULATION

News — *Free Press*

1,300,000 Combined *Detroit Free Press* and *Detroit News* Daily Circulation

— 125,000

— 30,000
— 12,000

• Weeklies

Geographic location and size of both daily and weekly newspapers are closely correlated with distribution of population. The heaviest concentration of both daily and weekly newspapers is in the Detroit metropolitan area. Detroit is the only city in the state with more than one newspaper, and the combined circulation of the two Detroit dailies, the morning **Detroit Free Press** and the evening **Detroit News,** exceeds total circulation of all other Michigan daily newspapers. The **Detroit Free Press** is one among a fairly limited number of regional newspapers published in the United States. It has a substantial circulation throughout Michigan and in nearby areas of Ontario.

The largest daily newspapers in Michigan are published in the heavily populated centers, the Detroit metropolitan area, Flint, and Grand Rapids. Newspapers tend to be noncompetitive because they are published in separate geographical areas and seek highly local audiences and advertising. Their location is as much a result of a concentration of retail business as it is of population. In larger cities, such as Detroit, dailies circulate throughout the metropolitan area. Smaller suburban dailies serve limited areas in suburban centers, and weekly papers serve neighborhoods or smaller cities.

FOREIGN LANGUAGE PUBLICATIONS
(NEWSPAPERS, MAGAZINES, JOURNALS)

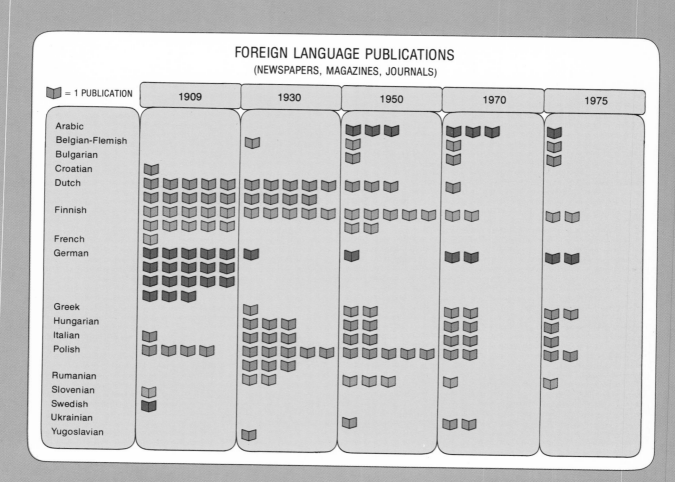

= 1 PUBLICATION

| | 1909 | 1930 | 1950 | 1970 | 1975 |

Arabic
Belgian-Flemish
Bulgarian
Croatian
Dutch
Finnish
French
German
Greek
Hungarian
Italian
Polish
Rumanian
Slovenian
Swedish
Ukrainian
Yugoslavian

PUBLICATIONS BY SPECIALTY

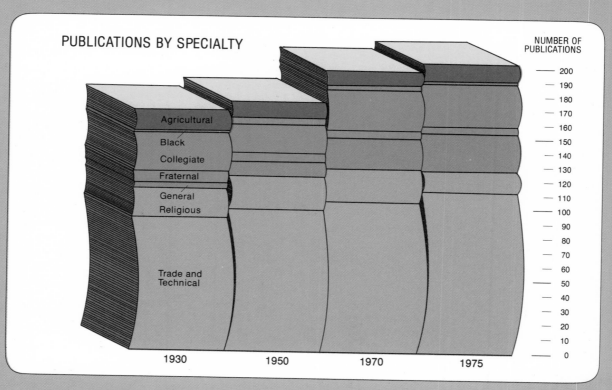

Agricultural
Black
Collegiate
Fraternal
General
Religious

Trade and
Technical

NUMBER OF
PUBLICATIONS

— 200
— 190
— 180
— 170
— 160
— 150
— 140
— 130
— 120
— 110
— 100
— 90
— 80
— 70
— 60
— 50
— 40
— 30
— 20
— 10
— 0

1930   1950   1970   1975

MICHIGAN TOMORROW

In this section some characteristics will be suggested for Michigan's economic, demographic, social, and political futures in the year 2000 and during the first decades of the twenty-first century. Many of these characteristics will also apply to the nation and society as a whole.

Michigan, and the entire nation, are entering what is termed a postindustrial state. In that society, most people will be employed in the service or tertiary sector, especially in transportation and communication, wholesale and retail trade, recreation, research and development, government services, and the professions. In turn, this sector will account for nearly three-fourths of the total income generated within the state. The life style, social values, and attitudes of the postindustrial society primarily will be based on its urban nature. This society will be marked by greater affluence, a greater appreciation for humanities and the arts, greater tolerance of acceptable life styles, and more leisure time. Shorter work weeks and earlier retirement will bring about more mobility and more time for leisure pursuits.

Growth and Patterns of Urban Population

Population growth will be greatest around the present urban areas and in the open spaces between them.

Suburban sprawl will expand into adjacent rural districts. Areas sparse in population and small towns and cities of less than 50,000 people between the metropolitan areas of Lansing and Grand Rapids, Flint and Saginaw, Ann Arbor and Jackson, or Kalamazoo and Battle Creek will undergo the greatest relative growth in urban southern Michigan, especially those small settlements along present or projected interstate highways. Even now cities are beginning to coalesce along highways I-96, I-94, and I-75. Agricultural regions and former rural trade centers along lines formed by Ann Arbor, Jackson, Battle Creek, Kalamazoo, and Benton Harbor, or by Lansing, Grand Rapids, and Muskegon, or by Ann Arbor, Flint, Saginaw, and Bay City are being transformed by new building developments. Highway interchanges have become the new residential and commercial centers. All of these complexes derive from the automobile-oriented society, in which people have learned to expect immediate access to their employment, shopping, or recreation.

The attraction of pleasant environmental surroundings will also contribute to changing population patterns. The pursuit of leisure, longer weekends, extended vacations, and early retirement (possibly after 25 or 30 years of work) will prompt some Michiganians and residents from surrounding states and Canada to come to the new communities near Lakes Michigan, Superior, and Huron, and to the state's national forest lands. Centers of new development will occur within a 50- or 100-mile (80 to 160 kilometers) radius of such regional centers as Marquette, Escanaba, Sault Sainte Marie, or Traverse City, where shopping, medical, educational, and cultural facilities exist. Some people will choose to live permanently in such areas and spend more than two hours each day commuting elsewhere to work, while others will decide to reside in an apartment in, say, Detroit or Chicago for four days of the week and commute to a townhouse or single-family dwelling somewhere in the Upper Peninsula for the long weekend. Hiking, skiing, snowmobiling, canoeing, and hunting, as well as the longing for clean air and open spaces, will also attract newcomers to the northern parts of the state. Within the next 50 years, coastal and interior areas north of a line from Bay City to Muskegon will grow relatively faster than the average for the rest of the state, as seasonal and permanent developments and communities are built and as regional trade centers develop economies based on recreation.

Communication and Travel

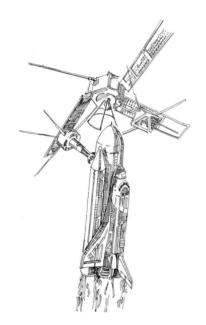

Improvements in communications, especially in television and the telephone, will increase Michigan's links with the rest of the world. With as many as 50 television channels carrying programs from the public sector, local private affiliates, and the major networks, the variety and scope of television as a medium of entertainment, learning, and business transaction will increase. In the future, the residents of Escanaba and Rogers City will be able to watch Detroit baseball, New York opera, Polish soccer, African travelogues, and United Nations General Assembly sessions just as easily as those living in Detroit and Kalamazoo. Channels will also carry the proceedings of a local city council, the state legislature, Congress, and the Canadian parliament. College credit even now can be earned from Michigan universities without leaving home. In the future examinations will be taken at home by means of computer-linked television sets. Lifelong learning in general will greatly increase in the years ahead.

Direct dialing and touch-tone phones provide fast and easy access to people around the world. Further advances in communications will reduce the need for face-to-face contact and for travel and may, in fact, make much business travel obsolete. Diminished need for personal contact will further change the economic rationale for central business districts.

More automation and computerization may permit tasks to be performed at home rather than at an office or industrial plant. Banking, car registration, catalog orders, information requests, and complaints can already be handled without leaving home. Television also offers a greater variety of programming for all age levels, from college art classes, up-to-date news, foreign languages, physical fitness, and gourmet cooking to child care, local government, weather forecasts, and travelogues. In the future, grocery shopping will be done by computer phone systems, much as mail ordering is done today. Messages sent via computers and satellites will replace letters. The link between the home computer and a regional medical center will allow physical and mental health to be monitored without patients leaving home. Voting could be accomplished by a centralized computer facility. These advances in telecommunications will have important effects on our travel patterns and thus on our styles of living.

Projected Characteristics of the Population

Michigan's population, 9.2 million people in 1975, will begin to level off at about 12 million in the early decades of the twenty-first century. Exactly when population growth will reach zero is impossible to predict because new migrants to Michigan must be considered along with the declining fertility and mortality rates. Michigan's birthrate can be expected to decline, as it has since the 1950s. With fewer children, fewer adults approaching childbearing years, smaller families, increased use of contraceptives, and more widespread acceptance of abortions there will be proportionately more older people in the state. Such a population will have decided economic and political effects on Michigan. Manufacturers who now produce items for a younger population—such as baby or breakfast foods, toys, television programs, records, and clothes—will face a greater market of middle-aged and senior citizens. Adult games, outdoor recreation, rejuvenating drugs, cosmetics, and special foods are likely to be designed to appeal to this older population. Smaller families and childless marriages will diminish the production and popularity of large automobiles and single-family dwellings. Small cars, apartments, townhouses, and condominiums will become more popular, not only because they will be cheaper and consume less energy, but because of greater demand.

An older population will produce political consequences in partisan and nonpartisan elections. Such a population is likely to be more conservative; to favor less experimental legislation and diminished funding for innovative programs aimed exclusively at younger groups. Programs covering dental and hospital care will be expanded. Payments will be higher, and social welfare benefits (unemployment, rent subsidies, food payments, and counseling) will include services not now considered under the federal government's aegis. Education programs will be developed that emphasize training for a second career, college credit, volunteer services, crafts and hobbies, and civic and consumer interests. Lifelong education will become a reality.

Government

The expansion of government's role in our lives and in society, which has been occurring for nearly 50 years, will continue. The public looks to governments, especially state and federal, as the chief supporters of social services and regulators of economic, consumer, and environmental policy. There is widespread public support for social programs that include education, health care and its delivery, housing, transportation, and environmental quality. Higher social security and medical payments, greater coverage for unemployment compensation, increased support for rent subsidies, urban renewal and homesteading, and more programs designed for rehabilitation rather than punishment for noncriminal acts are expected. Government will support education that is oriented toward the adult population, vocational interests, and cooperative extension. The federal government's leadership in such social programs will continue to attract the participation of various state and municipal agencies.

Much of the future success of Michigan's local, municipal, and state government will depend on the organizational framework established to identify and resolve problems and fund specific programs. Michigan's present organization—83 counties, 1,248 townships, and several hundred special districts (schools, police, soil conservation, water, hunting, parks, courts)—is needlessly inefficient and ineffective and is likely to be streamlined. Today's problems in energy conservation, consumer protection, land-use zoning, or spending differentials for public education are seldom identifiable at the local level or solvable by a single government agency. They are regional and have many origins. Townships and counties as units of government charged with meeting specific responsibilities may gradually be reduced and embraced by larger planning districts and regional governments that would have an advantage in working with problems overlapping present jurisdictional boundaries. State agencies will become fewer; they will be organized into districts that have uniform boundaries.

Michigan's future legislature will likely have a different composition and be faced with new responsibilities. The growth of urban and suburban populations in southern Michigan will increase this area's representation in the legislature. The one-person one-vote principle will continue to give greater representation to suburbs and fewer seats to declining inner-city areas. Representatives and regional councils will be asked to render decisions and develop major programs affecting land use, growth and development, consumer protection, citizen privacy, property rights, criminal rehabilitation, adult education, health delivery, scenic land protection, and environmental quality. A single legislative branch may evolve that could operate more efficiently and at less public expense than the present two. Governments at all levels will be held more accountable to public needs.

Future legislative action will not be limited just to problems that affect Michigan directly. More interstate transactions, at the urging of the federal government, will lead to greater cooperation with surrounding states. We may see the Michigan legislature or its subcommittees meet with their counterparts in Ohio, Indiana, Illinois, and Wisconsin to discuss mutual problems and form compacts in areas that transcend state boundaries, such as the environment, transportation, education, health, and criminal justice. Greater intergovernmental contact with Canada will help resolve common problems of energy allocation and costs, water pollution in and year-round shipping on the Great Lakes, and mass transit systems linking Michigan, Ontario, and the Northeast. With greater interregional planning and intergovernmental cooperation, regional councils among the states and between Michigan and Canada will be organized.

Planning for Future Land Use

Short- and long-range planning will become a major responsibility of future governments. Growth in population and urbanization in southern Michigan illustrates even now the need for effective planning. Precarious beach and forest environments need to be protected. Excellent agricultural lands in the southern half of the Lower Peninsula are being lost to housing, commercial, urban, and transportation developments. Agriculture is thus expanding to inferior lands where production is lower and capital investment higher. Suburban expansion, highways and interchanges, and vacation or resort developments have failed to protect some of the state's most scenic and potentially valuable dairy, corn, and horticultural lands. Anticipated population growth between now and the year 2000 and beyond will be roughly in these same kinds of areas unless they are protected.

In planning for future expansion, state, regional, and municipal governments must consider land uses as a package. In this way conflicting uses can be resolved; for example, by long-range planning the state can be assured that good dairy lands will not become speculative and sold to condominium developers or that scenic recreational areas will be protected from amusement parks, restaurant-motel complexes, or public utility installations. Land will be considered in terms of its best inherent qualities rather than as an item of transaction for capital gain. Property will be considered from the vantage point of the public good, not that of individuals or firms who will benefit if it is subject to speculation.

Rural Areas

By setting aside the best lands for agriculture, the state will assure its agricultural future. With proper planning the income generated from dairy products, cash grains, fruits, vegetables, and nursery stock will increase. That diverse base will provide necessary products to satisfy consumer demands in Michigan, the Middle West, Canada, and other parts of the nation. Fewer operators will be engaged full time in agriculture. Farms will become fewer but larger and more specialized. Agribusiness and corporate farming will likely link individual farms to other holdings and to supermarkets in an ever-expanding, vertically integrated economy. The headquarters for these agribusinesses may be in Chicago or New York, but they will be the source of planting, harvesting, and marketing decisions for the vineyards near Kalamazoo, the orchards around Traverse City, and the bean farms near Saginaw.

Marginal and submarginal agricultural lands in the northern half of the Lower Peninsula and in the Upper Peninsula may be left to revert to forest and brush or they may be developed for the burgeoning recreation and tourist economies. Not infrequently, old or abandoned farms and farmsteads will be used for historic amusement centers, backpacking camps, artists' colonies, summer camps, and ski lodges; for educational workshops in summer and hunting lodges in winter; or purchased for second homes.

Industrial Economies

Michigan's future industry will have to adjust to a new and different economy and society. The forest products industry will continue to enjoy success, but at the expense of cheaper and more durable substitutes for furniture and synthetics for newsprint and packaging materials. Higher costs and diminishing natural materials will make recycling more popular. Newspapers, magazines, and books will have to compete with television, tape systems, recording devices, home computers, and copying machines. Paper products will compete with plastics, aluminum, and newer, lighter metals for a variety of manufactured and consumer goods. Standardization in packaging will be popular. The consumer-oriented society will demand household appliances that are standardized, guaranteed for longer than a few years, and easily repairable.

Michigan's industrial development has been tied to the automobile more than to any single product. Both the automobile and the state's transportation industry are now the target of consumer interests and federal legislation. Safety, pollution, mileage, and size are becoming more important in selecting cars than weight, luxury, length, speed, and trim. The automobile will remain an essential mode of travel for some time, but the higher price of gasoline, smaller families, and the burgeoning commuter population will foster new automobile designs and alternative transportation systems. It is anticipated that the public will increasingly favor funding for mass transit systems and alternative transportation. The present bus and minibus experiments under way in several Michigan cities could be expanded. High-speed transit lines and commuter trains may be developed to link Ann Arbor and Detroit or Flint, Saginaw, and Bay City. High-speed bus lines might also evolve to permit easy travel throughout both peninsulas. Within metropolitan areas, bus networks could be expanded and lines could be developed to put every resident within 15 minutes of a park, shopping center, or hospital. Efficient and inexpensive public transportation would eliminate the need for many private automobiles. Former streets and parking lots could be torn up and replaced with gardens or used for playgrounds and parks.

The transportation industry will play an important part in Michigan's industrial future, but in a slightly different way than it does now. Vast automobile production may level off around the turn of the century, provided that meaningful alternative modes of transportation have become available and acceptable. Commuter trains, coaches, buses, minibuses, and minicars will be produced. The expanding recreation industry will call for more recreational vehicles of all types (boats, snowmobiles, airplanes, and even submarines), campers and portable campgrounds, and prefabricated houses. The recreational equipment industry has potential for economic growth in view of the state's year-round recreation and the already existing technology and skilled labor force.

Planning and developing a diversified economic base may help prevent the likelihood of serious downturns or lengthly periods of slow growth. Agriculture, industry, recreation, and the components of the tertiary sector represent a good mix for economic development. There will be demands for more computers, office machines, telecommunication equipment, and information retrieval and storage systems. These are basic to a postindustrial society, and their growth seems especially promising in view of the talent already here, the training available, and the research being carried out in Michigan's universities, industries, and private research foundations.

Economic Growth and Energy

The success an economy reaps is tied in large measure to its supplies and sources of energy. An expanding economy's need for more energy will probably lead to a greater reliance on nuclear energy. By the year 2000 it is anticipated that, with petroleum, coal, and gas supplies exhausted or unavailable at competitive costs or in the volume demanded, about 20 percent of our energy may come from atomic power. The problems of this form of energy — disposal of radioactive wastes, heating of Lake Michigan waters, leakage of nuclear particles, and environmental destruction — will have to be solved and the public protected by stiff, enforceable regulations. Assuming the problems can be resolved, the state will rely on nuclear power plants to operate industries, businesses, and homes. In the meantime, Michigan will continue to rely on coal, petroleum, and natural gas from Canada and elsewhere. Higher costs for these nonrenewable energy sources will hasten the search for cheaper, cleaner, and more abundant alternative renewable sources. Solar power is a long way from contributing meaningfully to the state's energy production, but it may produce a share as early as 2015 or 2025. The drilling for oil and gas in parts of the northern third of the Lower Peninsula already is yielding some positive results, and Lake Michigan represents potential for future energy as well.

Michigan's environment, economies, and energy need to be considered as an integrated and interlocking system. Our attitudes toward the natural environment, energy conservation, industrial development, and use of resources are important in policy making. Planning for the future must include measuring the damage done by pollution from steel plants and numerous other factories to Michigan's air, waters, and natural environment. Clashes between consumer, conservation, and commercial interests are certain to arise over the location of needed facilities such as new airports, nuclear power plants, power grid lines, and highways. Consumers' interests need to be weighed equally in future industrial and commercial expansion to ensure that standards for clean air and water are maintained and planning for incompatible use of land is avoided; that consumers are protected and environmental ethics are considered. Indicators that measure living standards, housing quality, justice, health, and a clean environment will become yardsticks of societal development just as industrial and agricultural production measure economic health.

Need for Continued Study

The state's future is of concern to all citizens. The need to study and plan the future can be carried out in informal discussions or formal workshops and seminars organized by the educational, religious, governmental, and business communities. A committee within the Michigan legislature to study the state's future in the Middle West, the nation, and the world might also stimulate thinking and planning. This proposal has already been discussed in legislative circles in Michigan and other states. Given government's greater authority and responsibility, it would be prudent for the legislature, working with the state's universities, to take a lead in discussing pressing problems and introducing sound legislation regarding Michigan's social, economic, and political future.

Stanley D. Brunn

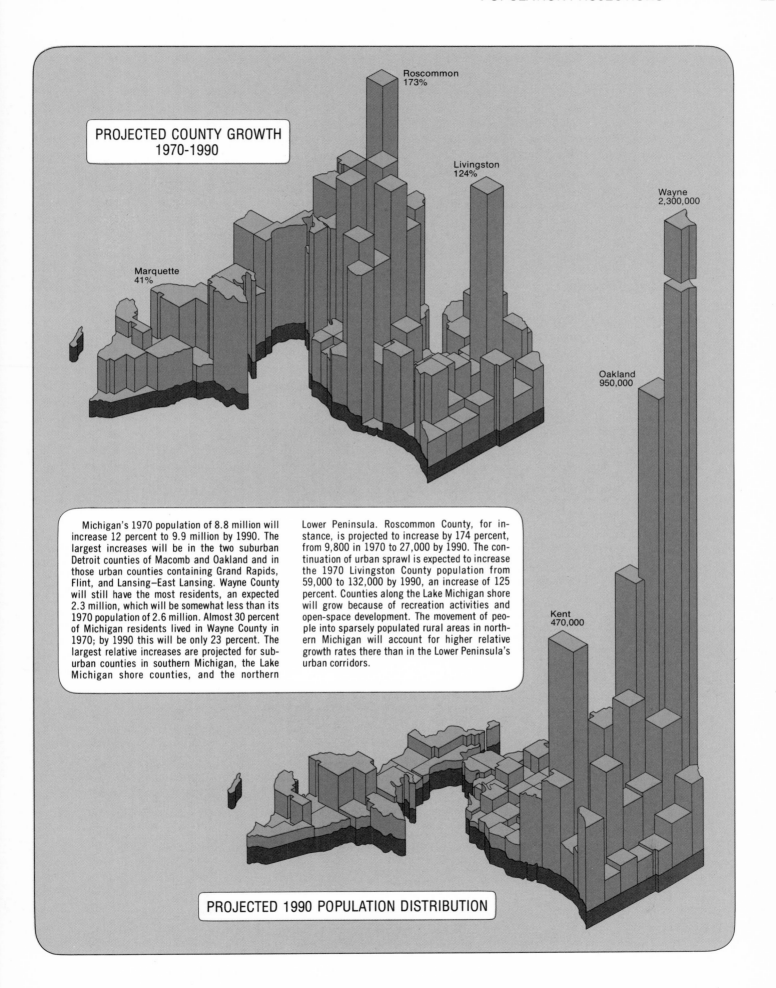

PROJECTED COUNTY GROWTH 1970-1990

Roscommon
173%

Livingston
124%

Wayne
2,300,000

Marquette
41%

Oakland
950,000

Kent
470,000

Michigan's 1970 population of 8.8 million will increase 12 percent to 9.9 million by 1990. The largest increases will be in the two suburban Detroit counties of Macomb and Oakland and in those urban counties containing Grand Rapids, Flint, and Lansing–East Lansing. Wayne County will still have the most residents, an expected 2.3 million, which will be somewhat less than its 1970 population of 2.6 million. Almost 30 percent of Michigan residents lived in Wayne County in 1970; by 1990 this will be only 23 percent. The largest relative increases are projected for suburban counties in southern Michigan, the Lake Michigan shore counties, and the northern Lower Peninsula. Roscommon County, for instance, is projected to increase by 174 percent, from 9,800 in 1970 to 27,000 by 1990. The continuation of urban sprawl is expected to increase the 1970 Livingston County population from 59,000 to 132,000 by 1990, an increase of 125 percent. Counties along the Lake Michigan shore will grow because of recreation activities and open-space development. The movement of people into sparsely populated rural areas in northern Michigan will account for higher relative growth rates there than in the Lower Peninsula's urban corridors.

PROJECTED 1990 POPULATION DISTRIBUTION

PROJECTED URBAN ENCROACHMENT ON PRIME AGRICULTURAL LANDS

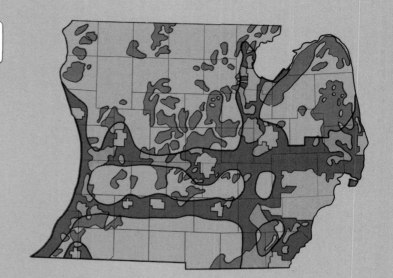

Existing Urban Land

Predicted Future Urban Land

Existing Prime Agricultural Land

Existing Prime Agricultural Land Within Area of Predicted Urban Expansion

Cities and suburbs in Michigan are expanding their populations and built-up areas, as is true in surrounding states and in the nation. The areas most affected by future growth in Michigan are south of the Bay City–Muskegon line. It is anticipated that future population and urban expansion will be around the major urban centers such as Muskegon, Grand Rapids, Lansing–East Lansing, Flint, Saginaw, Bay City, Midland, Kalamazoo, Battle Creek, Jackson, and Ann Arbor. The growth of the Detroit metropolitan area is expected to continue. The principal corridors of urban expansion will be along the major interstate highways—I-75, I-94, and I-96—and will include growth in the small towns and agricultural areas between the large cities. The desire for easy and rapid accessibility to the larger urban centers is responsible for the urban and suburban expansion into rural land near cities and highways.

Projected urban growth will likely occur in some of the state's prime agricultural lands. The best areas for dairying, livestock, field crops, fruits, and vegetables are often immediately adjacent to or near the sprawling suburbs of Michigan's largest cities. It is not only subdivisions that are appearing in former corn fields or cattle pastures, but industrial parks and complexes of motels, restaurants, and gasoline stations near the major highway interchanges. Within the past two decades the expanding Detroit area has usurped many former dairy farms as well as those raising fruits, vegetables, and field crops. Likewise, because of urban and commercial growth along the Lake Michigan shoreline, many orchard areas devoted to raising apples, cherries, plums, grapes, and blueberries have been sold, subdivided, and zoned for vacation homes, tourist accommodations, and commerce.

The need to plan for an effective and realistic policy for future urban growth is recognized by many private and government groups throughout the state. Because urban growth is projected to be within or adjacent to the state's best agricultural lands, sound land-use planning programs are needed. Local and regional planning units need to work together in devising programs to retain the best lands for dairying, field crops, or fruits and vegetables and to steer urban expansion to marginal and submarginal lands. Very good agricultural land within the state is limited in area, and further use of such spaces for urban growth

will force future agricultural production in marginal areas. The end result of such ventures will be more costly production of Michigan dairy products or fruits and vegetables.

Similar urban growth patterns can be projected for the lower Great Lakes. Doxiadis Associates, in their 1970 report on the future of the Detroit area, envisaged urban Michigan becoming an integral part of a larger urban system that would stretch from Pittsburgh to Chicago and into southern Ontario. Detroit would be a major center in this Great Lakes Megalopolis in which metropolitan corridors would extend from Toronto–Detroit–Chicago and Bay City–Saginaw–Detroit–Toledo to Cleveland–Pittsburgh. Eventually the urban system will include major and minor corridors that intricately link the urban nodes in southern Michigan with the Chicago area, northern Indiana, northern Ohio, and southern Ontario.

The emerging Great Lakes Megalopolis is one of several continuous urban regions that are expected to appear at the national level by the year 2000. In a federal report on population growth and America's future, 25 urban regions of varying sizes are identified. Many metropolitan areas in the Northeast and Middle West will grow together and cross state lines. The southern half of the Lower Peninsula is expected to become a part of a large urban region stretching from southeast Wisconsin, northeast Illinois, northern Indiana, and northern Ohio to western parts of Pennsylvania and New York. Outside the Great Lakes area a broad urban belt will reach from southern New England to southern Virginia. Southern and coastal California will form a large contiguous urban region, as will peninsular Florida. Smaller but significant metropolitan growth will occur along the Texas–Louisiana Gulf Coast; in the San Antonio–Dallas–Fort Worth area; and in the Tulsa–Oklahoma City and Denver–Boulder–Pueblo areas. Because of the large distances separating some metropolitan centers, their future urban growth will be an enlargement of their own sphere of influence, as in the case of Kansas City, Salt Lake City, Seattle, and Nashville. The interstate highway network is the underlying stimulus for projecting patterns of urban expansion for the nation, the Middle West, and Michigan.

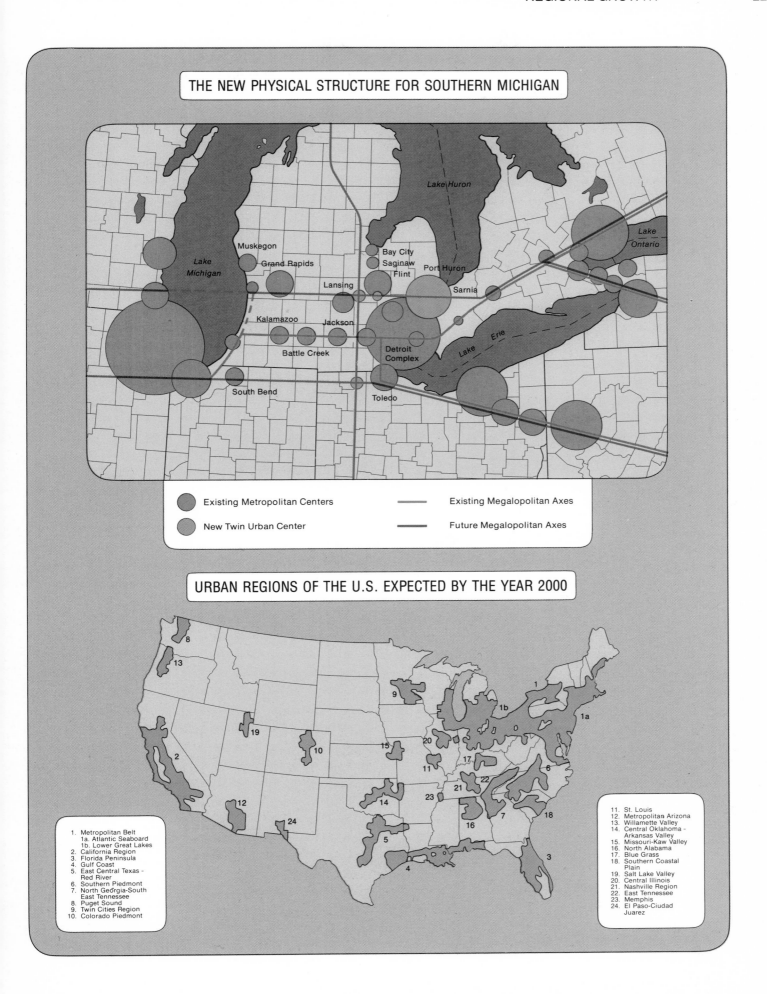

THE NEW PHYSICAL STRUCTURE FOR SOUTHERN MICHIGAN

Lake Huron

Lake Ontario

Muskegon

Lake Michigan

Grand Rapids

Bay City
Saginaw
Flint

Port Huron

Lansing

Sarnia

Kalamazoo

Jackson

Detroit
Complex

Lake Erie

Battle Creek

South Bend

Toledo

● Existing Metropolitan Centers
● New Twin Urban Center

―― Existing Megalopolitan Axes
―― Future Megalopolitan Axes

URBAN REGIONS OF THE U.S. EXPECTED BY THE YEAR 2000

8
13
9
1
1b
1a
20
19
15
10
11
17
6
2
22
21
23
14
18
12
7
24
16
5
4
3

1. Metropolitan Belt
   1a. Atlantic Seaboard
   1b. Lower Great Lakes
2. California Region
3. Florida Peninsula
4. Gulf Coast
5. East Central Texas -
   Red River
6. Southern Piedmont
7. North Georgia-South
   East Tennessee
8. Puget Sound
9. Twin Cities Region
10. Colorado Piedmont

11. St. Louis
12. Metropolitan Arizona
13. Willamette Valley
14. Central Oklahoma -
    Arkansas Valley
15. Missouri-Kaw Valley
16. North Alabama
17. Blue Grass
18. Southern Coastal
    Plain
19. Salt Lake Valley
20. Central Illinois
21. Nashville Region
22. East Tennessee
23. Memphis
24. El Paso-Ciudad
    Juarez

38 STATE PROPOSAL

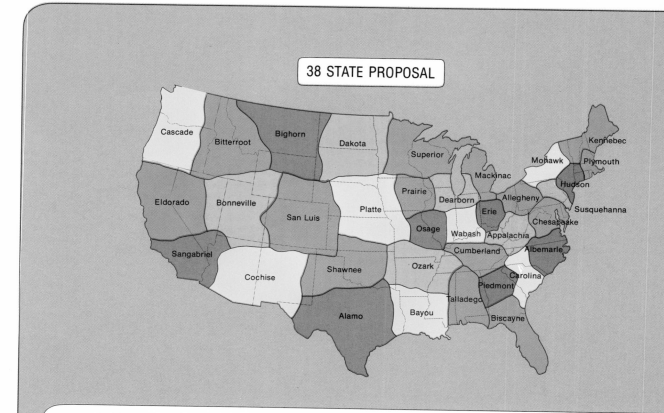

Political maps in the future may have a different appearance. Professor G. Etzel Pearcy, California State University in Los Angeles, recommended that 38 states replace the existing 50 states. In his proposal for a more realistic political order, Pearcy retains state government but gives his states new names and boundaries drawn to delimit the hinterlands or trade areas of major cities throughout the country. State names are based on dominant physical features in the region or cultural groups important in the area's heritage. Professor Stanley D. Brunn, Michigan State University, proposed that 16 administrative districts replace the states. With greater federal government legislation and funding for social welfare, environmental, and economic programs, and Supreme Court decisions that supersede varying state interpretations, he envisages states being replaced by broad administrative regions defined on the bases of economic orientation to major cities and social-political heritage. These districts will be responsible for dispensing federal programs to urban areas (that often cross state lines now) and to individuals.

16 DISTRICT PROPOSAL

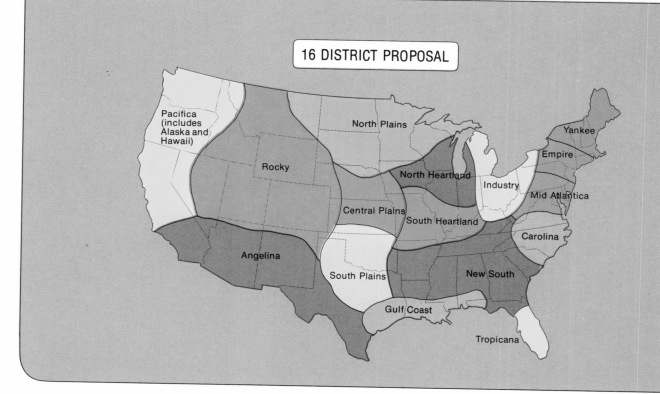

PAST, PRESENT, AND PROJECTED INTERNATIONAL HOURLY FLIGHT TIME FROM DETROIT

Since 1950 international communications have been facilitated by improved technological advances in telephone service and faster airplanes. A term that illustrates the shrinkage of spaces is "time-space convergence"; it measures the rate at which places are moving closer together in travel or communication time. Actual distances, of course, remain the same, but the amount of time it takes to travel from one location to another decreases with faster and more efficient technological breakthroughs in transportation. One way to demonstrate the shrinkage of air space between major cities is to measure how long air flights took from Detroit to selected world cities in 1950 and 1975 and how long they will take in the year 2000.

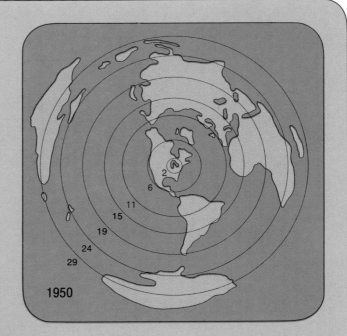

1950

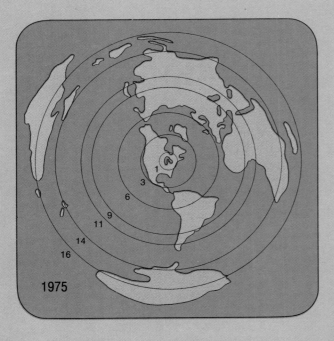

1975

In 1950 the fastest commercial plane, the DC7, traveled about 350 miles per hour. Toronto could be reached in one hour of flying from Detroit; Miami, Houston, and Denver in 3 to 4 hours; and Los Angeles in slightly more than 5 hours. It took 10 hours to get to London and Lima, Peru and more than 20 hours to travel to Tokyo and Teheran. Direct flights from Detroit to Singapore, Bangkok, and Melbourne would have taken more than 24 hours. By 1975 the larger and faster commercial planes further reduced the flying time from Detroit to major cities. The 747 jumbo jets could fly almost 640 miles per hour. West European and northern South American cities could be reached in 6 hours from Detroit. A flight from Detroit to Rio de Janeiro took 15 hours in 1950 but only 9 hours in 1975. Nairobi and Calcutta were 23 hours away in 1950 but only 13 in 1975.

Supersonic transport speeds will be possible for the commercial aircraft of the year 2000. The Concorde now flies at maximum speeds approaching 2,000 miles per hour. Eventually this plane will further shrink the direct flying time from Detroit to major world cities in Europe, East and South Asia, Africa, and Australia. Widespread use of supersonic planes by 2000 will link Detroit to Denver, Houston, and New York within one hour and to Los Angeles, Caracas, and Mexico City within two hours. Most European capitals, including Berlin, Rome, and Moscow, will be reached in four hours. Even the cities that were almost a day's direct flying time from Detroit in 1950—Capetown, Hong Kong, Nairobi, Bangkok, Singapore, and Melbourne—will be reachable in six to eight hours.

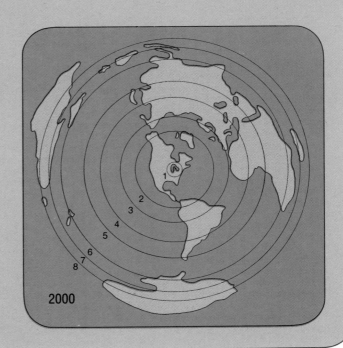

2000

SELECTED STATISTICS BY COUNTY

BIBLIOGRAPHY

INDEX

SELECTED STATISTICS BY COUNTY

Counties	Land Area (Square Miles)	Total Population 1970	Total Population 1975	Percent Population Change 1970-1975	Percent Urban Population 1970	Total Civilian Labor Force 1970	Median Number School Years Completed by Population over 25, 1970
ALCONA	678	7,113	8,500	19.7	0.0	2,074	10.6
ALGER	905	8,568	8,800	2.9	42.9	2,989	11.4
ALLEGAN	826	66,575	71,600	7.6	22.5	25,432	11.5
ALPENA	565	30,708	33,100	7.8	44.9	10,312	12.0
ANTRIM	476	12,612	15,000	19.3	0.0	4,389	12.0
ARENAC	367	11,149	13,300	19.4	0.0	3,879	10.4
BARAGA	901	7,789	8,000	2.9	32.6	2,510	11.0
BARRY	554	38,166	41,100	7.6	17.0	14,483	12.1
BAY	447	117,339	119,700	2.0	66.8	43,868	11.7
BENZIE	316	8,593	9,900	15.5	0.0	3,161	12.1
BERRIEN	580	163,875	170,800	4.2	46.4	66,769	12.1
BRANCH	506	37,906	37,900	0.0	24.0	14,212	11.9
CALHOUN	709	141,963	141,300	−0.5	59.6	58,415	12.1
CASS	491	43,312	45,600	5.4	20.6	17,338	12.0
CHARLEVOIX	414	16,541	18,400	11.3	39.2	6,342	12.1
CHEBOYGAN	721	16,573	19,300	16.5	33.5	5,598	11.9
CHIPPEWA	1,590	32,412	36,200	11.5	66.2	9,000	12.1
CLARE	571	16,695	21,300	27.5	15.8	5,558	11.2
CLINTON	572	48,492	53,200	9.7	21.3	18,521	12.1
CRAWFORD	561	6,482	8,100	24.8	0.0	2,342	12.0
DELTA	1,177	35,924	39,500	10.0	57.4	12,244	11.9
DICKINSON	757	23,753	25,100	5.7	71.6	8,197	12.0
EATON	571	68,892	75,700	9.9	42.1	27,330	12.3
EMMET	461	18,331	21,300	16.4	34.6	6,835	12.2
GENESEE	642	445,589	450,400	1.1	77.3	168,389	12.1
GLADWIN	503	13,471	16,600	23.0	0.0	4,424	10.9
GOGEBIC	1,107	20,676	20,700	0.0	69.0	6,897	12.0
GRAND TRAVERSE	462	39,175	45,100	15.1	46.1	14,743	12.3
GRATIOT	566	39,246	39,700	1.3	42.4	14,770	12.1
HILLSDALE	600	37,171	40,700	9.5	20.8	14,659	12.2
HOUGHTON	1,017	34,652	36,700	6.0	39.7	10,658	11.2
HURON	819	34,083	35,600	4.5	8.8	11,652	10.4
INGHAM	559	261,039	270,900	3.8	85.7	111,542	12.4
IONIA	575	45,848	47,100	2.8	33.4	16,544	12.1
IOSCO	544	24,905	28,800	15.5	41.8	6,070	12.2
IRON	1,171	13,813	14,300	3.4	19.4	4,533	11.7
ISABELLA	572	44,594	50,800	14.0	46.0	16,833	12.1
JACKSON	698	143,274	147,100	2.7	54.8	55,328	12.1
KALAMAZOO	562	201,550	203,100	0.8	75.5	82,997	12.3
KALKASKA	566	5,272	8,000	49.4	0.0	1,657	11.2
KENT	857	411,044	427,100	3.9	83.3	166,035	12.2
KEWEENAW	538	2,264	2,100	−6.1	0.0	605	9.0
LAKE	571	5,661	6,700	18.2	0.0	1,816	10.1
LAPEER	658	52,361	62,000	18.3	12.0	18,040	12.1
LEELANAU	345	10,872	12,300	13.0	0.0	3,864	12.1
LENAWEE	753	81,951	86,700	5.8	40.3	32,959	12.1
LIVINGSTON	572	58,967	78,500	33.1	11.0	22,166	12.2
LUCE	906	6,789	7,300	7.7	0.0	2,183	10.6
MACKINAC	1,014	9,660	10,600	10.2	29.9	3,056	11.4
MACOMB	480	625,309	669,600	6.9	92.2	240,015	12.1
MANISTEE	553	20,094	21,600	6.1	38.4	7,508	11.9
MARQUETTE	1,828	64,686	70,300	8.7	65.1	20,986	12.2
MASON	490	22,612	24,500	8.2	39.9	8,623	12.1
MECOSTA	560	27,992	35,200	25.9	42.9	10,275	12.2
MENOMINEE	1,038	24,587	25,500	3.8	43.7	8,720	11.7
MIDLAND	520	63,769	67,500	5.8	54.8	23,470	12.5
MISSAUKEE	565	7,126	8,700	22.7	0.0	2,472	10.5
MONROE	557	118,479	126,500	6.1	35.0	44,086	11.4
MONTCALM	712	39,660	44,300	11.6	18.9	15,064	11.9
MONTMORENCY	555	5,247	6,900	31.9	0.0	1,579	10.8
MUSKEGON	501	157,426	156,700	−0.4	69.1	60,084	11.6
NEWAYGO	849	27,992	31,000	10.7	12.4	9,631	11.3
OAKLAND	867	907,871	967,500	6.6	90.0	363,528	12.4
OCEANA	536	17,984	20,900	16.3	0.0	6,330	11.8
OGEMAW	571	11,903	14,800	24.6	0.0	3,653	11.0
ONTONAGON	1,316	10,548	11,300	7.0	0.0	3,626	12.0
OSCEOLA	581	14,838	17,300	16.4	0.0	5,522	11.5
OSCODA	563	4,726	6,100	29.7	0.0	1,444	11.2
OTSEGO	527	10,422	13,400	28.6	28.9	3,922	12.2
OTTAWA	563	128,181	140,500	9.6	48.3	50,183	12.0
PRESQUE ISLE	648	12,836	14,100	9.9	33.3	3,794	10.3
ROSCOMMON	521	9,892	14,400	45.2	0.0	3,031	11.6
SAGINAW	814	219,743	226,800	3.2	69.7	80,572	12.0
ST. CLAIR	734	120,175	130,500	9.4	46.0	44,456	12.0
ST. JOSEPH	506	47,392	51,200	8.0	35.1	19,211	12.1
SANILAC	961	35,181	38,500	9.5	0.0	12,764	11.5
SCHOOLCRAFT	1,181	8,226	8,600	4.8	52.6	2,623	11.1
SHIAWASSEE	540	63,075	69,700	10.5	37.5	24,248	12.1
TUSCOLA	815	48,603	53,700	10.5	13.4	16,788	11.6
VAN BUREN	603	56,173	62,100	10.5	21.6	21,147	11.6
WASHTENAW	711	234,103	256,400	9.5	78.2	102,749	12.6
WAYNE	605	2,669,604	2,536,700	−5.0	98.2	1,061,985	11.7
WEXFORD	559	19,717	22,000	11.5	50.7	7,039	12.0

SOURCES: David I. Verway, ed., *Michigan Statistical Abstract* (East Lansing, Mi.: Division of Research, Graduate School of Business Administration, Michigan State University, 1976). U.S., Department of Commerce, Bureau of the Census, *County and City Data Book, 1972 (Statistical Abstract Supplement)* (Washington, D.C.: Government Printing Office, 1973).

Median Family Income 1969	Families with Income below Poverty Level, 1969	Percent Employed in Agriculture 1973	Total Earnings in Agriculture, 1974 (Thousands of Dollars)	Value Added by Manufacture, 1972 (Millions of Dollars)	Retail Sales per Capita	Total Population per Doctor of Medicine, 1970	Percent Wage and Salary Employment in Government, 1973
$ 5,842	18.1	17.51	$ 1,025	$ 2.7	$1,634	3,557	23.37
8,014	11.1	4.47	420	12.5	1,673	1,714	19.66
9,309	9.5	17.26	21,425	154.2	1,698	2,219	13.92
8,765	10.3	5.40	2,592	85.8	2,625	1,097	16.71
8,043	9.9	10.34	2,526	19.4	1,755	2,522	16.00
8,320	12.2	15.67	6,874	...*	2,203	3,716	14.35
8,045	12.4	5.70	372	12.0	1,749	1,558	26.85
9,704	8.7	14.66	8,304	60.7	1,198	1,659	14.75
10,408	6.6	4.91	29,162	201.7	2,320	1,210	11.45
7,760	11.2	11.31	1,160	7.4	2,205	955	17.03
10,056	9.5	6.46	28,476	546.2	2,291	942	9.55
9,325	9.0	12.33	10,888	58.9	1,984	1,264	22.50
10,789	7.5	9.28	12,351	635.0	2,316	1,029	9.69
9,781	8.3	12.52	9,479	59.2	1,337	2,707	14.30
8,535	10.7	4.81	1,236	45.4	1,965	1,182	13.56
7,660	13.9	3.98	721	22.1	2,886	1,657	11.77
7,131	15.2	3.71	1,231	3.1	1,945	1,351	16.85
7,547	15.4	8.95	1,930	10.0	2,344	4,174	17.68
11,014	5.2	24.00	19,335	35.2	1,532	4,849	18.95
7,930	12.5	.40	−6	7.8	2,833	720	16.14
8,779	10.6	3.75	2,803	40.7	2,274	1,382	13.77
8,316	10.2	2.41	3,062	22.2	2,523	819	13.12
11,423	5.4	13.58	12,866	59.9	2,673	3,626	18.02
8,610	10.3	3.42	1,396	13.3	3,757	258	12.64
11,255	6.7	.92	5,800	...*	2,465	956	10.22
8,157	10.7	15.30	1,294	7.9	1,743	3,368	16.36
7,236	13.2	1.37	409	12.4	2,131	1,880	17.19
9,542	7.3	5.47	4,134	48.8	3,574	359	17.13
8,891	9.0	14.40	27,599	77.1	2,100	1,154	10.62
8,895	9.0	15.90	10,592	85.1	1,569	2,323	12.83
6,300	21.0	3.05	986	9.3	1,824	1,283	26.41
7,785	15.0	21.52	45,504	29.6	1,950	1,482	15.80
11,193	6.5	1.32	12,502	814.7	2,509	571	27.80
9,578	7.4	14.44	18,228	71.6	1,669	2,183	17.86
7,165	13.3	3.89	1,769	11.8	2,059	1,779	10.36
7,443	10.6	3.38	1,037	1.7	2,009	1,535	27.58
9,207	10.0	10.63	11,969	10.2	1,705	1,143	30.95
10,726	6.6	3.39	11,933	377.9	2,228	1,077	12.99
11,037	5.8	1.86	8,100	672.0	2,372	535	16.38
6,686	18.5	8.84	811	1.3	2,060	1,757	21.33
10,692	6.6	1.55	23,567	1,198.8	2,703	642	7.76
4,809	21.8	.32	6	.5	837	0	30.91
6,000	22.9	19.33	344	.9	1,279	944	21.07
10,388	8.3	16.13	17,346	39.6	1,673	2,275	27.15
8,278	11.3	8.85	23,491	2.6	1,524	1,359	14.34
10,027	6.7	24.21	4,081	251.7	2,494	1,149	10.45
11,551	5.1	9.50	6,964	64.0	1,727	1,685	20.44
8,974	9.5	1.41	367	2.8	1,666	522	56.85
7,273	12.8	2.92	561	2.2	2,315	3,220	21.92
12,110	3.6	.86	12,714	1,746.6	2,392	1,281	10.01
8,365	11.8	9.46	5,253	42.2	1,999	1,116	15.62
8,562	8.7	.46	688	16.3	1,626	799	18.55
8,476	9.4	9.81	4,651	44.5	2,424	780	12.51
7,902	11.8	10.98	8,035	13.9	1,731	1,750	33.99
7,703	12.9	8.76	3,705	29.2	1,472	2,049	11.88
11,618	5.2	2.98	8,998	...*	2,127	671	8.90
6,820	17.6	25.67	4,457	.4	1,433	2,375	20.67
11,398	5.7	8.94	20,077	189.3	1,611	1,881	14.36
8,526	10.1	13.80	22,092	79.6	2,249	1,889	12.97
5,851	18.4	7.58	820	10.9	2,003	0	15.06
9,757	7.8	1.78	8,854	392.3	2,105	1,202	10.88
8,121	11.9	17.44	13,879	39.4	1,534	1,866	14.89
13,826	3.8	.39	4,923	2,070.0	2,925	430	10.53
8,000	14.9	28.77	8,066	9.2	1,618	1,798	17.82
6,545	18.8	11.53	2,349	19.7	2,723	1,190	18.56
8,421	8.2	4.10	727	...*	1,829	1,758	14.14
7,961	13.3	12.21	3,632	30.5	1,433	2,120	16.27
6,411	18.8	8.48	486	2.7	1,426	1,575	21.81
9,413	9.0	4.08	872	19.4	3,111	651	16.39
10,445	4.6	6.11	19,304	315.6	1,853	1,257	10.13
7,889	15.9	12.47	3,306	1.4	1,846	4,279	18.18
6,895	14.9	1.40	−13	7.2	3,293	989	25.17
10,878	7.7	3.32	38,315	921.1	2,304	872	9.28
10,125	8.5	5.36	10,088	174.2	2,040	1,167	12.91
9,686	8.0	7.46	10,117	200.8	2,095	1,394	11.05
8,583	11.5	25.22	33,370	50.4	1,676	2,492	12.82
7,692	13.5	2.12	139	4.1	2,080	1,175	24.07
10,540	7.0	10.52	13,765	74.2	1,848	1,705	13.09
9,558	8.8	17.22	44,122	46.9	1,672	2,314	20.85
8,735	11.2	19.45	22,562	83.0	1,779	1,560	14.06
12,294	5.1	1.81	10,374	907.0	2,504	193	28.66
11,351	8.1	.08	4,011	7,697.8	2,182	800	10.18
8,024	12.4	4.26	1,771	44.8	3,001	789	15.39

*Data not available

BIBLIOGRAPHY

The sources in this bibliography are arranged according to the order of the sections of the atlas. In general, they are sources of data from which the maps and other illustrations were derived. The numbers in parentheses at the end of each entry indicate the pages for which the entry was used as a source for an illustration or map.

INTRODUCTION

Michigan. Department of State Highways and Transportation. State Highway Commission. "Official Michigan Highway Map." Lansing, 1976. (10-12)

U.S. Department of Agriculture. Agricultural Stabilization and Conservation Service. *Index to Air Photo Coverage in Michigan.* (13)

———. Department of the Interior. Geological Survey. *Index to Topographic Maps of Michigan.* 1975. (Available from the Geological Survey, Department of Natural Resources, State of Michigan, Lansing.) (13)

NATURAL ENVIRONMENT

Blair, R. Baxter. "Michigan Physical-Political Wall Map." Chicago: Denoyer-Geppert, 1956. (26)

Brown, Claudeous J. D. *Michigan Streams.* Ann Arbor, Mi.: Institute for Fisheries Research, University of Michigan, 1944. (41)

Dorr, John A., and Eschman, Donald F. *Geology of Michigan.* Ann Arbor, Mi.: University of Michigan Press, 1970. (31)

Farrand, W. R., and Eschman, D. F. "Glaciation of the Southern Peninsula of Michigan: A Review." *Michigan Academician,* Vol. 7, No. 1, 1975. (28-29)

Flint, Richard F. *Glacial and Pleistocene Geology.* New York: John Wiley and Sons, Inc., 1957. (28-29)

———, et al. "Glacial Map of the U.S. East of the Rocky Mountains." Scale 1:1,750,000. Geological Society of America, 1959. (2 sheets) (32)

Gifford, A. R., and Humphrys, C. R. "Lake Shore Classifications—Southern Peninsula of Michigan." Department of Resource Development and the Agricultural Experiment Station, Michigan State University, East Lansing, Mi., 1966. (33)

Hough, J. L. *Geology of the Great Lakes.* Urbana, Ill.: University of Illinois Press, 1958. (40)

Humphrys, C. R. "Shoretype Classification of Ontonagon County and Gogebic County, Michigan." Department of Resource Development and the Agricultural Experiment Station, Michigan State University, East Lansing, Mi., 1958. (33)

Kapp, Ronald O. "National Areas for the Protection of Endangered Species." Paper presented in zoology section, Michigan Academy of Science, Arts, and Letters, April 4, 1975. (59)

Michigan. Department of Agriculture. Michigan Weather Service. "Michigan Tornado Fact Sheet, 1918-1973"; and "Michigan Tornado Occurrences, 1900-1970." Lansing. (52)

———. Department of Natural Resources. Fisheries Division. "Michigan's Twenty Largest Inland Lakes." Lansing, 1974. (Pamphlet) (41)

———. Department of Natural Resources. Geological Survey Division. "Bedrock of Michigan: Map." Lansing, 1968. (30)

———. Department of Natural Resources. Geological Survey Division. "The Glacial Lakes around Michigan." Bulletin 4, by R. W. Kelley and W. R. Farrand. Lansing, 1967. (28-29)

———. Department of Natural Resources. Geological Survey Division. "Map of the Surface Formations of the Southern Peninsula of Michigan," Publication 49 by H. Martin, 1957; "Sand Dunes of Michigan, Map," by R. W. Kelley, 1962; and "Sinks and Caves of Michigan," by I. Kuehner (personal communication). Lansing. (33)

———. Department of Natural Resources. Resources Planning Division and Water Resources Commission. "Water Holding Capacity and Infiltration Rates of Soils in Michigan," by I. F. Schneider and A. E. Erickson. Michigan Agricultural Extension Project 413. Lansing, n.d. (39)

Michigan Statistical Abstract. Edited by David I. Verway. East Lansing, Mi.: Division of Research, Graduate School of Business Administration, Michigan State University, 1976. (47)

Pawling, J. W. "Morphometric Analysis of the Southern Peninsula of Michigan." Ph.D. dissertation, Michigan State University, 1969. (27)

Rieck, R. "Drumlins of Michigan." 1969. (Manuscript map) (33)

———. "Morphology, Structure, and Formation of Eskers with Illustrations from Michigan: A Bibliographical Index to Esker Literature." Unpublished M.A. thesis, Wayne State University, 1972. (33)

U.S. Army Corps of Engineers. U.S. Survey of Northern and Northwestern Lakes. "General Chart of the Great Lakes, Chart No. 0, 1970." (42-43)

———. Department of Agriculture. North Central Forest Experiment Station. "The Growing Timber Resource of Michigan—1966." Resource Bulletin NC-9. St. Paul, Minn., 1970. (45)

———. Department of Agriculture. Soil Conservation Service et al. "Prime Lands of Michigan." 1973. (Map) (38)

———. Department of Commerce. Environmental Science Service Administration. National Weather Service, Silver Spring, Md. Various weather maps. (55-57)

———. Department of Commerce. National Oceanographic and Atmospheric Administration. Environmental Data Service. *Climatological Data—Michigan, Annual Summary 1970-74.* Vols. 85-89. Asheville, N.C.: NOAA. (46-51, 53)

———. Department of Commerce. National Oceanographic and Atmospheric Administration. National Ocean Survey. *Great Lakes Water Levels, 1860-1970; Great Lakes Water Level, 1971;* and *Great Lakes Water Level, 1972.* Detroit, Mi.: Lake Survey Center. (42-43)

———. Department of Commerce. National Oceanographic and Atmospheric Administration in cooperation with the Michigan Weather Service. *Climate of Michigan by Stations,* by N. D. Strommen. Asheville, N.C.: NOAA. (46-51, 53)

———. Department of the Interior. Geological Survey. "General Availability and Quality of Groundwater in the Bedrock Deposits in Michigan" (map); and "General Availability of Groundwater in the Glacial Deposits in Michigan" (map), both by F. R. Twenter. (44)

———. Department of the Interior. Geological Survey. *Pleistocene of Indiana and Michigan and the History of the Great Lakes.* Monograph #53, by F. Leverett and F. B. Taylor. 1915. (28-29)

———. Department of the Interior. Geological Survey. "State of Michigan, Map." 1970. (41)

———. Department of the Interior. Geological Survey. "Water Resources Data for Michigan." USGS office, Okemos, Mi. (54)

Veatch, J. O. "Presettlement Forest in Michigan." Department of Resource Development, Michigan State University, East Lansing, Mi., 1959. (Map) (45)

PEOPLE AND SOCIETY

Beegle, J. A.; Wang, Ching-li; and Lepper, Carol. "Michigan Age-Sex Composition, 1970." Rural Sociology Studies #5. Agricultural Experiment Station, Michigan State University, East Lansing, Mi., July 1974. (86)

Johnson, D. W.; Picard, P. R.; and Quinn, B. *Churches and Church Membership in the United States: 1971.* Washington, D.C.: Glenmary Research Center, 1974. (79)

Michigan. Department of Education. Bureau of Administrative Services. "Enrollments by Grades for Selected Years," 1975; and "Total Michigan School Districts," Bulletin No. 1011, 1975. Lansing. (80)

_____ . Department of Education. Office of the Community College Coordinator. "Existing Community College Districts." Lansing, 1975. (Map) (81)

_____ . Department of Education. Superintendent of Public Instruction. *Annual Report*, 1900, 1910, 1920, 1930, 1940, 1950. Lansing. (81)

_____ . Department of Management and Budget. Planning and Policy Analysis Division. "Population Projections for the Counties of Michigan." Lansing, 1974. (74)

_____ . Department of Natural Resources. Air Pollution Control Division. "Air Quality Report, 1974." Lansing, 1974. (Mimeo) (91)

_____ . Department of Natural Resources. "Wayne County Report, 1974." Lansing. (91)

_____ . Department of Public Health. Bureau of Health Care Administration. *Michigan State Plan for Hospital and Medical Facilities Construction, 1974-75.* Lansing, 1975. (92)

_____ . Department of Public Health. Center for Health Statistics. *Michigan Health Statistics, 1973.* Lansing, 1973. (88-90)

_____ . Department of Public Health. Planning and Evaluation Unit. *Health in Michigan: A Profile 1973-74.* Lansing, 1974. (90)

_____ . Department of Social Services. *Annual Report, Fiscal Year 1970; and Program Statistics, 1974.* Lansing. (95)

_____ . State Police. "Uniform Crime Report" (Michigan). Lansing, 1974. (97)

Michigan Health Council. "Health Manpower in Michigan." East Lansing, Mi. Spring 1975. (Newsletter) (93)

Michigan State University. Office of the Registrar. Evaluation and Research. "Enrollment Report, East Lansing Campus." Special internal composite report, East Lansing, Mi., Fall 1975. (82)

Michigan Statistical Abstract. Edited by David I. Verway. East Lansing, Mi.: Division of Research, Graduate School of Business Administration, Michigan State University, 1974. (71, 81, 92, 94)

Thaden, J. F. "Ethnic Settlements in Rural Michigan." *Michigan State University Agricultural Experiment Station Quarterly Bulletin,* Vol. 29, No. 2, 1946. (78)

University of Michigan. Office of the Registrar. Statistical Service. "Geographic Distribution of Residence Credit Students by Unit and Geographic Location, Fall Term 1975." Ann Arbor, Mi., November 1975. (82)

U.S. Department of Commerce. Bureau of the Census. *Census of Housing: 1970.* Vol. I, pt. 24: *Michigan.* Chap. A: "General Housing Characteristics." (96)

_____ . Department of Commerce. Bureau of the Census. *Census of Housing.* U.S. Summary for the years 1930, 1940, 1950, 1960, 1970. (96)

_____ . Department of Commerce. Bureau of the Census. *Census of Population: 1930.* Vol. III, pt. 1: *General Population Characteristics.* Section on Michigan. (70)

_____ . Department of Commerce. Bureau of the Census. *Census of Population: 1940.* Vol. II: *Characteristics of the Population.* Pt. 3: "Kansas-Michigan." Section on Michigan. (80)

_____ . Department of Commerce. Bureau of the Census. *Census of Population: 1950.* Vol. II: *Characteristics of the Population.* Pt. 22: *Michigan.* Chap. B: "General Characteristics." (70)

_____ . Department of Commerce. Bureau of the Census. *Census of Population: 1970.* Vol. I: *Characteristics of the Population.* Pt. 1: *U.S. Summary.* (80)

_____ . Department of Commerce. Bureau of the Census. *Census of Population: 1970.* Vol. I: *Characteristics of the Population.* Pt. 24: *Michigan.* Chap. B: "General Population Characteristics" (68-70, 74, 85, 87); Chap. C: "General Social and Economic Characteristics" (75, 80, 83, 94, 95); Chap. D: "Detailed Characteristics" (76-77).

_____ . Department of Commerce. Bureau of the Census. *Census of Population: 1970.* Vol. II: *Subject Reports.* Report PC (2)-2B: *Mobility for States and the Nation.* 1973. (83, 84)

_____ . Department of Commerce. Bureau of the Census. *Statistical Abstract of the U.S., 1974.* (89)

_____ . Department of Commerce. Bureau of the Census. *Thirteenth Census of the United States Taken in the Year 1910.* Vol. II: *Population 1910, Alabama—Montana.* Section on Michigan. 1913. (70)

_____ . Department of Health, Education and Welfare. Office of Education. Bureau for Education Personnel Development. "Detroit Area Ethnic Groups 1971," by Bryan Thompson. Grant No. OEG-0-70-2030 (725). (78)

Wayne State University. Office of the Registrar. "Residence of Students Registered in Credit Programs." Quarterly report. Detroit, Mi., Fall 1975. (82)

HISTORY AND CULTURE

Andrews, Wayne. *Architecture in Michigan.* Detroit, Mi.: Wayne State University, 1967. (133)

Bald, F. Clever. *Detroit's First American Decade, 1796 to 1805.* Ann Arbor, Mi.: University of Michigan Press, 1948. (110-11)

_____ . *Michigan in Four Centuries.* New York: Harper, 1961. (110-11)

Black, Albert G. *Michigan in Novels: An Annotated Bibliography.* Ann Arbor, Mi.: Michigan Council of Teachers of English, 1963. (134)

Burkhart, C. A. "French Explorations and Settlements in the Old Northwest." Map MH #1 in *Burkhart Michigan History Series.* Chicago: A. J. Nystrom Co., 1926. (112)

Craven, Wayne. *Sculpture in America.* New York: Crowell, 1968. (132)

Dodge, Roy L. *Michigan Ghost Towns.* 3 vols. Oscoda, Mi.: Amateur Treasure Hunters Association, 1970-73. (125)

Dunbar, W. F. *Michigan: A History of the Wolverine State.* Grand Rapids, Mi.: Wm. B. Eerdmans, 1973. (108-9)

Field, Arthur. "Road Patterns of Southern Michigan." *Papers, Michigan Academy of Sciences,* Vol. 14, 1930. (108-9)

Hinsdale, Wilbert B. *Archaeological Atlas of Michigan.* University Museums, Michigan Handbook Series, No. 4. Ann Arbor, Mi.: University of Michigan Press, 1931. (108-9)

Hudgins, Bert. *Michigan: Geographic Backgrounds in the Development of the Commonwealth.* Ann Arbor, Mi.: Edwards Brothers, 1961. (123-24)

Karpinski, L. C. *Bibliography of the Printed Maps of Michigan, Up to 1888.* Lansing, Mi.: Michigan Historical Commission, 1931. (107)

Michigan. Adjutant General's Department. *Record of Service of Michigan Volunteers in the Civil War 1861-1865.* Published by the Authority of the Senate and House of Representatives of the Michigan Legislature, Lansing, Mi., 190? (122)

_____ . Department of Education. State Library Services. "County Evolution in Michigan, 1790-1897." Occasional Paper No. 2, by R. W. Welsh. Lansing, 1972. (118-19)

"Michigan in Novels." Greenville Public Library, Greenville, Mi., 1972. (Pamphlet) (134)

Mumford, L. Quincy. *Michigan: Sesquicentennial of the Territory 1805-1955: An Exhibition in the Library of Congress.* Washington, D.C.: Library of Congress, 1955. (114-15)

Paullin, Charles O. *Atlas of Historical Geography of the United States.* New York: American Geographical Society; Washington, D.C.: Carnegie Institute, 1932. (116, 128-29)

Romig, W. *Michigan Place Names.* Grosse Pointe, Mi.: W. Romig and Co., 1973. (113)

Rummel, Walt. "Ghost Towns are Everywhere." *Michigan Motor News,* September 1975. (125)

Scammon, Richard. *America at the Polls.* Pittsburgh, Pa.: University of Pittsburgh Press, 1965. (128-29)

_____ . "America Votes." *Congressional Quarterly,* Vol. 8, 1968, and Vol. 10, 1972. (128-29)

U.S. Department of Commerce. Bureau of the Census. *Census of Population: 1940.* Vol. II: *Characteristics of the Population.* Pt. 3: "Kansas-Michigan." Section on Michigan. (120-21)

_____ . Department of Commerce. Bureau of the Census. *Thirteenth Census of the United States Taken in the Year 1910.* Vol. I: *Population 1910, General Report and Analysis,* 1913. (120-21)

_____ . Department of the Interior. Census Office. *Report on the Manufactures of the United States at the Tenth Census (June 1, 1880) Embracing General Statistics.* Section on Michigan. 1883. (124)

_____ . Department of the Interior. Census Office. *Statistics of the Population of the United States at the Tenth Census (June 1, 1880).* 1883. (120-21)

_____ . Secretary of the Interior. *The Statistics of the Population of the United States, Embracing the Tables of Race, Nationality, Sex, Selected Ages, Occupations ... compiled from the Original Returns of the Ninth Census (June 1, 1870).* 1872. (120-21)

_____ . Superintendent of the United States Census. *Statistical View of the Seventh Census (1850).* Washington, D.C.: A. O. P. Nicholson, Public Printer, 1854. (120-21)

———. Works Project Administration, Michigan. "Michigan Log Marks, Their Function and Use During the Great Michigan Pine Harvest." Memoir Bulletin No. 4, Michigan Agricultural Experiment Station, 1941. (124)

Vanderhill, C. W. *Settling the Great Lakes Frontier: Immigration to Michigan 1857-1924.* Lansing, Mi.: Michigan Historical Commission, 1970. (120-21)

ECONOMY

Advertising Age. 1973. (Newspaper) (166)

American Motors Corporation. *American Motors Corporation 1974 Annual Report.* Detroit, Mi.: The Corporation, 1974. (162-64)

Barlowe, Raleigh. "Project '80: Land and Water Resources." Research Report #52, Agricultural Experiment Station and the Cooperative Extension Service, Michigan State University, East Lansing, Mi., 1970. (151)

Chrysler Corporation. *Chrysler Corporation 1974 Annual Report.* Detroit, Mi.: The Corporation, 1974. (162-64)

Directory of Michigan Manufacturers, 1971. Detroit, Mi.: Manufacturers Publishing Co., 1971. (165)

Gardner, Philip D., and Kimball, William J. "Michigan's Land Use Picture." Department of Resource Development, Agricultural Experiment Station, and the Cooperative Extension Service, Michigan State University, East Lansing, Mi., 1976. (146-47)

General Motors Corporation. *1975 Information Handbook.* Flint, Mi.: The Corporation, 1975. (162-64)

The Handbook of Basic Economic Statistics. Washington, D.C.: Bureau of Economic Statistics, Inc., 1975. (162-64)

Manthy, Robert S.; James, Lee M.; and Huber, Henry H. "Michigan Timber Production—Now and in 1985." Research Report #192. Agricultural Experiment Station and the Cooperative Extension Service, Michigan State University, East Lansing, Mi., 1973. (154-55)

Michigan. Bureau of State Lottery. *Annual Report, 1973-74.* Lansing. (168)

———. Department of Agriculture. "Michigan Agricultural Land Requirements: A Projection to 2000 A.D." Lansing, 1973. (Mimeo) (153)

——— Department of Labor. Michigan Employment Security Commission. Office of Research and Statistics. "Civilian Labor Force Estimates, Michigan by County, 1974 Annual Average." Lansing. (141)

———. Department of Management and Budget. Financial reports and statements for the years 1973-76. (168)

———. Department of Natural Resources. Geological Survey Division. "Michigan Mineral Producers, 1974" (pamphlet); "Michigan Oil and Gas Fields, Southern Peninsula" (map); and "Michigan's Oil and Gas Fields, 1973" (pamphlet). Lansing. (157, 159)

———. Department of Natural Resources. Office of Planning Services. *Michigan Recreation Plan,* 1971, 1974. Lansing. (154-55)

———. Department of Treasury. *Michigan County Government, Financial Report,* 1969, 1971, 1972, 1973. Lansing. (169)

———. Governor, Executive office of. "Report to Governor William G. Milliken by the Special Commission on Energy." Lansing, February 1974. (158)

Michigan National Guards (Army and Air). "Station List and Miscellaneous Directory." Lansing, 1975. (145)

Michigan Statistical Abstract. Edited by David I. Verway. E. Lansing, Mi.: Division of Research, Graduate School of Business Administration, Michigan State University, East Lansing, Mi., 1974. (143, 145, 162-64, 167)

Motor Vehicle Manufacturers Association. *Automobile Facts and Figures.* Detroit, Mi.: The Association, various years. (162-64)

National Science Foundation. *Research and Development in Industry.* Surveys of Science Resource Series. Washington, D.C.: The Foundation, 1962-72. (161)

U.S. Department of Agriculture. North Central Forest Experiment Station. "Primary Forest Products Industry and Timber Use, Michigan." St. Paul, Minn., 1972. (154-55)

———. Community Services Administration for Executive Office of the President. *Federal Outlays in Michigan, Fiscal Year 1975.* (161)

———. Department of Commerce. Bureau of the Census. *Census of Agriculture.* Michigan and U.S. Summary for the years 1950, 1964, 1969. (148-53)

———. Department of Commerce. Bureau of the Census. *Census of Manufactures: 1972.* Vol. IV: *Area Series.* Section on Michigan. (160)

———. Department of Commerce. Bureau of the Census. *Census of Population.* Michigan and U.S. Summary for the years 1910, 1920, 1930, 1940, 1950, 1960, 1970. (160)

———. Department of Commerce. Bureau of the Census. *Census of Population: 1970.* Vol. I: *Characteristics of the Population.* Pt. 24: *Michigan.* Chap. C: "General Social and Economic Characteristics" (144); Chap. D: "Detailed Characteristics" (142).

———. Department of Commerce. Bureau of the Census. *Construction Reports—Housing Authorized by Building Permits and Public Contracts, 1974.* (167)

———. Department of Commerce. Bureau of the Census. Social and Economic Statistics Administration. *Survey of the Origin of Exports of Manufacturing Establishments in 1972.* (170)

———. Department of Commerce. Commissioner of Patents. *1973 Annual Report.* (161)

———. Department of the Interior. Geological Survey. *National Atlas of the United States.* 1970. (159)

———. Office of Economic Opportunity. *Federal Outlays, Fiscal Year 1968.* Compiled for the Office of the President. Clearing House of Federal Scientific and Technical Information, National Bureau of Standards, Springfield, Va., 1969, 1970. (161)

Ward's Communications, Inc. *Ward's Automotive Yearbook,* 1958-75. Detroit, Mi.: Ward's Communications, Inc. (162-64)

RECREATION

Automobile Club of Michigan. *Michigan Outdoor Guide.* Dearborn, Mi.: Touring Department and Motor News, AAA, 1975. (182)

Detroit Free Press. "Winter Scene," October 26, 1975. (194)

Dice, Gene. "Supply-Demand in Michigan Campgrounds." Extension Bulletin E-895, Cooperative Extension Service, Michigan State University, East Lansing, Mi., September 1975. (196)

Gogebic Community College. "1973-74 Michigan Snowmobile Survey." A survey conducted by the college. Ironwood, Mi. (194)

Lansing, City of. Lansing City Council and Park Board. "Lansing Parks and Recreation—Facility Guide and Map." (200)

Michigan. Department of Commerce. Michigan Tourist Council. "Michigan Calendar of Travel Events." Lansing, 1975 and 1976. (Pamphlets) (202)

———. Department of Conservation. Research and Development Division. *History of Michigan Deer Hunting.* Report No. 85, by C. L. Bennett, Jr., et al. Lansing, 1966. (193)

———. Department of Natural Resources. Administrative Services. License Control. "Fishing License Sales by County," 1974; and "History of Fishing License and Park Permit Sales, 1914-1974." Lansing. (Mimeos) (188-89)

———. Department of Natural Resources. Information and Education Division. *Michigan Natural Resources,* Vol. 44, March-April 1975. (198)

———. Department of Natural Resources. "Michigan's Natural River System." Lansing. (Unpublished map) (185)

———. Department of Natural Resources. Office of Planning Services. *Michigan Recreation Plan,* 1971, 1974. Lansing. (181-84, 185, 195)

———. Department of Natural Resources. Office of Planning Services. "Recreation Resource Reports, Regions 1-14." Lansing, 1975. (197)

———. Department of Natural Resources. Office of Surveys and Statistical Services. "Great Lakes Trout and Salmon Angler Days at Destination Counties," 1973; and "Inland Waters Fishing Days by Destination," 1975. Computer-generated tables in the Michigan Sport Fishing Survey. Lansing. (188-89)

———. Department of Natural Resources. Parks Division. "State Park Attendance, 1974 and 1975." Lansing. (Mimeo) (181)

———. Department of Natural Resources. Wildlife Division. "Firearm Deer Hunting Statistics," 1973 (mimeo); "Relative Density of Deer —Early 1970s," (map); and "Small Game Ducks, Snowshoes, Cottontails—Hunter Days," in *Small Game Kill Estimates,* 1973. Lansing. (190-91, 193)

———. Waterways Commission and Department of Natural Resources. "Michigan Harbors Guide, 1975." Lansing, 1975. (195)

Michigan Travel Commission. "Charter Boat Captains, by Port." 1975. (Pamphlet) (188)

U.S. Department of Commerce. Bureau of the Census. *Census of Governments: 1972.* Vol. III: *Public Employment.* (197)

———. Department of Interior. Fish and Wildlife Service. "Michigan Permanent Water Areas." (Map) (192)

———. Department of Interior. National Park Service. "Isle Royale," 1968 (brochure); "Pictured Rocks," 1975 (brochure); "Pictured Rocks National Lakeshore General Development Plan," 1975; and "Sleeping Bear Dunes, National Lakeshore, Michigan," National Park Service, Denver Service Center, Denver, Colo., n.d. (184)

Upper Peninsula Travel and Recreation Association. "Waterfalls Guide." Iron Mountain, Mi., 1975. (186)

TRANSPORTATION AND COMMUNICATION

Ayer Directory ... for the years 1930, 1950, 1970, 1975. Philadelphia, Pa.: Ayer Press. (219-20)

Broadcasting Yearbook, 1976. Washington, D.C.: Broadcasting Publications, Inc., 1976. (216-18)

Detroit Free Press. "Free Press Wins Circulation Lead," November 23, 1975. (219)

Michigan. Department of State. "Revenue and Fee Collections for July 1974 through June 1975; License Plate Registrations by County; Registration, Licenses and Titles Since 1916." Lansing, 1975. (209)

———. Department of State Highways and Transportation. Bureau of Transportation Planning. Aviation Planning Section. *Air Carrier Statistics, Fiscal Year 1974-75; Aviation Statistics;* and *Registered Aircraft by State Planning and Development Regions, 1970-75.* Lansing: The Bureau, 1975. (210-11)

———. Department of State Highways and Transportation. "545 Zone Statewide Transportation Modeling System Instate Zone Map." Lansing, 1974. (207)

———. Department of State Highways and Transportation. Michigan Aeronautics Commission. *Licensed Class A, Class B, and Class C Commercial Airports, February 1, 1975;* "Michigan Air Carrier Routes (January 1971)," in *State Airport Plan, 1971;* and "Registered Aircraft 1946-75." Lansing: The Commission, 1975. (210-11)

———. Department of State Highways and Transportation. "Official Railway Map of the State of Michigan, January 1976." Lansing, 1976. (214)

———. Department of State Highways and Transportation. Railway Planning Section. "Rail FRA Density Bandwidth Plot." Lansing, 1975. (Map) (214)

———. Department of State Highways and Transportation. "Traffic Flow Map." Lansing, 1973. (208)

Michigan Newspaper Coop, Inc. *Michigan Newspaper Directory and Ratebook.* East Lansing, Mi.: Michigan Press Association, 1975. (219)

1975 Editor and Publisher International Yearbook. New York: The Editor and Publisher Co., Inc., 1975. (219)

Paule, Milton, ed. *Working Press of the Nation—Radio and Television Directory.* Burlington, Iowa: National Research Bureau, Inc., 1975. (218)

Saint Lawrence Seaway Development Corporation. "1974 U.S. Great Lakes Ports Statistics for Overseas and Canadian Waterborne Commerce." Washington, D.C., 1975. (212)

U.S. Army Corps of Engineers. *Annual Report to the Chief of Engineers.* Part II: *Commercial Statistics, Waterborne Commerce of the United States.* (213)

———. Department of Commerce. Bureau of the Census. *Thirteenth Census of the United States Taken in the Year 1910: Abstract of the Census...with Supplement for Michigan.* (220)

———. Department of Commerce. Office of Telecommunications. "Geographical Areas Serviced by Bell and Independent Telephone Companies in the United States," by B. A. Hart. 1973. (Pamphlet) (215)

———. Federal Communications Commission. "Statistics of Communication Common Carriers." February 1973. (Transmittal sheets) (215)

———. Postal Service. *1974 National Zip Code Directory.* Washington, D.C.: Government Printing Office, 1974. (215)

MICHIGAN TOMORROW

Commission on Population Growth and the American Future. *Population and the American Future.* Washington, D.C.: The Commission, 1972. (229)

C. A. Doxiadis Associates. *Emergence and Growth of an Urban Region, The Developing Urban Detroit Area.* Vol. 3. Detroit, Mi.: Detroit Edison Co., 1970. (229)

Michigan. Department of Management and Budget. "Population Projections for the Counties of Michigan." Lansing, 1974. (227)

U.S. Department of Agriculture. Soil Conservation Service et al. "Prime Lands of Michigan." 1973. (Map) (228)

INDEX

Numbers in boldface type are
references to map pages.